ANTHROPOLOGICAL PAPERS OF
THE UNIVERSITY OF ARIZONA
NUMBER 77

The Ceramic Sequence of the Holmul Region, Guatemala

Michael G. Callaghan, *University of Central Florida*

Nina Neivens de Estrada, *Tulane University*

vessel and sherd drawings by
Fernando Alvarez Andaverde

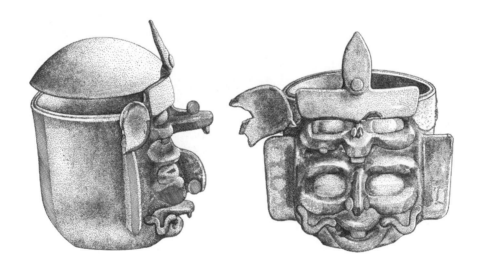

THE UNIVERSITY OF
ARIZONA PRESS
TUCSON

The University of Arizona Press
www.uapress.arizona.edu

© 2016 The Arizona Board of Regents
All rights reserved. Published 2016

Printed in the United States of America

21 20 19 18 17 16   6 5 4 3 2 1

ISBN-13: 978-0-8165-3194-3 (paper)

Editing and indexing by Linda Gregonis
Content editing by Laura Kosakowsky
InDesign layout by Douglas Goewey

Library of Congress Cataloging-in-Publication Data
Names: Callaghan, Michael G., author. | Neivens de
    Estrada, Nina, author.
Title: The ceramic sequence of the Holmul region,
    Guatemala / Michael G. Callaghan, University of
    Central Florida, Nina Neivens de Estrada, Tulane
    University.
Other titles: Anthropological papers of the University of
    Arizona ; no. 77.
Description: Tucson : University of Arizona Press, 2016.
    | Series: Anthropological papers of the University of
    Arizona ; 77 | Includes bibliographical references and
    index.
Identifiers: LCCN 2016004473 | ISBN 9780816531943
    (pbk. : alk. paper)
Subjects: LCSH: Maya pottery—Catalogs. | Excavations
    (Archaeology)—Guatemala—Holmul Site—Catalogs.
    | Holmul Site (Guatemala)—Catalogs. | Mayas—
    Antiquities. | LCGFT: Catalogs.
Classification: LCC F1435.1.H7 C35 2016 | DDC
    972.81/016—dc23 LC record available at http://lccn.loc
    .gov/2016004473

About the Authors

MICHAEL G. CALLAGHAN is Assistant Professor of Anthropology at the University of Central Florida. He earned his bachelor's degree (1998) and doctorate (2008) from Vanderbilt University. Michael specializes in complex societies of Mesoamerica with a specific emphasis on prehistoric ceramic analysis, economy, and its articulation with politics and ritual. His research interests also include gender in archaeology. He has published his ceramic work on Holmul in *Ancient Mesoamerica, The Archaeological Papers of the American Anthropology Association,* and recent edited volumes including *Ancient Maya Pottery: Classification, Analysis, and Interpretation* edited by Jim Aimers, and *Gendered Labor in Specialized Economies* edited by Sophia Kelley and Traci Ardren. Along with his wife, Brigitte Kovacevich, he co-directs the Holtun Archaeological Project located in the department of Petén, Guatemala. Michael currently resides in Orlando with Brigitte and their daughter Caroline.

Michael G. Callaghan, Department of Anthropology, University of Central Florida, 4000 Central Florida Blvd Howard Phillips Hall Rm 309, Orlando, FL 32816-1361, michael.callaghan@ucf.edu.

NINA NEIVENS DE ESTRADA is a doctoral candidate at Tulane University. She received her bachelor's degree from Columbia University in 2003 and master's degree from Tulane in 2008. Her current research focuses on the typological and modal analysis of the pre-Mamom pottery in the Maya lowlands. Nina has published preliminary findings on pre-Mamom material at Holmul in Geoffrey Braswell's recent edited volume, *The Maya and Their Central American Neighbors: Settlement Patterns, Architecture, Hieroglyphic Texts and Ceramics.* She has experience excavating at Maya sites in the Holmul region, Guatemala (at Holmul, La Sufricaya, Cival, and Dos Aguadas) as well as Copán, Honduras. She specializes in ceramic analysis and excavation of monumental architecture. Nina is mother to son Manolo and daughter Bella.

Nina Neivens de Estrada, 26 East 93rd Street, New York, NY 10128, ninaneivens@yahoo.com

Cover

Illustration in foreground is Unnamed Modeled (Aguila Group) (HOL.T.84.11.02.02); illustration in background is Unnamed Polychrome (Chak 1) plate (HOL.L.20.21). Photos by Michael G. Callaghan.

Title page

Illustration on title page is Unnamed Modeled and Painted (Chak 2–3) vessel from Stela 7, Ruin X at Holmul (drawing by Fernando Alvarez, Holmul Archaeological Project).

Contents

FIGURES

TABLES

Acknowledgments

We would like to thank Francisco Estrada-Belli for giving us the opportunity to work on the Holmul ceramic material and for all his advice and support during the research process. Michael would also like to thank Susan H. Haskell, Curatorial Associate for Special Projects at the Peabody Museum of Archaeology and Ethnology at Harvard University, for facilitating his research at the Peabody Museum. Michael's visit to the Museum in November 2006 was invaluable and he greatly appreciates Ms. Haskell's help. A number of scholars greatly aided both of us during the classification process. Many of this help came in the form of informal conversations and emails about the material and we would like to thank these scholars for helping us formulate our methodology and informing our interpretations. These scholars include Will Andrews, James Brady, David Cheetham, John Clark, Pat Culbert, Donald Forsyth, Richard Hansen, Laura Kosakowsky, Lisa LeCount, Marion Poponoe de Hatch, Dorie Reents-Budet, and Debra Walker. Funding for this research was provided in part by grants awarded to Michael including a National Science Foundation Dissertation Enhancement Grant (#0707244) and a Vanderbilt University College of Arts and Sciences Graduate Dissertation Enhancement Grant. The majority of funding came from the Holmul Region Archaeological Project, with funds raised by Francisco Estrada-Belli. We thank the series editor of the Anthropological Paper Series, T.J. Ferguson; the Editor in Chief of the University of Arizona Press, Allyson Carter; and the board of review responsible for agreeing to publish this manuscript. Despite the importance of ceramic sequences for archaeological research, they are becoming decreasingly popular to publish and we greatly appreciate their willingness to print our study. Michael is sincerely grateful for the work of Laura Kosakowsky and Linda Gregonis who painstakingly edited for content and copy respectively. It was truly a Herculean task and he is forever in their debt. We also thank two anonymous reviewers for their substantive and helpful critiques, which helped us to greatly revise this manuscript. Many special thanks to artist and friend, Fernando Alvarez Andaverde, whose stunning sherd and vessel drawings appear in this study. We also thank Diana Méndez-Lee for her sherd illustrations and beautiful composite photographs. We thank the following American and Guatemalan graduate and undergraduate students for their help during the editorial phases of the project: namely, Diana Méndez-Lee and Dawn Crawford. Finally, we thank our families for all their support and sacrifice during the many years it took to assemble this study—we could not have done this without you.

CHAPTER ONE

Introduction

Michael G. Callaghan

Ceramic classification is essential for the archaeological investigation of many complex pre-Columbian societies. It allows archaeologists to quickly establish two important parameters of investigation: temporal range and spatial relations. Once determined, archaeologists are able to test hypotheses about past human behavior using other classes of artifacts along broad spectrums of theoretical inquiry. In the southern Maya area ceramicists have used modal (Sharer 1978; Smith 1955, 1971), type: variety-mode (Adams 1971; Ball 1977; Forsyth 1983, 1989; Gifford 1976; Kosakowsky 1987; Sabloff 1975), and contextual (Chase 1994; Chase and Chase 2013) ceramic classifications to create temporal-spatial frameworks that enable archaeologists to understand local and regional culture-historical events and to reconstruct the lifeways of a broad range of ancient Maya peoples. Although several subregions of the Maya lowlands contain at least one site where a sequence has been defined, there are still many areas where the ceramic record is undefined. One of these important and understudied areas is the Holmul region located in the northeastern department of Petén, Guatemala. Due to its strategic location between the central lowlands and the Belize River Valley and the number of large sites spanning the Middle Preclassic through Terminal Classic periods, ceramic research in the Holmul region has the potential to refine and reshape our ideas about many aspects of ancient Maya cultural practice and process.

This classification was created in an effort to accomplish three primary goals. The first was to use ceramic artifacts to establish site-wide and regional chronological and spatial frameworks for the Holmul region. The second was to compare site and regional temporal-spatial frameworks to other sites in the southern Maya lowlands and to a lesser extent the northern Maya lowlands, southern Maya highlands, and Pacific coast. The third goal was to address specifically defined issues within particular ceramic complexes. These issues are (1) establishing when pottery was adopted and how it was used in the early Middle Preclassic period, (2) assessing the social and ecological reasons for qualitative changes in production patterns between Preclassic period ceramic complexes, (3) determining the function and meaning of the first polychrome painted ceramics of the Terminal Preclassic period, (4) assessing the strength and nature of ceramic influences from the central Mexican city of Teotihuacan in the Early Classic period, (5) understanding the role of Holmul in interregional politics as seen through cream polychrome ceramics during the Late Classic period, and 6) using ceramics to understand the timing and possible reasons for permanent abandonment of sites in the Holmul region during the Terminal Classic period. Although I attempted to address the preceding issues using ceramic data, the final product tends toward the descriptive rather than interpretive. Excavations in the Holmul region are ongoing and, like all ceramic sequences, the Holmul region sequence (and interpretation based on its classifications) is subject to revision. The current Holmul region sequence is the product of what Trigger (2006:30–31) defines as low-level theory (i.e., looking for patterns in archaeological data generated from artifact analysis). Although seemingly absent of theory, classification is guided by a number of implicit theoretical assumptions and is the foundation upon which the answers to mid and high level questions of theory regarding human behavior rest. One cannot emphasize how important ceramic classification and sequence building still is to Maya archaeology today. And this is one of the reasons it was so important to undertake and complete this study.

In order to address issues of time, spatial relations, and cultural process and practice, I needed to employ a classification system that would enable the creation of a sensitive temporal-spatial framework for sites within the Holmul region, and to compare that framework to other sites in the Maya area. I decided that a type: variety-mode classification would fulfill these needs. This study is largely the result of my previous establishment and subsequent revisions of the type: variety-mode classification for Holmul region ceramics (see Callaghan 2005, 2008). Table 1.1 lists the ware, group, type, and variety equivalencies for each complex. In Chapter 2, Nina Neivens de Estrada describes pre-Mamom wares and type: varieties,

some of which are revisions to my descriptions in a previous work (Callaghan 2008:240–270). In Chapters 3 through 7 wares and type: varieties for early Middle Preclassic Yax Te Complex, Late Preclassic Itzamkanak Complex, Terminal Preclassic Wayab Subcomplex, Early Classic K'ak Complex, and Late to Terminal Classic Chak Complex ceramics are described. In Chapter 8, I summarize our work and discuss ceramics within the context of Holmul region history.

The following sections explain the reasons for using type: variety-mode classification, discuss the quality and quantity of the ceramic sample, and present the method behind the classification including particular revisions to previous type: variety-mode classification systems. Before addressing these issues, however, it will be helpful to provide some information on sites in the Holmul region and a history of archaeological excavations in the area.

Table 1.1. Alphabetical Listing of Holmul Types and Varieties with Callaghan (2008) Equivalent

Callaghan and Neivens de Estrada *Type: Variety*	Callaghan (2008) *Type: Variety*
Aac Red-on-buff: Aac Variety	Aac Red on Buff: Variety Unspecified
Accordian Incised: Accordian Variety	Accordion Incised: Variety Unspecified
Accordian Incised: Variety Unspecified (Wayab)	Accordion Incised: Variety Unspecified
Achiotes Unslipped: Achiotes Variety	Achiotes Unslipped: Variety Unspecified
Achiotes Unslipped: Variety Unspecified (Itzamkanak)	Achiotes Unslipped: Unnamed Scratched Variety
Achote Black: Achote Variety	Achote Black: Variety Unspecified
Actuncan Orange Polychrome: Actuncan Variety	Actuncan Orange Polychrome: Variety Unspecified
Actuncan Orange Polychrome: Variety Unspecified (Wayab)	Actuncan Orange Polychrome: Variety Unspecified
Aguila Orange: Aguila Variety	Aguila Orange: Variety Unspecified
Aguila Orange: Variety Unspecified (Wayab)	Aguila Orange: Variety Unspecified
Altamira Fluted: Altamira Variety	Altamira Fluted: Variety Unspecified
Ante Incised: Ante Variety	(not represented)
Asote Orange: Asote Variety	Asote Orange: Variety Unspecified
Baadz Tan: Incised Variety	Variegated Incised: Variety Unspecified
Balanza Black: Balanza Variety	Balanza Black: Variety Unspecified
Bocul Orange-on-cream: Bocul Variety	Aguila Orange: Buff and Polished Variety
Bocul Orange-on-cream: Variety Unspecified	Aguila Orange: Buff and Polished Incised Variety
Boleto Black-on-orange: Boleto Variety	Boleto Black-on-Orange: Variety Unspecified
Boxcay Brown: Boxcay Variety	Boxcay Brown: Variety Unspecified
Cabcoh Striated: Cabcoh Variety	(not represented)
Cabrito Cream Polychrome: Cabrito Variety	Cabrito Cream Polychrome: Variety Unspecified

Table 1.1. (*continued*)

Callaghan and Neivens de Estrada Type: Variety	Callaghan (2008) Type: Variety
Calam Buff: Calam Variety	Calam Buff: Variety Unspecified
Caldero Buff Polychrome: Caldero Variety	Caldero Buff Polychrome: Variety Unspecified
Cambio Unslipped: Cambio Variety	Cambio Unslipped: Variety Unspecified
Cameron Incised: Cameron Variety	Cameron Incised: Variety Unspecified
Cameron Incised: Variety Unspecified	(not represented)
Canhel Unslipped: Canhel Variety	Unnamed Unslipped Impressed: Tecomates
Centenario Fluted: Centenario Variety	Centenario Fluted: Variety Unspecified
Chacchinic Red-on-orange-brown: Chacchinic Variety	Chacchinic Red on Orange-Brown: Variety Unspecified
Chaquiste Impressed: Chaquiste Variety	Chaquiste Impressed: Variety Unspecified
Chicin'a Black: Chicin'a Variety	(not represented)
Chicin'a Black: Incised Variety	(not represented)
Chinja Impressed: Floresas Variety	Chinja Impressed: Form A Variety
Chinja Impressed: Tuspán Variety	Chinja Impressed: Form B Variety
Chito Red-and-unslipped: Chito Variety	Muxanal Red on Cream: Variety Unspecified
Chito Red-and-unslipped: Variety Unspecified	Muxanal Incised: Variety Unspecified
Chunhinta Black: Chunhinta Variety	Chunhinta Black: Variety Unspecified
Deprecio Incised: Deprecio Variety	Deprecio Incised: Variety Unspecified
Desvario Chamfered: Desvario Variety	Desvario Chamfered: Variety Unspecified
Desvario Chamfered: Horqueta Variety	Desvario Chamfered: Variety Unspecified
Dos Arroyos Orange Polychrome: Dos Arroyos Variety	Dos Arroyos Orange Polychrome: Variety Unspecified
Dos Hermanos Red: Dos Hermanos Variety	Dos Hermanos Red: Variety Unspecified
Eknab Black: Eknab Variety	Chi Black: Variety Unspecified
Eknab Black: Incised Variety	Chi Black Incised: Variety Unspecified
Encanto Striated: Encanto Variety	Encanto Striated: Variety Unspecified
Flor Cream: Flor Variety	Flor Cream: Variety Unspecified
Flor Cream: Variety Unspecified (Wayab)	Flor Cream Group
Guitara Incised: Guitara Variety	Guitarra Incised: Guitarra Variety
Guitara Incised: Noctún Variety	Guitarra Incised: Variety Unspecified
Ixcanrio Orange Polychrome: Ixcanrio Variety	Ixcanrio Orange Polychrome: Ixcanrio Variety
Ixcanrio Orange Polychrome: Turnbull Variety	Ixcanrio Orange Polychrome: Turnbull Variety
Ixcanrio Orange Polychrome: Variety Unspecified (Wayab)	Ixcanrio Orange Polychrome: Variety Unspecified
Japon Resist: Japon Variety	Japon Resist: Variety Unspecified
Jobal Red: Incised Variety	(not represented)
Jobal Red: Jobal Variety	(not represented)
Jocote Orange-brown: Jocote Variety	Jocote Orange-Brown: Variety Unspecified
Joventud Red: Ixtoc Variety	Joventud Red: Variety Unspecified
Joventud Red: Joventud Variety	Joventud Red: Joventud Variety

continued

Table 1.1. (*continued*)

Callaghan and Neivens de Estrada Type: Variety	Callaghan (2008) Type: Variety
K'atun Red: Incised Variety	Kitam Incised: Variety Unspecified
K'atun Red: K'atun Variety	Uck Red: Variety Unspecified
K'atun Red: Lak Variety	Aac Red on Buff: Variety Unspecified
K'atun Red: Lak'ek Variety	Aac Red on Buff: Variety Unspecified
Kitam Incised: Kitam Variety	Kitam Incised: Variety Unspecified
Laguna Verde Incised: Grooved-incised Variety	Laguna Verde Incised: Groove-Incised Variety
Laguna Verde Incised: Laguna Verde Variety	Laguna Verde Incised: Variety Unspecified
Lak'in Red-on-white: Incised Variety	(not represented)
Lak'in Red-on-white: Lak'in Variety	(not represented)
Lechugal Incised: Lechugal Variety	Lechugal Incised: Variety Unspecified
Lucha Incised: Lucha Variety	Lucha Incised: Variety Unspecified
Lucha Incised: Variety Unspecified	Lucha Incised: Variety Unspecified
Maquina Brown: Maquina Variety	Maquina Brown: Variety Unspecified
Miseria Appliquéd: Miseria Variety	Miseria Applique: Variety Unspecified
Mo' Mottled: Fluted Variety	(not represented)
Mo' Mottled: Mo' Variety	(not represented)
Muxanal Red-on-cream: Muxanal Variety	Muxanal Red on Cream: Muxanal Variety
Nitan Composite: Nitan Variety	Nitan Composite: Variety Unspecified
Ochkin Orange: Incised Variety	(not represented)
Ochkin Orange: Ochkin Variety	(not represented)
Palmar Orange Polychrome: Palmar Variety	Palmar Orange Polychrome: Variety Unspecified
Paso Danto Incised: Paso Danto Variety	Paso Danto Incised: Paso DantoVariety
Paxbán Unslipped: Paxbán Variety	Unnamed Unslipped: Censerware
Pita Incised: Pita Variety	Pita Incised: Variety Unspecified
Pital Cream: Pital Variety	Pital Cream: Pital Variety
Polvero Black: Polvero Variety	Polvero Black: Variety Unspecified
Positas Modeled: Positas Variety	Positas Modeled: Variety Unspecified
Quintal Unslipped: Quintal Variety	Quintal Unslipped: Variety Unspecified
Quintal Unslipped: Variety Unspecified	Quintal Unslipped: Variety Unspecified
Ramonal Unslipped: Variety Unspecified	(not represented)
Reforma Incised: Reforma Variety	Reforma Incised: Variety Unspecified
Repasto Black-on-red: Variety Unspecified	(not represented)
Sak White: Incised Variety	(not represented)
Sak White: Sak Variety	Cocoyol Cream: Variety Unspecified
Sapote Striated: Sapote Variety	Sapote Striated: Variety Unspecified
Savana Orange: Savana Variety	Savanna Orange: Variety Unspecified
Saxche Orange Polychrome: Saxche Variety	Saxche Orange Polychrome: Variety Unspecified

Table 1.1. (*continued*)

Callaghan and Neivens de Estrada Type: Variety	Callaghan (2008) Type: Variety
Sierra Red: Sierra Variety	Sierra Red: Sierra Variety
Sierra Red: Variety Unspecified (Wayab)	Sierra Red: Sierra Variety
Society Hall: Society Hall Variety	Society Hall: Variety Unspecified
Tierra Mojada Resist: Tierra Mojada Variety	Tierra Mojada Resist: Tierra Mojada Variety
Tinaja Red: Tinaja Variety	Tinaja Red: Variety Unspecified
Trapiche Incised: Trapiche Variety	Trapiche Incised: Variety Unspecified
Triunfo Striated: Triunfo Variety	Triunfo Striated: Variety Unspecified
Triunfo Striated: Variety Unspecified	Triunfo Striated: Variety Unspecified
Unnamed Black-on-orange (Chak 1)	(not represented)
Unnamed Black-on-orange (Chak 2-3)	Unnamed Black-on-Orange: Variety Unspecified
Unnamed Dichrome (Sierra Group)	(not represented)
Unnamed Modeled (Aguila Group)	(not represented)
Unnamed Modeled (Sierra Group)	(not represented)
Unnamed Modeled and Painted (Chak 2-3)	Unnamed Modeled and Painted
Unnamed Modeled (Molded)-carved (Chak 3)	Unnamed Modeled-Carved: Variety Unspecified
Unnamed Polychrome (Chak 1)	(not represented)
Unnamed Polychrome (Chak 2-3)	Unnamed Polychrome: Variety Unspecified
Unnamed Polyhcrome (K'ak)	Unnamed
Unnamed Punctated (Sierra Group)	(not represented)
Unnamed Red Slipped (K'ak 2-3)	Unnamed
Unnamed Red-and-unslipped (Sierra Group)	(not represented)
Unnamed Red-on-cream (Chak 2-3)	Unnamed Red-on-Cream Carved: Variety Unspecified
Unnamed Red-on-cream Incised (Pital Group)	Muxanal Incised: Variety Unspecified
Unnamed Red-on-orange (Caramba Group)	(not represented)
Unnamed Trickle-on-gray (Zapatista Group)	(not represented)
Unnamed Unslipped (pre-Mamom)	Unnamed Unslipped: Jars (pre-Mamom)
Unnamed Unslipped and Modeled (K'ak)	(not represented)
Unnamed Unslipped Red Paste (pre-Mamom)	(not represented)
Urita Gouged-Incised: Urita Variety	Urita Gouged-Incised
Xaman Red-on-white: Xaman Variety	(not represented)
Xpokol Incised: Xpokol Variety	(not represented)
Zacatel Cream Polychrome: Zacatel Variety	Zacatel Cream Polychrome: Variety Unspecified
(not represented)	Variegated: Variety Unspecified (Itzamkanak)
(not represented)	Variegated Incised: Variety Unspecified (Itzamkanak)
(not represented)	Imitation Fine Orange (Kisin)
(not represented)	Unnamed Thin Walled Orange (Kisin)

THE HOLMUL REGION

The Holmul Region is located in the northeastern Department of the Petén, Guatemala (Figure 1.1). The region is composed of eight recorded sites varying in size, with dates of occupation spanning approximately 1900 -years, beginning in the Early Middle Preclassic period (1000 BC) and ending in the Terminal Classic period (AD 900). This area is defined as an archaeological region because the sites are located on uplands bounded by low, wet areas, and share characteristics of material culture, particularly in terms of ceramic inventories. The Holmul region is north of Naranjo and south of Witzna.

The eight sites include the two major civic-ceremonial centers of Holmul and Cival as well as the intermediate-sized and smaller centers of Hamontun, Hahakab, T'ot, La Sufricaya, Riverona, and K'o (Figure 1.2). All sites are located on a karstic hilly upland plateau bounded on the north, west, and south by low seasonally inundated areas locally known as *bajos*. These *bajos* are further bounded on the north, west, and south by an approximate 200m high escarpment, which forms one larger geographical basin. The Río Holmul, is today a seasonal river; it flows from south to north during the wettest periods of the year and drains the southern and western *bajos*. The river runs southwest to northeast and splits the upland plateau where the archaeological sites are located. Annual precipitation is approximately 200 cm with the strongest rainfall occurring in June, September through October, and December and January (Estrada-Belli and Koch 2007; Wahl et al. 2013). Drainages, including the Rio Holmul, usually flow for short periods of time during the wettest periods of the year, but do not run during the dry season (approximately February through May). Modern vegetation varies with topography and drainage. Well-drained upland areas containing archaeological sites are characterized by high, dense canopy composed of ramon (*Brosimum alicastrum*), cedar (*Cedrela* spp.), ficus (*Ficus glaucensces*), chico zapote (*Manilkara zapota*) and mahogany trees (*Swietenia macrophylla*) (Ford 1986; Wahl et al. 2013). Palm species such as corozo (*Orbignya cohune*), escoba (*Cryosophila argentea*), and guano palm (*Sabal* spp.) grow in the areas between upland zones and *bajos* (Wahl et al. 2013). *Bajo* vegetation varies depending on the amount of water present year-round. In less frequently inundated areas, vegetation consists of leguminous scrub species, like the palo tinto (*Haematoxylum campechianum*). Herbaceous vegetation such as grasses, rushes, and sedges predominate in the lowest and perennially inundated parts of the *bajos*, which are called *civales*. Finally, riparian forests composed of palms, upland trees, and thorny bamboo groves characterize the land along rivers and streams.

The ceramics classified in this study were discovered in surface and subsurface contexts in the civic-ceremonial centers of six of the eight main sites located in the Holmul region: Holmul, Cival, Hamontun, T'ot, La Sufricaya, and K'o. Material recovered from smaller settlements outside and between civic-ceremonial centers were also classified, as were whole pots from recent excavations in the civic-ceremonial center of Dos Aguadas, which is just outside the Holmul region.

The site of Holmul is located on the west side of the Río Holmul. The civic-ceremonial core of Homul is approximately 800 m by 600 m and is comprised of three main acropolis-type groups (Figure 1.3). Holmul was first mapped and excavated in 1911 by Raymond Merwin (Merwin and Vaillant 1932), but was not investigated again until Francisco Estrada-Belli initiated a regional-scale project in 2000 (Estrada-Belli 2000, 2010). Notable contexts at Holmul include Merwin's original excavations into Building B, Group II, where he discovered a sequence of superimposed tombs containing ceramic material spanning the Late Preclassic through early facet Early Classic periods (AD 0–550). Among these materials were examples of the earliest polychrome painted pottery in the Maya lowlands, which dates to the Terminal Preclassic period (AD 120–230). More recently, Late Preclassic period stucco masks were discovered on substructures beneath Building B (Estrada-Belli 2010). Recent excavations into Building A, also on the Group II platform, have uncovered an early Late Classic period building adorned with a stucco frieze containing a hieroglyphic inscription that mentions political interactions between the Late Classic period site of Naranjo and Holmul (Estrada-Belli 2013; Estrada-Belli and Tokovinine 2016). A possible royal tomb was discovered inside this building and a burial was uncovered underneath the main staircase. The Holmul ceramics used in this report come from early Middle Preclassic through Terminal Classic contexts (1000 BC–AD 900) that are listed in Appendix B.

Figure 1.1. Map showing the location of the Holmul region (by Michael G. Callaghan, Holmul Archaeological Project).

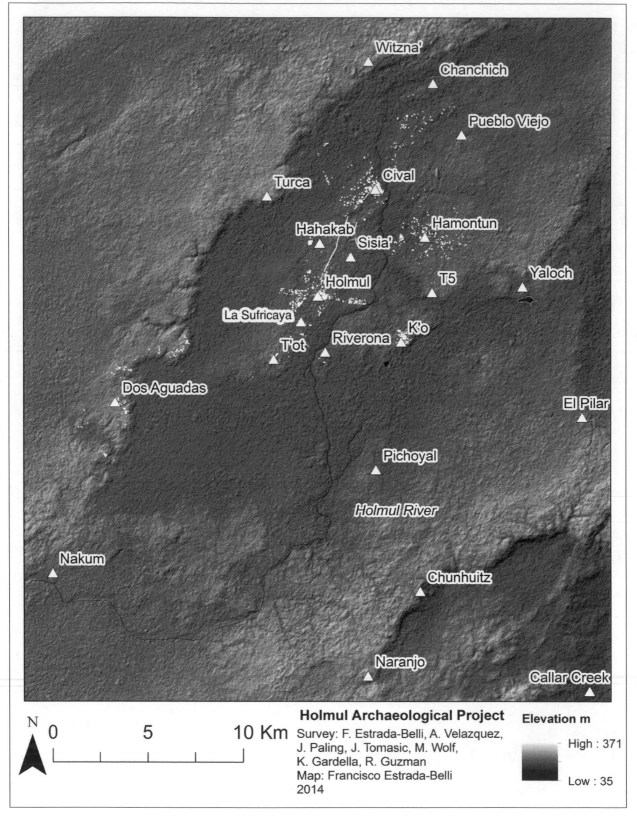

Figure 1.2. Shaded relief map of the Holmul region (Holmul Archaeological Project. Elevation data courtesy of NASA/Japan ASTER-GDEM2 program).

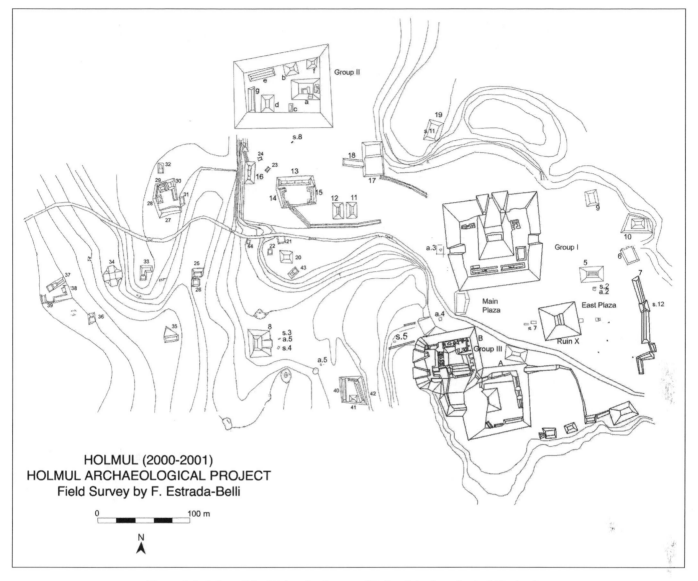

Figure 1.3. Map of the Holmul epicenter (Holmul Archaeological Project).

Cival is a large civic-ceremonial center located adjacent to a natural pond (*cival*) approximately 6.5 km north of Holmul on the west side of the Río Holmul (Figures 1.2 and 1.4). According to Estrada-Belli (2001:10), Ian Graham originally mapped the site in 1984, but excavations did not begin until 2001. The site center is approximately 750 m by 1000 m with architecture and plazas centered on a main group consisting of a Preclassic period triadic platform and an E-Group complex. Cival is notable for contexts uncovered in its E-Group plaza and triadic platform. In 2003, archaeologists Molly Morgan and Jeremy Bauer discovered a series of caches in the main E-Group plaza. The stratigraphically lowest cache was in a cruciform-shaped cut dug into bedrock. It and contained ceramic jars and jade (celts and pebbles) (Morgan and Bauer 2003). A fragmentary Late Preclassic period stela (Cival Stela 2) was also found in the E-Group plaza (Estrada-Belli 2003). In the triadic group adjacent to the E-Group compound, Estrada-Belli discovered a series of masks representing celestial deities that date to the Late Preclassic period (Estrada-Belli 2006b). Ceramic material used in this report comes from contexts at Cival that are listed in Appendix B. These contexts date from the early Middle Preclassic through the Late Classic periods (1000 BC–AD 800).

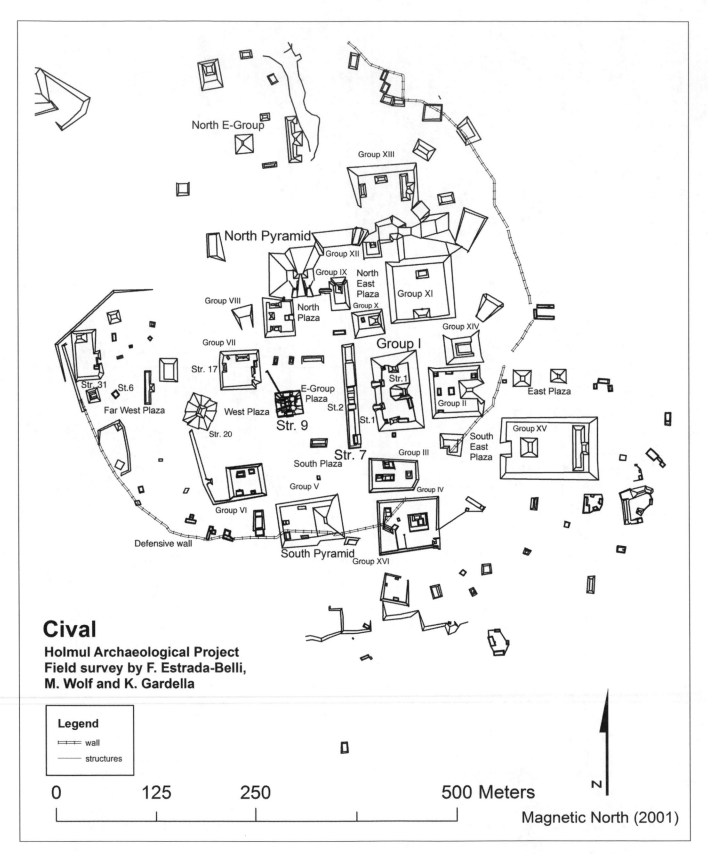

North E-Group

Group XIII

North Pyramid

Group XII

Group IX

North East Plaza

Group VIII

Group X

North Plaza

Group XI

Group XIV

Group VII

Group I

Str. 17

Str. 1

East Plaza

Str. 31

St.6

E-Group Plaza

St.2

Group II

Far West Plaza

West Plaza

St.1

Group XV

Str. 9

Str. 20

South East Plaza

Str. 7

Group III

South Plaza

Group V

Group IV

Group VI

South Pyramid

Defensive wall

Group XVI

Cival

**Holmul Archaeological Project
Field survey by F. Estrada-Belli,
M. Wolf and K. Gardella**

Legend

wall

structures

0   125   250   500 Meters

N

Magnetic North (2001)

Figure 1.4. Map of the Cival epicenter (Holmul Archaeological Project).

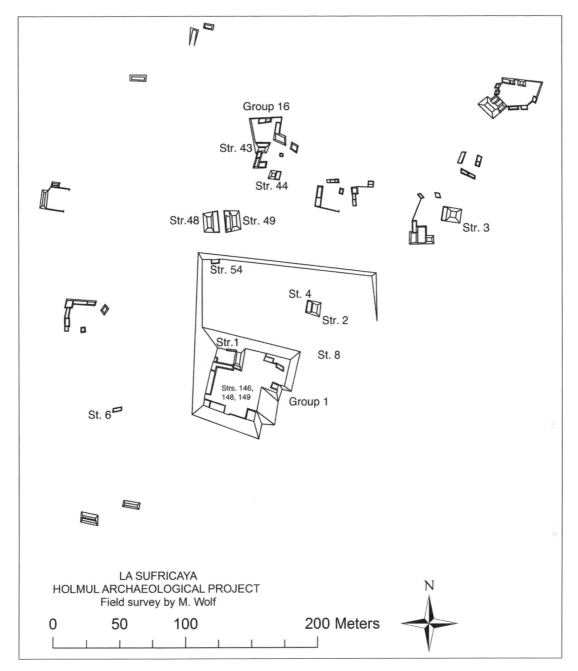

Figure 1.5. Map of La Sufricaya epicenter (Holmul Archaeological Project).

The smaller Early Classic center of La Sufricaya is located on the west side of the Río Holmul approximately 1.2 km west of Holmul (Figures 1.2 and 1.5). According to Estrada-Belli (2001:12), the site was discovered and its monuments first documented by Ian Graham in 1984. The area mapped in 2001 and subsequent field seasons is approximately 400 m by 320 m, but the majority of architecture at the site sits atop a narrow, 150-m-long ridge that runs southwest to northeast. The site is best known for its seven fragmentary stelae and a palace structure with painted murals (Estrada-Belli 2001; Estrada-Belli et al. 2009; Tokovinine and Estrada-Belli 2015). The murals and stelae date to the Early Classic period and document historical events occurring around AD 378, the time of the arrival of the elite Teotihuacan culture in the southern Maya lowlands. Ceramic material used in this

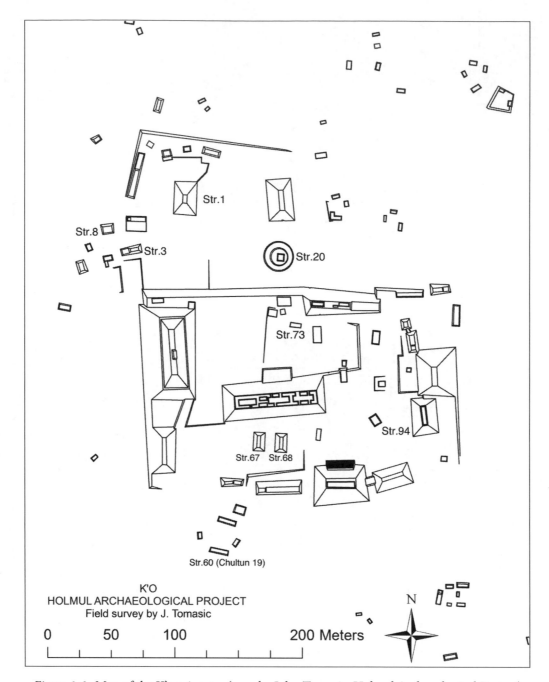

Figure 1.6. Map of the K'o epicenter (map by John Tomasic, Holmul Archaeological Project).

report comes from the contexts at La Sufricaya listed in Appendix B. These contexts date from the Late Preclassic period through the Late Classic period (300 BC–AD 800).

The site of K'o (previously named "Lechugal") is located approximately 4.6 miles southeast of Holmul on the east side of the Río Holmul (Figures 1.2 and 1.6). K'o contains a civic-ceremonial center measuring approximately 400 m by 480 m. The site is most notable for its Middle to Late

Preclassic period *chultun* found beneath Structure 60 in Patio Group 4 just south of the main civic-ceremonial core (Tomasic 2009; Tomasic and Bozarth 2011). The *chultun* contained a single extended burial with seven vessels, one of which is an incised effigy bowl picturing an anthropomorphic face wearing a possible trefoil jewel headband. Ceramic material used in this report comes from the contexts at K'o listed in Appendix B. These contexts date from

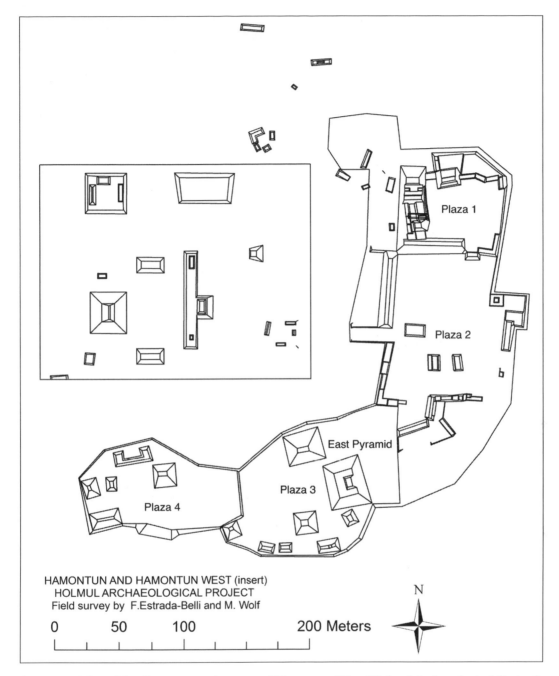

Figure 1.7. Map of the Hamontun epicenter and Hamontun West (Holmul Archaeological Project).

the late Middle Preclassic period through the Terminal Classic period (600 BC–AD 900).

The site of Hamontun is located approximately 1.5 km from the east bank of the Río Holmul and 5 km northeast of the site of Holmul (Figures 1.2 and 1.7). Hamontun is a densely populated settlement containing a civic-ceremonial center with an E-Group compound. The site was discovered by Estrada-Belli (2002) and later investigated by Jason Paling (Estrada-Belli 2009; Paling et al. 2011). Only surface finds discovered in Estrada-Belli's initial reconnaissance of the site were included in this report. Ceramic material used in this report comes from the contexts at Hamontun listed in Appendix B. Ongoing work at Hamontun suggests that the site dates from the late Middle Preclassic period through the Terminal Classic period (600 BC–AD 900).

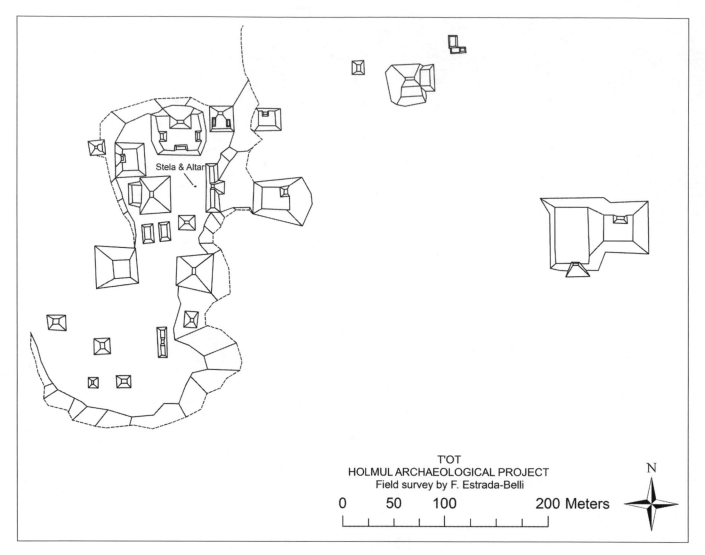

Stela & Altar

T'OT
HOLMUL ARCHAEOLOGICAL PROJECT
Field survey by F. Estrada-Belli

0   50   100   200 Meters

N

Figure 1.8. Map of the T'ot epicenter (Holmul Archaeological Project).

The site of T'ot (previously known as Caracol) is located 4 km southwest of Holmul on the west side of the Río Holmul (Figures 1.2 and 1.8). The site is located on a narrow, 160- to 170-m high ridge. T'ot is comprised of a settlement that surrounds a civic-ceremonial center containing Late Preclassic period. Architecture. The site was not part of any intensive excavation at the time of our research, so only surface finds from reconnaissance in 2001 were included in our analysis. Ceramic material used in this report comes from the contexts at T'ot listed in Appendix B. The small sample from T'ot used in this study contains dates from the Late Preclassic period (400 BC–AD 230).

Riverona is a little-studied site in the Holmul region. It is located 3.4 km south of Holmul on the east side of the Río Holmul (Figures 1.2 and 1.9). It contains three main groups within an approximate 400-m by 150-m area as well as four plain stelae. Ceramic material from Riverona is not reported in this study.

Hahakab is another less-studied site in the Holmul region. It is located 3.5 km north of Holmul on the west side of the Río Holmul (Figures 1.2 and 1.10). The site consists of a small civic-ceremonial center including an E-Group; it was mapped and sampled by Justin Ebersole (Estrada-Belli 2002). Ceramic material from Hahakab is not reported in this study.

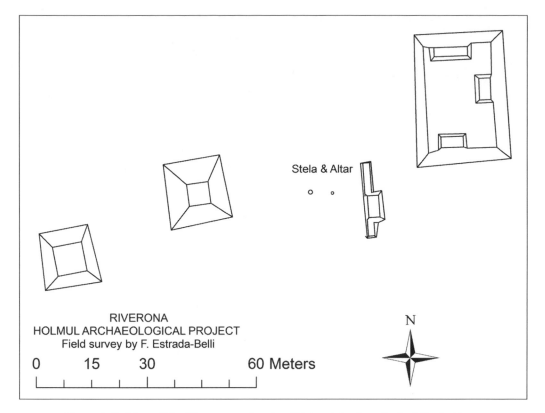

Figure 1.9. Map of the Riverona epicenter (Holmul Archaeological Project).

Dos Aguadas is located outside the Holmul region on the ridge that makes up the western escarpment enclosing the Holmul Basin (Figures 1.2 and 1.11). The site is located approximately 13 km southwest of Holmul. Dos Aguadas contains a large civic-ceremonial center concentrated around an E-Group compound, as well as a dense surrounding settlement. The site was the subject of mapping and excavation in 2012 (Estrada-Belli 2012). Only whole pots associated with burial contexts (listed in Appendix B) are reported in this study. Ongoing work at Dos Aguadas suggests that the site dates from the Late Preclassic period through the Terminal Classic period (400 BC–AD 900).

HISTORY OF RESEARCH

This study includes ceramic material recovered in Merwin's 1911 investigations at Holmul as well as multiple years of the Holmul Regional Archaeological Project directed by Estrada-Belli (2000, 2001, 2002, 2003, 2004, 2005, 2007, 2008, 2009, 2012, 2013). Merwin's 1911

investigations included the mapping and sampling of monumental architecture in the civic-ceremonial center at Holmul (Merwin and Vaillant 1932). Most notable among Merwin's initial finds was the discovery and excavation of Building B in Group II at Holmul. The building and substructures contained a series of superimposed tombs with ceramic material dating from the Late Preclassic period, Terminal Preclassic period, and early facet Early Classic period (see also Callaghan 2013; Callaghan et al. 2013). Unfortunately, Merwin passed away before he was able to fully complete his report on the 1911 excavations. George Vaillant later co-published Merwin's findings with his own analyses of material discovered during Merwin's initial excavations and created the first ceramic sequence for Holmul (Merwin and Vaillant 1932). Vaillant was also able to use material recovered by Merwin from Building B, Group 2, along with early excavation data from other sites in the Maya lowlands, to create the first interregional lowland Maya ceramic sequence (Vaillant 1927). Although the pottery recovered by Merwin in 1911 continued to be the subject of archaeological inquiry

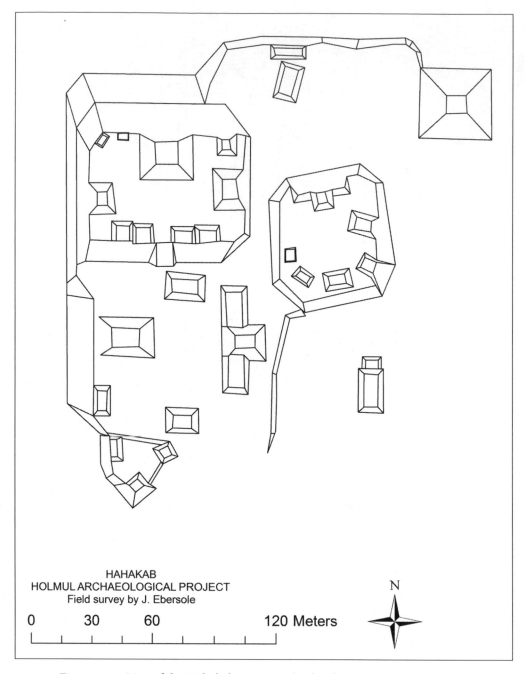

Figure 1.10. Map of the Hahakab epicenter (Holmul Archaeological Project).

through the late 1990s, excavation did not take place at the site of Holmul for nearly 90 years.

Estrada-Belli began investigation of the Holmul region in the Spring of 2000. The project was initiated with the goal of building on Merwin's original research in an effort to understand the evolution of ancient Maya political institutions from the Preclassic to Classic periods. The region was an appropriate area to test hypotheses concerning the evolution of ancient Maya politics not only because of Merwin's previous discovery of continuous occupation from the Late Preclassic through Classic periods, but also because the Holmul region was located at an important geographical and political crossroads between the large and powerful

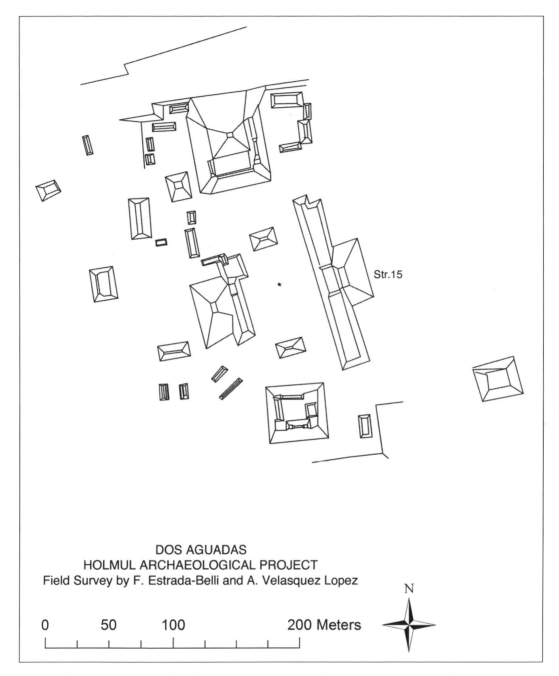

Str.15

DOS AGUADAS
HOLMUL ARCHAEOLOGICAL PROJECT
Field Survey by F. Estrada-Belli and A. Velasquez Lopez

N

0   50   100   200 Meters

Figure 1.11. Map of the Dos Aguadas epicenter (Holmul Archaeological Project).

site of Tikal and other important Classic period sites to the north, east, and south (i.e., Naranjo, Yaxha, Nakum, Xultun, El Pilar, Buenavista del Cayo, and Xunantunich) (Estrada-Belli 2001) (Figure 1.12). It was expected that investigations in the Holmul region would not only provide information on the evolution of local political institutions, but would contribute to the understanding of interregional political developments in the southern Maya lowlands.

Investigation began with mapping, clearing of looters' trenches, and small-scale excavation at the site of Holmul in 2000 (Estrada-Belli 2000). The scale of the project expanded in 2001 to include mapping and sampling of Cival, T'ot, Riverona, La Sufricaya, and K'o (Estrada-Belli

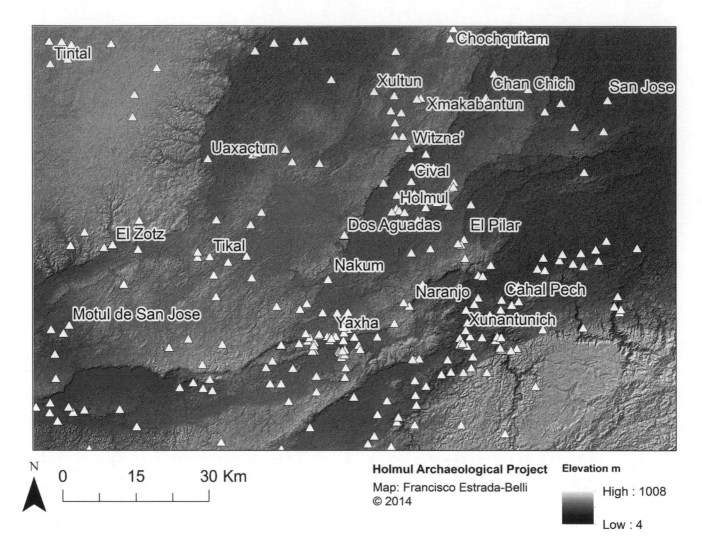

Figure 1.12. Shaded relief map showing the location of Holmul in relation to other Preclassic and Classic-period capitals (Holmul Archaeological Project, Elevation data courtesy of NASA/Japan ASTER-GDEM2 program).

2001). In 2002, investigation continued at the sites of Holmul, La Sufricaya, Cival, and K'o. Study also expanded to include the mapping and sampling of Hahakab. Extensive excavation and conservation took place in the civic-ceremonial centers of Holmul, Cival, and La Sufricaya in 2003 through 2008 (Estrada-Belli 2002, 2003). K'o became the focus of investigation in 2007 and 2008 (Tomasic 2009). In 2008, the focus at Cival shifted to GPS mapping and sampling of groups around the civic-ceremonial core of that site while investigations continued at Homul and K'o (Estrada-Belli 2008). Mapping and sampling at Hamontun became the focus of investigations in 2009 along with continued excavation and conservation at Holmul (Estrada-Belli 2009). Studies

of human-environmental interaction were initiated in 2010 with the goal of reconstructing climate and environmental conditions during human occupation of the Holmul region in the late Holocene (Wahl et al. 2013). These data were later compared to settlement histories of sites in the Holmul region to gain a better understanding of the growth and decline of populations and political institutions in relation to environmental factors (Wahl et al. 2013). An emphasis on human-environmental interactions continued in 2011 and 2012 with the project expanding to map and sample the site of Dos Aguadas, as well as to take cores in water features around that site (Estrada-Belli 2012; Wahl et al. 2013). Excavation also continued at Holmul. In 2013, mapping and excavation of substructure architecture continued at Holmul and Cival (Estrada-Belli 2013). The present study contains classification and interpretations of all sherds and whole vessels from the 2000 to 2005 field seasons, a sample of sherds and whole vessels from the 2007 field season, and whole vessels from the 2008 to 2013 field seasons.

EPIGRAPHIC HISTORY

Due to the limited number of monuments in the Holmul region, few historical data are available. It is, however, helpful to present what is known about the Holmul region from epigraphic sources, as this information bears on the relationship between the ceramics classified in this study and cultural-historical events in the region and larger Maya lowlands. The earliest inscribed monument in the Holmul region, Stela 2, comes from the site of Cival and has been dated stylistically to the Preclassic period (Estrada-Belli 2002, 2006a; Estrada-Belli et al. 2003). Several inscribed monuments and painted murals were found at the site of La Sufricaya (all from Structure 1 in Group 1). These murals and monuments date to the Early Classic period, and their texts and images imply a relationship between La Sufricaya, Tikal, and the central Mexican polity of Teotihuacan (Estrada-Belli et al. 2009; Tokovinine and Estrada-Belli 2015). Some monuments and murals reference the AD 378 date of the purported arrival of Teotihuacan elites at Tikal. This date is recorded at several lowland Maya sites and is usually related to the presence of Teotihuacan-style iconography and material culture, such as ceramics, at the sites where it is mentioned (Braswell 2004).

Alexandre Tokovinine (2005) has pieced together fragments of the Late and Terminal Classic political history of the Holmul region from portable artifacts discovered in Merwin's 1911 excavations, Holmul Project excavations directed by Francisco Estrada-Belli from 2000 to 2006, and pieces in various museums and private collections. The record is scarce, but Tokovinine (2005) identifies potential links between the site of Naranjo and Holmul in the Late and Terminal Classic periods. He also identifies the presence of a local title, *Chak-Tok-Wayab*, that extends from Early Classic times to the Terminal Classic period at Holmul (see Estrada-Belli et al. 2009). One specific mention of this title was found on a stingray spine associated with the burial of an elite individual in Room 1, Building B, Group II at Holmul. The pottery associated with this burial dates to the Tzakol 2 facet of the Tzakol sphere and will be discussed in the type-descriptions and summary chapter. In 2013, an intact stucco frieze was discovered on a substructure beneath Building A, Group II at Holmul. The frieze depicts three individuals and there is a hieroglyphic text below them. The center figure is believed to be a local Holmul ruler, while the two figures seated on either side of him are suggested to be supernatural figures (Estrada-Belli 2013). The text is complicated, but Tokovinine believes it records the seating of a local Holmul ruler under the auspices of the founder of the Late Classic dynasty at Naranjo (a king named *Aj Wosal*) (see Estrada-Belli and Tokovinine 2016).

Taken together, these epigraphic data suggest that sites in the Holmul region played an important role in larger politics of the Preclassic and Classic periods, an assertion predicted by Merwin's original finds at Holmul and the region's location at a crossroads between Tikal and its powerful neighbors to the east and north. What these data also reveal is that the epigraphic record is insufficient to tell us about the evolution of political systems in the region (much less the daily lives of ordinary people), and more lines of evidence are needed to answer the many questions about culture-history and process in the area. This is why ceramic classification continues to be an important part of the Holmul Regional Archaeological Project and one of the many reasons we sought to undertake and publish this study.

TYPOLOGICAL METHOD AND SAMPLE

Principles and Terminology within Modal and Type: Variety Classification Systems

This study is based upon the principles of a combined type: variety-mode classification system (see Forsyth 1983, 1989; Gifford 1976; Kosakowsky 1987; Sabloff 1975). Rice (2013:11–15) summarizes the procedures inherent in systems of classification. Classification begins with grouping (i.e., physically sorting) objects into units based upon similar characteristics. Rice recognizes two kinds of grouping procedures, categorization and identification. Categorization involves the assignment of objects into completely new groups, whereas identification involves the assignment of objects into previously existing groups. The majority of descriptions in the present study detail ceramics grouped according to identification (i.e., placement of ceramic material into previously existing type: varieties and modes). However, the study also includes descriptions of categorizations (i.e., the assigning of ceramics to new groups).

After grouping comes classification proper, or paradigmatic classification, which leads to the creation of a typology or "a conceptual structure of attributes relating to theoretical needs" (Rice 2013:14). The type: variety-mode classification model creates a hierarchical taxonomic typology based on ceramic attributes of surface, paste, and form in that order. For most ceramicists and archaeologists employing type: variety-mode analysis, the typology is related to theoretical needs regarding temporal-spatial frameworks within and among sites and regions. Data from these typologies can then be used to address other mid- and high-level theoretical questions.

Type: variety-mode analysis is based upon the principles of two conceptually distinct, yet often combined, systems of classification that employ different procedures for creating groups. Rice (1987:277) and Rouse (1960) suggest that type: variety classification is primarily taxonomic, while modal classification is analytic. Both systems of classification involve the placing of ceramic material into groups based upon ceramic attributes. A ceramic attribute is a single characteristic related to the paste preparation, forming, firing, or finishing/decoration of a piece of pottery. According to Gifford (1976:9), "Attributes are the fundamental observational working data of pottery and represent the most rudimentary factors of manufacture of which the artisan could have been conscious."

Although modal and type: variety classifications both create groupings based upon ceramic attributes, the way analysts use those classifications stem from different conceptual frameworks. In modal classification, categorization and identification are what Rouse (1960) and Rice (1987) term "analytical" and involve the grouping of ceramic material into units based on form, paste, surface, and firing attributes—the constituent parts that make up a pot. Meaningful analytical units are referred to as "modes." A mode encompasses both a physical and a social dimension. Rouse (1960:313) explains that,

> By the term "mode" is meant any standard, concept, or custom which governs the behavior of the artisans of a community, which they hand down from generation to generation, and which may spread from community to community over considerable distances (Rouse 1939). Such modes will be reflected in the artifacts as attributes which conform to a community's standards, which express its concepts, or which reveal its customary ways of manufacturing and using artifacts. Analytic classification focuses on

these attributes and, through them, attempts to get at the standards, concepts, and customs themselves. In effect, it attempts to read such modes out of the artifacts.

Rice (1987:277) uses a similar definition of mode stating that "modes are certain attributes the analyst judges to reflect communitywide standards for manufacturing and using the ancient artifacts. . . . Modes represent efforts to achieve some isomorphism between categories of devised classifications and those of the ancient makers and users of the pottery—that is, to replicate ancient folk classifications." I have always been uncomfortable with the previous definitions of ceramic mode. I hesitate to imply a relationship between a frequently occurring ceramic attribute and some kind of community standard or cultural ideal. Therefore, in this study I employ the more neutral definition provided by Forsyth (1983:9): "A mode is a ceramic attribute or cluster of attributes that demonstrates significance in its own right. Modes may cross-cut [*sic*] types and varieties, but remain unaltered in each case. Modes are, of themselves, important aspects of analysis." This definition more closely resembles Smith, Willey, and Gifford's (1960:331) definition in their initial application of type: variety classification to Maya ceramic units.

It can be argued that influential early classifications of pottery in the Maya area were "modal" in nature including Kidder, Jennings, and Shook's (1946) classification of ceramics from Kaminaljuyu, Smith's (1955) seminal publication on the ceramics from Uaxactun, Longyear's (1952) classification of pottery from Copan, and Thompson's (1958) classification of modern Yucatecan pottery (see also Sharer 1978 for Chalchuapa; Smith 1971 for Mayapan). In these publications, ceramic material was categorized into groups based upon modes of form and decoration, which were in turn assigned to larger categories termed "wares." In these earlier publications, analysts conceptualized wares as combinations of paste, form, and surface modes (but, not always in that order). Modal classifications using this concept of ware are rare at sites in the Maya lowlands today, but have been published and are still being used in other areas of Mesoamerica (see Caso et al. 1967; Love 2002; Poponoe de Hatch 1997; Rattray 2001).

Type: variety classification was formulated by archaeologists working in the American southwest (Colton and Hargrave 1937; Gladwin and Gladwin 1930; Wheat et al. 1958). The method was later adopted by archaeologists working in the American Southeast (Phillips 1958) and subsequently revised by archaeologists working in the Maya area (Gifford 1960; Smith et al. 1960; Willey et al. 1967). Traditional type: variety classification is ideally a "taxonomic process" (Rice 1987:277; Rouse 1960) in which the goal is to group ceramic material into a hierarchical system emphasizing attributes related primarily to surface finish and decoration. Before continuing, it is important to note that, in practice, modal and type: variety classifications are not as dichotomous as they may appear. Analysts who have employed type: variety often record and make note of other modes—specifically form and paste—in their studies (see Gifford 1976; Kosakowsky 1987; Forsyth 1983, 1989; Sabloff 1975). Therefore, instead of labeling this classificatory approach simply as "type: variety," it is often more useful and appropriate to term it "type: variety-mode" as it is used today. In addition, the reader will note that in this publication I use the nomenclature "type: variety-mode" as opposed to "type-variety-mode" or "type-variety." Here I follow Aimers's (2013:xiv–v) reasoning that "there is probably a good argument to be made to use *type: variety* and *type: variety-mode*, because the colon between the first two terms reflects the intimate connection between types and their varieties and is also used in notation (e.g., San Felipe Brown: San Felipe Variety), whereas the hyphen nicely indicates the less consistent and potentially separable inclusion of modal data in type variety."

Within type: variety classification emphasis is placed upon the creation and ordering of types and varieties. A ceramic type is the combination of ceramic attributes (i.e., two or more modes, or even single or combined ceramic attributes) that are believed to have temporal and spatial significance (Forsyth 1983:8; Gifford 1960:341). Varieties are, "a component of the type. Varieties within the type are distinguished from one another by a relatively small number of attributes and or minor temporal and/or spatial variations." (Forsyth 1983:8). Varieties, then, are subgroupings of types defined by minor yet consistent and classifiable variations in ceramic attributes.

Types are combined with other types into larger units based on similarities in surface, form, and paste characteristics called "groups." Groups, "demonstrate a distinctive homogeneity in range of variation concerning form, base color, technological, and other allied attributes." (Gifford 1963b:23). Groups are then combined with one another and classified into categories of "ware," which ideally represent a combination of technological characteristics, but in practice are usually defined by shared surface and/or

paste attributes (Forsyth 1983:9; Rice 1976). Wares and groups can then be integrated into larger temporal-spatial units. These units include subcomplexes (Ball 1977:3–4), complexes (Forsyth 1983:9), horizons (Forsyth 1983:9; Willey et al. 1967:305), systems (Forsyth 1983:9; Gifford 1976:12), traditions (Forsyth 1983:9; Gifford 1963b:29), macro-traditions (Bill 2013:33), and spheres (Forsyth 1983:9; Willey et al. 1967:305). In part, it was the comparative power of these larger temporal-spatial concepts that led us to use type: variety classification in the present study. The study returns to these concepts often, so it is useful to define them here.

In this report I use Ball's (1977:3–4) definition of subcomplex and complex. Ball (1977:3) argues that a subcomplex represents "ceramic assemblages of lesser stature, defined on the basis of assumed or apparent pertinence to a particular functional class. Thus, types that consistently occur in burial, dedicatory, offertory, or ceremonial contexts may be classified into mortuary, cache vessel, or censer subcomplexes." An example of a subcomplex in the Holmul region would be Terminal Preclassic period polychrome serving vessels that regularly appear as whole pots in burial and ritual contexts.

Subcomplexes differ from ceramic complexes proper. Complexes are "ceramic assemblages with specific temporal, spatial, and cultural integrity and boundaries" (Ball 1977:3) or, "the sum total of the ceramic content of an archaeological unit or phase. The ceramic complex has a definite setting in time and space" (Forsyth 1983:9). That is, a ceramic complex consists of all utilitarian, serving, and trade ware types that are temporally and spatially bounded. I separate the ceramic sequence in the Holmul region into a description of Early Middle Preclassic pre-Mamom ceramics, four succeeding ceramic complexes, and one subcomplex spanning the Late Middle Preclassic through Terminal Classic periods.

In this report I use Forsyth's (1983:9) definition of ceramic horizon, which "consists of ceramic complexes that contain a common set of horizon markers. A horizon marker consists of 'distinctive and chronologically significant modes shared by two or more ceramic complexes' [Willey et al. 1967:305]." The term ceramic horizon defines a short-lived but expansive distribution of pottery with a specific set of paste, form, firing, and surface modes (i.e., horizon markers). A notable ceramic horizon occurs during the Terminal Preclassic period in the Maya lowlands (AD 150–250) when some widely distributed sites in the central and eastern Maya area contain ceramics with distinct modes of form and decoration including, composite silhouette bowl forms, bulbous mammiform supports, and black-and-red-on-orange polychrome painting.

Ceramic systems and traditions are also temporally and spatially bounded groupings of ceramic types. In this study ceramic systems are defined as a group of "roughly contemporaneous types that range over a wide [geographically continuous] area and that are related to one another in particular from the standpoint of decorative treatment, design style, and surface manipulation" (Gifford 1976:12). The terms "tradition" and "macro-tradition" add depth of time and breadth of types to the system concept. In this report I follow Forsyth's (1983:9) definition of ceramic tradition or a set of "modes that can be shown to persist through time. The 'stress is upon a mode as the constant element in a pottery tradition as opposed to the pottery type' [Gifford 1963a:20]. The ceramic tradition thus represents modes that have a relatively long temporal span and that can often and do crosscut types." Bill (2013:33) incorporates ceramic systems and traditions into her definition of a "macro-tradition," stating "the term macro-tradition is suggested here to refer to these specific types of long-lived widely shared ceramic systems that, (1) continue over very long periods of time, indeed, often over the entire occupational history of a region . . . (2) maintain the same geographic boundaries over time . . . and (3) the ceramics (that is, pottery types and modes) associated with these long-lived systems are not generally found outside of those boundaries except as occasional imports or with rare, and explainable, exceptions." Bill explains that fine black serving vessels in the southern Maya area are an example of a macro-tradition spanning many complexes at many sites in the southern Maya lowlands. The concepts of horizon, system, tradition, and macro-tradition are valuable. They have the power to inform our ideas about a prehistoric people's cultural values, social interactions, and technological choices and, in turn, allow researchers to address mid- and high-level theoretical concepts pertinent to the ancient Maya. These terms are employed in this volume in an effort to quantify and qualify ceramic interaction among sites in the Holmul region and between the Holmul region and other areas.

Finally, in this study I use Willey's and colleagues' (Willey et al. 1967:306) definition of ceramic sphere. Specifically, "a ceramic sphere exists when two or more complexes share a majority of their most common types. Whereas the horizon need imply no more than a few connections at the modal level, the sphere implies high content similarity at the typological level." As with horizons, systems, traditions, and macro-traditions, ceramic spheres are temporally and spatially bounded distributions of ceramics that are thought to be the product of cultural interaction. An example of a ceramic sphere would be the well-defined Chicanel sphere, which is composed of multiple site-complexes sharing the majority of their types during the Late Preclassic period in the southern Maya lowlands.

Advantages and Disadvantages of Modal and Type: Variety-Mode Systems

There are advantages and disadvantages to using type: variety-mode vs. modal or other "nonhierarchical systems" of classification (see Sagebiel 2005). Modal and other nonhierarchical systems create groups based on attributes related to each separate stage of the production process (namely, paste preparation, forming, firing, and surface finish/decoration). This makes modal classification an excellent choice if goals of ceramic classification are related to production studies. Because modal classification emphasizes grouping by individual modes, it allows for intrasite and intersite comparison of ceramics along multiple separate lines of inquiry (i.e., paste, form, firing, and surface) (see also Culbert and Rands 2007). Modes, however, are not the most reliable indicators of temporal or spatial boundaries (Sabloff 1975:3-4). Many sites within a region (or different regions) can share ceramics with the same modes, thereby masking differences that could be identified by looking at combinations of modes.

Individual modes may also have a tendency to persist in time through periods of great cultural change, whereas combinations of modes can be more reliable indicators upon which to build chronological frameworks. Because the type: variety-mode system classifies ceramic material according to clusters of attributes (i.e., two or more modes), it allows for the creation of varieties and types that may be more sensitive to change over time and influence from other sites or regions. Because the type: variety-mode system classifies material based upon combinations of modes, it allows the analyst to sort more material in less time than does a strictly modal classification where each piece of material must be coded for multiple modes. While modal and other nonhierarchical systems may be an ideal form of classification, in practice they can be more time-consuming than traditional type: variety-mode classification, which itself is no speedy endeavor.

For these reasons, a combined type: variety-mode approach to classify ceramics of the Holmul region is employed. This type of approach allowed researchers (1) classify a large amount of material in a relatively short period of time, (2) meet the objectives of the larger research strategy by creating a sensitive regional temporal-spatial framework that could be compared to data from other sites, and (3) undertake separate analyses of paste, form, firing, and surface modes that can help answer questions related to cultural practice and process. I recognize there are still a number of problems with using this particular form of classification. Those problems are addressed in the next section. But first, the method of classification used in this study is briefly outlined.

Sample and Method

This classification is the result of 15 years of continuous work on ceramic material from sites in the Holmul region. Type: variety-mode classification was begun in 2000 by Laura Kosakowsky (2001), who defined the late Middle Preclassic through Terminal Classic complexes (600 BC–AD 900) using material recovered in the first season of excavations at the site of Holmul. Ceramic classification continued with the help of Bernard Hermes who identified material in an effort to date excavation contexts from the 2001 to 2004 field seasons. Hermes initially identified a handful of sherds belonging to a possible early Middle Preclassic (1000–840 BC) ceramic complex at the sites of Holmul and Cival. I began work on the classification in 2005. Working with collections from previous years, I sorted and recorded all contexts from the 2000 to 2005 field seasons. Classification began in field laboratory facilities in Melchor de Mencos in May 2005 and later moved to permanent labs in Antigua, Guatemala, in June 2005. Sorting and recording of all material continued through the 2006 field season. In 2007, I began a strictly modal analysis of Late Preclassic, Terminal Preclassic, and early-facet Early Classic types (Callaghan 2005, 2008; Callaghan et al. 2013). In 2008 through 2015, Nina Neivens de Estrada and Diana Méndez-Lee focused on classification of pre-Mamom ceramics in the region (Neivens de Estrada 2014). Neivens de Estrada, Méndez-Lee, and Sylvia Alvarado continued sorting and classificatory work from select contexts excavated between the years 2008 and 2013. The present classification is based on 47,761 diagnostic samples including 151 whole vessels, and incorporating vessels from Merwin's original excavations (see Merwin and Vaillant 1932).

The procedure for classifying sherds ideally followed a five-step process that involved washing, labeling, sorting, counting, and recording. Archaeologists bagged ceramic material according to archaeological context in the field. Archaeological contexts were labeled on bags according to site name, site operation number, sub-operation, excavation unit, lot, archaeological context, date of collection, and excavator's initials. A non-exhaustive list of archaeological contexts includes wall-fall, humus, midden, plaza fill, construction fill, burial, and special deposit, among others. The field archaeologist determined archaeological context. In the field, archaeological lots were excavated in natural layers of deposition. After collection, ceramics were washed and dried. Ideally all ceramics were then labeled. Clear nail polish or whiteout was used to create an even surface on which to write, then context numbers were written on the sherds using black ink. Sorting took place on large tabletops in labs. Analysts sorted ceramics by lots within units within operations. The stratigraphically lowest lot in a unit was sorted first, then progressed through the uppermost lot, which contained humus or surface material. Sorting occurred by first culling eroded ceramics. Completely eroded, unidentifiable ceramics were separated from potential diagnostic sherds. Depending on the context, eroded sherds could outnumber diagnostic pieces. Although eroded sherds were not counted I estimate that they amounted to between three and five times the number of diagnostic sherds classified in this study (some 150,000 to 250,000 sherds). Because the type: variety-mode classification was used, sorting of diagnostic sherds began by first identifying type-classes or "all pottery upon which a particular kind of surface treatment appears" (Gifford 1963a:35; see also Gifford 1976:25 and Forsyth 1983:10). Examples of type-classes include red, black, cream, and polychromes. Type-classes were then separated into types, varieties, groups, and wares (in that order). Counts were recorded first on paper ledgers and the data were later entered into a Microsoft Access database. Sherds were then bagged according to variety with a tag placed in the bag noting the variety. Bags of varieties were then bagged by type and types bagged into groups. All bags were then placed back into the original excavation bags and stored. Exceptions to the bagging procedure took place for two reasons: (1) if certain varieties or types were being subject to separate modal analyses, or (2) if sherds were chosen as diagnostics for the laboratory type collection. Complete or restored whole vessels and diagnostic sherds were photographed and drawn.

As in any type: variety-mode classification of Maya ceramics, we encountered some problems with classification and existing type: variety definitions. I discuss these problems and our particular strategies to address them next.

REVISIONS TO TYPE: VARIETY-MODE CLASSIFICATION

Despite its utility in classifying ceramic material, there are a number of well-documented critiques of the type: variety-mode system (see for example Aimers 2013; Forsyth 1983:229-241; Rice 2013). The discussion in this section does not address every problem that previous analysts have expressed in relation to type: variety classification, only those that relate to the immediate study. These problems include (1) "pigeonholing" or misclassification due to differential fragmentation of vessels, (2) miscounting whole vessels or inaccurate representations of MNI, (3) emphasis on surface characteristics over attributes related to form, paste, and firing, (4) creating new type names for each ceramic complex despite the tendency for old types to persist through new complexes, and (5) definition and integration of the ware concept into type: variety-mode classification.

One of the most frequently discussed issues in using the type: variety-mode classification is the potential to misclassify and miscount type: varieties (Bryant et al. 2005; Demarest 1986; Foias and Bishop 2013:44; Gifford 1976:6; Hammond 1972). The following scenario is often used to illustrate this problem. Analysts have suggested that when a vessel contains a decoration on a portion of its surface and is fragmented, this results in the creation of sherds belonging to two specific ceramic types (i.e., a plain type and a decorated type). If a vessel contains multiple types of decoration and is fragmented, it then creates sherds of multiple ceramic types (i.e., a plain type or variety and multiple decorated types or varieties). A similar problem occurs when a sherd displays more than one type of decoration (e.g., both black and red slip). Forsyth (1983:231–232) refers to this problem as pigeonholing. Essentially, an analyst is forced to pigeonhole or classify a sherd into one type: variety despite the fact that a sherd displays multiple modes of decoration, or that the sherd could come from a whole vessel with multiple forms of decoration. This problem is created because type: variety was conceptualized to identify or classify whole vessels, but the actual sample that analysts work with is composed of vessel fragments, or sherds (see

Gifford 1976:6). Of course, when large enough samples of sherds with consistent multiple decorative attributes are discovered this problem can be ameliorated with the creation of a new variety designation (as is the case when whole vessels are present as well). The problem persists, however, in the case of fragmented vessels with multiple forms of surface decoration.

Some investigators have tried to address this misclassification problem by classifying ceramics at the level of the group (see for example Foias and Bishop 2013:46; Forsyth 1989; Urban et al. 2013). Analysts argue that this strategy is particularly useful in relation to problems created by large samples of eroded sherds, as well as breakage of vessels into plain and decorated sherds. Analysts argue that when plain sherds are classified on the level of type: variety, this artificially inflates the plain type: variety within a given ceramic group. Proponents of this approach argue that classifying plain sherds on the level of the group solves the problem of artificial inflation of plain type: varieties. This strategy was not used in the present study because it does not necessarily solve the misclassification problem. If all plain sherds were counted on the group level, no plain type: variety would exist for any given group, making type: variety counts unusable for analysis and interpretation, and essentially undermining the utility of the entire classification. Because much of the analysis and interpretation of classification occurred on the level of the group (which encompasses all type-varieties both plain and decorated within that group), misidentification at the type: variety level should not dramatically affect any conclusions.

Somewhat related to this issue is the reconstruction of vessel counts based on a sample of vessel fragments. In an effort to accurately calculate the number of whole vessels in each type: variety category, rims were counted separately from bodies. Ceramic group frequencies were determined by rim counts, not total number of sherds. Rim count is a more reliable indicator of minimum number of vessels than is the count of body sherds. When possible I applied procedures of contextual classification in which stratigraphic/cultural contexts were studied together in the chance that pieces of the same pots would appear in different lots and units of a larger operation. Specifically, rim and body sherds that could be refitted to one another were counted as one rim or one body (Chase and Chase 2013).

Ceramicists have often remarked that systems of classification based on type: variety principles emphasize modes of surface characteristics over modes associated with paste, form, and firing (Culbert and Rands 2007; Foias 2004:144). The potential result is loss of important information about nonsurface-related modes. Because modal studies of paste, form, and firing were another important goal of the larger ceramic study at Holmul, this type of information could not be lost in the baseline typology. In order to alleviate this problem sherds and whole vessels were coded for attributes of paste, form, and firing mode in addition to type-variety. Principal identifying nonsurface-related attributes were listed in our type descriptions and were searchable in the Access database built for the project. Note that not all sherds underwent intensive modal analysis, only those used in my study of Late Preclassic, Terminal Preclassic, and Early Classic material (Callaghan 2008; Callaghan et al. 2013).

Another common critique of the type: variety classification system is that new type names can be used for types that crosscut ceramic complexes (Adams 1971:30; Forsyth 1983:5; Lincoln 1985). Forsyth (1989:8) uses the example of plain unslipped types of the Middle and Late Preclassic periods. Traditionally, the unslipped utilitarian type of the Middle Preclassic period is labeled Achiotes Unslipped, whereas the unslipped type of the Late Preclassic period is labeled Paila Unslipped. Forsyth found little difference between unslipped ceramics of the Middle and Late Preclassic periods at El Mirador, which led him to collapse the two types into one group—namely, the Achiotes Unslipped Group. In the present classification I made similar modifications including the deletion of Paila Unslipped. Other specific revisions can be seen in the type-descriptions. It is important to note that I did not follow Forsyth (1989:7–10) in collapsing many other wares, groups, or types as the sample did not warrant it.

Finally, another complicated aspect of traditional type: variety classification has been the definition and analytical integration of the "ware" concept (Aimers 2013; Ball 1977:3; Rice 1976; Willey et al. 1967:304). Many analysts agree that ware is defined by technological characteristics of a sherd, particularly those characteristics related to surface finish and paste composition (Ball 1977:3; Gifford 1976:14; Forsyth 1983:9; Sabloff 1975:27; Sabloff and Smith 1972:98; Willey et al. 1967:304). Some analysts—most notably Rice (1976, 2013)—disagree with this definition and propose using only surface finish to define ware with a separate "paste ware" classification. Analysts also disagree on how ware should be integrated into type: variety-mode classifications. While Smith (Willey et al. 1967:304) suggested that ware be integrated into type: variety classification as a hierarchical category

above the level of group, type, and variety, other analysts believe that ware should be abstracted from the group, type, variety taxonomy, because ware (i.e., technological characteristics) usually crosscut varieties on the lowest taxonomic level of analysis (see Ball 1977:3; Gifford 1976:14).

In this study, classification of the late Middle Preclassic (Mamom), Late Preclassic (Chicanel), Terminal Preclassic ("Protoclassic"), Early Classic (Tzakol), and Late Classic (Tepeu) complexes and subcomplexes follows Ball (1977:3; Ball and Taschek 2003), abstracting the concept of ware from the typological hierarchy. Classification of Holmul region material revealed that, although it is helpful as a potential technological analytical category, ware is not hierarchically related to groups and actually crosscut types and varieties. The most striking example comes in the form of Middle Preclassic period Joventud Group material. As I explain in chapter 3, I classified Joventud Group material into two wares: (1) a local Unspecified Ware characterized by glossy red slip and yellow-orange paste with volcanic ash inclusions, and (2) the established lowland Maya Flores Waxy Ware characterized by waxy or soapy red slip and crystalline calcite and/or grog inclusions. In this instance, surface and paste technology crosscut what is inarguably the same "type" of ceramic material. Although unconventional, this methodology is not without precedent. Ball and Taschek (2003:199–203) have noted a similar distinction in wares that crosscut the Joventud Group in the Middle Preclassic period of the Belize River Valley. There, they recognize an established Joventud Red that belongs within the Flores Waxy Ware, as well as local type: varieties that they claim belong to a new ware, which they call Yesoso Orange Paste Ware (Ball and Tashchek 2003). Related to this last point an effort was made to decrease confusion related to how wares are defined (i.e., based on surface characteristics or paste characteristics), when defining established type: varieties of wares that have been defined previously based on paste characteristics. The term "Paste Ware" (for example, "Mars Orange Paste Ware") was added in order to qualify and call a distinction between this established "Paste Ware" and other established wares defined by surface finish (such as "Flores Waxy Ware" or "Uaxactun Unslipped Ware"). In this way, I follow Rice (1976) and Ball and Taschek (2003), who suggest that analysts be more explicit in how they determine a specific ware—that is, by technology associated with surface finish or paste. In the event that a new type: variety is being defined, the descriptions make explicit whether the ware is being determined by characteristics of surface finish or paste. In her discussion of the Pre-Mamom material in the Holmul region (Chapter 2), Neivens de Estrada uses different criteria.

THE CERAMIC COMPLEXES

The current Holmul region ceramic sequence is presented in relation to other Maya area sequences in Figure 1.13. Vaillant's original complex names (i.e., Holmul I–V) were not retained as they began in the Terminal Preclassic period (Holmul I) and ended in the Late Classic period (Holmul V), and in some instances did not represent true breaks or changes in complexes. The Holmul sequence was created by using a combination of absolute and relative dating techniques including (1) carbon dating of organic material found in association with whole vessels in sealed, well-stratified contexts (Table 1.2), (2) ceramic seriation of modes and types of pottery found in Holmul region excavations, and (3) cross-dating ceramic modes and types of Holmul region pottery with pottery found in other Maya sites.

Neivens de Estrada and Estrada-Belli named the ceramic complexes through a combination of god-names and Maya concepts. Neivens de Estrada tentatively names the early Middle Preclassic presence of Pre-Mamom material K'awil after God K, who is associated with maize and the dawn of Maya complex society (Taube 1985). This early Middle Preclassic material dates between 1000 and 840 BC. The following late Middle Preclassic Yax Te Complex is named after a combination of *yax* or the color green and *te* referring to a count of time (Mathews and Biro 2006). This complex was named after a special deposit found in the plaza of the main E-Group at Cival. The deposit contained a cruciform cache of greenstone celts and pebbles, along with five smashed water jars (see Morgan and Bauer 2003). The Yax Te Complex dates between 840 and 400 BC. The Late Preclassic complex dates between 400 BC and AD 230 and was named Itzamkanak after the Maya creator deity Itzamna (Mathews

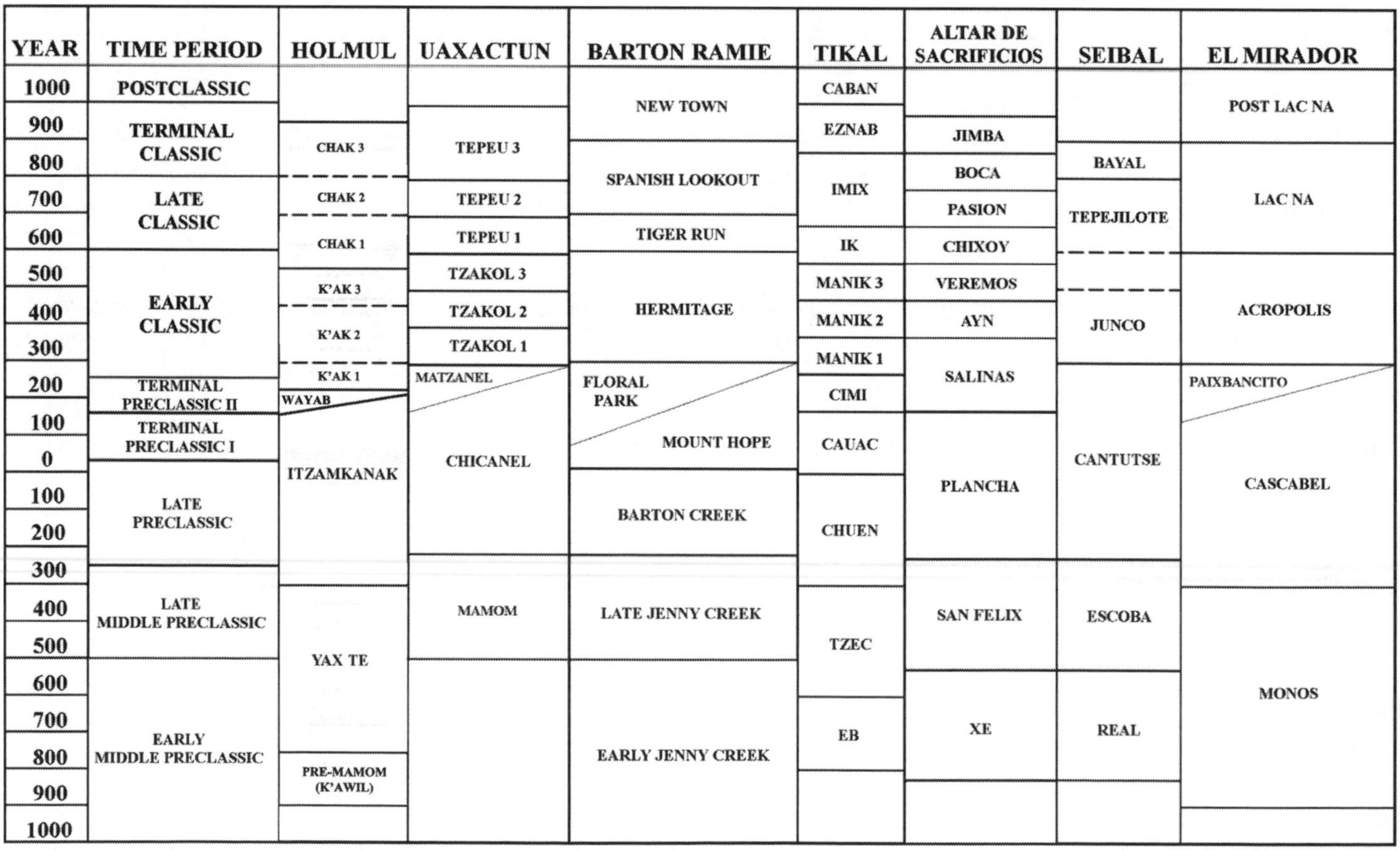

YEAR	TIME PERIOD	HOLMUL	UAXACTUN	BARTON RAMIE	TIKAL	ALTAR DE SACRIFICIOS	SEIBAL	EL MIRADOR
1000	POSTCLASSIC				CABAN			POST LAC NA
900	TERMINAL CLASSIC			NEW TOWN	EZNAB	JIMBA		
800		CHAK 3	TEPEU 3			BOCA	BAYAL	
700	LATE CLASSIC	CHAK 2	TEPEU 2	SPANISH LOOKOUT	IMIX	PASION	TEPEJILOTE	LAC NA
600		CHAK 1	TEPEU 1	TIGER RUN	IK	CHIXOY		
500	EARLY CLASSIC	K'AK 3	TZAKOL 3		MANIK 3	VEREMOS		
400			TZAKOL 2	HERMITAGE	MANIK 2	AYN	JUNCO	ACROPOLIS
300		K'AK 2	TZAKOL 1		MANIK 1			
200	TERMINAL PRECLASSIC II	K'AK 1 / WAYAB	MATZANEL	FLORAL PARK	CIMI	SALINAS		PAIXBANCITO
100	TERMINAL PRECLASSIC I			MOUNT HOPE	CAUAC		CANTUTSE	
0		ITZAMKANAK	CHICANEL			PLANCHA		CASCABEL
100	LATE PRECLASSIC			BARTON CREEK	CHUEN			
200								
300								
400	LATE MIDDLE PRECLASSIC		MAMOM	LATE JENNY CREEK		SAN FELIX	ESCOBA	
500		YAX TE			TZEC			
600								MONOS
700					EB	XE	REAL	
800	EARLY MIDDLE PRECLASSIC	PRE-MAMOM (K'AWIL)		EARLY JENNY CREEK				
900								
1000								

Figure 1.13. The Holmul region ceramic sequence compared to other Maya area sequences (by Michael G. Callaghan).

Table 1.2. Radiocarbon Dates and Ceramic Complexes within the Holmul Region, Guatemala

Context	Uncalibrated	1-Sigma	2-Sigma	Complex	Reference
Cival, Burial 33	2670+/-40 BP	895–840 BC	900–790 BC	Pre-Mamom	Estrada-Belli 2008:44
Cival, Cache 4	2520+/-40 BP	680–550 BC	800–520 BC	Yax Te	Estrada-Belli 2006b:44
Holmul, Building B, Group II, Phase I	2300+/-40 BP	400–340 BC	----	Itzamkanak	Estrada-Belli 2008:15
Cival, Structure 1, Phase 4	2170+/-40 BP	260–160 BC	360–90 BC	Itzamkanak	Estrada-Belli 2006b:65
Holmul, Building B, Group II, Burial 10	1840+/-40 BP	AD 120–230	AD 80–250	Wayab (Sub)	Estrada-Belli 2006a:4

and Biro 2006). The succeeding Terminal Preclassic period subcomplex was named Wayab, which translates to "sleep or dream" (see Mathews and Biro 2006) and is closely related phonetically to Wayeb, the last five days in the Maya Haab calendar system. These last five days are considered by the ancient Maya to be a mysterious and unpredictable time of year—much like our present knowledge of the events in the Terminal Preclassic period itself. This subcomplex dates between AD 120 and 230. The Early Classic complex was named K'ak, which often means fire or tongues of fire (Mathews and Biro 2006) and dates between AD 230 and 550. This is the time period in which the first rival polities and Classic period dynasties appeared in the Maya lowlands. K'ak is split into three facets: namely, K'ak 1 (AD 230–300), K'ak 2 (AD 300–450), and K'ak 3 (AD 450–550). Lastly, the Late Classic to Terminal Classic period complex was named Chak, which represents the rain and thunder deity of the Classic period (Mathews and Biro 2006) and dates between AD 550 and 950. This larger complex is also split into three facets: namely, Chak 1 (AD 550–693), Chak 2 (AD 693–800), and Chak 3 (AD 800–900).

Versions of the Holmul Region sequence have appeared in previous publications (Callaghan 2005, 2008, 2013; Kosakowsky 2001). Revisions to the most recently published version of the sequence (Callaghan 2013) include the deletion of the previously defined Ixim Complex, which would have occurred between the tentative K'awil Complex and Yax Te Complex. Initially, it was thought that the local expressions of previously established Mamom Complex types were chronologically older than the conventional Mamom types. But a more in-depth contextual analysis of deposits containing potential Ixim material that were stratigraphically beneath or mixed in with Yax Te material, showed that the material previously thought to represent an earlier ceramic complex (similar to the Tzec Complex defined at Tikal by Culbert 1993, 2003) was actually contemporaneous with Yax Te material. What was being called Ixim material proved instead to be previously unclassified types of local Mamom Complex ceramics. The current study reflects this revision.

TYPE: VARIETY-MODE PRESENTATION

Ceramic complexes are presented with a brief introduction, followed by a complete list of ceramic types and varieties. Type descriptions are then presented. The descriptions include the following terms and analytic categories:

Type: variety Name: This term provides the type: variety name based upon the type: variety classification system established by Smith, Willey, and Gifford (1960) for the Maya lowlands. Names can be either (1) established type: varieties previously defined by other analysts or (2) new type: varieties developed during the course of this classification. Established type: variety names were used when the sherd or whole vessel could be positively classified as an established type: variety based on paste, form, firing, and surface attributes identical to established type: varieties defined and illustrated in published reports or studied in person by the volume authors. In the case of classifying sherds or whole vessels as established type: varieties, sherd frequency was not taken into account. In this report, however, new type: varieties were created using different frequency criteria. Despite differences of opinion on establishing new types, the volume authors broke from established type: variety protocols and chose to define new type: varieties based on more than just surface attributes. Combinations of surface, form, and paste attributes were used to define new type: varieties in the chapters describing Middle Preclassic period ceramics. Specific arguments for creating new types appear in the "comments" section for each type.

In the chapters dedicated to the description of material from the late Middle Preclassic (Yax Te), Late Preclassic (Itzamkanak), Terminal Preclassic (Wayab), Early Classic (K'ak), and Late Classic (Chak) new types or varieties were created and named according to criteria established by Ball (1977). To paraphrase, new varieties and new types were created when an attribute or attributes consistently differed from established varieties or types and were "believed to have chronological, areal, or functional significance" (Ball 1977:4). If a new type: variety consistently differed from an established type: variety and numbered less than 50 rim sherds, the variety was classified as "Unspecified." This system is more conservative than that used by Ball (1977:4), who used a count of 50 total sherds to exceed the threshold of "Unspecified" variety. New type: variety names in these complexes were created in accordance with standards outlined by Phillips and Gifford (1959:22–24), and Smith, Willey, and Gifford (1960). Namely, the type: variety name consists of two terms: the type name, composed of a geographical term and a descriptive term, as well as a variety name composed of a noun and in some cases a descriptive term (e.g. Bocul Orange-on-cream: Bocul Variety). The category "Unnamed" is used for new types with small samples for which there is no discernable link to prior designated type: varieties. In her contribution outlining the Pre-Mamom material in the Holmul region, Neivens de Estrada employed different criteria from the standards outlined here. This has enabled her to create new type: varieties using smaller sample sizes and nontraditional nomenclature (see also Bryant et al. 2005:12–17).

Established: This term provides a reference to when, where, and by whom the type and variety were established.

Group: This term indicates the ceramic group name in which the type: variety is included.

Ware: This term refers to the classification of ceramic material based on technological characteristics related to surface finish or paste attributes (Ball 1977:3; Gifford 1976:14; Forsyth 1983:9; Sabloff 1975:27; Sabloff and Smith 1972:98; Willey et al. 1967:304). In the chapters discussing late Middle Preclassic through Late Classic material, I define ware on the basis of surface finish alone, unless established wares have been defined by paste characteristics. In that case the term "Paste Ware" was used. In Chapter 2 Neivens de Estrada uses different criteria, which are defined in that chapter.

Ceramic Complex: This term places a specific type: variety into a temporally defined ceramic unit within the Holmul region.

Sphere: This term refers to the ceramic sphere affiliation for the complex and type: variety.

Ceramic Group Frequency: Sample frequencies include the number of rims, the number of whole vessels (if present), the number of bodies, the total number of sherds, the type: variety percent of its respective ceramic group, and the type: variety percent of ceramic complex. Ceramic group frequencies are based on rim counts (including whole vessels), which I think are a better representation of minimum number of individual vessels than the total number of sherds.

Principal Identifying Attributes: This is a list of the most common attributes identified for the type and variety.

Paste, Firing, and Temper: This category provides a description of paste texture, color, inclusions, and any evidence left of the firing process. Paste texture refers to the classification of the overall size of inclusions in the paste ranging from Very Fine Sand (1/16 to 1/8 mm) to Very Coarse Sand (1.0 to 2.0 mm) as defined by the Wentworth (1922) scale. Paste color is defined both in qualitative terms (e.g., yellow, red, black, etc.) and quantitative terms using the Munsell Soil Color Chart (2012). Color readings were taken outside in daylight or inside with the use of a daylight bulb. Inclusions are considered to be any nonplastic particles visible with an Omano stereo-zoom microscope with magnification up to 70×. Overall paste classification or inclusion classification falls into three types: calcite-based, volcanic ash-based, or mixed calcite and volcanic ash. Note that I use the term "ash" rather than "glass" in reference to volcanic pastes. I consider "ash" to be very fine glass-like volcanic inclusions that appear as spicules or small tubes under magnification up to 70×. Firing characteristics refer to hardness, and the presence or absence, location, relative color, and size of a firing core.

Surface Finish and Decoration: In this category, surface finish technique and decorative attributes are described. Attributes of surface finishing include evidence of smoothing, slipping, polishing, or tooling. Slip and unslipped color were recorded both on a relative scale (i.e., yellow, red, black, etc.) and in quantitative terms using the Munsell Soil Color Chart (2012). Color readings were taken outside in daylight or inside with the use of a daylight bulb. Evidence of firing technology as it pertains to surface appearance was also recorded and included the presence or absence, location, size, and color of fire clouds as well as the presence or absence and extent of slip crackling. Decorative attributes and painting were also recorded and qualified or quantified using metric measurements and the Munsell Soil Color Chart. Methods of decoration and types of design follow Smith (1955 v.1:37–74).

Forms: This category provides a description of vessel form. Vessel forms encompass five general categories: plate, dish, bowl, vase, and jar. Vessel form and all other terminology pertaining to vessel morphology (e.g., rim form, wall form, lip form, base form, support form, etc.) adhere to categories used by Sabloff (1975:22–27) for his analysis of ceramics from the site of Seibal, Guatemala. Aspects of vessel form were determined from morphologically diagnostic sherds such as rims, bases, and appendages. Vessel forms and their associated attributes related to lip and rim treatments and wall and base morphology are listed in descending order of frequency. Rim diameters, wall thickness below the lip, and height (when possible) are provided.

Intraregional Locations and Contexts: This category provides information on where the type: variety was found within the Holmul region. The location is noted at the site level. A brief description of the contexts can be found in Appendix B. Specific burials, caches, and large fill or midden deposits are mentioned when appropriate.

Interregional Locations and Contexts: This category lists references to descriptions of the type: variety from other regions and sites in the Maya area. The references are by no means exhaustive; they include published monographs and some dissertations, mostly from lowland Maya sites. Publications from sites outside of the lowlands are referenced when similarities are noted between Holmul type: varieties and type: varieties at sites in other regions. A more generalized discussion of ceramic sphere affiliations can be found in Chapter 8. Although intersite locations and comparisons are one of the most important categories in regard to ceramic descriptions, such comparisons were, unfortunately, often difficult to formulate. That is because ceramic classifications have few printings and are rarely distributed widely. The authors of this volume made a concerted effort to obtain reports and visit collections as best we could.

Comment: If included, a comment provides a brief statement on some significant aspect of the type: variety in the Holmul region and, when applicable, its relation to material from other sites.

Illustration: Figure numbers for drawings and photos in the present work are included under this category. See Figure 1.14 for color conventions for line drawings.

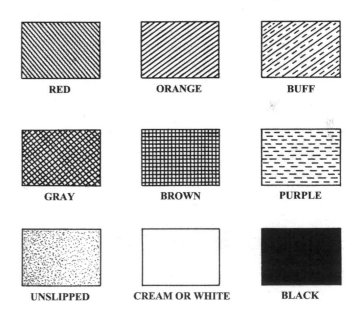

Figure 1.14. Color conventions for line drawings (by Michael G. Callaghan adapted from Smith 1955 v2:ix).

CHAPTER TWO

K'awil Complex

Nina Neivens de Estrada

Pre-Mamom ceramics are the earliest found in the Holmul region. This conclusion was reached by typological comparisons with sites in other regions. Although these ceramics have not been found in stratigraphically isolated contexts, the name K'awil Complex has been assigned to them. It is assumed that further work will produce more pre-Mamom ceramics in the region. Callaghan and I have estimated the start and end dates of this complex through a combination of radiocarbon sampling and type: variety-mode classification. There is no carbon sample currently associated with the beginning of the K'awil Complex, but there is a sample associated with the beginning of the succeeding Yax Te (Mamom) Complex. Burial 33 at Cival, which included a complete Guitara Incised: Noctún Variety bowl, was found below a collapsed *chultun* containing a large Yax Te deposit (Estrada-Belli 2008:38–44). A radiocarbon sample associated with the deposit returned a calibrated date of 895 to 840 BC (Estrada-Belli 2008:44). Recent proxy studies of pollen indicating early settlement in the Holmul region show that the region was initially populated by approximately 1300 BC (Wahl et al. 2013). Based on these lines of evidence, as well as typological similarities with other pre-Mamom complexes that are discussed later in this chapter, Callaghan and I have tentatively placed pre-Mamom pottery between 1000 and 840 BC.

The K'awil Complex is distinguished from the following Yax Te Complex in terms of form, surface finish, and paste. The most common forms in the K'awil Complex are plates and dishes with outcurving sides that also have either exterior thickened rims and pointed lips or wide everted rims. Jars tend to have short, outcurving or vertical necks. Tecomates are also present. The surface finish of slipped ceramics is generally dull. Red-colored slip predominates, with some examples showing signs of specular particles on the surface. In some examples, the red slip lends itself to purple, while in other cases the red tends towards orange. The predominant paste variant in red-slipped ceramics contains volcanic ash.

The descriptions of K'awil material included in this study are derived from analyzing 1,271 rim sherds and 560 diagnostic body sherds for a total of 1,831 sherds. The K'awil Complex is defined by 4 definable wares, 12 groups, and 30 type-varieties (Table 2.1). The majority of type-varieties are decorated serving vessels that are slipped (73.5%) or burnished (18.2%). Unslipped utilitarian vessels account for only 8.3 percent of the sherds. The reader will notice the small quantity of unslipped utilitarian pottery in this study. This is because it has been difficult to chronologically isolate unslipped ceramics without sealed stratified deposits. Analysis of the K'awil material was conservative. Based on surface, paste, and form attributes, only those sherds that could be dated with certainty to the early Middle Preclassic were included in developing the descriptions. Future studies will likely reveal a larger component of unslipped utilitarian types in the tentative K'awil Complex. In addition, pre-Mamom complexes tend to have fewer utilitarian vessels than decorated serving vessels. This is true for the Real Xe (80.5% slipped, 9.5% unslipped), Cunil (percentages not published), and Swasey (91% slipped vs. 9% unslipped) complexes. This suggests that these early ceramics were introduced primarily as serving vessels.

The K'awil Complex is defined on the basis of this classification. K'awil includes varieties of types present in the Cunil Complex of the neighboring Belize River

Table 2.1. Ceramic Wares, Groups, Types, and Varieties of the Early Middle Preclassic Period (K'awil Complex)

Ware	Group (% of complex)	Type: Variety	Numbers			Percentages	
			Rims	Bodies	Vessels	Group	Complex
K'an Slipped	K'an (36.7%)	K'atun Red: K'atun Red Variety	182	208	0	39.0	14.3
		K'atun Red: Incised Variety	104	67	0	22.3	8.2
		K'atun Red: Lak Variety	128	10	0	27.4	10.1
		K'atun Red: Lak'ek Variety	53	8	0	11.3	4.2
	Ochkin (1.1%)	Ochkin Orange: Ochkin Variety	7	2	0	50.0	0.6
		Ochkin Orange: Incised Variety	7	4	0	50.0	0.6
	Baadz (0.2%)	Baadz Tan: Incised Variety	2	1	0	100.0	0.2
	Sak (15.3%)	Sak White: Sak Variety	119	60	0	61.3	9.4
		Sak White: Incised Variety	22	9	0	11.3	1.7
		Lak'in Red-on-white: Lak'in Variety	50	2	0	25.8	3.9
		Lak'in Red-on-white: Incised Variety	3	4	0	1.5	0.2
	Eknab (4.0%)	Eknab: Eknab Variety	46	10	0	90.2	3.6
		Eknab: Incised Variety	5	10	0	9.8	0.4
Belize Valley Dull	Uck (9.2%)	Mo' Mottled: Mo' Variety	44	2	0	37.6	3.5
		Mo' Mottled: Fluted Variety	12	1	0	10.3	0.9
		Kitam Incised: Kitam Variety	61	6	0	52.1	4.8
La Lila Burnished	Calam (18.2%)	Calam Buff: Calam Variety	193	101	0	83.5	15.2
		Ante Incised: Ante Variety	33	14	0	14.3	2.6
		Aac Red-on-buff: Aac Variety	5	15	0	2.2	0.4
Rio Holmul Slipped	Jobal (5.7%)	Jobal Red: Jobal Variety	56	5	0	76.7	4.4
		Jobal Red: Incised Variety	17	12	0	23.3	1.3
	Ainil (0.3%)	Xpokol Incised: Xpokol Variety	4	0	0	100.0	0.3
	Chicin'a (0.6%)	Chicin'a Black: Chicin'a Variety	4	2	0	57.1	0.3
		Chicin'a Black: Incised Variety	3	3	0	42.9	0.2
	Unnamed (0.4%)	Xaman Red-on-white: Xaman Variety	5	2	0	100.0	0.4

continued

Table 2.1. (continued)

Ware	Group (% of complex)	Type: Variety	Numbers			Percentages	
			Rims	Bodies	Vessels	Group	Complex
Unspecified	Canhel (3.5%)	Canhel Unslipped: Canhel Variety	44	2	0	100.0	3.5
	Cabcoh (0.4%	Cabcoh Striated: Cabcoh Variety	5	0	0	100.0	0.4
	Unnamed (4.5%)	Ramonal Unslipped: Variety Unspecified	28	0	0	49.1	2.2
		Unamed Unslipped	9	0	0	15.8	0.7
		Unnamed Unslipped Red Paste	20	0	0	35.1	1.6
		TOTALS	**1271**	**560**	**0**		

Valley (e.g., Mo' Mottled and Kitam Incised) and the Eb Complex of Tikal (Calam Buff), but the presence of these types is not enough to include it within the Cunil or Eb Spheres. K'awil is roughly contemporaneous with the Early Eb Complex at Tikal (Culbert 1993, 2003, 2006; Laporte and Fialko 1995; Laporte and Valdes 1993), the Cunil Complex at Cahal Pech (Awe 1992; Cheetham 1995, 1996, 2005; Cheetham et al. 2003; Clark and Cheetham 2002) and Xunantunich (Strelow and LeCount 2001), Kanocha at Blackman Eddy (Garber et al. 2002), the Early Ah Pam Complex in the Lake Yaxha region (Rice 1979), Xe at Altar de Sacrificios (Adams 1971), Real at Seibal (Sabloff 1975; Inomata et al. 2013, Inomata et al. 2015), the Swasey Complex at Cuello originally defined by Pring (1977b) and later split into Swasey and Bladen by Kosakowsky (1987), Bolay at Colha (Valdez 1987), and Ek/Ch'oh in the Northern Yucatan (Andrews and Bey 2011.). K'awil ceramics were found in greatest quantities at the site of Holmul in subplatform excavations in Buildings B, N, and F in Group II (see Estrada-Belli 2008; Neivens de Estrada 2014). A few diagnostic sherds have been found in construction fill in the epicenter of Cival. It is important to note that, to date, K'awil material has not been found in isolation in the Holmul region. Although it has been found in relatively large quantities in substructure fill beneath Group II at Holmul, K'awil sherds were associated with late Middle Preclassic Yax Te Complex and Late Preclassic Itzamkanak Complex material. This situation adds to the confusion regarding the beginning date of this complex. Despite this material not having been found in an isolated context, I still believe K'awil ceramics represent the presence of a true pre-Mamom complex in the Holmul region.

Descriptions of wares and types are now presented. Initial interpretations about the pre-Mamom sample represented by the K'awil Complex can be found in Chapter 8.

K'AN SLIPPED WARE

K'an Slipped Ware is characterized by a thick slip that adheres well so that examples tend to be well-preserved. The ware includes slips of all major colors common to the lowland Maya, including red (K'atun Group), black (Eknab Group), white (Sak Group), orange (Ochkin Group), and tan (Baadz Group). It is similar to Río Pasión Slipped Ware and Belize Valley Dull Ware in the presence of dull or matte slips. It differs from these in that it is defined based on local types and shows greater diversity in decoration (e.g., more slip colors, more varieties with incised decoration). It is most similar to Belize Valley Dull Ware, which also includes volcanic ash in the paste. It differs from Belize Valley Dull Ware in the color of the slips (e.g., the red group exhibits a darker red rather than orange-red, the black group is more common, and the white is distinct in color and in the presence of an incised variety).

The paste is a yellow color that is usually consistent throughout the body of the sherd, although sometimes a darker gray core is present. Some sherds exhibit an entirely gray paste color that is interpreted as the result of differing firing conditions. Either the vessel was insufficiently fired (temperature too low), or the vessel was fired in a reducing atmosphere (black-slipped vessels). Paste inclusions are well-sorted and scarce, especially in comparison to the contemporary ceramics of Seibal (Río Pasión Ware). Inclusions include ash, mica, and ferruginous particles. These occur in small and regular quantities, indicating that they were part of the original clay matrix rather than having been added as temper to the clay during production. A small quantity of the sample reacts to hydrochloric acid, indicating the presence of calcite. There is little or no organic matter in the paste. K'an Slipped Ware contains the following types:

> K'atun Group
>> K'atun Red: K'atun Variety
>> K'atun Red: Incised Variety
>> K'atun Red: Lak Variety
>> K'atun Red: Lak'ek Variety
> Ochkin Group
>> Ochkin Orange: Ochkin Variety
>> Ochkin Orange: Incised Variety
> Baadz Group
>> Baadz Tan: Incised Variety
> Sak Group
>> Sak White: Sak Variety
>> Sak White: Incised Variety
>> Lak'in Red-on-white: Lak'in Variety
>> Lak'in Red-on-white: Incised Variety
> Eknab Group
>> Eknab Black: Eknab Variety
>> Eknab Black: Incised Variety

LA LILA BURNISHED WARE

La Lila Burnished Ware is based on the Calam Buff paste defined by Culbert (2006:6–7) at Tikal and it is defined here as a ceramic ware. It is essentially identical to the paste of K'an Slipped Ware but differs in that vessel surfaces are burnished but not slipped. La Lila Burnished Ware differs significantly from other unslipped wares in terms of function. Most unslipped wares are utilitarian vessels, while La Lila Burnished Ware consists primarily of serving vessels. La Lila Burnished Ware includes four types:

> Calam Buff Group
>> Calam Buff: Calam Variety
>> Ante Incised: Ante Variety
>> Aac Red-on-buff: Aac Variety

RÍO HOLMUL SLIPPED WARE

Río Holmul Slipped Ware is found in the K'awil Complex at Holmul and Cival. This ware is characterized by a thick dull slip that adheres well to the surface. It also has a compact paste with medium-coarse texture. The ware differs from K'an Slipped ware in characteristics of the paste; its gritty texture is more similar to paste of Río Pasión Slipped Ware. The paste of Río Holmul Slipped Ware is dark brown (10YR5/3, 6/6, 5/6, 4/4, 6/8, 4/6, 5/4, 5/8; 7.5YR4/6, 5/8, 5/6) or gray (7.5YR6/1). Inclusions in the paste include organic matter and crystalline calcite (reacts to hydrochloric acid), ash, mica, and round red ferruginous particles. Firing cores are present, especially in bases of dishes and bowls. Vessel walls tend to be thinner than those in K'an Slipped Ware, and surfaces tend to be harder. The ware contains the following types:

> Jobal Group
>> Jobal Red: Jobal Variety
>> Jobal Red: Incised Variety
> Unnamed White Group
>> Xaman Red-on-white: Xaman Variety
> Ainil Goup
>> Xpokol Incised: Xpokol Variety
> Chicin'a Group
>> Chicin'a Black: Chicin'a Variety
>> Chicin'a Black: Incised Variety.

BELIZE VALLEY DULL WARE

This ware was developed from the analysis of ceramics that Awe (1992) identified as pre-Mamom pottery at Cahal Pech, Belize. Cheetham, Forsyth, and Clark (2003) presented an early description of Belize Valley Dull Ware that was later revised by Sullivan and Awe (2013). Belize Valley Dull Ware is characterized by red, black, cream, orange, and mottled (7.5YR5/4; 5YR5/6, 4/6, 5/4; 2.5YR4/4, 5/6) color slips. Decoration includes incision, zone-incision, fluting, and resist. Surfaces are polished to a dull or low shine. Pastes are fine textured and yellow in color (10YR7/4; 10YR7/6; 7.5YR8/6). Common paste inclusions are volcanic ash, calcite, quartz, and mica. Type: varieties within the Holmul region sample include:

> Uck Group
>> Mo' Mottled: Mo' Variety
>> Mo' Mottled: Fluted Variety
>> Kitam Incised: Kitam Variety

UNSPECIFIED WARES

The early Middle Preclassic sample also includes type: varieties that do not belong to the above-mentioned wares. Because of the limited size of the sample, specific wares for these type: varieties cannot be defined at this time. These type: varieties are unslipped and include:

Canhel Group
    Canhel Unslipped: Canhel Variety
Cabcoh Group
    Cabcoh Striated: Cabcoh Variety
Unnamed Groups
    Ramonal Unslipped: Variety Unspecified
    Unnamed Unslipped (pre-Mamom)
    Unnamed Unslipped Red Paste (pre-Mamom)

TYPE DESCRIPTIONS

K'atun Red: K'atun Variety

Established: Neivens de Estrada in this study.
Group: K'atun
Ware: K'an Slipped
Complex: K'awil
Sphere: Unaffiliated
Ceramic Group Frequency: 182 rims, 208 bodies, 390 total, 39 percent of group, 14.3 percent of complex.
Principal identifying attributes: (1) Dull red slip on interiors and exteriors, and (2) fine yellow paste.
Paste, firing, and temper: There are a number of paste variants in the K'atun Red Group. The most diagnostic is fine textured with volcanic ash and yellow (10YR7/4, 7/6; 7.5YR8/6) in color. Other paste variants contain crystalline calcite as the main inclusions or are a combination of crystalline calcite and volcanic ash. No sherd temper has been observed in K'atun Red pastes. Firing cores are rare in the volcanic pastes, but do occur in the calcite pastes.
Surface finish and decoration: Vessel surfaces are well-smoothed and polished to a low shine. The slip is red (10R4/6; 7.5R4/6) and includes shiny micaceous particles. The presence of these micaceous particles distinguishes K'atun Red from other red types such as Uck Red from Cahal Pech and Abelino Red from Ceibal.
Forms:
    1. Plates with outcurved sides and exterior folded or thickened rims with pointed lips; rim diameters are 25 to 30 cm and wall thicknesses range from 0.7 to 1.1 cm;

2. bowls with flaring sides and direct rims with rounded or squared lips; rim diameters measure 20 to 30 cm and wall thicknesses 0.7 to 0.9 cm;
3. bowls with slightly incurved sides, direct or interior thickened rims with rounded lips; rim diameters are 20 to 30 cm and wall thicknesses 0.5 to 0.8 cm;
4. bowls with rounded sides, direct rims and rounded lips; rim diameters measure 10 to 20 cm, and wall thicknesses 0.5 to 0.8 cm;
5. jars with outcurved or vertical necks, direct rims, and pointed or rounded lips; rim diameters measure 10 to 15 cm and wall thicknesses 0.7 to 1.2 cm;
6. tecomates with direct rims, rounded lips, and 0.7 to 0.8-cm thick walls; and
7. mushroom stands (no measurements available).

Intraregional locations and contexts: K'atun Red: K'atun Variety has been found at Holmul in mixed deposits in excavations into the platforms of Building B, Group II; Building F, Group II; and Building N, Group II. The type: variety is most commonly found in phase 1 contexts of Building F, and phases 1 and 2 contexts of Buildings B and N. It has also been found at Cival in mixed deposits in the Group 1 platform, in Structure 1, a midden in the northern area of the epicenter, the plaza in front of the North Pyramid, Structure 20 (i.e., West Pyramid), the defensive wall, Structure 17 in Group 7, and beneath Stela 6.
Interregional locations and contexts: K'atun Red is similar, but not identical, to the Uck Red type at Cahal Pech (Awe 1992; Sullivan et al. 2009; Sullivan and Awe 2013), and Abelino Red at Seibal (Sabloff 1975) and Altar de Sacrificios (Adams 1971). Similarities are seen in the use of dull or matte slip, and similar forms such as the outcurved plate with exterior folded rim and pointed lip. Abelino Red is different from K'atun Red because it has a much coarser paste with more inclusions and in that the vessels tend to be smaller overall, with thinner vessel walls. Uck Red is different from K'atun Red because its surface slip lacks the micaceous particles and the red color tends more towards orange. K'atun Red is also similar to Kolok Red from the Yaxha-Sacnab region. The similarity with Kolok Red: Kolok Variety (Rice 1979) is primarily in a common form: the flaring sided dish with exterior-thickened rim (personal observation 2011). K'atun Red also shows similarities to Consejo Red: Consejo Variety from Cuello, Belize (Kosakowsky 1987).
Comment: K'atun Red: K'atun Variety was initially typed as Uck Red by Callaghan (2008:254–255) and is here represented by a new type and variety designation.
Illustration: Figure 2.1 a-b.

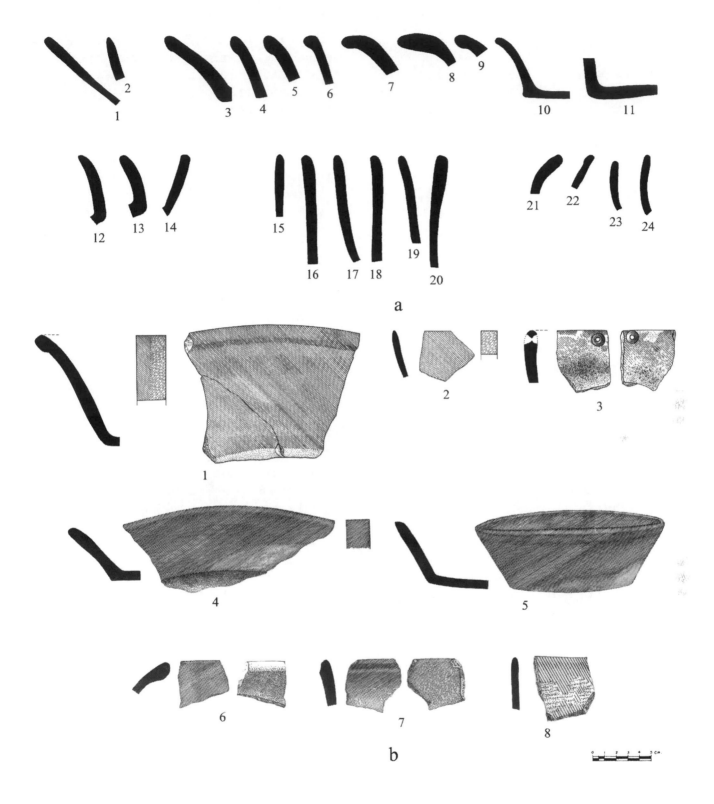

Figure 2.1. K'atun Red: K'atun Variety: (a1) CIV.L.01.06, (a2) HOL.T.63.08, (a3) HOL.T.71.71, (a4) HOL.T.75.24, (a5) HOL.T.63.01, (a6) CIV.L.01.01, (a7) HOL.T.71.26, (a8) HOL.T.71.43, (a9) HOL.T.71.57, (a10) HOL.T.71.58, (a11) HOL.T.71.35, (a12)HOL.T.71.28, (a13) HOL.T.71.26, (a14) HOL.T.71.57, (a15) HOL.T.71.71, (a16) HOL.T.74.26, (a17) CIV.L.01.01, (a18) HOL.T.75.24, (a19) HOL.T.71.71, (a20) HOL.T.63.20, (a21) HOL.T.71.30, (a22) HOL.T.63.08, (a23) HOL.T.71.30, (a24) HOL.T.71.07, (b1) CIV.T.28.110, (b2) CIV.T.28.110, (b3) CIV.T.69.05, and (b4–8) Unknown provenance. Drawings by Diana Méndez-Lee (a) and Fernando Alvarez (b) (Holmul Archaeological Project).

K'atun Red: Incised Variety

Established: Neivens de Estrada in this study.
Group: K'atun
Ware: K'an Slipped
Complex: K'awil
Sphere: Unaffiliated
Ceramic Group Frequency: 104 rims, 67 bodies, 171 total, 22.3 percent of group, 8.2 percent of complex.
Principal identifying attributes: (1) Dull red slip on interiors and exteriors, (2) fine yellow paste, (3) post slip incision on interiors, exteriors, or both.
Paste, firing, and temper: Paste, firing, and temper are identical to K'atun Red.
Surface finish and decoration: Monochrome red slip with addition of post slip-incised decoration. The most common incised designs are single, double, or triple lines encircling the rim; these are often combined with a set of specific motifs. Motifs include the "music bracket," "cleft head," "shark's tooth," "mat" and "tassel" (Cheetham et al. 2003). Geometric forms include U-shapes, L-shapes, double merlons, triangles (often with triangle shape repeated inside), circles, and semi-circles. Designs also include distinct combinations of motifs, such as a rounded square around a rounded star with circle inside.
Forms:

1. Plates with outcurving sides, everted rims, rounded lips; rim diameters measure 20 to 35 cm and wall thicknesses 0.7 to 1.1 cm;

2. plates with flaring sides, exterior folded rims, rounded or pointed lips (no measurements available);

3. bowls with slightly incurved sides, direct rims, and rounded or pointed lips; rim diameters measure 20 to 30 cm and wall thicknesses 0.7 to 1.1 cm;

4. bowls with flaring sides, direct rims, and pointed lips (no measurements available);

5. tecomates with exterior-folded and incised rims, and rounded lips; rim diameters are 20 to 25 cm and wall thicknesses 0.6 to 1.3 cm; and

6. bowls with round sides, direct rims, and pointed lips; rim diameters are 15 to 30 cm and wall thicknesses 0.5 to 0.8 cm.

Intraregional location and contexts: K'atun Red: Incised Variety pottery has been found at Holmul in mixed deposits in excavations into the platforms of Building B, Group II; Building F, Group II; and Building N, Group II. It has also been found at Cival in mixed deposits in the Group 1 platform, in Structure 1, a midden in the northern area of the epicenter, the plaza in front of the North Pyramid, Structure 20 (i.e., West Pyramid), Structure 7 (i.e., east structure of the main E-Group), the defensive wall, and beneath Stela 2.

Interregional locations and contexts: K'atun Red: Incised Variety is most similar to Baki Red-incised: Baki Variety at Cahal Pech (Sullivan et al. 2009; Sullivan and Awe 2013). It is distinct from Baki Red-incised: Baki Variety because the latter usually has a dark gray paste that is revealed through the incision, while K'atun Red: Incised Variety usually has a light-colored paste revealed through incision (personal observation 2009, 2010). It is also very similar to Pico de Oro Incised: Pico de Oro Variety from Seibal (Sabloff 1975) where similarities are found in the method of incision and content of the incised decoration. K'atun Red: Incised Variety is similar to Backlanding Incised: Backlanding Variety in the content of incised design (Kosakowsky 1987). Similarities to Kin Orange-Red: Incised Variety include the method of incision and the presence of cross-hatching, although Kin Orange-Red: Incised Variety tends to consist of straight-sided bowls with incision on the exterior (Andrews and Bey 2011).

Comment: K'atun Red: Incised Variety is one of the most remarkable types in the K'awil Complex. All of the pre-Mamom complexes include a monochrome red with incised decoration. The incisions were usually made after the vessel was slipped. The content of the decoration includes various geometric patterns that are often created with single or double lines encircling the vessel. The designs may be found on the exterior of bowls or on the interior of wide everted-rim dishes and bowls. The characteristic incision makes it easily recognizable even if the slip has been completely eroded away. Because these designs occur during the same time period (~1000-800 BC) and have been recorded on ceramics found in sites on the south coast of Guatemala (see Love's Melendrez White [2002:Figures 48e2, 50f], Melendrez Black [2002:Figures 54b, 56e, 62f, 62j], Cuca Red-on-Buff [2002:Figures 68c, e1, e3], and Ramirez Fine-White [2002:Figures 78-80]), and through the Pasión River region, the Central Petén, Belize Valley, and northern Belize, Cheetham (2005:27) calls this a horizon style. Dating for these types is still under question in the Holmul region, but the ceramics do seem to fit the pattern of the period. K'atun Red: Incised Variety was initially typed as Kitam Incised by Callaghan (2008:256–258) and is here represented by a new type and variety designation.

Illustration: Figures 2.2–2.5. Note that some illustrations appear to be unslipped. These sherds are not unslipped, but eroded.

Figure 2.2. K'atun Red: Incised Variety. Photo by Diana Méndez-Lee (Holmul Archaeological Project).

K'atun Red: Lak Variety

Established: Neivens de Estrada in this study.
Group: K'atun
Ware: K'an Slipped
Complex: K'awil
Sphere: Unaffiliated
Ceramic Group Frequency: 128 rims, 10 bodies, 138 total, 27.4 percent of group, 10.1 percent of complex.
Principal identifying attributes: (1) Dull red slip on vessel interiors and rim of vessel exteriors with remaining exterior surfaces unslipped and (2) plates with exterior folded rims and pointed lips.
Paste, firing, and temper: Paste is similar to others in the K'atun Group; it is fine with volcanic ash inclusions

and is yellow (10YR7/4) to buff (10YR8/2) in color. This paste is also relatively compact. Firing clouds are rare to non-existent.
Surface finish and decoration: Vessel interiors and the exteriors of folded rims are slipped red (10R4/6; 2.5YR6/4; 7.5R4/6). Exteriors are unslipped but are well-smoothed and burnished to a buff or pinkish gray color (5YR7/2; 10YR7/3; 7.5YR6/3).
Forms: Form is restricted to plates with flaring sides, exterior bolstered or folded rims, and flat bases. Rim diameters range from 30 to 35 cm and wall thickness 0.8 to 1 cm.
Intraregional location and contexts: K'atun Red: Lak Variety has been found at Holmul in mixed deposits in

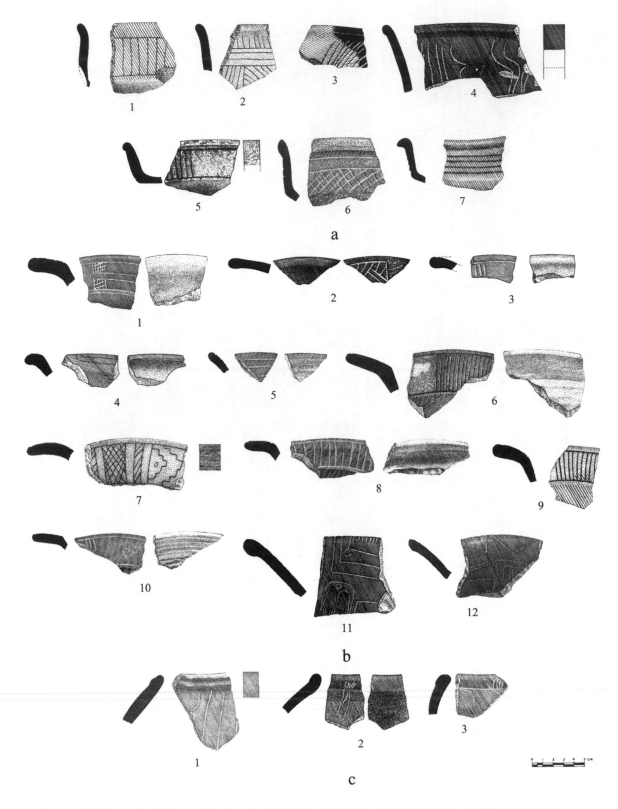

Figure 2.3. K'atun Red: Incised Variety: (a1–3) HOL.L.63.20, (a4) HOL.T.75.18, (a5) HOL.T.75.26, (a6) HOL.T.63.98, (a7) Unknown provenance, (b1) CIV.T.28.110, (b2) HOL.T.75.08, (b3) CIV.T.55.13, (b4) CIV.T.67.07, (b5) HOL.T.63.105, (b6) HOL.T.71.35, (b7) HOL.T.106.01.01, (b8–12) Unknown provenance, (c1) HOL.T.74.02, (c2) HOL.T.75.05, and (c3) CL.04.01. Drawings by Fernando Alvarez (Holmul Archaeological Project).

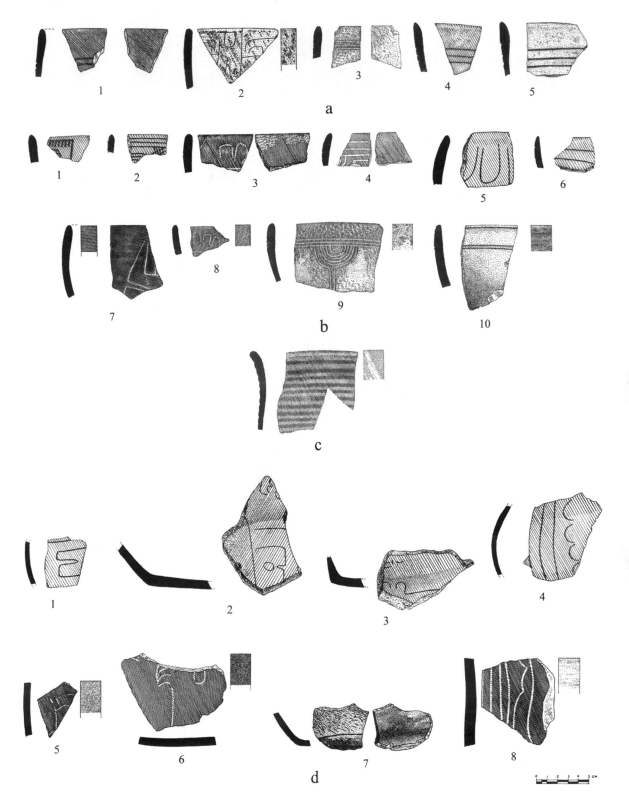

Figure 2.4. K'atun Red: Incised Variety: (a1) CIV.T.62.07, (a2) HOL.T.75.26, (a3) HOL.T.71.35), (a4–5) Unknown provenance, (b1–2) Unknown provenance, (b3) HOL.T.76.01, (b4) CIV.T.28.110, (b5) HOL.L.63.20, (b6) Unknown provenance, (b7) HOL.L.23.09, (b8) HOL.T.71.26, (b9) HOL.T.71.35, (b10) HOL.T.106, (c1) HOL.T.24.24, (d1–4) HOL.T.63.20, and (d5–8) HOL.T.75.10. Drawings by Fernando Alvarez (Holmul Archaeological Project).

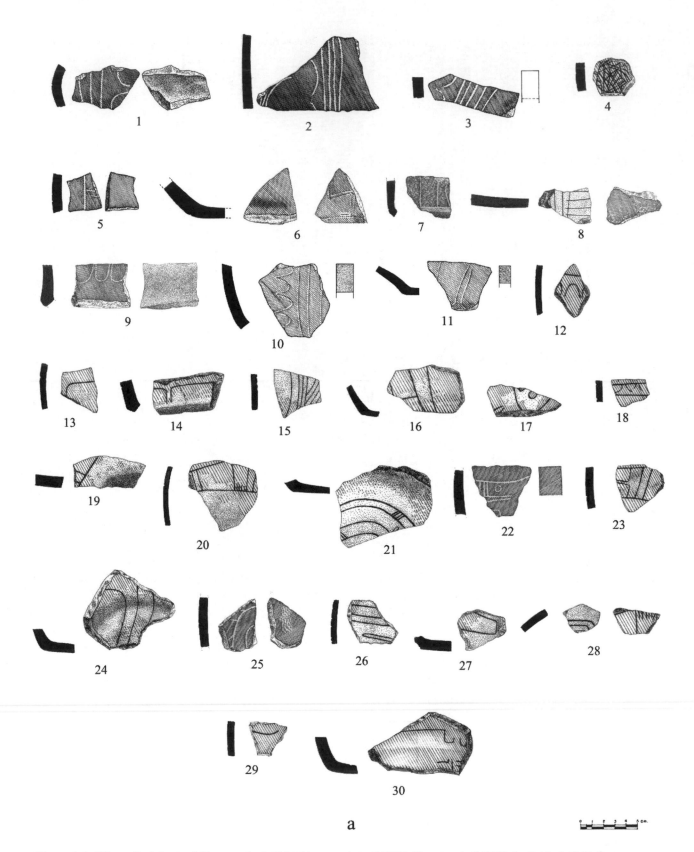

a

Figure 2.5. K'atun Red: Incised Variety: (a1) HOL.T.75.05, (a2–3) HOL.T.75.26, (a4) HOL.L.63.20, (a5) Unknown provenance, (a6) CIV.T.29.07, (a7) HOL.T.63.05, (a8) HOL.T.75.01, (a9) HOL.T.76.15, (a10) HOL.L.23.21, (a11) HOL.L.23.06, and (a12–30) HOL.L.63.20. Drawings by Fernando Alvarez (Holmul Archaeological Project).

the fill of the platforms of Building B, Group II; Building F, Group II; and Building N, Group II. It is most common in phase 1 of Building F and phases 1 and 2 of Building N. It has also been found at Cival in mixed deposits in the Group 1 platform, in Structure 1, and in Structure 20 (i.e., West Pyramid).

Interregional locations and contexts: K'atun Red: Lak Variety is a form variation of K'atun Red. This form is common in monochrome red types from other pre-Mamom sites but it has not been defined at any other site.

Comment: K'atun Red: Lak Variety was initially typed as Aac Red-on-Buff by Callaghan (2008:252–253) and is here represented by a new type and variety designation. This variety is defined by form, because of its consistency in shape and size. Future studies may find that it is a variation within K'atun Red: K'atun Variety but I chose to separate it in this study because it will be simpler for future scholars to lump these two varieties than to split them.

Illustration: Figure 2.6a.

K'atun Red: Lak'ek Variety

Established: Neivens de Estrada in this study.
Group: K'atun
Ware: K'an Slipped
Complex: K'awil
Sphere: Unaffiliated
Ceramic Group Frequency: 53 rims, 8 bodies, 61 total, 11.3 percent of group, 4.2 percent of complex.

Principal identifying attributes: (1) Dull red slip on interiors and the rims of exteriors with remaining exterior surface smudged black and (2) plates with exterior folded rims and pointed lips.

Paste, firing, and temper: Paste is identical to K'atun Red: K'atun Variety.

Surface finish and decoration: Interior vessel surfaces and exterior folded rims are slipped red (10R4/6; 2.5YR6/4; 7.5R4/6); colors are similar to others in the K'atun Group. Exteriors are well-smoothed and smudged black.

Forms: Form is restricted to plates with flaring sides, exterior bolstered or folded rims, and flat bases. Rim diameters measure 30 to 35 cm and wall thicknesses 0.8 to 1 cm.

Intraregional location and contexts: K'atun Red: Lak'ek Variety has been found at Holmul in mixed deposits in the platforms of Building B, Building F, and Building N, in Group II. The type: variety is most commonly found in phase 1 contexts in Buildings F, B, and N. One sherd was also found in in mixed deposits in Structure 9 (the western structure of the main E-Group) at Cival.

Interregional locations and contexts: K'atun Red: Lak'ek Variety is similar in form to sherds in the monochrome red group at Yaxha-Sacnab (e.g., Kolok Red: Kolok Variety; see Rice 1979) and Seibal (Abelino Red: Abelino Variety; see Sabloff 1975).

Comment: K'atun Red: Lak'ek Variety was not classified in Callaghan's (2005, 2008) initial typologies, but was included under the comment subhead for Aac Red-on-Buff (Callaghan 2008:253). Finally, there may be an incised type-variety of K'atun Red: Lak'ek Variety, which has been included in K'atun Red: Incised Variety. There are currently only four rims and one body, so I simply note this observation here and direct the reader to Figure 2.6c.

Illustration: Figure 2.6b.

Ochkin Orange: Ochkin Variety

Established: Neivens de Estrada in this study.
Group: Ochkin
Ware: K'an Slipped
Complex: K'awil
Sphere: Unaffiliated
Ceramic Group Frequency: 7 rims, 2 bodies, 9 total, 50 percent of group, 0.6 percent of complex.

Principal identifying attributes: (1) Orange slip on vessel exteriors and interiors; (2) bowls with outcurving sides, direct rims, and rounded lips; and (3) yellow paste with volcanic ash inclusions.

Paste, firing, and temper: Paste, firing, and temper are similar to K'atun Red: K'atun Variety.

Surface finish and decoration: Interior and exterior surfaces are well-smoothed, slipped orange (2.5YR5/6, 5/8, 6/6; 5YR6/6, 7/6), and have a relatively matte finish. Ochkin Orange is distinguished from the K'atun Red group by its surface color, which is a true orange color and lacks the micaceous particles found in the K'atun Group slip. It may have a cream underslip that produces this very orange color.

Forms:

1. Bowls with outcurving side, exterior thickened rims, pointed lips, and flat bases; rim diameters are 25 cm and wall thicknesses 0.7 to 1.1 cm; and

2. plates with outcurving sides, direct rims, rounded lips, and flat bases; rim diameters measure 25 to 40 cm and wall thicknesses 0.9 to 1.1 cm.

Intraregional location and contexts: Ochkin Orange: Ochkin Variety has been found at Holmul in mixed deposits in the platforms of Building B, Group II and Building F, Group II.

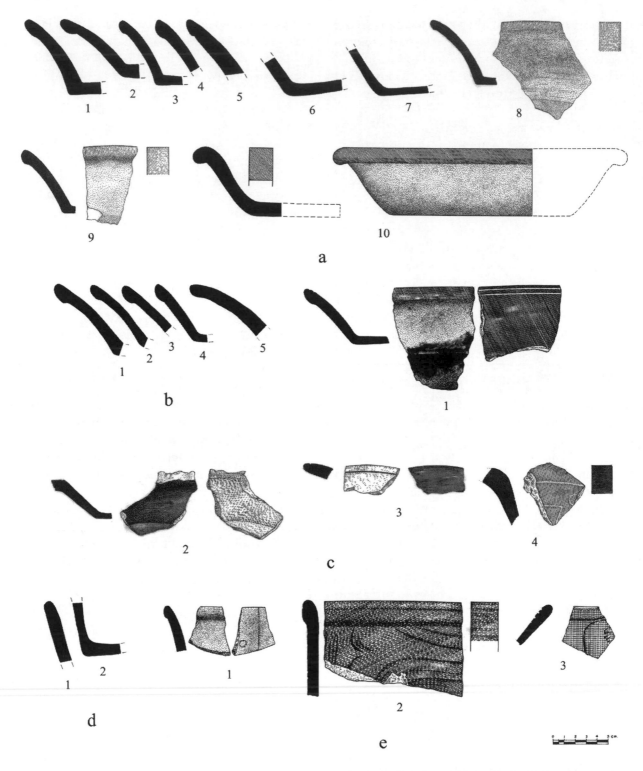

Figure 2.6. K'atun Red: Lak Variety: (a1) HOL.T.75.26, (a2) HOL.T.14.12A, (a3–4) HOL.T.75.26, (a5) HOL.T.71.26, (a6) HOL.T.71.01, (a7) HOL.T.71.57, (a8) HOL.T.71.58, (a9) HOL.T.63.105, and (a10) CIV.T.28.110. K'atun Red: Lak'ek Variety: (b1) HOL.T.75.26, (b2) CIV.L.01.01, (b3) HOL.T.75.24, (b4) HOL.T.74.28, and (b5) HOL.T.71.77. K'atun Red: Lak'ek Incised Variety: (c1) HOL.T.75.18, (c2) HOL.T.71.36, (c3) HOL.T.71.26, and (c4) HOL.T.71.58. Ochkin Orange: Ochkin Variety: (d1) HOL.T.74.26 and (d2) HOL.T.75.10. Baadz Tan: Incised Variety: (e1) HOL.T.75.24, (e2) HOL.T.75.25, and (e3) HOL.L.63.20. Drawings by Diana Méndez-Lee (a1–a7, b1–b5, d1–d2) and Fernando Alvarez (a8–a10, c1–c4, e1–e3) (Holmul Archaeological Project).

Interregional locations and contexts: Ochkin Orange is rare, but similar in surface color and form to contemporaneous types from Northern Belize and Mexico. It is similar to Kin Orange-red from Komchen and Kiuic in Mexico (Andrews and Bey 2011). It is also similar to Chicago Orange from Cuello (Kosakowsky 1987).

Illustration: Figure 2.6d.

Ochkin Orange: Incised Variety

Established: Neivens de Estrada in this study.
Group: Ochkin
Ware: K'an Slipped
Complex: K'awil
Sphere: Unaffiliated
Ceramic Group Frequency: 7 rims, 4 bodies, 11 total, 50 percent of group, 0.6 percent of complex.
Principal identifying attributes: (1) Orange slip on vessel exteriors and interiors, (2) bowls and plates with outcurving sides, (3) yellow volcanic ash paste, and (4) post-slip incision.
Paste, firing, and temper: Paste, firing, and temper are similar to Ochkin Orange and K'atun Red.
Surface finish and decoration: Interior and exterior surfaces are well-smoothed, slipped orange (2.5YR5/6, 5/8, 6/8; 10R4/8, 5/8, 6/6; 5YR6/8) and relatively matte. Ochkin Orange: Incised Variety is identical to Ochkin Orange: Ochkin Variety with the addition of post-slip incision. The most common motif consists of curvilinear lines found on the interior or exterior of vessel bodies; one line is combined with a circle and continuous notches. Vertical lines are found on vessel exteriors on the rim, the body, or both. Single and multiple lines are present. The single line encircling the vessel was combined with various geometric forms, in one case with a curving line on the vessel's exterior rim and in another case with continuous vertical lines on the interior of an everted rim. One rectangular cleft head was combined with a group of vertical lines on the vessel's exterior rim. The collection also includes a circle on an interior body sherd, an unidentified geometric form on the interior of the body, and vertical scratching on exterior rim.

Forms:

1. Plates with outcurving sides, wide everted rims, and 0.8- to 1.4-cm thick walls;

2. bowls with vertical sides and direct, 15-cm diameter rims; wall thicknesses are 0.6 to 0.7 cm; and

3. tecomates with exterior folded rims, and pointed lips; rim diameters are 20 cm and wall thicknesses 0.8 cm.

Figure 2.7. Ochkin Orange: Incised Variety. Photo by Diana Méndez-Lee (Holmul Archaeological Project).

Intraregional location and contexts: Ochkin Orange: Incised Variety has been found at Holmul in mixed deposits in the platforms of Building B, Group II, and Building N, Group II.

Interregional locations and contexts: Ochkin Orange: Incised Variety is most similar to Kin Orange-red: Incised Variety from Komchen (Andrews and Bey 2011).

Illustration: Figure 2.7.

Baadz Tan: Incised Variety

Established: Baadz Tan type named by Culbert (1993:5, 2006) at Tikal; Variety by Neivens de Estrada in this study.
Group: Baadz
Ware: K'an Slipped
Complex: K'awil
Sphere: Unaffiliated
Ceramic Group Frequency: 2 rims, 1 body, 3 total, 100 percent of group, 0.2 percent of complex.
Principal identifying attributes: (1) Tan slip, (2) secondary decoration with post-slip incision, and (3) plates with flaring or outcurving sides and exterior folded rims.
Paste, firing, and temper: Similar to K'atun Red and others in the K'an Slipped Ware.
Surface finish and decoration: Tan slip with post-slip incision depicting geometric patterns.

Forms: Plates with flaring or outcurving sides and exterior folded rims. Rim diameters measure 20 to 40 cm and wall thicknesses 0.8 to 1.0 cm.

Intraregional Locations and Contexts: Baadz Tan: Incised Variety has been found at Holmul in mixed deposits in the platforms of Buildings B, N, and F, in Group II.

Interregional Locations and Contexts: Ceramics within the Baadz Group are also found at Tikal (Culbert 2006:24–25).

Comment: Noting the distinctions in paste, Culbert has suggested that Baadz Tan may be a trade type (Culbert 2006:24).

Illustration: Figure 2.6e. Note that the color conventions for some sherds appear to be buff. These sherds are not buff; they are brown.

Sak White: Sak Variety

Established: Neivens de Estrada in this study.
Group: Sak
Ware: K'an Slipped
Complex: K'awil
Sphere: Unaffiliated
Ceramic Group Frequency: 119 rims, 60 bodies, 179 total, 61.3 percent of group, 9.4 percent of complex.

Principal identifying attributes: Matte-white to matte-gray slip.

Paste, firing, and temper: Paste is well-sorted with few inclusions. Primary inclusions are fine to medium-grained crystalline calcite, medium-grained white calcite, and volcanic ash. Paste color can be light gray or light brown (10YR7/1, 6/3) when well-fired and hard. Color can also be light yellowish brown (10YR6/4) when less fired and softer, sometimes with gray firing core. This paste is similar to that of the K'atun Group.

Surface finish and decoration: Matte-white slip (10YR8/1, 8/2, 7/1, 7/2, 7/3, 6/1; 5YR8/1, 7/2) often poorly applied, leading to erosion. The paste color can be seen underneath the slip and where the slip has eroded. A monochrome color is found on the interiors and exteriors of vessels, depending upon form. Plates with outcurving sides are slipped only on the interior.

Forms:

1. Plates with outcurving sides and exterior thickened or folded rims; rim diameters measure 20 to 30 cm, wall thicknesses 0.4 to 1.0 cm, and, where available, vessel heights are 3 to 5 cm;

2. plates with outcurving sides, direct rims, and rounded or pointed lips; rim diameters measure 20 to 30 cm, wall thicknesses 0.4 to 1.0 cm, and, where available, vessel heights 3 to 5 cm;

3. plates with outcurving sides and everted rims; rim diameters are 20 to 30 cm, wall thicknesses 0.4 to 1.0 cm, and, where available, vessel heights range from 3 to 5 cm;

4. bowls with flaring sides, exterior folded or thickened rims, and rounded lips, rim diameters measure 25 to 40 cm and wall thicknesses 0.6 to 1.1 cm;

5. bowls with slightly incurving side, direct rims, and rounded or pointed lips; rim diameters measure 25 to 40 cm and wall thicknesses 0.6 to 1.1 cm;

6. tecomates with 20- to 30-cm diameter rims and 0.8 to 0.9-cm thick walls; and

7. jars with outcurving necks; rim diameters measure 12 to 15 cm and rim thicknesses 0.6 to 0.9 cm.

Intraregional location and contexts: Sak White: Sak Variety has been found at Holmul in mixed deposits in excavations into the platforms of Buildings B, N, and F, Group II. It occurs most commonly in phase 1 contexts of Building F and phases 1 and 2 contexts of Building N. It is also found at Cival in mixed deposits in Structure 20 (West Pyramid).

Interregional locations and contexts: Sak White is very similar to Cocoyol Cream found at Cahal Pech (Awe 1992:231; Sullivan and Awe 2013), and Bil White at Tikal (Culbert 2006). In both cases Sak White is similar in the presence of ash in the paste and in the matte quality of the white slip. It is contemporaneous with Huetche White of Seibal (Sabloff 1975:53–55) and Altar de Sacrificios (Adams 1971:25). In the Lake Yaxha-Sacnab region Rice (1979: Figure 4a-c) identified a similar monochrome white and called it Huetche White. Similarities between Sak White and Huetche White are found in the true white color of the slip (later slips tend towards a cream color) and in the matte surface texture.

Comment: Sak White was initially typed as Cocoyol White by Callaghan (2008:258–259) and is here represented by a new type and variety designation.

Illustration: Figure 2.8a.

Sak White: Incised Variety

Established: Neivens de Estrada in this study.
Group: Sak
Ware: K'an Slipped
Complex: K'awil
Sphere: Unaffiliated

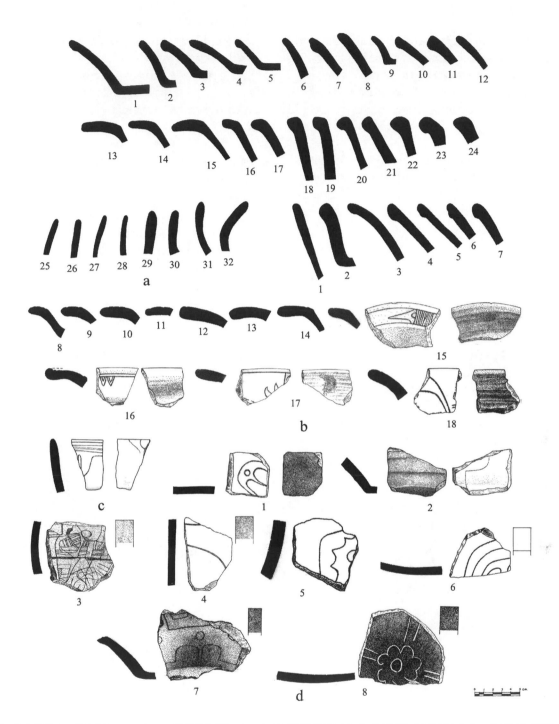

Figure 2.8. Sak White: Sak Variety: (a1–a2) HOL.T.75.26, (a3) HOL.T.75.10, (a4) HOL.T.71.57, (a5–a6) HOL.T.75.10, (a7) HOL.T.63.20, (a8) HOL.T.71.11, (a9) HOL.T.71.57, (a10) HOL.T.71.58, (a11) HOL.T.75.24, (a12) HOL.T.71.57, (a13) HOL.T.63.20, (a14) HOL.T.71.30, (a15) HOL.T.63.00, (a16) HOL.T.71.57, (a17) HOL.T.71.30, (a18) HOL.T.71.71, (a19) HOL.T.71.26, (a20) HOL.T.77.57, (a21–a22) HOL.T.77.05, (a23) HOL.T.63.20, (a24) HOL.T.63.98, (a25) HOL.T.71.57, (a26–a27) HOL.T.76.02, (a28) HOL.T.75.02, (a29) HOL.T.71.12, (a30) HOL.T.71.30, and (a31–a32) HOL.T.71.57. Sak White: Incised Variety: (b1) HOL.T.71.30, (b2) HOL.T.71.60, (b3) HOL.T.71.71, (b4) HOL.T.71.11, (b5) HOL.T.71.57, (b6) HOL.T.71.30, (b7) HOL.T.63.05, (b8) HOL.T.71.30, (b9) HOL.T.71.26, (b10) HOL.T.75.10, (b11) HOL.T.76.15, (b12) HOL.T.63.105, (b13) HOL.T.75.15, (b14) HOL.T.63.105, (b15) HOL.T.21.76, (b16) CIV.T.54.11, (b17) HOL.T.71.35, (b18) HOL.T.75.08, (c1) HOL.L.20.19, (d1) HOL.L.23.21, (d2) HOL.L.20.18, (d3) HOL.T.75.05, (d4) HOL.T.75.24, (d5–d6) HOL.T.75.10, (d7) HOL.T.74.12A, and (d8) HOL.T.75.26. Drawings by Diana Méndez-Lee (a, b1-14) and Fernando Alvarez (b15-18, c-d) (Holmul Archaeological Project).

Ceramic Group Frequency: 22 rims, 9 bodies, 31 total, 11.3 percent of group, 1.7 percent of complex.

Principal identifying modes/attributes: (1) Matte-white slip and (2) post-slip incised decoration in complex or simple motifs, or combinations thereof.

Paste, firing, and temper: The paste is identical to Sak White.

Surface finish and decoration: The surface finish is identical to Sak White, with the addition of post-slip incised decoration. Incised lines often form complex motifs such as cleft heads, shark's teeth, geometric forms, and double merlons. Incised decoration also occurs in simple designs such as single or double lines encircling vessel on the interiors and rims, sometimes in combination with more complex motifs. The majority of the incisions are fine, 0.4 to 0.8 mm in width, although there are two examples of grooved-incision.

Forms:

1. Plates with wide everted rims and rounded lips; with rim diameters measure 25 to 40 cm, wall thicknesses are 0.7 to 0.9 cm, and, where available, vessel heights are 4 cm;

2. plates with exterior folded rims, and pointed lips; rim diameters measure 25 to 40 cm, wall thicknesses are 0.7 to 0.9 cm, and, where available, vessel heights are 4 cm; and

3. bowls with slightly incurving sides, direct rims, and rounded lips; rim diameters are 15 cm and wall thicknesses 0.4 to 0.6 cm

Intraregional location and contexts: Sak White: Incised Variety has been found at Holmul in mixed deposits in the platforms of Buildings B, N, and F, Group II. The type: variety is found most commonly in phase 2 contexts of Building N.

Interregional locations and contexts: Sak White: Incised Variety is similar to Comistun Incised of Seibal (Sabloff 1975:53–55) and Altar de Sacrificios (Adams 1971:25). Comistun Incised sometimes includes preslip grooved-incision in combination with post-slip incision; this is not seen in Sak White: Incised Variety. It is also similar to Bil White: Incised Variety from Tikal (Neivens de Estrada personal observation, 2011). Although there are strong similarities between Sak White and Cocoyol White from Cahal Pech, no examples of an incised white type have yet been identified in the Belize River Valley.

Illustration: Figures 2.8b–d and 2.9. Note color conventions on some of the sherd drawings appear to be unslipped. These sherds are eroded and not unslipped.

Figure 2.9. Sak White: Incised Variety. Photo by Diana Méndez-Lee (Holmul Archaeological Project).

Lak'in Red-on-white: Lak'in Variety

Established: Neivens de Estrada in this study.
Group: Sak
Ware: K'an Slipped
Complex: K'awil
Sphere: Unaffiliated
Ceramic Group Frequency: 50 rims, 2 bodies, 52 total, 25.8 percent of group, 3.9 percent of complex.
Principal identifying attributes: (1) Matte-white slip and (2) matte-red slip painted over white slip.
Paste, firing, and temper: Paste, temper, and firing are identical to Sak White.
Surface finish and decoration: The general surface finish is identical to Sak White: Sak Variety with the addition of a red slip similar to K'atun Red: K'atun Variety. Red lines show sharp edges that demarcate red versus white space. Red slip is most often found only on vessel interiors or on the interiors and around the exteriors of rims. Also present are sherds that are slipped on exterior and interior rims, and sherds slipped only on the rims. There is one example of a vertical line painted from the rim on the vessel exterior. Body sherds show vertical and curving lines.
Forms:
    1. Plates with outcurving sides, and direct rims, and rounded or pointed lips; rim diameters measure 20 to 30 cm and wall thicknesses 0.6 to 1.1 cm;
    2. plates with exterior thickened rims and pointed lips (no measurements available);
    3 plates with wide everted rims (no measurements available); and
    4. bowls with vertical or slightly incurving side, direct rims, and rounded lips; rim diameters measure 20 cm and wall thicknesses 0.7 to 1 cm.

Intraregional location and contexts: Lak'in Red-on-white: Lak'in Variety is found at Holmul in the platforms of Buildings B and N, Group II. It is found most commonly in phase 1 contexts of Building F.
Interregional locations and contexts: Lak'in Red-on-white is similar to Toribio Red-on-cream from Altar de Sacrificios (Adams 1971), to the Unnamed Red-on-buff in the Cocoyol Group at Cahal Pech (Sullivan and Awe 2013: 116–117) and to Tower Hill Red-on-cream from the Bladen phase at Cuello (Kosakowsky 1987). Lak'in Red-on-white is also similar to Bil White Group Unnamed Red-on-white from Tikal (personal observations 2011). Red-on-white is common in other parts of Mesoamerica at this time, including Meledrez Red-on-white from the Pacific coast of Guatemala, and Xola Red-on-white from the Salama Valley (personal observation 2011). Lak'in Red-on-white is also similar to San Jose Red-on-white from the Valley of Oaxaca (Flannery et al. 1994). These non-Maya types have a white primary slip with the addition of bands of red paint around the exterior rims of plates and in vertical lines on vessel exteriors.
Comment: Lak'in Red-on-white represents a true red-on-white slip type and a possible precursor to later Muxanal Red-on-cream of the Middle Preclassic Yax Te Complex in the Holmul area.
Illustration: Figure 2.10a.

Lak'in Red-on-white: Incised Variety

Established: Neivens de Estrada in this study.
Group: Sak
Ware: K'an Slipped
Complex: K'awil
Sphere: Unaffiliated
Ceramic Group Frequency: 3 rims, 4 bodies, 7 total, 1.5 percent of group, 0.2 percent of complex.
Principal identifying attributes: (1) Matte-white slip, (2) matte-red slip painted over white slip, and (3) post-slip incised decoration.
Paste, firing, and temper: Paste is identical to Sak White.
Surface finish and decoration: Identical to Lak'in Red-on-white: Lak'in Variety with the addition of post-slip incision. Most examples use incision to demarcate red-and-white-slipped space. Also present are simple lines and one example of a more complex motif.
Forms:
    1. Plates with outcurving sides, exterior thickened rims, and pointed lips; rim diameters are 40 cm and wall thicknesses 0.8 to 0.9 cm and
    2. bowls with slightly incurving sides, direct rims, rounded lips, and 0.5-cm-thick walls.

Intraregional location and contexts: Lak'in Red-on-white: Incised Variety is found at Holmul in mixed deposits in the platforms of Buildings B, N, and F, Group II.
Interregional locations and contexts: Lak'in Red-on-white has currently been identified only in the Holmul region.
Illustration: Figure 2.10b. Note that color conventions on some sherds appear to be unslipped. These sherds are not unslipped, but they are eroded.

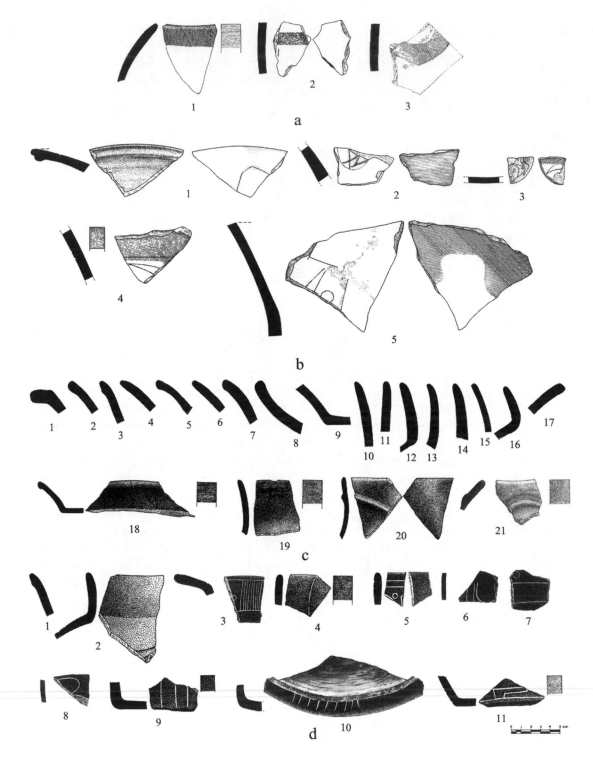

Figure 2.10. Lak'in Red-on-white: Lak'in Variety: (a1) HOL.T.75.05, (a2) HOL.T.75.24, and (a3) HOL.T.77.00. Lak'in Red-on-white: Incised Variety: (b1) HOL.L.23.06, (b2) CIV.T.12.50, (b3) CIV.T.65.01, and (b4–b5) HOL.L.23.06. Eknab Black: Eknab Variety: (c1) HOL.T.71.57, (c2) HOL.T.71.51, (c3) HOL.T.63.106, (c4) HOL.T.74.24, (c5) HOL.T.75.26, (c6) HOL.T.71.11, (c7–c8) HOL.T.63.20, (c9) HOL.T.71.57, (c10) HOL.T.75.25), (c11) HOL.T.71.51, (c12) CIV.L.01.01, (c13) CIV.L.01.06, (c14) HOL.T.63.20, (c15) HOL.T.75.25, (c16) HOL.T.71.35, (c17) HOL.T.75.24, (c18) HOL.T.75.26, (c19–c20) HOL.T.75.25, and (c21) HOL.T.63.106. Eknab Black: Incised Variety: (d1) HOL.T.71.43, (d2) HOL.T.74.17, (d3) Unknown provenance, (d4) HOL.T.75.26, (d5) CIV.T.28.110, (d6–d8) HOL.T.63.20, (d9) HOL.T.76.15, (d10) HOL.T.63.20, and (d11) HOL.T.76.15. Drawings by Fernando Alvarez (a–b, c17–c21, d2–11) and Diana Méndez-Lee (c1–17, d1) (Holmul Archaeological Project).

Eknab Black: Eknab Variety

Established: Neivens de Estrada in this study.
Group: Eknab
Ware: K'an Slipped
Ceramic Complex: K'awil
Sphere: Unaffiliated
Ceramic Group Frequency: 46 rims, 10 bodies, 56 total, 90.2 percent of group, 3.6 percent of complex.
Principal identifying attributes: (1) Gray-black to light black thin slip and (2) gray paste.
Paste, firing, and temper: Paste color is gray to gray-back, well-sorted with crystalline calcite as the primary inclusion. Ferruginous particles are frequent.
Surface finish and decoration: Exterior surfaces are well-smoothed and slip color is light black to gray-black (7.5YR 6/1, 4/0, 3/0, 5/0; 10YR5/1, 6/1, 4/1; 2.5YR3/0). Jar rims often have a band of orange or red around the lip.
Forms:
   1. Jars with outcurving necks, direct rims, and rounded lips; rims are 10 to 18 cm in diameter and 0.7 to 1.1 cm thick;
   2. bowls with flared or slightly incurving sides, direct rims, and rounded lips; rim diameters measure 20 to 30 cm and wall thicknesses 0.6 to 1.0 cm;
   3. plates with outcurving sides, exterior folded or direct rims, and rounded or pointed lips; rim diameters measure 20 to 30 cm and wall thicknesses 0.7 to 0.9 cm; and
   4. tecomates with direct rims, and rounded lips; rim diameters measure 15 to 20 cm and wall thicknesses 0.5 to 1.4 cm.

Intraregional location and contexts: Eknab Black is found at Holmul in mixed deposits in the platforms of Buildings B, N, and F, Group II. It is found in greatest abundance in phase 1 contexts of Building F, and phase 2 contexts of Building B.
Interregional locations and contexts: Eknab Black appears identical to Early Eb phase Lamat Black at Tikal (personal observation 2011). Eknab Black shows strong similarities to Chi Black from Cahal Pech (Sullivan and Awe 2013), although the latter is very rare and the Chi Group does not include an incised type. Eknab Black is similar in slip color and forms to Crisanto Black from Seibal (Sabloff 1975:57) and Altar de Sacrificios (Adams 1971:24), but differs in paste composition. The incised examples of these groups differ significantly. Chompipi Incised of the Crisanto Group usually has grooved-incision that is often created preslip, while Eknab Black: Incised Variety occurs exclusively with post-slip incision.
Comment: Eknab Black was typed initially as Chi Black by Callaghan (2008:260) and is here represented by a new type and variety designation.
Illustration: Figure 2.10c. Note that color conventions on some sherds indicate unslipped surfaces; these sherds are black.

Eknab Black: Incised Variety

Established: Neivens de Estrada in this study.
Group: Eknab
Ware: K'an Slipped
Complex: K'awil
Sphere: Unaffiliated
Ceramic Group Frequency: 5 rims, 10 bodies, 15 total, 9.8 percent of group, 0.4 percent of complex.
Principal identifying attributes: (1) Gray-black to light black thin slip, (2) gray paste, and (3) post-slip incision.
Paste, firing, and temper: Paste is identical to Eknab Black.
Surface finish and decoration: Identical to Eknab Black: Eknab Variety with the addition of post-slip incised decoration. The incised decoration displays a number of motifs including three lines encircling the vessel, double lines encircling, and a double-line register encasing continuous vertical lines. Also present are diagonal music brackets, geometric lines, and circles. One sherd shows a more complex configuration of motifs including a bird's beak, three circles, and geometric forms. These incised designs are found on the interior of open serving vessels and the exterior of more restricted forms.
Forms:
   1. Plates with outcurving sides, outflared everted rims or exterior folded rims, and rounded lips; rim diameters measure 25 to 30 cm and wall thicknesses 1.0 to 1.2 cm;
   2. jars with ourcurving rims rounded lips, 12-cm rim diameters, and 0.8-cm thick walls; and
   3. tecomates with exterior folded and incised 18-cm diameter rims, rounded lips, and 08-cm-thick walls.

Intraregional location and contexts: Eknab Black is found at Holmul in mixed deposits in the platforms of Buildings B, N, and F, Group II. It is found most commonly in phase 1 contexts of Building F.
Interregional locations and contexts: Eknab Black: Incised Variety is contemporaneous with Chompipi Incised from Seibal (Sabloff 1975:57) and Altar de

Sacrificios (Adams 1971:42), but differs in paste composition and vessel form.

Comment: Eknab Black: Incised Variety was initially typed as Chi Black: Incised Variety by Callaghan (2008:261–262) and is here represented by a new type designation.

Illustration: Figure 2.10d.

Mo' Mottled: Mo' Variety

Established: Sullivan et al. (2009) at Cahal Pech.
Group: Uck
Ware: Belize Valley Dull Ware
Complex: K'awil
Sphere: Cunil
Ceramic Group Frequency: 44 rims, 2 bodies, 46 total, 37.6 percent of group, 3.5 percent of complex.
Principal identifying attributes: (1) Mottled slip color ranging from brown to red to white, (2) fine yellow paste, and (3) small serving bowls and dishes.
Paste, firing, and temper: Paste, firing, and temper are similar to K'atun Red. The most diagnostic paste is a fine-textured variant with volcanic ash inclusions that is yellow in color (10YR7/4; 10YR7/6; 7.5YR8/6). Paste variants contain crystalline calcite or have mixed calcite and volcanic ash.
Surface finish and decoration: Vessel surfaces are well-smoothed and polished to a low shine. Slip is mottled with much variability. Primary slip color is an orange-brown, but can range to red and even white (7.5YR5/4; 5YR5/6, 4/6, 5/4; 2.5YR4/4, 5/6). .
Forms:
  1. Plates with outcurving sides and exterior thickened or exterior folded rims; rim diameters measure 20 to 35 cm and wall thicknesses 0.6 to 1.2 cm;
  2. plates with outcurving sides, direct rims, and rounded or pointed lips; rim diameters measure 20 to 35 cm and wall thicknesses 0.6 to 1.2 cm;
  3. bowls with slightly incurving sides, direct rims, and rounded lips; rim diameters measure 20 to 30 cm and wall thicknesses 0.5 to 1.0 cm; and
  4. plates with outflared everted rims and rounded lips; rim diameters measure 25 to 35 cm and wall thicknesses 0.9 to 1.0 cm.

Intraregional location and contexts: Mo' Mottled: Mo' Variety is found at the site of Holmul in mixed deposits in platforms of Buildings B and N, Group II. It is found with greatest frequency in phase 1 contexts of Buildings F and B and phases 1, 2, and 4 contexts of Building N.

Interregional locations and contexts: Mo' Mottled: Mo' Variety was established at Cahal Pech (Sullivan et al. 2009) and is part of the Cunil Complex at Cahal Pech, Belize.
Illustration: Figure 2.11a.

Mo' Mottled: Fluted Variety

Established: Type by Sullivan et al. (2009) at Cahal Pech, Variety by Neivens de Estrada in this study.
Group: Uck
Ware: Belize Valley Dull
Complex: K'awil
Sphere: Cunil
Ceramic Group Frequency: 12 Rims, 1 body, 13 total, 10.3 percent of group, 0.9 percent of complex.
Principal identifying attributes: (1) Surface color and finish identical to Mo' Mottled and (2) fluting on exterior walls below rim.
Paste, firing, and temper: Identical to Mo' Mottled and similar to K'atun Red.
Surface finish and decoration: Identical to Mo' Mottled with addition of fluting on exterior body.
Forms: Dishes with outcurving sides and narrow, outflaring everted rims with rounded lips; the fluting occurs just below the rim. ; Rim diameters measure 20 to 35 cm and wall thicknesses 0.6 to 1.2 cm.
Intraregional location and contexts: Mo' Mottled: Fluted Variety is found at the site of Holmul in mixed deposits in platforms of Buildings F and N, Group II. It is most common in Phase 1 and 4 contexts of Building N.
Illustration: Figure 2.11b.

Kitam Incised: Kitam Variety

Established: Sullivan et al. (2009:164) at Cahal Pech.
Group: Uck
Ware: Belize Valley Dull
Complex: K'awil
Sphere: Cunil
Ceramic Group Frequency: 61 rims, 6 bodies, 67 total, 52.1 percent of group, 4.8 percent of complex.
Principal Identifying Attributes: (1) Surfaces similar to Mo' Mottled and (2) incision and grooved-incision.
Paste, firing, and temper: Paste, firing, and temper are similar to K'atun Red and others in the Uck Group. The most diagnostic paste is a fine-textured variant with volcanic ash and yellow in color (10YR7/4, 7/6; 7.5YR8/6).
Surface finish and decoration: Identical to Mo' Mottled with the addition of incision, grooved-incision, or a combination of both on exteriors. Kitam Incised:

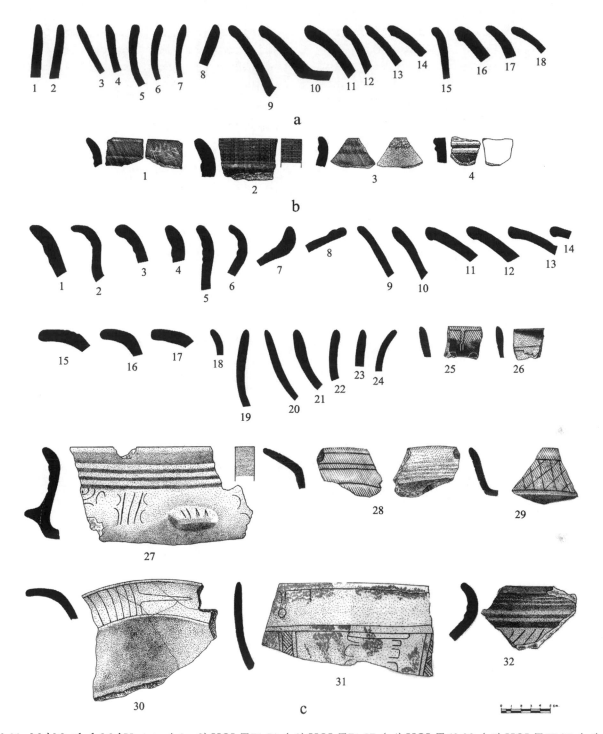

Figure 2.11. Mo' Mottled: Mo' Variety: (a1–a2) HOL.T.71.51, (a3) HOL.T.71.57, (a4) HOL.T.63.00, (a5) HOL.T.77.05, (a6) HOL.T.71.57, (a7) HOL.T.63.37, (a8) HOL.T.63.20, (a9) HOL.T.71.57, (a10) CIV.L.01.01, (a11) HOL.T.76.15, (a12) HOL.T.75.10, (a13) HOL.T.71.35), (a14) HOL.T.74.26, (a15) HOL.T.63.20, (a16) HOL.T.63.00, (a17) HOL.T.71.35, and (a18) HOL.T:71.56. Mo' Mottled: Fluted Variety: (b1) HOL.T.75.10, (b2) HOL.T.77.04, (b3) HOL.T.75.05, and (b4) HOL.T.75.10. Kitam Incised: Kitam Variety: (c1) HOL.T.71.12, (c2) HOL.T.75.26, (c3) HOL.T.71.27, (c4) HOL.T.77.04, (c5) HOL.T.71.20, (c6) HOL.T.71.57, (c7) HOL.T.71.75, (c8) HOL.T.71.12, (c9) HOL.T.63.20, (c10) HOL.T.77.05, (c11) CIV.L.01.01, (c12–c13) HOL.T.71.57, (c14) HOL.T.71.58, (c15) HOL.T.71.30, (c16) HOL.T.71.57, (c17) HOL.T.77.05, (c18) HOL.T.71.24, (c19) HOL.T.71.57, (c20) HOL.T.63.106, (c21) HOL.T.71.57, (c22) HOL.T.71.01, (c23) HOL.T.71.56, (c24) HOL.T.63.106, (c25–c26) Unknown provenance, (c27) HOL.T.75.26, (c28–29) Unknown provenance, (c30) HOL.L.63.20, and (c31–c32) Unknown provenance. Drawings by Diana Méndez-Lee (a, c1–24) and Fernando Alvarez (b, c25–32) (Holmul Archaeological Project).

Kitam Variety shows more complex incised motifs than other incised types during the early Middle Preclassic in the Holmul area. Simple incised decorations include the double lines encircling the vessel, which are often used to define space containing further decoration. More complex motifs include woven lines, continuous diagonal lines, L-shapes, U-shapes, circles, music brackets, rounded flowers with cruciform lines, fish fins, and shark's teeth. Cleft heads are also common including several distinct styles: rectangular, square, triangular, and profile. Cleft heads are often combined with other geometric forms; two of the rectangular cleft heads are combined with square cleft heads on one sherd, and on another with a double encircling line and a group of horizontal lines. The circular cleft heads are combined with a circle and L-shape on one sherd, and with a rounded rectangle on another sherd. The profile cleft head from this collection also includes a rectangular eye and a triangular bird's beak.

Forms:

1. Plates with outflared everted rims;

2. bowls with incurving sides and direct, and rounded rims; rim diameters measure 20 to 35 cm and wall thicknesses 0.8 to 1.0 cm;

3. plates with outflaring sides and exterior thickened rims; rim diameters measure 20 to 35 cm and wall thicknesses 0.8 to 1.0 cm;

4. bowls with flared sides and direct rims; rim diameters measure 23 to 30 cm and wall thicknesses 0.7 to 0.8 cm; and

5. tecomates with 12-cm diameter rims and 0.7-cm thick walls.

Intraregional Locations and Contexts: Kitam Incised: Kitam Variety is found at Holmul in mixed deposits in the platforms of Buildings F, B, and N, at Group II.

Interregional Locations and Contexts: Kitam Incised: Kitam Variety was defined at Cahal Pech (Sullivan et al. 2009). It is nearly identical to Kitam Incised: Kitam Variety from Holmul, differing only in its local paste composition. Kitam Incised: Kitam Variety has been observed in Tikal collections (personal observation 2011). It is very distinct from K'atun Red: Incised Variety because of its mottled slip color that is never a monochrome red, but often ranging from red to orange to brown. Mottling can also include white patches.

Comments: Callaghan (2008:256–258) identified Kitam Incised: Variety Unspecified in previous work at Holmul.

Illustration: Figures 2.11c, 2.12a, and 2.13. Note that color conventions on the drawings of some sherds indicate unslipped surfaces; these sherds are not unslipped, but eroded.

Calam Buff: Calam Variety

Established: Type named by Rice (1979) at Yaxha-Sacnab, Variety by Culbert (1993; 2006) at Tikal.

Group: Calam

Ware: La Lila

Complex: K'awil

Sphere: Eb

Ceramic Group Frequency: 193 rims, 101 bodies, 294 total, 83.5 percent of group, 15.2 percent of complex.

Principal identifying attributes: (1) Burnished, unslipped, buff or yellow surfaces and (2) exterior bolstered rims and flat base.

Paste, firing, and temper: Callaghan (2008:251) identified two paste variants in Calam Buff. The first is fine with volcanic ash inclusions and yellow (10YR7/4) to buff (10YR8/2) in color. This paste is relatively compact. The second variant is medium-textured with rounded gray calcite and less rounded crystal calcite inclusions. This variant is less compact and more porous. Color is buff (10YR8/2; 10YR8/3), and firing cores are almost nonexistent.

Surface finish and decoration: Interior and exterior surfaces are well-smoothed and burnished. Surface color is buff, similar to the paste color (10YR7/1-4 and 5YR7/3). In many cases, it appears that a light buff or cream wash was applied to vessel surfaces, but microscopic analysis does not reveal any additional surface treatment. This suggests that this effect was created through burnishing. The more porous calcite pastes seem to correlate with well-burnished exteriors.

Forms:

1. Plates with outflaring sides, exterior folded rims, and pointed or rounded lips; rim diameters are 20 to 40 cm and wall thicknesses 0.8 to 1.4 cm;

2. plates with flared sides, direct rims, and rounded lips; rim diameters measure 20 to 40 cm and wall thicknesses 0.8 to 1.4 cm;

3. plates with round sides and direct rims; rim diameters measure 20 to 40 cm and wall thicknesses 0.8 to 1.4 cm;

4. bowls with round or slightly incurving sides and direct rims; rim diameters measure 10 to 45 cm and wall thicknesses 0.7 to 1.3 cm; and

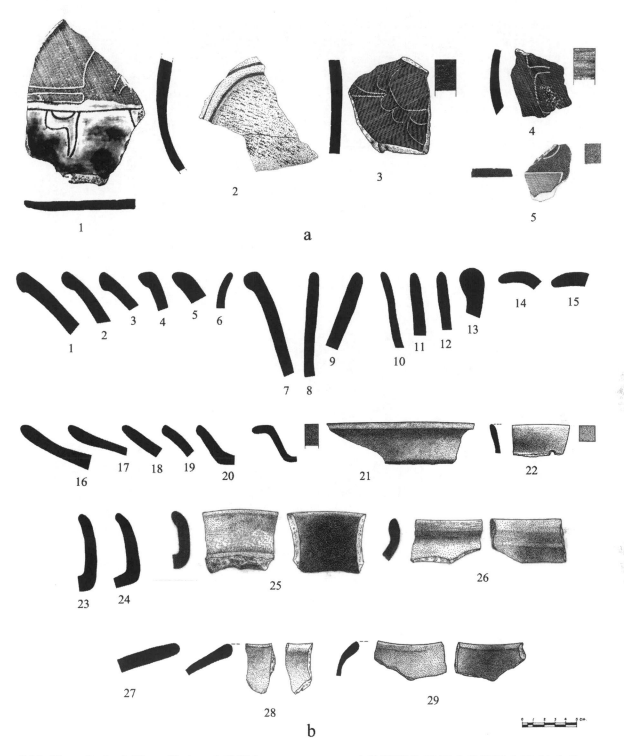

Figure 2.12. Kitam Incised: Kitam Variety: (a1) Unknown provenance (a2) HOL.L.63.20, (a3) HOL.L.75.24, (a4) HOL.T.75.10, and (a5) HOL.T.76.15. Calam Buff: Calam Variety: (b1) HOL.T.63.00, (b2) HOL.T.71.51, (b3) HOL.T.71.20, (b4) HOL.T.75.24, (b5) HOL.T.63.20, (b6) CIV.L.01.01, (b7) HOL.T.71.30, (b8–b9) CIV.L.01.01 , (b10) HOL.T.75.08, (b11) HOL.T.71.51, (b12) HOL.T.76.15, (b13) HOL.T.71.30, (b14) HOL.T.63.20, (b15) HOL.T.71.30, (b16) HOL.T.61.06, (b17) HOL.T.74.07, (b18–b19) HOL.T.63.01, (b20) HOL.T.71.20, (b21) CIV.T.68.39, (b22) CIV.T.57.07, (b23) HOL.T.71.02, (b24) HOL.T.63.20, (b25–b26) HOL.T.71.26, (b27) CIV.L.01.01, (b28) HOL.L.51.20, and (b29) HOL.L.10.08. Drawings by Fernando Alvarez (a, b21–29) and Diana Méndez-Lee (b1–20) (Holmul Archaeological Project).

0   CM   10

Figure 2.13. Kitam Incised: Kitam Variety. Photo by Diana Méndez-Lee (Holmul Archaeological Project).

5. jars with outcurving necks; direct, 15-cm diameter rims, and rounded lips; rim thicknesses are 0.7 to 0.9 cm.

Intraregional location and contexts: Calam Buff: Calam Variety has been found at the site of Holmul in mixed deposits in the platforms of Buildings B, F, and N, Group II. It is most abundant in Phase 1 contexts of Building F, Phase 1 and 2 contexts of Building B, and Phases 1, 2, and 4 contexts of Building N. The pottery is also at Cival in the platform of Group 1, Structure 1, Structure 9 (the west pyramid of the main E-Group complex) and Structure 7 (the east platform of main E-Group complex), a midden in the northern area of the epicenter, Structure 20 (i.e., West Pyramid), Structure 31, beneath Stela 2, and in the collapsed chultun that contained Burial 33.

Interregional locations and contexts: Culbert's (2006) description of Calam Buff from University of Pennsylvania excavations is very similar to the Calam material at Holmul and so are illustrated forms from PD 1 at Tikal (Culbert 1993: Figure 117a, b, c, d). Laporte and Valdes (1993:55) report finding similar material in problematical deposits 6, 12, and 13 in the Mundo Perdido Complex at Tikal as does Cheetham (n.d.). The type is found at Lake Yaxha-Sacnab in the Ah Pam Complex (see Rice 1979: Figure 5j). Calam material appears to be absent in the Belize Valley and northern Belize.

Comment: Calam Buff may have been a unique Central Petén burnished pottery type. Its form, surface, and occasionally paste modes are very similar across sites in the Central Petén. Callaghan (2008:250–252) identified Calam Buff: Variety Unspecified in previous work. In this study Calam Buff: Calam Variety is placed in La Lila Burnished Ware on the basis of paste, form, and surface characteristics.

Illustration: Figures 2.12b, 2.14a, b. Note that the color conventions on some sherds indicate unslipped; these sherds are burnished and buff in color.

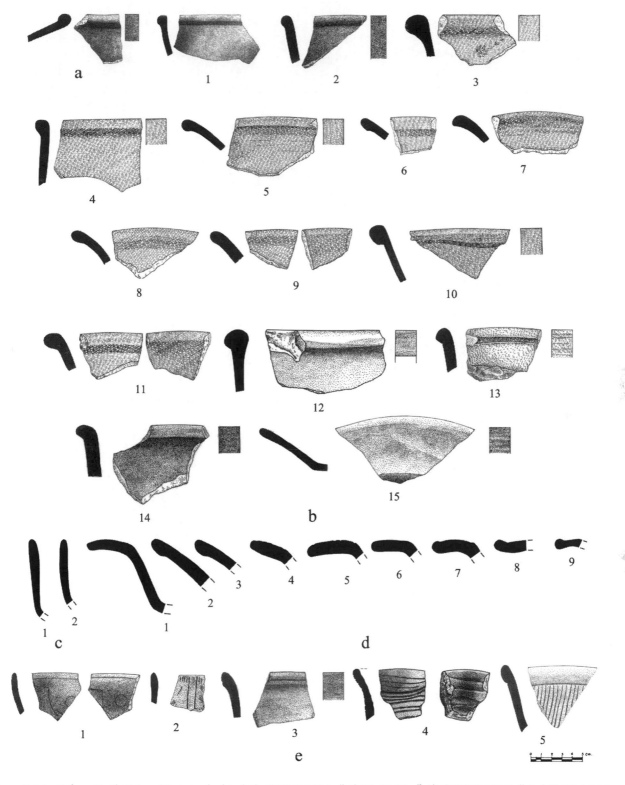

Figure 2.14. Calam Buff: Calam Variety: (a, b1–b2) CIV.T.28.110, (b3) CL.04.01, (b4) CIV.T.28.110, (b5–b8) CL.04.01, (b9–b11) CIV.T.28.110, (b12) HOL.L.10.13, (b13) HOL.T.63.100, (b14) Unknown provenance, and (b15) HOL.T.71.35. Ante Incised: Ante Variety: (c1) HOL.T.71.12, (c2) CIV.L.01.06, (d1) HOL.L.63.20, (d2) HOL.T.76.02, (d3) HOL.T.77.05, (d4) HOL.T.63.20, (d5) CIV.L.01.01, (d6) HOL.T.63.20, (d7) HOL.T.63.00, (d8) HOL.T.76.15, (d9) HOL.T.75.08, (e1) HOL.T.63.106, (e2) Unknown provenance, (e3) HOL.T.63.105, (e4) HOL.T.01.10, and (e5) HOL.T.77.05. Drawings by Fernando Alvarez (a, b, e) and Diana Méndez-Lee (c, d) (Holmul Archaeological Project).

Ante Incised: Ante Variety

Established: Laporte and Valdes (1993:55–59) at Tikal.
Group: Calam
Ware: La Lila
Complex: K'awil
Sphere: Eb
Ceramic Group Frequency: 33 rims, 14 bodies, 47 total, 14.3 percent of group, 2.6 percent of complex.

Principal identifying attributes: (1) Burnished, unslipped, buff or yellow surfaces and (2) post-slip incised design.

Paste, firing, and temper: Paste, firing, and temper is similar to Calam Buff: Calam Surface finish and decoration: Surface finish and appearance is identical to Calam Buff: Calam Variety, with the addition of incision or grooved-incision (less frequent). One sherd displays grooved-incision around the everted rim and incision on the interior body and rim. The most common motif found on Ante Incised: Ante Variety vessels is the shark's tooth, which usually occurs on the interior rim of wide, everted-rim dishes and the exterior rim of bowls. Other motifs include cleft heads, music brackets, L-shapes, circles, and crossed bands. Simple incised designs include double or single lines encircling the vessel, often delineating spaces for further complex designs, groups of vertical or diagonal lines, and other geometric forms.

Forms:

1. Plates with outflaring sides, wide everted rims, and rounded lips; rim diameters measure 25 to 40 cm and wall thicknesses 0.7 to 1.0 cm;

2. plates with outflaring, exterior-folded rims and pointed lips; rim diameters measure 25 to 40 cm and wall thicknesses 0.7 to 1.0 cm; and

3. bowls with slightly incurving sides, direct rims, and rounded lips; rim diameters measure 20 to 30 cm and wall thicknesses 0.6 to 0.8 cm.

Intraregional location and contexts: Ante Incised: Ante Variety is found at the site of Holmul in mixed deposits in platforms of Buildings B, F, and N, Group II. It is most common in Phase 1 contexts of Building N and Phase 2 contexts of Building B.

Interregional locations and contexts: Ante Incised: Ante Variety is common at Tikal (Hermes 1993 refers to it as "Aute" Incised; Laporte and Valdes 1993). At Tikal Ante Incised: Ante Variety often combines grooved-incision with post-slip incision, while at Holmul grooved-incision is rare.

Illustration: Figures 2.14c–e, 2.15, 2.16, and 2.17a.

Figure 2.15. Ante Incised: Ante Variety. Photo by Diana Méndez-Lee (Holmul Archaeological Project).

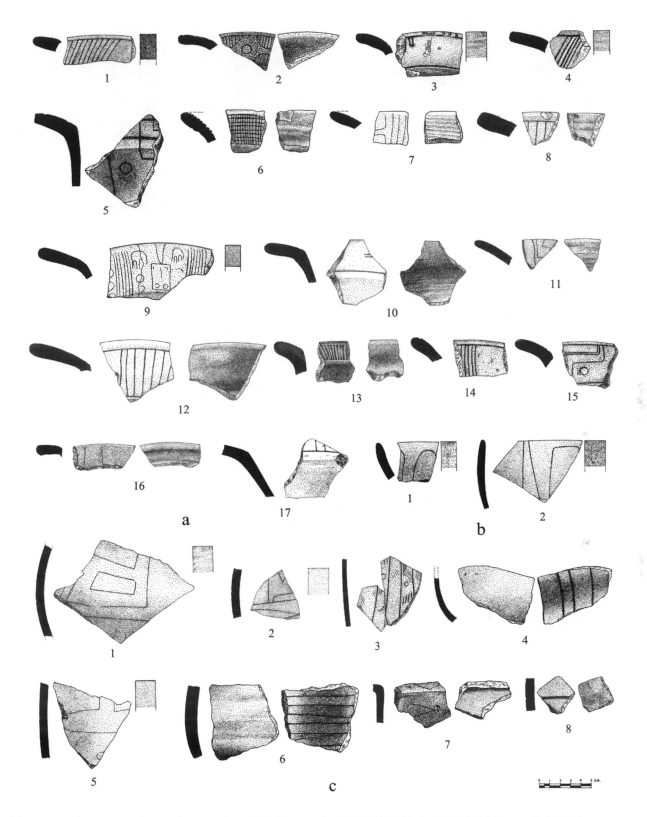

Figure 2.16 Ante Incised: Ante Variety: (a1) HOL.T.76.15, (a2) HOL.T.75.05, (a3) HOL.T.76.15, (a4) HOL.T.77.01, (a5) HOL.T.74.19, (a6) CIV.T.53.12, (a7) CIV.T.55.13, (a8) HOL.T.63.106, (a9) HOL.T.01.10, (a10–12) HOL.T.63.105, (a13–17) Unknown provenance, (b1) HOL.T.76.15, (b2) HOL.L.01.06, (c1) HOL.T.63.106, (c2–c3) Unknown provenance, (c4) HOL.T.75.10, (c5) HOL.T.75.26, (c6–c7) HOL.T.74.19, and. (c8) HOL.T.75.26. Drawings by Fernando Alvarez (Holmul Archaeological Project).

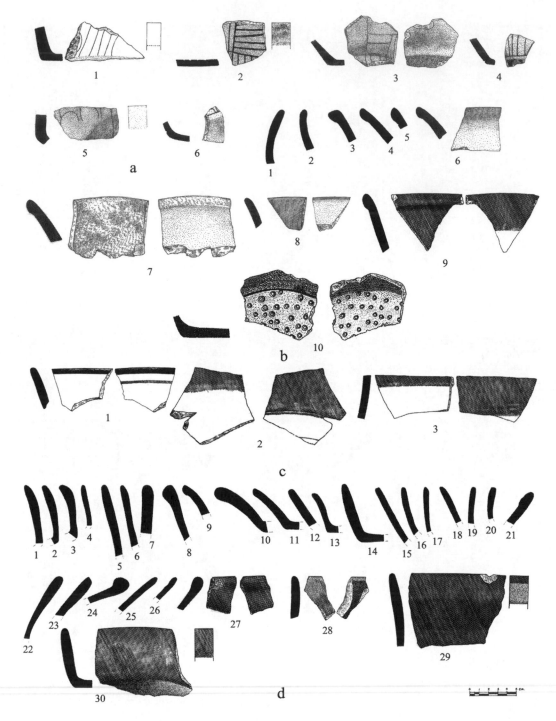

Figure 2.17. Ante Incised: Ante Variety: (a1) HOL.T.75.25, (a2) HOL.T.75.05, and (a3–a6) Unknown provenance. Aac Red-on-buff: Aac Variety: (b1–b3) HOL.T.75.26, (b4) HOL.T.75.28, (b5) HOL.T.63.98, (b6) HOL.T.106, (b7) HOL.T.71.26, (b8) Unknown provenance, (b9) HOL.T.75.24, and (b10) Unknown provenance. Aac Red-on-buff (Incised): (c1) CIV.L.04.01, and (c2–c3) HOL.T.75.24. Jobal Red: Jobal Variety: (d1) HOL.T.75.24, (d2) HOL.T.75.26, (d3) HOL.T.63.38, (d4) HOL.T.74.26, (d5) HOL.T.75.27, (d6) HOL.T.71.22, (d7) HOL.T.76.09, (d8) HOL.T.71.57, (d9) HOL.T.71.51, (d10) CIV.L.01.01, (d11) HOL.T.71.57, (d12) HOL.T.74.25, (d13) CIV.L.01.01, (d14) HOL.T.75.24, (d15) HOL.T.63.98, (d16) HOL.T.74.24, (d17) CIV.L.01.01, (d18) HOL.T.71.57, (d19) HOL.T.74.26, (d20) CIV.L.01.01, (d21) HOL.T.75.26, (d22) HOL.T.63.20, (d23) HOL.T.71.57, (d24) HOL.T.63.106, (d25) HOL.T.71.51, (d26) HOL.T.75.05, (d27) HOL.T.75.01, (d28) HOL.T.75.05, and (d29–d30) HOL.T:75.24. Drawings by Fernando Alvarez (a, b6–b10, c, d27–30) and Diana Méndez-Lee (b1–b5, d1–26) (Holmul Archaeological Project).

Aac Red-on-buff: Aac Variety

Established: Type named by Rice (1979:13) at Yaxha Sacnab, Variety named by Culbert (1993, 2006) at Tikal.
Group: Calam
Ware: La Lila Burnished
Complex: K'awil
Sphere: Eb
Ceramic Group Frequency: 5 rims, 15 bodies, 20 total, 2.2 percent of group, 0.4 percent of complex.
Principal identifying attributes: (1) Burnished, unslipped, buff colored surface; (2) band of red slip around rim on exterior and interior of vessel; and (3) bands of red slip encircling vessel exterior.
Paste, firing, and temper: The paste, firing, and temper are similar to Calam Buff: Calam Variety.
Surface finish and decoration: The surface finish is identical to Calam Buff: Calam Variety with the addition of red (7.5R4/6; 10R5/3) bands of slip around rims and exteriors. The slip was sometimes applied in streaks lacking definitive boundaries.
Forms:

1. Plates with outflared sides; wide, everted 25-cm diameter rims; and rounded lips; wall thicknesses are 0.8 to 1.2 cm;

2. bowls with slightly incurving sides, direct rim, and round lips; rim diameters are 15 to 20 cm and wall thicknesses 0.7 to 0.8 cm; and

3. plates with outflaring sides; direct, 25-cm diameter rims rounded lips; and 0.8- to 1.2-cm thick walls.

Intraregional location and contexts: Aac Red-on-buff is found at Holmul in mixed deposits in the platforms of Building B, and F in Group II.
Interregional locations and contexts: Aac Red-on-buff was first identified by Rice (1979) at Yaxha Sacnab in the Ah Pam Complex. It is also found at Tikal where it is common in the Proyecto Nacional de Tikal collection (personal observation 2011).
Comment: There may be an incised variety of this type. Five body sherds were recovered that display the same paste, surface, and form modes with the addition of incision enclosing red bands of slip. But I am hesitant to create another type without rim sherds. Therefore, I simply include this observation. See Figure 2.17c for illustrations of these incised sherds. Note that color conventions indicate a cream slip, these surfaces are buff-colored.
Illustration: Figure 2.17b.

Jobal Red: Jobal Variety

Established: Neivens de Estrada in this study.
Group: Jobal
Ware: Río Holmul Slipped Ware
Complex: K'awil
Sphere: Unaffiliated
Ceramic Group Frequency: 56 rims, 5 bodies, 61 total, 76.7 percent of group, 4.4 percent of complex.
Principal identifying attributes: (1) Monochrome dark red to purple slip and (2) compact dark gray to brown paste.
Paste, firing, and temper: Paste is compact and dark brown (10YR4/4, 4/6, 5/3-4, 5/6, 5/8, 6/6, 6/8; 7.5YR4/6, 5/6, 5/8) or gray (7.5YR6/1). Inclusions consist of organic matter and crystalline or sparitic calcite, volcanic ash, mica, and round red ferruginous particles. Firing cores are present, especially in the bases of dishes and bowls.
Surface finish and decoration: Surfaces are well-smoothed and burnished to a dull shine. Monochrome red slip ranges in color from true red to purple-red (7.5R3/8, 4/4, 4/6, 5/6, 5/8; 2.5YR4/6, 4/8, 5/4, 5/6, 5/8, 6/4; 10R4/4, 4/6, 4/8, 5/6, 5/8). The slip appears to be well-preserved and is rarely eroded, indicating a strong bond between slip and vessel body. Jobal Red: Jobal Variety is distinguished from K'atun Red: K'atun Variety in slip color; it is a darker red and sometimes purplish. The paste is more compact and dark brown to gray in color.
Form:

1. Bowls with slightly incurving sides, direct rims, and rounded or pointed lips; rim diameters are 15 to 30 cm and wall thicknesses 0.6 to 1.1 cm;

2. jars with outcurving necks, direct rims, and rounded lips; rim diameters measure 12 to 20 cm and rim thicknesses 0.6 to 0.9 cm;

3. plates with outcurving sides and direct or exterior folded rims; rim diameters measure 20 to 30 cm and wall thicknesses 0.7 to 1.0 cm;

4. tecomates with interior or exterior thickened rims that are 15 to 40 cm in diameter; wall thicknesses are 0.5 to 1.0 cm; and

5. dish with flared sides, direct 12- to 20-cm-diameter rims, and 0.6- to 1.1-cm-thick walls.

Intraregional location and contexts: Jobal Red is found at the site of Holmul in mixed deposits in platforms of Buildings B, F, and N, Group II. It is found most commonly in phase 1 contexts of Building F, phase 2 contexts of Building N, and phases 1 and 2 contexts of Building B.

Interregional locations and contexts: Jobal Red is also found at Tikal (personal observation, 2011). The purplish red slip color is not found at other pre-Mamom sites in the Maya lowlands but is common in contemporary collections on the Pacific Coast of Guatemala in types such as Victoria Red and Meledrez Red.

Illustration: Figure 2.17d.

Jobal Red: Incised Variety

Established: Neivens de Estrada in this study.
Group: Jobal
Ware: Río Holmul Slipped
Complex: K'awil
Sphere: Unaffiliated
Ceramic Group Frequency: 17 rims, 12 bodies, 29 total, 23.3 percent of group, 1.3 percent of complex.
Principal identifying attributes: (1) Monochrome dark red to purple slip, (2) compact dark gray to black paste, and (3) post-slip incision.
Paste, firing, and temper: Paste, firing, and temper are identical to Jobal Red: Jobal Variety. Surface finish and decoration: Surface finish is identical to Jobal Red with the addition of post-slip incision. The incising includes one or more vertical lines, diagonal lines, double encircling lines, and double line registers. Lines can be combined with other motifs such as double merlons, shark teeth, continuous vertical lines, stepped frets, and cross hatching. There are also cleft heads, sometimes found in combination with circles. Geometric motifs include U-shapes, semi-circles, and teardrop shape. There is also one example of a diagonal music bracket, as well as a tassel shape combined with diagonal lines.
Forms:
   1. Bowls with slightly outcurving sides, direct rims, and rounded lips; rim diameters measure 15 to 30 cm and wall thicknesses 0.4 to 0.8 cm;
   2. plates with outcurving sides, exterior folded rims, and pointed lips; rim diameters measure 15 to 35 cm and wall thicknesses 0.7 to 0.9 cm; and
   3. plates with outcurving sides, outflared everted rims, and rounded lips; rim diameters measure 15 to 35 cm and wall thicknesses 0.7 to 0.9 cm.

Intraregional location and contexts: Jobal Red: Incised Variety is found at the site of Holmul in mixed deposits in the platforms of Buildings B, F, and N, Group II. It is most common in phase 2 contexts of Building N.
Interregional locations and contexts: Jobal Red: Incised Variety is also found at Tikal (personal observation, 2011). Jobal Red: Incised Variety is similar to Huiscoyol Incised from the Pacific Coast of Guatemala.

Illustration: Figures 2.18 and 2.19a. Note that the color convention on some of the drawings indicates unslipped; these sherds are not unslipped, but are eroded.

Xpokol Incised: Xpokol Variety

Established: Typed named by Culbert (1993:5, 2006) at Tikal, Variety by Neivens de Estrada in this study.
Group: Ainil
Ware: Río Holmul Slipped Ware
Complex: K'awil
Sphere: Eb
Ceramic Group Frequency: 4 rims, 0 bodies, 4 total, 100 percent of group, 0.3 percent of complex.
Principal identifying attributes: (1) Deep orange slip, (2) incised decoration, and (3) thin walled bowls.
Paste, firing, and temper: The paste is compact with medium-coarse inclusions. Paste color is dark brown (10YR4/4, 4/6, 5/3, 5/4, 5/6, 5/8, 6/6, 6/8; 7.5YR4/6, 5/6, 5/8) or gray (7.5YR6/1). Inclusions are organic matter, crystalline calcite, volcanic ash, and mica.
Surface finish and decoration: Vessel surfaces are well-smoothed and burnished. Slip color is deep orange (7.5YR5/4; 5YR6/6) and well preserved. Both incision and grooved-incision are present. One example displays grooved-incision with double lines encircling the exterior rim. Two examples have incision, one with geometric forms and a circle, the other with a rectangular cleft head and a rounded rectangle. The incising on both is located on the exterior rim and upper body of the vessels.
Forms:
   1. Bowls with slightly incurving sides; direct 15-cm-diameter rims; rounded lips; and 0.5- to 0.9-cm-thick walls;
   2. bowls with vertical sides; direct, 15-cm-diameter rims, rounded lips; and 0.5- 0.9-cm thick walls.

Intraregional location and contexts: Xpokol Incised was recovered in mixed deposits in phase 1 contexts of Buildings F and B, Group II at Holmul.
Interregional locations and contexts: Ainil Orange and Xpokol Incised were both defined by Culbert (1993:5; 2006) at Tikal.
Comment: One Ainil Orange: Ainil Variety sherd has been found at Holmul. It is a slightly rounded bowl with a direct rim and rounded lip.
Illustration: Figure 2.19b.

Figure 2.18. Jobal Red: Jobal Incised Variety. Photo by Diana Méndez-Lee (Holmul Archaeological Project).

Xaman Red-on-white: Xaman Variety

Established: Neivens de Estrada in this study.
Group: Unnamed
Ware: Río Holmul Slipped Ware
Complex: K'awil
Sphere: Unaffiliated
Ceramic Group Frequency: 5 rims, 2 bodies, 7 total, 100 percent of group, 0.4 percent of complex.
Principal identifying attributes: (1) Dense, compact, dark gray to black paste, (2) thin-walled bowls or vases, and (3) white slip with red slip painted onto interior and in lines on exterior.
Paste, firing, and temper: The paste, firing, and temper are similar to Jobal Red: Jobal Variety.
Surface finish and decoration: Xaman Red-on-white combines a base white slip (10YR6/1, 8/1-2; 5YR8/1) with the addition of Jobal Red slip (7.5R3/8, 4/6; 2.5YR4/6) on vessel interiors and in bands on vessel exteriors, often in horizontal encircling lines around vessel rims. The red slip sometimes includes specular hematite. This type is easily distinguished from Sak Group red-on-white because of the distinct paste and dark red to purple slip.
Form:

1. Bowls or vases with vertical sides, direct rims, and rounded or pointed lips; rim diameters measure 20 to 30 cm and wall thicknesses 0.7 cm;

2. bowls with slightly incurving sides, direct rims, and rounded lips; rim diameters measure 20 to 30 cm and wall thicknesses 0.7 cm; and

3. plate with outcurved sides; direct, 25-cm-diameter rims; rounded lips; and 0.9-cm thick walls.

Intraregional location and contexts: Xaman Red-on-white material comes from phase 1 contexts in the sub-platform of Building B, Group II at Holmul.
Interregional locations and contexts: Xaman Red-on-white is currently only found in the Holmul region.
Illustration: Figure 2.19c.

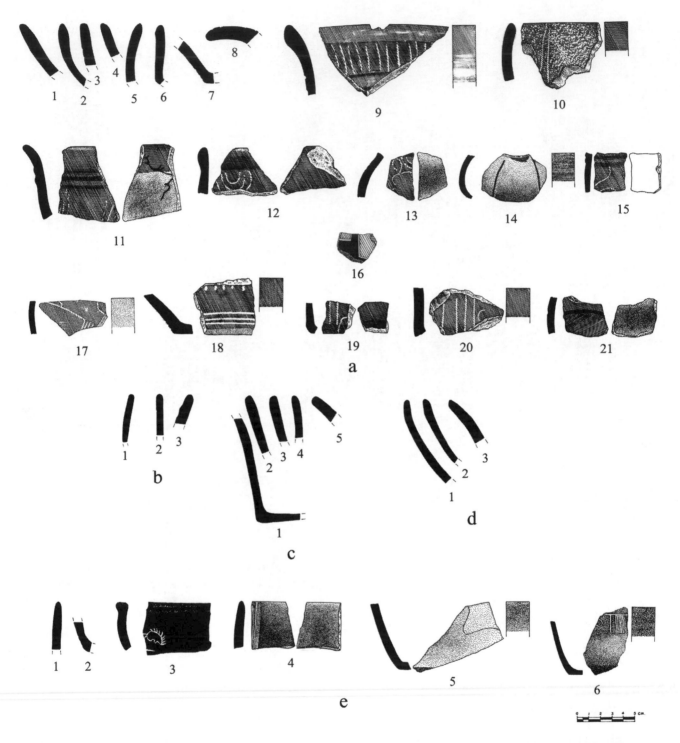

Figure 2.19. Jobal Red: Incised Variety: (a1–a3) HOL.T.71.57, (a4) HOL.T.63.20, (a5) HOL.T.71.51, (a6) HOL.T.71.57, (a7) HOL.T.75.25, (a8) HOL.T.63.106, (a9) HOL.T.75.24), (a10) HOL.T.71.05, (a11) HOL.T.75.18, (a12) HOL.T.71.00, (a13) HOL.T.74.19, (a14) HOL.T.75.24, (a15) HOL.T.75.09, (a16) Unknown provenance, (a17) HOL.T.75.18, (a18) HOL.T.75.25, and (a20–a21) HOL.T.75.10. Xpokol Incised: Xpokol Variety: (b1) HOL.T.75.25 and (b2–b3) HOL.T.63.08. Xaman Red-on-white: Xaman Variety: (c1) HOL.T.75.10, (c2) HOL.T.75.76, (c3) HOL.T.63.100, (c4) HOL.T.63.00, and (c5) HOL.T.75.26. Chicin'a Black: Chicin'a Variety: (d1) CIV.L.01.01, (d2) HOL.T.71.57, and (d3) HOL.T.75.24. Chicin'a Black: Incised Variety: (e1) HOL.T.75.24, (e2) HOL.T.76.15, (e3) Unknown provenance, (e4) HOL.T.75.24, (e5) HOL.T.75.18, and (e6) HOL.T.75.25. Drawings by Diana Méndez-Lee (a1–8, b, c, d, e1–2) and Fernando Alvarez (a9–a21, e3–e6) (Holmul Archaeological Project).

Chicin'a Black: Chicin'a Variety

Established: Neivens de Estrada in this study.
Group: Chicin'a
Ware: Río Homul Slipped Ware
Complex: K'awil
Sphere: Unaffiliated
Ceramic Group Frequency: 4 rims, 2 bodies, 6 total, 57.1 percent of group, 0.3 percent of complex.
Principal identifying attributes: (1) Monochrome black slip, (2) dark gray to black paste, and (3) thin bowls with incurving sides.
Paste, firing, and temper: The paste is compact and dark brown (10YR4/4, 4/6, 5/3-4, 5/6, 5/8, 6/6, 6/8; 7.5YR4/6, 5/6, 5/8) or gray (7.5YR6/1). Inclusions are organic matter and crystalline calcite, volcanic ash, and mica. Chicin'a Black: Chicin'a Variety is distinguished from Eknab Black: Eknab Variety based on paste characteristics. This paste is darker, more compact, and has medium-coarse particles. Vessel walls tend to be thinner than in Eknab Black: Eknab Variety.
Surface finish and decoration: The black slip (2.5YR4/0; 5YR3/0-1; 7.5YR4/0; 10YR4/1) is not uniformly applied, so that each sherd displayed a slightly different color.
Forms:
1. Bowls with slightly incurving sides, direct rims, and rounded lips; rim diameters measure 20 to 30 cm and wall thicknesses 0.4 to 0.6 cm and
2. plates with outcurving sides, direct rims, and pointed or rounded lips; rim diameters measure 15 to 17 cm and wall thicknesses 0.4 to 0.9 cm

Intraregional location and contexts: The small sample of Chicin'a Black material comes from mixed deposits in the subplatform of Building F, Group II at Holmul.
Interregional locations and contexts: At present, Chicin'a Black has only been found in the Holmul region.
Illustration: Figure 2.19d.

Chicin'a Black: Incised Variety

Established: Neivens de Estrada in this study.
Group: Chicin'a
Ware: Río Holmul Slipped Ware
Complex: K'awil
Sphere: Unaffiliated
Ceramic Group Frequency: 3 rims, 3 bodies, 6 total, 42.9 percent of group, 0.2 percent of complex.
Principal identifying attributes: (1) Monochrome black slip, (2) dark gray to black paste, and (3) post-slip incision.

Paste, firing, and temper: Paste, temper, and firing are identical to Chicin'a Black: Chicin'a Variety.
Surface finish and decoration: The surface finish is identical to Chicin'a Black: Chicin'a Variety, with the addition of fine-line post-slip incision. Motifs identified to date include a rounded–star design and curvilinear lines.
Form:
1. Bowls or dishes with vertical sides, direct rims, and rounded lips; rim diameters measure 20 to 30 cm and wall thicknesses 0.4 to 0.7 cm and
2. bowls with slightly incurving sides, direct rims, and rounded lips; rim diameter measure 20 to 30 cm and wall thicknesses 0.4 to 0.7 cm.

Intraregional location and contexts: The small sample of Chicin'a Black: Incised Variety material comes from mixed deposits in the subplatform of Building F, Group II at Holmul.
Interregional locations and contexts: Chicin'a Black: Incised Variety is currently only found in the Holmul region.
Illustration: Figure 2.19e. Note that the color convention on some sherds indicates unslipped surfaces. These surfaces are not unslipped, they are eroded.

Canhel Unslipped: Canhel Variety

Established: Culbert (1993:6; 2006) at Tikal.
Group: Canhel
Ware: Unspecified
Complex: K'awil
Sphere: Eb
Ceramic Group Frequency: 44 rims, 2 bodies, 46 total, 100 percent of group, 3.5 percent of complex.
Principal identifying attributes: (1) Unslipped vessel surfaces, (2) light brown color, (3) slightly incurving bowls with rounded bases, and (4) occasional decoration in the form of impression.
Paste, firing, and temper: The paste is medium texture, with few inclusions of white calcite and silica. It is light brown in color (7.5YR6/4).
Surface finish and decoration: The surface is unslipped, with a color similar to the paste, although somewhat lighter (10YR7/2 and 7.5YR6/4). Vessel interiors are more smoothed than vessel exteriors. There is occasional decoration in the form of impressions.
Forms: Bowls with incurving walls, direct rims, and rounded bases. Rim diameters are 20 to 35 cm and walls are 0.7 to 1.2 cm thick.

Intraregional location and contexts: Canhel Unslipped has been found at Holmul in mixed deposits in the platforms of Building B, Group II; Building F, Group II; and Building N, Group II. It is found most commonly in phase 1 and 2 contexts of Buildings N and F, as well as phase 4 contexts of Buildings N and B.

Interregional locations and contexts: Canhel Unslipped is also found at Tikal, where it was established by Culbert (2006; see illustrations in Culbert 1993:Figure 119). Laporte and Valdes (1993:60, Figure 32) identified Canhel Unslipped with impressions in PNT06 and 13 in Mundo Perdido at Tikal. Canhel Unslipped in the Holmul area is very similar to Ardagh Orange-Brown: Ardagh Variety from Cahal Pech in surface color (Sullivan and Awe 2013).

Comment: Two sherds in the current Holmul sample display red paint on the exterior of the upper shoulder of the vessel. This is common at Tikal within the Canhel Unslipped group but was not defined by Culbert (2006) because most examples come from the Proyecto National de Tikal project that post-dated Culbert's study. This could indicate another variety of Canhel Unslipped.

Illustration: Figure 2.20a, b.

Cabcoh Striated: Cabcoh Variety

Established: Culbert (1993:6; 2006) at Tikal.
Group: Cabcoh
Ware: Unspecified
Sphere: Unaffiliated
Complex: K'awil
Ceramic Group Frequency: 5 rims, 5 total, 100 percent of group, 0.4 percent of complex.
Principal identifying attributes: (1) Unslipped vessel surfaces, (2) light brown color, (3) striations on vessel exteriors, and (4) bowls with incurved or recurved sides and outcurving necks.
Paste, firing, and temper: The paste is medium texture, with few inclusions of white calcite and silica. The paste is light brown in color (7.5YR6/4).
Surface finish and decoration: The surface is unslipped with a similar color to the paste, light to medium brown (7.5YR6/2, 5YR6/2). Vessels have striations, most notably on the upper portion of exteriors. In some cases lower parts of the vessel are smoothed.
Forms: Bowls with incurved or recurved sides, outcurving necks, and rounded bases. Rims are 25 to 40 cm in diameter and walls are 0.8 cm thick.
Intraregional location and contexts: Cabcoh Striated has been found at Holmul in mixed deposits in the platforms of Building B, Group II; Building F, Group II; and

Building N, Group II. It is found most commonly in phase 1 and 2 contexts of Building F, and phase 1 and 4 contexts of Building B.

Interregional locations and contexts: Cabcoh Striated is also found at Tikal, where it was established by Culbert (1993:5, Figure 119; 2006).

Illustration: Figure 2.20c.

Ramonal Unslipped: Variety Unspecified

Established: Neivens de Estrada in this study.
Group: Unnamed
Ceramic Group Frequency: 28 rims, 28 total, 2.2 percent of complex.
Ware: Unspecified
Complex: K'awil
Sphere: Unaffiliated (possibly Eb)
Principal identifying attributes: (1) Unslipped surfaces, (2) light yellow to buff color, (3) slightly incurving bowls with direct or exterior thickened rims, and (4) jars with outcurving necks.
Paste, firing, and temper: The paste is medium in texture with rounded gray calcite and less rounded crystal calcite inclusions. It is yellow (10YR7/4) to buff (10YR8/2) in color. This type is similar to Calam Buff but its paste is less compact and more porous. Firing cores are almost nonexistent.
Surface finish and decoration: The surface is coarse and unslipped, with surface color identical to the paste color.
Forms:

  1. Slightly incurving sided bowls that have direct or exterior thickened rims that are 20 to 30 cm in diameter; wall thicknesses are 0.9 to 1.2 cm;

  2. jars with outcurving necks with 10- to 20-cm-diameter rims and 0.8- to 1.1-cm-thick walls; and

  3. tecomates with 10- to 20-cm-diameter rims and 0.4- to 0.9-cm-thick walls.

Intraregional location and contexts: Ramonal Unslipped has been found at Holmul in mixed deposits in the platforms of Building B, Group II; Building F, Group II; and Building N, Group II. It is found most commonly in phase 1 and 2 contexts of Buildings N and F, as well as phase 4 contexts of Buildings N and B.

Interregional locations and contexts: This type is also found at Tikal where it is abundant in the Proyecto Nacional de Tikal collections.

Comment: This type is extremely similar to Calam Buff: Calam Variety in terms of paste and surface color. The major distinction is that Ramonal Unslipped is not

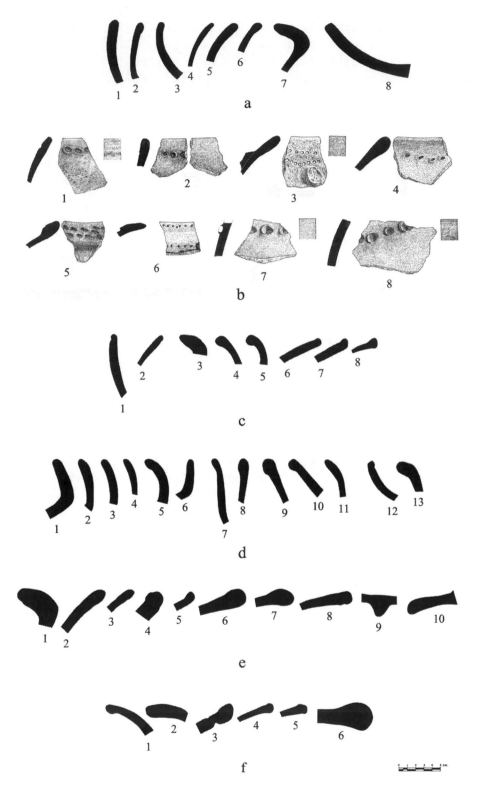

Figure 2.20. Canhel Unslipped: Canhel Variety: (a1–a8) Unknown provenance. Canhel Unslipped: Variety Unspecified: (b1) Unknown provenance, (b2) CIV.T.28.110, (b3–b5) CL.04.01, (b6) HOL.L.63.20, and (b7–b8) CIV.T.28.110. Cabcoh Striated: Cabcoh Variety: (c1 –c8) Unknown provenance. Ramonal Unslipped: Variety Unspecified: (d1–d13) Unknown provenance. Unnamed Unslipped: Variety Unspecified: (e1–e10) Unknown provenance. Unnamed Red Paste Unslipped: Variety Unspecified: (f1–f6) Unknown provenance. Drawings by Diana Méndez-Lee (a, c, d, e, f) and Fernando Alvarez (b) (Holmul Archaeological Project).

burnished. The two types blend into one another. Some Calam Buff sherds are less well smoothed or are eroded and some Ramonal Unslipped pottery is well smoothed or otherwise decorated (incised or with addition of red paint).

Illustration: Figure 2.20d. Note that 2.20d12 and d13 are red-on-unslipped forms.

Unnamed Unslipped (pre-Mamom)

Established: Neivens de Estrada in this study.
Group: Unnamed
Ware: Unspecified
Complex: K'awil
Sphere: Unaffiliated (possibly Eb)
Ceramic Group Frequency: 9 rims, 9 total, 0.7 percent of complex.
Principal identifying attributes: (1) Unslipped vessel surfaces, (2) gray color, (3) tecomates, (4) incensarios, and (4) volcanic ash inclusions.
Paste, firing, and temper: The paste is medium coarse in texture, with many fine-grained inclusions of silica and few medium-sized red inclusions and volcanic ash. The paste is gray in color (5YR5/1).
Surface finish and decoration: The surface is unslipped and smoothed, with a darker color on the interior than the exterior. The surface color ranges from light brown to light gray (5YR8/1, 5YR7/1).
Forms:

1. Tecomates with exterior folded or interior thickened rims that are 18 to 30 cm in diameter; walls are 0.8 to 1.5 cm and

2. incensarios with annular supports (no measurements available).

Intraregional location and contexts: This Unnamed Unslipped type has been found at Holmul in mixed deposits in the platforms of Building B, Group II; Building F, Group II; and Building N, Group II. It is found most commonly in phase 1 and 2 contexts of Buildings N and B.
Interregional locations and contexts: This Unnamed Unslipped type is similar to examples of Achiotes Unslipped found at Tikal in the Early Eb Complex,

which becomes more common in the following Tzec complex (see Culbert 1993:5, 2006). These early forms of Achiotes Unslipped are also found at Seibal, where tecomates are common in pre-Mamom contexts (Sabloff 1975:46).

Illustration: Figure 2.20e.

Unnamed Unslipped Red Paste (pre-Mamom)

Established: Neivens de Estrada in this study.
Group: Unnamed
Ware: Unspecified
Complex: K'awil
Sphere: Unaffiliated
Ceramic Group Frequency: 20 rims, 20 total, 1.6 percent of complex.
Principal identifying attributes: (1) Unslipped vessel surfaces, (2) orange-red color, and (3) thin-walled tecomates with exterior folded rims.
Paste, firing, and temper: The paste is coarse-textured, with many medium-sized inclusions of quartz. The paste is red (2.5YR6/8).
Surface finish and decoration: The surface is unslipped with a similar color to the paste, ranging from red to light red and reddish brown (2.5YR6/6, 2.56/4, 10R4/8). Vessel interiors are more smoothed than vessel exteriors, and vessel exteriors are sometimes striated.
Forms:

1. tecomates with exterior folded or thickened rims that are 8 to 15 cm in diameter; walls are 0.4 to 0.7 cm thick; and

2. jars with short outcurving necks with wall thicknesses of 1.0 to 1.4 cm.

Intraregional location and contexts: This Unnamed Red Paste Unslipped type has been found at Holmul in mixed deposits in the platforms of Building B, Group II; Building F, Group II; and Building N, Group II. It is found most commonly in phase 1 and 2 contexts of Building F.
Interregional locations and contexts: This type resembles Amanecer Unslipped: Amanecer Variety, which is common at Tikal.
Illustration: Figure 2.20f.

CHAPTER THREE

Yax Te Complex

Michael G. Callaghan

The Yax Te Complex dates between 840 and 400 BC. Dating was determined through a combination of radiocarbon samples (Table 1.2; Estrada-Belli 2008:15, 144; 2006b:44) and typological comparisons to other sites. Radiocarbon dates associated with Burial 33 from CIV.T.28 (Estrada-Belli 2007:38–44) at Cival anchors the beginning of the Yax Te Complex between 895 and 840 BC (calibrated). Radiocarbon dates associated with Yax Te whole vessels in Cival Cache 4, or the cruciform cache, in CT.08.46 (Morgan and Bauer 2003) returned a calibrated date between 680 and 550 BC. Finally, the earliest radiocarbon date associated with Late Preclassic Itzamkanak (Chicanel) material comes from fill within the first phase of Building B, Group II at Holmul (400–340 BC calibrated).

Descriptions of Yax Te material included in this study come from 2,614 rim sherds, 5,666 diagnostic body sherds, and 20 whole vessels for a total of 8,300 samples. Four wares (1 Unspecified), 7 groups, and 21 type-varieties define the Yax Te Complex (Table 3.1). The majority of type-varieties are slipped (93.1%). Typologically, Yax Te ceramics resemble material of the Mamom Sphere during the Late Middle Preclassic period in the Maya lowlands and are contemporaneous with Mamom material at Uaxactun (Smith 1955), Tzec at Tikal (Culbert 1993, 2003, 2006), Monos at El Mirador (Forsyth 1989), Escoba at Seibal (Sabloff 1975), San Felix at Altar de Sacrificios (Adams 1971), Jenny Creek at Barton Ramie (Gifford 1976), Lopez at Cuello (Kosakowsky 1987), Boden at Chan (Kosakowsky 2012), the Bolay and Chiwa Complexes at Colha (Valdez 1987), Zihnal at Calakmul (Dominguez-Carrasco 1994), Kanluk at Cahal Pech (Awe 1992), Chaakk'ax at K'axob (Lopez Varela 2004), and Excarvado in the Petexbatun region (Foias and Bishop 2013).

The majority of Yax Te material was recovered from excavations at the site of Cival, although sherds have occasionally been found mixed into fill at the sites of Holmul, K'o, and La Sufricaya. The most notable deposit discovered outside of Cival was found in a *chultun* at K'o beneath Structure 60 in Patio Group 4, just south of the main civic-ceremonial core (Tomasic 2009). The chultun contained a single extended burial with seven vessels, one of which was an incised effigy Chunhinta Black bowl picturing an anthropomorphic face wearing a possible trefoil jewel headband (Tomasic and Bozarth 2011). The two largest deposits of Yax Te material were found at Cival. Operation CIV.T.28 was located in the plaza in front of the North Pyramid at Cival (see Figure 1.4). It included excavation of a test pit into the plaza and a collapsed chultun beneath the surface; both revealed sealed stratified layers of construction fill that contained pure deposits of Yax Te material (Estrada-Belli 2007:38–44). The second largest deposit of Yax Te material at Cival was found in operation CL.04. This is a trench located on the east side of Structure 31 (Leonard 2003:139–144). The excavation began as a looters' trench. Archaeologists cleaned the trench, revealing a pure deposit of Yax Te material used in construction fill.

Modally, the majority of Yax Te ceramic types resemble pre-Mamom ceramics in terms of paste, form, and surface treatment. Yax Te ceramics also include many types of contemporaneous established Mamom-sphere ceramics. There are, however, a notable number of

Table 3.1. Ceramic Wares, Groups, Types, and Varieties of the Late Middle Preclassic Period (Yax Te Complex)

Ware	Group (% of complex)	Type: Variety	Numbers			Percentages	
			Rims	Bodies	Vessels	Group	Complex
Uaxactun Unslipped	Achiotes (6.8%)	Achiotes Unslipped: Achiotes Variety	173	818	7	100.0	6.8
	Jocote (0.1%)	Jocote Orange-brown: Jocote Variety	2	97	0	66.7	3.2
		Chacchinic Red-on-orange-brown: Chacchinic Variety	1	3	0	33.3	0.04
Mars Orange Paste	Savana (12.0%)	Savana Orange: Savana Variety	197	921	0	62.3	7.5
		Reforma Incised: Reforma Variety	119	94	0	37.7	4.5
Unspecified	Joventud (64.6%)	Joventud Red: Ixtoc Variety	769	2681	5	45.5	29.4
		Guitara Incised: Noctún Variety	489	89	1	28.8	18.6
		Chito Red-and-unslipped: Chito Variety	95	41	0	5.6	3.6
		Chito Red-and-unslipped: Variety Unspecified	28	7	0	1.6	1.1
		Desvario Chamfered: Horqueta Variety	54	9	0	3.2	2.1
Flores Waxy	Joventud	Joventud Red: Joventud Variety	220	5	0	12.9	8.4
		Guitara Incised: Guitara Variety	12	0	0	0.7	0.5
		Desvario Chamfered: Desvario Variety	28	0	0	1.6	1.1
	Tierra Mojada (0.3%)	Tierra Mojada Resist: Tierra Mojada Variety	8	2	0	100.0	0.3
	Pital (5.1%)	Pital Cream: Pital Variety	107	124	1	80.6	4.1
		Paso Danto Incised: Paso Danto Variety	9	5	0	6.7	0.3
		Muxanal Red-on-cream: Muxanal Variety	14	4	1	11.2	0.6
		Unnamed Red-on-cream Incised	2	0	0	1.5	0.1
	Chunhinta (11.1%)	Chunhinta Black: Chunhinta Variety	187	683	4	65.4	7.3
		Deprecio Incised: Deprecio Variety	62	71	1	21.6	2.4
		Centenario Fluted: Centenario Variety	38	12	0	13.0	1.4
		TOTALS	**2614**	**5666**	**20**		

previously undefined local varieties of Mamom-sphere types within the Yax Te Complex. The implications of the differences and similarities between Yax Te ceramics and other Mamom-sphere complexes are discussed in the type descriptions in this chapter and in Chapter 8. Yax Te represents a continuation of local production technologies adopted during pre-Mamom times as well as participation in the burgeoning Mamom Sphere across the Maya lowlands. Yax Te Complex wares are briefly defined next, followed by type descriptions.

UAXACTUN UNSLIPPED WARE

Smith and Gifford (1966:169) established this ware at Uaxactun. It is characterized by roughly smoothed unslipped surfaces. Decoration is rare. Vessel surfaces are the color of the pastes (7.5YR5/2, 4/2). Pastes are coarse to medium in texture with primary inclusions of crystalline calcite. Type: varieties within Uaxactun Unslipped Ware dating to the Yax Te Complex include

Achiotes Group
    Achiotes Unslipped: Achiotes Variety
Jocote Group
    Jocote Orange-brown: Jocote Variety
    Chacchinic Red-on-orange brown: Chacchinic Variety

FLORES WAXY WARE

Smith and Gifford (1966:166) established this ware at Uaxactun. It is one of two slipped wares dating to the Yax Te Complex era. Flores Waxy Ware is characterized by highly polished or burnished surfaces that feel "greasy" or "waxy" to the touch. Slipped ceramics include red, black, cream, and red-on-cream colors. Surface decoration includes incision, grooved-incision, chamfering, fluting, modeling, applique, dichrome slips, and resist. Red slips tend toward orange (2.5YR5/8) and cream slips toward a more true white (10YR8/1) than in the later Paso Caballo Waxy Ware of the Late Preclassic Itzamkanak Complex. Pastes are medium in texture. Colors range from yellow (10YR6/4), to buff (10YR8/3), to pink (5YR7/4), or gray (10YR4/1). Primary paste inclusions are crystalline calcite, sherd temper (grog), burnt organics, and even shell. Although some analysts have chosen to collapse Flores Waxy Ware and Paso Caballo Waxy Ware due to the lack of qualitative and quantitative differences in technology between the two wares (see Forsyth 1989:13), typological

and modal data derived from the Holmul sample lead me to maintain the distinction between the two wares.

Groups and type: varieties within Flores Waxy Ware include
    Joventud Group
        Joventud Red: Joventud Variety
        Guitara Incised: Guitara Variety
        Desvario Chamfered: Desvario Variety
    Tierra Mojada Group
        Tierra Mojada Resist: Tierra Mojada Variety
    Pital Group
        Pital Cream: Pital Variety
        Paso Danto Incised: Paso Danto Variety
        Muxanal Red-on-cream: Muxanal Variety
        Unnamed Red-on-cream Incised (Pital Group)
    Chunhinta Group
        Chunhinta Black: Chunhinta Variety
        Deprecio Incised: Deprecio Variety
        Centenario Fluted: Cententario Variety

MARS ORANGE PASTE WARE

Smith and Gifford (1966:167) established "Mars Orange Ware" at Uaxactun (here referred to as Mars Orange Paste Ware). The primary distinguishing characteristic of Mars Orange Paste Ware is its bright orange-colored pastes (5YR5/8, 6/8), which contain volcanic ash or few discernible inclusions (occasionally very small pieces of calcite). Surfaces are perfectly smoothed and can be unslipped or slipped red (10R4/8). Decoration includes incision, grooved-incision, and chamfering.

Groups and type: varieties within Mars Orange Paste Ware include
    Savana Group
        Savana Orange: Savana Variety
        Reforma Incised: Reforma Variety

UNSPECIFIED WARE

This Unspecified Ware is unique to local type: varieties of the Joventud Group within the Yax Te Complex and has not been defined in previous publications. It is characterized by smooth vessel surfaces with a duller polish than Flores Waxy Ware. Slip colors are a true bright red (10R4/8). Paste is fine-textured, yellow (10YR7/3, 10YR7/4), and contains volcanic ash. Decoration includes grooved-incision, incision, and chamfering. This Unspecified Ware appears to be local to the Holmul region during Yax Te Complex times. It is an obvious outgrowth of, if not identical to, what Neivens de Estrada has named K'an Slipped Ware, which dates to the preceding pre-Mamom early Middle Preclassic period. I am reticent to name this new ware K'an Unslipped, however, as Neivens de Estrada's analysis is ongoing. As a note, it is not uncommon for two wares to be present within the same ceramic group within a specific ceramic complex (see Ball and Taschek 2003:199–203 and Joventud Red: Ixtoc Variety in this chapter). The presence of different wares crosscutting type: varieties within the Yax Te Complex is one reason why I have chosen not to integrate wares into the typology at a hierarchical level.

Groups and type: varieties within this Unspecified Ware include:

Joventud Group
    Joventud Red: Ixtoc Variety
    Guitara Incised: Noctún Variety
    Desvario Chamfered: Horqueta Variety
    Chito Red-and-unslipped: Chito Variety
    Chito Red-and-unslipped: Variety Unspecified

TYPE DESCRIPTIONS

Achiotes Unslipped: Achiotes Variety

Established: Smith and Gifford at Uaxactun (1966: 154, 170).
  Group: Achiotes
  Ware: Uaxactun Unslipped
  Complex: Yax Te
  Sphere: Mamom
  Ceramic Group Frequency: 173 rims, 818 bodies, 7 whole vessels, 988 total, 100 percent of group, 6.8 percent of complex.
  Principal identifying attributes: (1) Unslipped surface, (2) coarse-tempered paste, and (3) small globular short-necked and outcurving-necked jars.
  Paste, firing, and temper: The paste is coarse- to medium-textured and gray (7.5YR4/2) in color. The major inclusion in Achiotes pastes is crystalline calcite. Dark paste cores are not uncommon.
  Surface finish and decoration: Smoothed and unslipped vessel exteriors and interiors. Surfaces are roughly the color of the paste (7.5YR5/2, 4/2).
  Forms:
    1. Small jars with short-necks and outcurved rims; rim diameters measure 14 to 23 cm, neck heights 1.4 to 4.4 cm, wall thicknesses 0.7 to 1 cm, and
    2. possible lid (very rare—only one example with measurements unknown).

Intraregional locations and contexts: Achiotes Unslipped appears in largest quantities in Cival excavations and contexts from Building B, Group II at Holmul. At this point in time it is difficult to differentiate between Middle Preclassic Yax Te Achiotes material and Late Preclassic Itzamkanak material. Two potentially significant characteristics may be related to form. Yax Te vessels appear to have smaller diameters and are shorter in height. Furthermore, rim forms are less varied, with the most common form being direct and outcurving. Finally, there appear to be more examples of handles and handle scars on Yax Te Achiotes Unslipped material. The ceramic group frequencies and illustrations listed here include sherds from stratified Yax Te deposits from the site of Cival.

Interregional locations and contexts: Achiotes Unslipped appears at Uaxactun (Smith and Gifford 1966:154), Barton Ramie (Gifford 1976:108), Altar de Sacrificios (Adams 1971:18), Becan (Ball 1977:8), Seibal (Sabloff 1975:46), the Valle de Dolores (Laporte et al. 1993:65–66), El Mirador (Forsyth 1989:49), Tikal (Culbert 1993:Figures 6b-c, 8a 1, 11a 2, 121d; 2006), Piedras Negras (Muñoz 2004:10), and the Petexbatun region (Foias and Bishop 2013:56–57).
  Illustration: Figure 3.1a15–49.

Jocote Orange-brown: Jocote Variety

Established: Willey, Bullard, Glass, and Gifford at Barton Ramie (Willey et al. 1965), type originally named as tentative in Smith and Gifford at Uaxactun (1963:26–33).
  Group: Jocote
  Ware: Uaxactun Unslipped Ware
  Complex: Yax Te
  Sphere: Mamom
  Ceramic Group Frequency: 2 rims, 97 bodies, 99 total, 66.7 percent of group, 3.2 percent of complex.
  Principal identifying attributes: (1) Unslipped orange-brown surface and (2) appliqué-impressed filet on vessel exterior.
  Paste, firing, and temper: Pastes are relatively fine- to medium-textured. Paste colors are yellow (10YR7/5, 6/8), but appear to be orange-brown. Major inclusions consist of small crystalline calcite grains and undefined white inclusions.
  Surface finish and decoration: Vessel exteriors and interiors are unslipped. Surface color is due to the paste, which fires gray to orange-brown (10YR7/5, 6/8). Primary decoration on Jocote sherds is a thin, impressed, often "winding" appliqué filet on vessel exteriors.

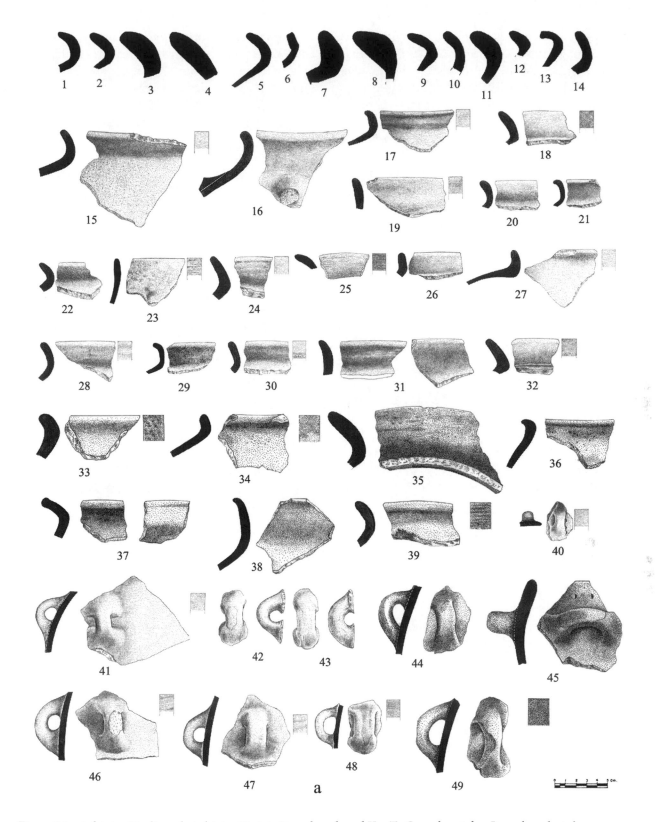

Figure 3.1. Achiotes Unslipped: Achiotes Variety Itzamkanak and Yax Te Complex styles. Itzamkanak styles: (a1–a2) CIV.T.16.02, (a3–a4) CIV.T.18:08, (a5–a7) CIV.T.15.02, (a8) HOL.T.56.01, (a9) HOL.T.56.01, (a10–a11) HOL.T.49.16, (a12) HOL.T.49:10, (a13) HOL.T.49.03, and (a14) HOL.T.49.16. Yax Te styles: (a15–a33) CIV.T.28.110, (a34–a39) CL.04.01, (a40–a43) CIV.T.28.110, (a44–a45) CL.04.01, (a46 –a48) CIV.T.28.110, and (a49) CL.04.01. Drawings by Michael G. Callaghan (a1–a14) and Fernando Alvarez (a15–49) (Holmul Archaeological Project).

Forms:

1. Small globular short neck jars (no form data);

2. thin-walled tecomates with 10- to 12–cm-diameter rims and 0.3- to 0.7-cm-thick walls; and

3. medium-sized incurving bowls (no measurements available).

Intraregional locations and contexts: This type: variety has been found at various contexts in the site of Cival, as well as in Middle Preclassic contexts at Holmul, specifically the substructure of Building B, Group II.

Interregional locations and contexts: Jocote Orange-brown appears at Barton Ramie (Gifford 1976:63–68) and in the Belize River Valley (Ball and Taschek 2003 as Tumbac Unslipped Ware), Cahal Pech (Awe 1992:237), and Chan (Kosakowsky 2012:62), as well as in northern Belize at Cuello (Kosakowsky and Pring 1998).

Illustration: Figure 3.2 c.

Chacchinic Red-on-orange-brown: Chacchinic Variety

Established: Sharer and Gifford (1970:446). Originally identified as an Unspecified Variety of Jocote Orange-brown by Willey, Bullard, Glass, and Gifford at Barton Ramie (Willey et al. 1965:Fig.189h).

Group: Jocote
Ware: Uaxactun Unslipped
Complex: Yax Te
Sphere: Mamom
Ceramic Group Frequency: 1 rim, 3 bodies, 4 total, 33.3 percent of group, 0.04 percent of complex.

Principal identifying attributes: (1) Red-orange wash or thin slip applied to upper portions of vessel exteriors and (2) thin, impressed appliqué filet.

Paste, firing, and temper: Pastes are fine- to medium-textured and are orange-yellow (10YR7/5, 6/8). Primary paste inclusions are small grains of crystalline calcite. Firing cores are not present in this small sample.

Surface finish and decoration: The surface finish is generally the same as Jocote Orange-brown. A thin, winding appliqué filet decorates the exterior vessel surface. The fillet is impressed with tiny vertical slits. In Chacchinic Red-on-orange-brown, however, a thin orange-red (2.5YR4/8) wash appears above the fillet on the vessel exterior and continues over the lip. The vessel is unslipped below the fillet on exteriors and the paste appears a bright orange-yellow.

Forms: The one rim sherd in the present collection is of a small, thin-walled, round-sided bowl with a rim diameter of 20 cm, and 0.6 to 0.8-cm thick walls.

Intraregional locations and contexts: This type: variety has been found at the sites of Cival and Holmul.

Interregional locations and contexts: Chacchinic Red-on-orange-brown also appears at Barton Ramie (Gifford 1976:68–69), in the Belize River Valley (Ball and Taschek 2003), and in northern Belize at Cuello (Kosakowsky and Pring 1998)

Illustration: Figure 3.2d.

Savana Orange: Savana Variety

Established: Smith and Gifford at Uaxactun (1966: 162, 170).

Group: Savana
Ware: Mars Orange Paste Ware
Complex: Yax Te
Sphere: Mamom
Ceramic Group Frequency: 197 rims, 921 bodies, 1118 total, 62.3 percent of group, 7.5 percent of complex.

Principal identifying attributes: (1) Fine, bright orange paste with few inclusions, (2) occasional red or cream slip, and (3) small bowls and jars with spouts.

Paste, firing, and temper: Two potential variants of Savana Orange pastes may exist in the present sample. The first is fine to very fine-textured with little or no volcanic ash inclusions. Paste color is bright orange (5YR5/8, 6/8) with no firing core. The second paste variant is also fine, but with many more inclusions (some rather large). The inclusions are mostly volcanic ash, with an occasional piece of crystalline calcite. This second paste color is also bright orange (5YR5/8, 6/8) with no firing core.

Surface finish and decoration: Surfaces are well-smoothed and highly polished (on preserved examples). Surfaces are usually eroded, but sometimes a lustrous, waxy well-preserved red (10R4/8) is present, which would make the sherd Savana Orange: Rejolla Variety.

Forms:

1. Bowls or dishes with thin, slightly flaring or outcurving sides, direct or slightly everted rims, and rounded lips; rim diameters measure 14 to 18 cm, and wall thicknesses 0.3 to 0.6 cm; and

2. possible jar or pitcher forms represented by some small spouts (no measurements available).

Intraregional locations and contexts: Savana Orange is found throughout the Holmul region at Cival, Ko, Holmul, and La Sufricaya.

Interregional locations and contexts: Mars Orange Paste Ware is found in the greatest quantities in northeastern Guatemala and the adjacent Belize River Valley.

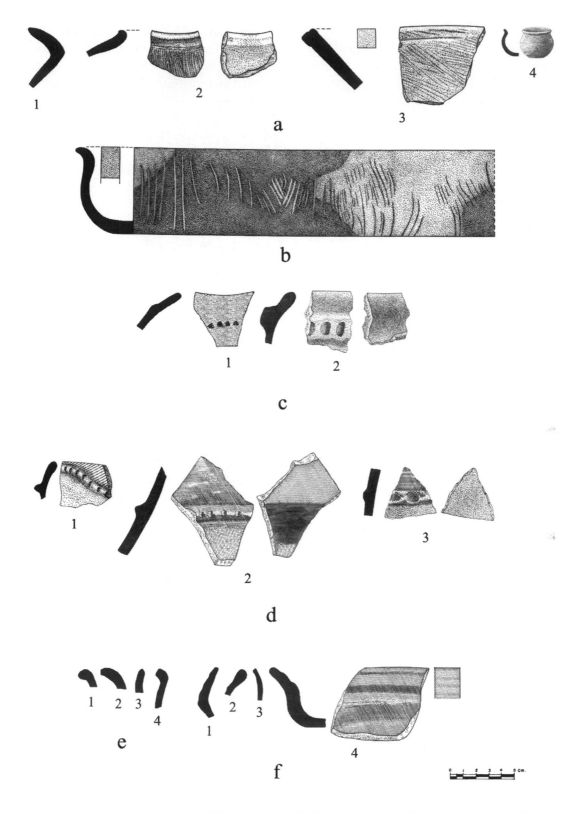

Figure 3.2. Sapote Striated: Sapote Variety: (a1) CIV.T.16.04, (a2) HOL.L.10.13, (a3) HOL.L.74.16, and (a4) KOL.T.34.24. Achiotes Unslipped: Variety Unspecified: (b1) CIV.T.17.07.56.03. Jocote Orange-brown: Jocote Variety: (c1) CIV.T.10.15 and (c2) HOL.T.74.12B. Chacchinic Red-on-orange-brown: Chacchinic Variety: (d1) CIV.T.16.04, (d2) CL.04.01, and (d3) HOL.T.74.01. Savana Orange: Savana Variety: (e1–e4) CIV.T.01.04. Reforma Incised: Reforma Variety: (f1–f3) CIV.T.01.04, (f4) CL.04.01. Drawings by Fernando Alvarez (a–d, f4) and Michael G. Callaghan (e, f1-3) (Holmul Archaeological Project).

Savana Orange appears at Uaxactun (Smith and Gifford 1966:167), Barton Ramie (Gifford 1976:73–76), Altar de Sacrificios (Adams 1971:80), Seibal (Sabloff 1975:74), Cahal Pech (Awe 1992:236–240), and Chan as the slipped Savana Orange: Rejolla Variety (Kosakowsky 2012:62).

Comment: The two paste variants of Savana Orange are interesting. Both variants are identified in the Savana Orange type from Barton Ramie (Gifford 1976:73–75) and may indicate that Savana was imported into the area, but this does not rule out local production. Ball and Taschek (2003) have found similar paste variants, also with red slip, at sites in the neighboring Belize Valley. They note that the forms are similar to Joventud Red and, therefore, place these fine-paste variants into the Joventud Group, classifying these sherds as Yesoso Orange Paste Ware.

Illustration: Figure 3.2e.

Reforma Incised: Reforma Variety

Established: Smith and Gifford at Uaxactun (1966: 161, 170).

Group: Savana
Ware: Mars Orange Paste Ware
Complex: Yax Te
Sphere: Mamom
Ceramic Group Frequency: 119 rims, 94 bodies, 213 total, 37.7 percent of group, 4.5 percent of complex.
Principal identifying attributes: Same as Savana Orange with the addition of thin grooved-incision on vessel exteriors.
Paste, firing, and temper: Same as Savana Orange.
Surface finish and decoration: Vessel exteriors are smoothed and burnished to a dull shine. Thin grooved-incision creates horizontal bands and geometric patterns on vessel exteriors. On well-preserved examples, a red-orange slip is still visible.
Forms:

1. Bowls or dishes with flaring or outcurving sides, direct or slightly everted rims, and rounded lips; rim diameters measure 18 to 30 cm and wall thicknesses 0.5 to 1.1 cm;

2. bowls with composite, incurving sides with sharp medial angles, direct rims, and rounded lips; rim diameters are 14 to 18 cm, and wall thicknesses 0.3 to 0.6 cm; and

3. possible jar or pitcher forms indicated by some small spouts (no form data).

Intraregional locations and contexts: Reforma Incised: Reforma Variety is almost as widely distributed as Savana Orange: Savana Variety. It has been found mostly at Cival, but also Holmul, K'o, and La Sufricaya.

Interregional locations and contexts: Unsurprisingly, the distribution of Reforma Incised corresponds to the distribution of Savana Orange. It appears at Uaxacatun (Smith and Gifford 1966:161), Barton Ramie (Gifford 1976:75–77), Chan (Kosakowsky 2012:48-9, 63), and Seibal (Sabloff 1975:74).

Illustration: Figure 3.2f.

Joventud Red: Ixtoc Variety

Established: Type named by Smith and Gifford at Uaxactun (1966:158, 170), Variety named by Callaghan in this study.

Group: Joventud
Ware: Unspecified
Complex: Yax Te
Ceramic Group Frequency: 769 rims, 2,681 bodies, 5 whole vessels, 3,455 total, 45.5 percent of group, 29.4 percent of complex.
Principal identifying attributes: (1) Red slip, (2) slightly glossy yet dull finish, and (3) fine, yellow volcanic ash-based paste.
Paste, firing, and temper: The only paste variant of Joventud Red: Ixtoc Variety is similar to a variety of earlier K'atun Red pastes. This is a fine-textured yellow (10YR7/3, 7/4) paste with volcanic ash inclusions. Firing cores are present in the sample, but infrequent. This type of paste is associated with a thin flaky red slip and low polish that is also similar to K'atun Group ceramics.
Surface finish and decoration: Surfaces are well-smoothed, slipped bright red (10R4/8), and polished to a dull shine. This surface is not waxy like the red-orange surfaces of Joventud Red: Joventud Variety common at other lowland sites and found in small quantities in the Holmul region during this time.
Forms:

1. Bowls with incurving sides, 10- to 23-cm-diameter rims and 0.4- to 0.7-cm-thick walls;

2. small bowls with flaring or outcurving sides, direct rims, and rounded lips; rim diameters measure 14 to 22 cm and wall thicknesses 0.5 to 0.7 cm;

3. round-sided bowls with 14- to 20-cm diameter rims and 0.5- to 0.7-cm-thick walls;

4. wide-everted rim dishes with flat bases, 14- to 35-cm-diameter rims and 0.7- 1.1-cm-thick walls;

5. jars with vertical necks, 8- to 13-cm-diameter rims, 0.7- to 1.1-cm-thick walls, and 3- to 5-cm-high necks;

6. large tecomates with bolstered rims, 13- to 22-cm-diameter rims, and 0.5- to 1-cm-thick walls; and

7. recurving bowls with direct rims and rounded lips; rim diameters measure 14 to 22 cm and wall thicknesses 0.5 to 0.7 cm.

Intraregional locations and contexts: Joventud Red: Ixtoc Variety is currently found at Cival and in Building B, Group II at Holmul. One complete Joventud Red: Ixtoc Variety jar was found in Cache 4 at Cival (Estrada-Belli 2006b).

Interregional locations and contexts: Joventud Red: Ixtoc Variety is a local variety of Joventud Red and to date has not been found outside of the Holmul region. Joventud Red: Yellow Paste Variety (Culbert 2006) exhibits a similar paste color, however; it is restricted to early Eb contexts at Tikal. Ball and Taschek (2003:199–203) have also identified a local variety of Joventud Red in the Belize River Valley. They identify Joventud Red: Sampopero Variety as part of a newly defined ware they call Yesoso Orange Paste Ware. Characteristics of the ware and the Joventud Red: Sampopero Variety are similar to Joventud Red: Ixtoc Variety in the Holmul region. Namely, both varieties are defined by a dull glossy surface finish with a red slip that is qualitatively different from the established Joventud variety (e.g., 10R4/8 compared to 2.5YR5/8); both have volcanic ash-based yellow-orange pastes. Although I hesitate to name a new ware at this time, I am certain that Joventud Red: Ixtoc Variety does not conform to Smith and Gifford's (1966:166–167) original definition of Flores Waxy Ware. Forms including outcurving bowls and dishes, incurving shallow bowls, composite bowls, and jars with short, vertical necks are almost identical to established Joventud variety examples. Finally, although qualitatively different, principal identifying attributes are clearly consistent with general trends observable in the established Joventud Variety. That is, no ceramicist who has seen this material in the Holmul lab has ever remarked that it was anything other than Joventud Red. The differences that separate it from the established type: variety of Joventud are at the varietal level, which is why it is classified as such. Joventud Red is not alone within the Joventud Group as being made from a local ware—a similar situation involving the creation of new varieties appears with Guitara Incised and Desvario Chamfered as explained later in this chapter.

Comment: As noted in Chapter 1 and the introduction to the Yax Te Complex, Joventud Red: Ixtoc Variety represents a local and more popular variety of monochrome red-slipped serving ceramics at the site of Cival and Holmul. It was previously classified as Joventud Red: Variety Unspecified and was part of the now deleted Ixim Complex in earlier publications by Callaghan (2005:234, 2008:279–280, 2013). The presence of this variety in the Holmul region indicates a local ceramic system of red-slipped pottery that is part of a larger tradition related to earlier material of the pre-Mamom period. The dull glossy red slip, yellow-orange ash-based paste, and forms of Joventud Red: Ixtoc Variety represent a clear continuity in pottery making tradition from pre-Mamom times. I prefer not to use the ware defined by Neivens de Estrada for pre-Mamom material, however because her study is ongoing and not yet complete. Therefore, the ware for Joventud Red: Ixtoc Variety remains "unspecified" (as it also does for Guitara Incised: Noctún Variety, Chito Red-and-unslipped, and Desvario Chamfered: Horqueta Variety). The presence of Joventud Red: Ixtoc Variety supports my argument that ware cannot be integrated into type: variety-mode classification in a hierarchical manner. In this case, ware crosscuts varieties of Joventud Red and cannot be integrated above the level of type: varieties, much less ceramic groups. Finally, analysts may question why I chose to create a new variety within an unspecified ware, and not an entirely new group of red-slipped ceramics. At this time, I do not believe that the differences between the local varieties and established varieties of Joventud Red warrant the creation of a new group. This material is clearly a local manifestation of an established tradition of pottery making and if I were to create a new group and ware designation, I would highlight the differences between the two more than the similarities, leading readers to believe the Holmul region was somehow more isolated from the rest of the lowlands during the late Middle Preclassic period than it actually was. I do not think this is the case. If anything, the presence of these local varieties of established types indicates contact (at the least) and appropriation (at the most) of a ceramic system outside of the immediate geographical area.

Illustration: Figure 3.3, 3.4a.

Guitara Incised: Noctún Variety

Established: Type named by Smith and Gifford (1966) at Uaxactun; Variety named by Callaghan in this study.

Group: Joventud

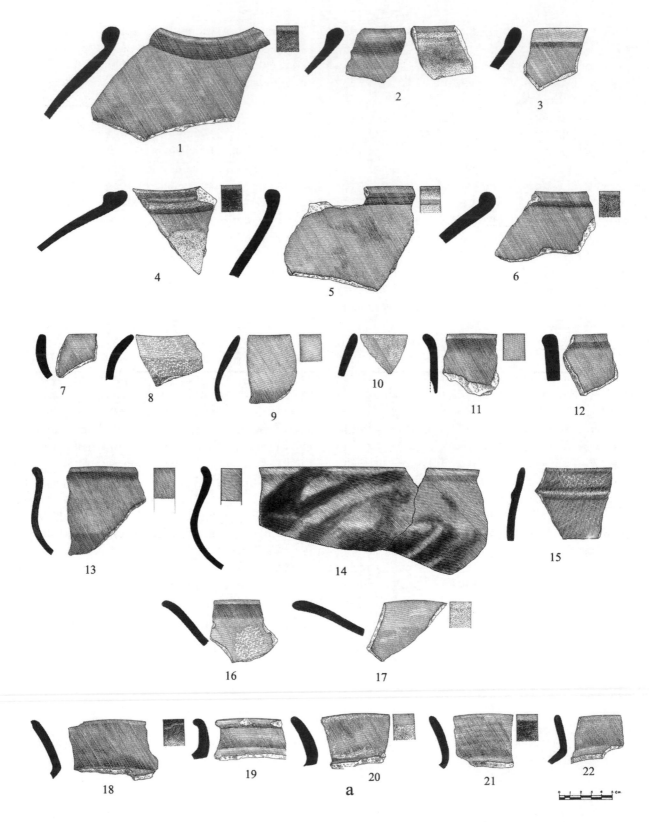

Figure 3.3. Joventud Red: Ixtoc Variety: (a1) HL.58.38.41, (a2–a3) CIV.T.28.110, (a4) CIV.T.28.120, (a5) CL.04.01, (a6) CIV.T.28.110, (a7) CL.04.01, (a8) CIV.T.28.110, (a9–a10) CL.04.01, (a11–a14) CIV.T.28.110, (a15) HOL.T.71.58, (a16–a17) CL.04.01, and (a18–a22) CIV.T.28.110. Drawings by Fernando Alvarez (Holmul Archaeological Project).

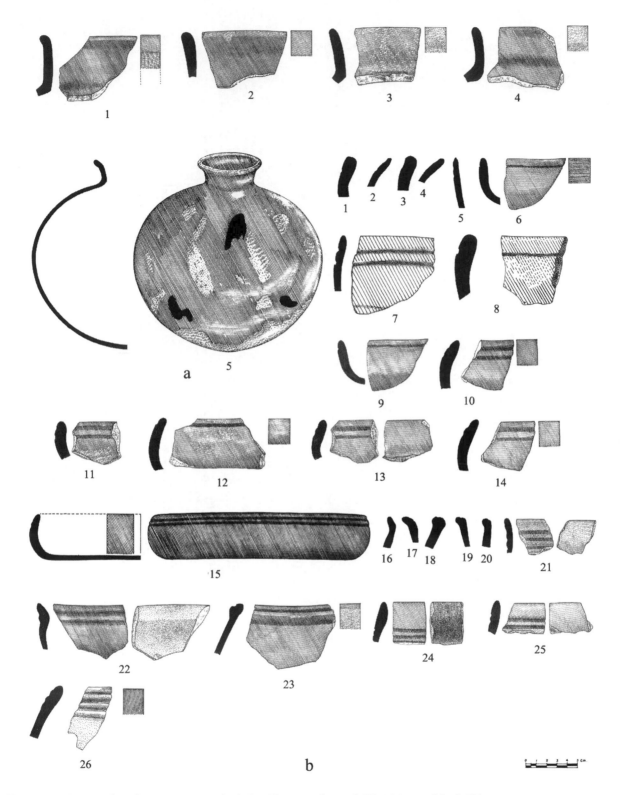

Figure 3.4. Joventud Red: Ixtoc Variety: (a1) CIV.T.28.110, (a2–a4) CL.04.01, and (a5) CT.08.49.02.01.02. Guitara Incised: Noctún Variety: (b1–b4) CIV.T.11.03, (b5) CIV.T.10.10, (b6) CIV.T.28.110, (b7–b8) CIV.T.11.03, (b9–b14) CIV.T.28.110, (b15) CIV.T.28.W, (b16–b17) CL.04.01, (b18–b20) CIV.T.11.03, (b21) CL.04.01, (b22) CIV.T.28.110, (b23–b25) CL.04.01, and (b26) HOL.T.71.35. Drawings by Fernando Alvarez (a, b6–b15, b21–b26) and Michael G. Callaghan (b1–5, b16–b20) (Holmul Archaeological Project).

Ware: Unspecified (see Joventud Red: Ixtoc Variety)
Complex: Yax Te

Sphere: Mamom

Ceramic Group Frequency: 489 rims, 89 bodies, 1 whole vessel, 579 total, 28.8 percent of group, 18.6 percent of complex.

Principal identifying attributes: (1) Red slip, (2) slightly glossy yet dull finish, (3) fine yellow volcanic ash based paste, and (4) horizontal bands of grooved-incision on vessel exteriors.

Paste, firing, and temper: The paste is identical to Joventud Red: Ixtoc Variety.

Surface finish and decoration: Surfaces are well-smoothed, covered with a thin flaky red (10R4/8) slip, and polished to a low shine. Incision takes the form of circumferential bands of grooved-incised lines below the rim on closed forms and one or two bands encircling wide-everted rims.

Forms:

   1. Incurved bowls with direct rims, round or square lips, and slightly concave bases; rim diameters are 30 to 40 cm, wall thicknesses 0.8 to 1.2 cm, and vessel heights 6 to 8.5 cm;

   2. wide-everted rim dishes with rounded lips and flat bases; rim diameters measure 20 to 40 cm, wall thicknesses 0.7 to 1 cm, and vessel heights 5 to 6.5 cm;

   3. round-sided bowls with direct rims and rounded lips; rim diameters measure 20 to 25 cm and wall thickness 0.7 to 0.9 cm; and

   4. tecomates with direct rims and rounded lips; rim diameters measure 13 to 22 cm and wall thicknesses 0.5 to 1 cm.

Intraregional locations and contexts: Rim sherds of Guitara Incised: Noctún Variety are easily identifiable; they have been found at Cival, Holmul, La Sufricaya, and K'o.

Interregional locations and contexts: Guitara Incised: Noctún Variety is a local variety of Guitara Incised that to date has not been found outside of the Holmul region.

Comment: Guitara Incised: Noctún Variety is a local and more popular type: variety of incised monochrome red-slipped serving ceramics at Cival and many other sites in the Holmul region (see discussion of Joventud Red: Ixtoc Variety). It was previously classified as Guitara Incised: Variety Unspecified within the now deleted Ixim Complex (Callaghan 2005:234–235, 2008:280–281, 2013), but is presented as a new variety of Guitara in this study.

Illustration: Figure 3.4b, 3.5a 1–4.

Chito Red-and-unslipped: Chito Variety

Established: Callaghan in this study.

Group: Joventud

Ware: Unspecified

Complex: Yax Te

Sphere: Mamom

Ceramic Group Frequency: 95 rims, 41 bodies, 136 total, 5.6 percent of group, 3.6 percent of complex.

Principal identifying attributes: (1) Red slip similar to Joventud Red: Ixtoc Variety on vessel interiors and unslipped exteriors or vice versa and (2) dichrome effect created by the differential application of red slip to various sides and the rim of the vessel.

Paste, firing, and temper: The primary paste variant is similar to Joventud Red: Ixtoc Variety, but ranges from yellow (10YR7/4) to buff (10YR8/2) in color.

Surface finish and decoration: The interior and exterior surfaces were well-smoothed, after which a thin red slip (10R4/8) was applied to either the interior or exterior of the vessel. The slip can continue up over the rim and partially down the opposite side. The rest of the vessel is unslipped. The slipped surface was polished to a low gloss or dull shine. The unslipped surface appears smooth and yellow (10YR7/4) to buff (10YR8/2) in color.

Forms:

   1. Bowls with incurving sides, direct rims and rounded or squared lips; rim diameters are 35 to 36 cm and wall thicknesses 1 to 1.2 cm; and

   2. bowls with outcurving sides, direct or gradually everted rims, rounded lips, and flat bases; rim diameters measure 14 to 35 cm and wall thicknesses 0.7 to 1.1 cm.

Intraregional locations and contexts: Chito Red-and-unslipped: Chito Variety pottery has been found mainly in Middle Preclassic architecture and other contexts at Cival, but sherds have also been found mixed in construction fill at Holmul.

Interregional locations and contexts: Chito Red-and-unslipped: Chito Variety is a local type within the Joventud Group, which to date has been found only in the Holmul region. Pring (1977b) identified a Bobo Red-and-unslipped at Cuello as part of the Joventud Group, but I have not viewed this material.

Comment: Chito Red-and-unslipped displays a surface and technology similar to earlier Aac Red-on-buff. Similarities include the ash-based paste-variant of Aac Red-on-buff and the differential application of red slip

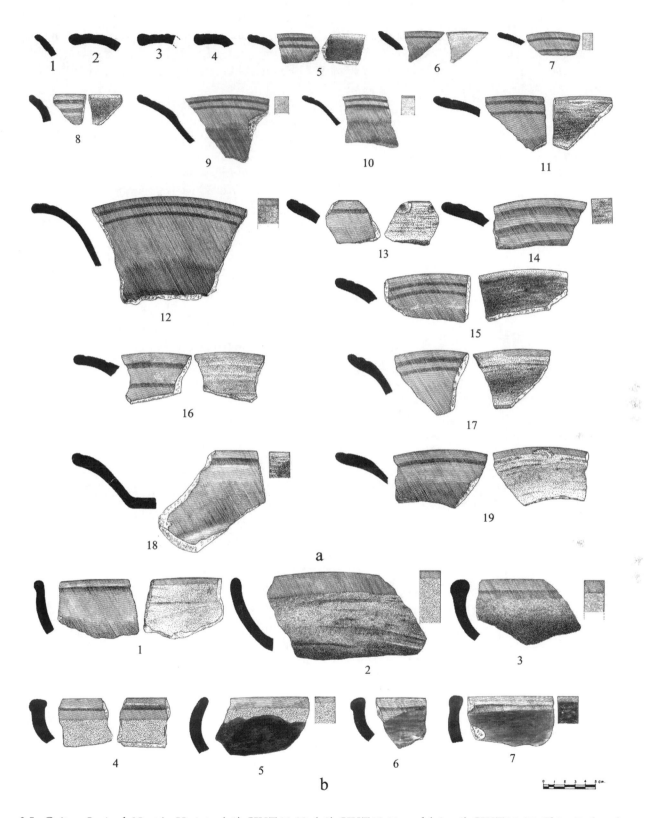

Figure 3.5. Guitara Incised: Noctún Variety: (a1) CIV.T.11.03, (a2) CIV.T.10.11, and (a3–a4) CIV.T.11.05. Chito Red-and-unslipped: Variety Unspecified: (a5–a7) CIV.T.28.110, (a8) CL.04.01, (a9–a12) CIV.T.28.110, (a13–a18) CL.04.01, and (a19) CIV.T.28.110. Chito Red-and-unslipped: Chito Variety: (b1–b3) CIV.T.28.110, (b4–b5) CL.04.01, (b6) CIV.T.28.110, (b7) CL.04.01. Drawings by Michael G. Callaghan (a1–a4) and Fernando Alvarez (a5–19, b) (Holmul Archaeological Project).

to vessel interiors and exteriors, usually including the rim and portions of the opposite side of the vessel. Chito Red-and-unslipped appears as if it bridges the earlier Aac Red-on-buff and the established Middle Preclassic type of Muxanal Red-on-cream. The type described here as Chito Red-and-unslipped: Chito Variety was previously classified as a possible earlier variety of Muxanal Red-on-cream (Callaghan 2005:235, 2008:283–284), but is presented as a new type in this study. Further analysis and comparison to Muxanal Red-on-cream showed that there is no cream slip or wash present on Chito Red-and-unslipped, which led me to classify it as a new type.

Illustration: Figures 3.5b, 3.6a.

Chito Red-and-unslipped: Unspecified Variety

Established: Callaghan in this study.
Group: Joventud
Ware: Unspecified
Complex: Yax Te
Sphere: Mamom
Ceramic Group Frequency: 28 rims, 7 bodies, 35 total, 1.6 percent of group, 1.1 percent of complex.

Principal identifying attributes: Same as Chito Red-and-unslipped with the addition of preslip, grooved-incision on vessel rim and lip.

Paste, firing, and temper: Paste is identical to Chito Red-and-unslipped: Chito Variety. Fire clouding is not uncommon on the base and lower exteriors of incurving bowl forms. The clouding may have served as decoration, thereby making it intentional.

Surface finish and decoration: Surface finish is identical to Chito Red-and-unslipped: Chito Variety, with the addition of grooved-incision on vessel exteriors. Interior and exterior surfaces were well-smoothed before a thin red (10R4/8) slip was applied to either the interior or exterior of the vessel. The slipped surface was then polished to a low gloss or dull shine. The slip is flaky. Incision on these sherds takes the form of preslip grooved-incision and varies in placement dependent on vessel form. On incurving bowls, incision appears as one circumferential band just below the rim on vessel exteriors. On gradually wide-everted bowls, it appears as single or double bands on the everted rim of vessel interiors. The interior color may extend over the lip and slightly down the exterior rims.

Forms:
1. Bowls with incurving sides, direct rims, and rounded or squared lips; rim diameters measure 35 to 36 cm and wall thicknesses 1 to 1.2 cm; and

2. bowls with outcurving sides, direct or gradually everted rims, rounded lips, and flat bases; rim diameters are 14 to 35 cm and wall thicknesses 0.7 to 1.1 cm.

Intraregional locations and contexts: Chito Red-and-unslipped: Unspecified Grooved-incised Variety has been found at Cival, but also occurs in smaller quantities at Holmul.

Interregional locations and contexts: Chito Red-and-unslipped: Unspecified Variety is a local type within the Joventud group and to date has been found only in the Holmul region.

Comment: The type described here as Chito Red-and-unslipped: Unspecified Variety was previously classified as a possible earlier incised variety of Muxanal Red-on-cream(Callaghan 2008:284–286), but is presented as an unspecified new variety of Chito Red-and-unslipped in this study. As noted in the description for Chito Red-and-unslipped, after further analysis and comparison to Muxanal Red-on-cream there is no evidence of cream slip on Chito Red-and-unslipped, which lead me to define a new type. Also like Chito Red-and-unslipped, the Unspecified Variety may also bridge the earlier Aac Red-on-buff type and later Muxanal Red-on-cream.

Illustration: Figure 3.5a5–19, 3.6b.

Desvario Chamfered: Horqueta Variety

Established: Type named Smith and Gifford at Uaxactun (1966:157); Variety named by Callaghan in this study.
Group: Joventud
Ware: Unspecified
Complex: Yax Te
Sphere: Mamom
Ceramic Group Frequency: 54 rims, 9 bodies, 63 total, 3.2 percent of group, 2.1 percent of complex.

Principal identifying attributes: (1) Red slip similar to Joventud Red: Ixtoc Variety, (2) chamfered exterior walls, and (3) bowls with incurving sides.

Paste, firing, and temper: The paste is identical to Joventud Red: Ixtoc Variety.

Surface finish and decoration: Surfaces are well smoothed, covered in a thin, flaky red (10R4/8) slip that has been polished to a low shine. Chamfering appears on exterior walls near the rim on bowls or vases with incurving sides and all the way down the sides on bowls or dishes with flaring sides.

Forms: Bowls with incurving sides, direct rims, and rounded lips. rim diameters are 10 to 24 cm and wall thicknesses 0.7 to 0.9 cm

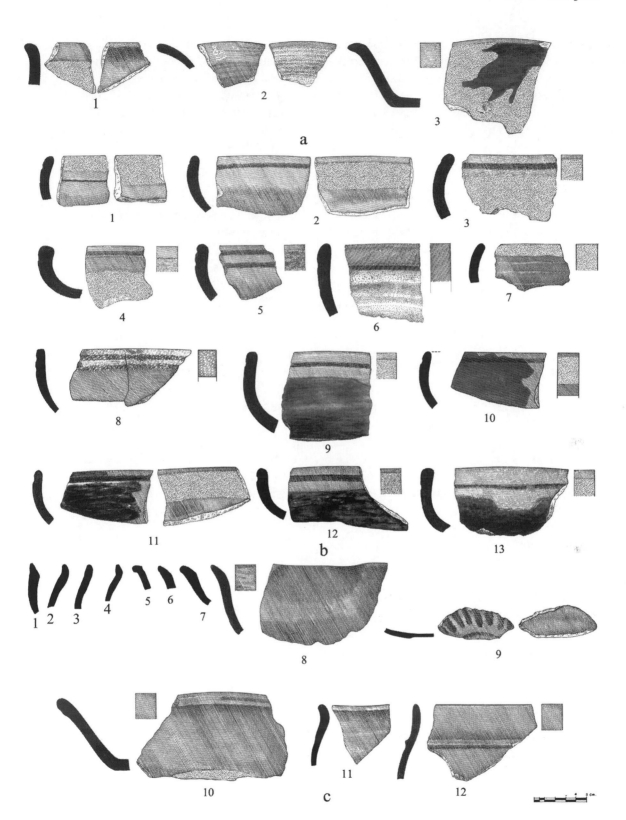

Figure 3.6. Chito Red-and-unslipped: Chito Variety: (a1–a3) CL.04.01. Chito Red-and-unslipped: Variety Unspecified: (b1–b3) CL.04.01, (b4–b5) CIV.T.28.110, (b6) Unknown provenance, (b7) CL.04.01, (b8) CIV.T.28.110, (b9) CL.04.01, (b10–b12) CIV.T.28.110, and (b13) CL.04.01. Joventud Red: Joventud Variety: (c1–c4) CIV.T.11.05, (c5) CIV.T.11.03, (c6–c7) CIV.T.11.05, (c8–c9) CIV.T.28.110, (c10) CL.04.01, and (c11–c12) CIV.T.28.110. Drawings by Fernando Alvarez (a, b, c8–c12) and Michael G. Callaghan (c1–c7) (Holmul Archaeological Project).

Intraregional locations and contexts: Desvario Chamfered: Horqueta Variety has been found in small quantities at Cival.

Interregional locations and contexts: Desvario Chamfered: Horqueta Variety is a local variety of Desvario Chamfered and to date has been found only in the Holmul region.

Comment: The type described here as Desvario Chamfered: Horqueta Variety was previously classified as Desvario Chamfered: Variety Unspecified within the now deleted Ixim complex (Callaghan 2008:282), but is presented as a new variety of Desvario in this report. Desvario Chamfered: Horqueta Variety displays the same paste and surface characteristics as Joventud Red: Ixtoc Variety, Guitara Incised: Noctún Variety, and Chito Red-and-unslipped. It belongs to the same local Unspecified Ware as these other new type: varieties.

Illustration: Figure 3.7d.

Joventud Red: Joventud Variety

Established: Smith and Gifford at Uaxactun (1966: 158, 170).

Group: Joventud
Ware: Flores Waxy
Complex: Yax Te
Sphere: Mamom
Ceramic Group Frequency: 220 rims, 5 bodies, 225 total, 12.9 percent of group. 8.4 percent of complex.

Principal identifying attributes: (1) Lustrous waxy finish, (2) orange-red slip, and (3) calcite and sometimes grog-based paste.

Paste, firing, and temper: The major paste variant is similar to Late Preclassic period Sierra Red. These pastes cluster around yellow (10YR6/4) and are carbonate based with various inclusions including crystalline calcite, sherd, shell, and burnt organics. Firing cores are frequent. This type of paste correlates to a thick, waxy orange-red slip.

Surface finish and decoration: Surfaces are well smoothed, slipped an orange-red (2.5YR5/8) and polished to a lustrous "waxy" shine.

Forms:

1. Small bowls with flaring or outcurving sides, direct rims, and rounded lips; rim diameters are 22 to 35cm and wall thicknesses 0.6 to 0.9 cm;

2. everted rim dishes with flat bases, 16- to 32-cm-diameter rims, and 0.6- to 0.9-cm-thick walls;

3. round-sided bowls with 20- to 25-cm-diameter rims and 0.6- to 0.9-cm-thick walls;

4. large tecomates with bolstered 13- to 20-cm-diameter rims and 0.7- to 1.1-cm-thick walls;

5. recurving bowls with direct rims and rounded lips; rim diameters measure 20 to 25 cm and wall thickness 0.6 to 0.9 cm; and

6. jars with vertical necks, 8- to 12-cm-diameter rims, 0.7- to 0.9-cm-thick walls, and 2.9- to 4-cm-high necks.

Intraregional locations and contexts: Joventud Red: Joventud Variety is has been found in Structure 1 at Cival and in Buildings B, F and N of Group II of Holmul. Joventud Red: Joventud Variety also occurs in small quantities at La Sufricaya and K'o.

Interregional locations and contexts: Joventud Red: Joventud Variety occurs at Uaxactun (Smith and Gifford 1966:158), Tikal (Culbert 1993:13, 2006), Barton Ramie (Gifford 1976:78–79), Altar de Sacrificios (Adams 1971:20), Becan (Ball 1977:17–18), El Mirador (Forsyth 1989:13–15), Cuello (Kosakowsky 1987:42–43), Calakmul (Dominguez-Carrasco 1994:51), and as an Unspecified Variety at K'axob (Lopez Varela 2004), Chan (Kosakowsky 2012:62), Piedras Negras (Muñoz 2004:10), and the Petexbatun region (Foias and Bishop 2013:59–60.). It has been defined as Palmasito Variety at Colha (Valdez 1987:81–82) and Cuello (Kosakowsky1987:42–43; Pring 1977b).

Illustration: Figure 3.6c, 3.7a.

Guitara Incised: Guitara Variety

Established: Smith and Gifford at Uaxactun (1966: 158, 170).

Group: Joventud
Ware: Flores Waxy
Complex: Yax Te
Sphere: Mamom
Ceramic Group Frequency: 12 rims, 0 bodies, 12 total, 0.7 percent of group, 0.5 percent of complex.

Principal identifying attributes: (1) Orange-red slip similar to Joventud Red: Joventud Variety, (2) lustrous waxy surface treatment, and (3) thin, preslip grooved-incision in geometric patterns.

Paste, firing, and temper: Identical to Joventud Red: Joventud Variety.

Surface finish and decoration: Surfaces are well-smoothed, slipped an orange-red (2.5YR5/8), and polished to a lustrous "waxy" shine. Thin, preslip grooved-incision of cross-hatching or other geometric designs appears on incurving rim bowls or slightly everted-rim dishes.

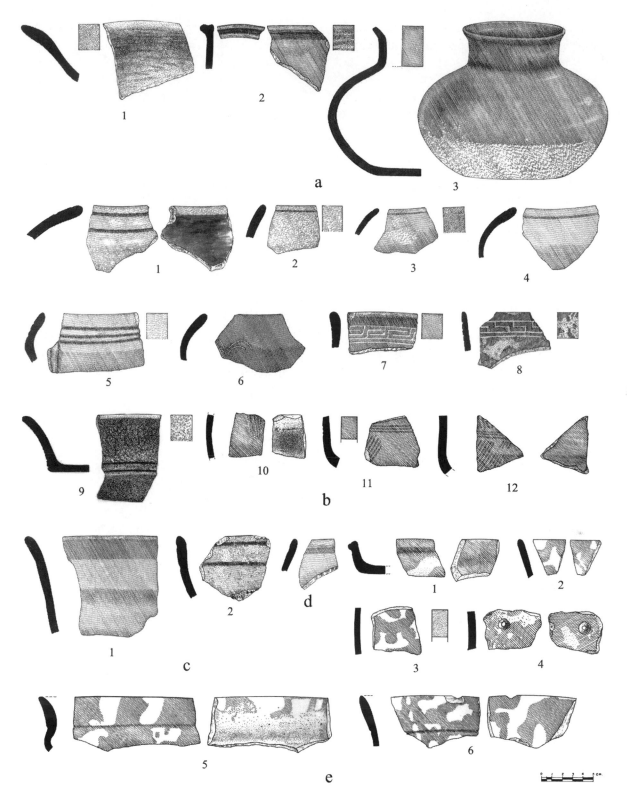

Figure 3.7. Joventud Red: Joventud Variety: (a1) CIV.T.28.110, (a2) CL.04.01, and (a3) KOL.T.34.26. Guitara Incised: Guitara Variety: (b1–b7) CL.04.01, (b8) ST.18.22, (b9) HOL.T.71.58, (b10) CIV.T.55.06, (b11) CIV.T.12.50, and (b12) CIV.T.12.41. Desvario Chamfered: Desvario Variety: (c1–c2) CL.04.01. Desvario Chamfered: Horqueta Variety: (d) CL.04.01. Tierra Mojada Resist: Tierra Mojada Variety: (e1) CIV.T.53.07, (e2) CIV.T.55.06, (e3) HOL.T.74.12, (e4) CIV.T.61.02, (e5) CIV.T.67.07, and (e6) CIV.T.75.18. Drawings by Fernando Alvarez (Holmul Archaeological Project).

Forms:

1. Incurving rim dishes or bowls with direct rims, round lips, and flat bases; rim diameters are 14 to 25 cm and wall thicknesses 0.6 to 0.9 cm;

2. round-sided bowls with direct rims and rounded lips; rim diameters are 15 to 20 cm and wall thicknesses 0.6 to 0.9 cm;

3. tecomates with direct rims and rounded lips; rim diameters are 15 to 20 cm and wall thicknesses 0.7 to 0.9 cm;

4. everted rim dishes with rounded lips and flat bases (no measurements available); and

5. jars with vertical necks, direct rims, and rounded lips; rim diameters measure 18 to 22 cm and wall thicknesses 0.7 to 0.9 cm.

Intraregional locations and contexts: Rim sherds of Guitara are easily identifiable, yet rare, and come from Cival, Holmul, La Sufricaya, and K'o.

Interregional locations and contexts: Guitara Incised: Guitara Variety appears at Uaxactun (Smith and Gifford 1966:170), Altar de Sacrificios (Adams 1971:42), Seibal (Sabloff 1975:62, 65–66), Becan (Ball 1977:82), Cuello (Kosakowsky 1987:43–45), El Mirador (Forsyth 1989:15–16), Tikal (Culbert 1993:13; 2006), the Petexbatun region (Foias and Bishop 2012:60–61), K'axob (Lopez Varela 2004); as a Grooved-Incised Variety at Colha (Valdez 1987:82–85), Cuello (Kosakowsky 1987:43–44), and Chan (Kosakowsky 2012:62); and as Pollo Desnudo Variety at Piedras Negras (Muñoz 2004:10).

Illustration: Figure 3.7b.

Desvario Chamfered: Desvario Variety

Established: Smith and Gifford at Uaxactun (1966: 157, 170).

Group: Joventud
Ware: Flores Waxy
Complex: Yax Te
Sphere: Mamom
Ceramic Group Frequency: 28 rims, 0 bodies, 28 total, 1.6 percent of group, 1.1 percent of complex.
Principal identifying attributes: (1) Orange-red slip identical to Joventud Red: Joventud Variety, (2) waxy surface finish, and (3) chamfered exterior walls.
Paste, firing, and temper: Paste is identical to Joventud Red: Joventud Variety.
Surface finish and decoration: Surfaces are well smoothed, covered in a waxy red-orange (2.5YR5/8) slip.

Chamfering appears on exterior walls on bowls with flaring sides.

Forms:

1. Bowls with flaring sides, direct rims, and rounded lips; rim diameters measure 16 to 24 cm and wall thicknesses 0.7 to 0.9 cm;

2. bowls with rounded sides; 20- to 22-cm-diameter rims, and 0.7- to 0.9-cm-thick walls.

Intraregional locations and contexts: Desvario Chamfered: Desvario Variety is rare, but has been found at Holmul and Cival.

Interregional locations and contexts: Desvario Chamfered: Desvario Variety is a strong Mamom Sphere diagnostic marker that has been found at Uaxactun (Smith and Gifford 1966:170), Cuello (Kosakowsky 1987:45–46), the Petexbatun region (Foias and Bishop 2013:62–64), Seibal (Sabloff 1975:62), and Colha (Valdez 1987:85); and as Unspecified Varieties at Becan (Ball 1977:91), El Mirador (Forsyth 1989:16), and K'axob (Lopez Varela 2004).

Illustration: Figure 3.7c.

Tierra Mojada Resist: Tierra Mojada Variety

Established: Sabloff (1975:71–73) at Seibal.
Group: Tierra Mojada
Ware: Flores Waxy
Complex: Yax Te
Sphere: Mamom
Ceramic Group Frequency: 8 rims, 2 bodies, 10 total, 100 percent of group, 0.3 percent of complex.
Principal identifying attributes: Orange-red slip with cream or yellow-brown resist splotches.
Paste, firing, and temper: Paste is similar to Joventud Red: Joventud Variety. The paste texture is medium with mixed carbonate (crystal calcite, white calcite), sherd, and burnt organic inclusions. The paste color is yellow (10YR6/4).
Surface finish and decoration: Vessel surfaces are smoothed and slipped an orange-red (2.5YR5/8). Patches or streaks of cream or yellow (10YR7/6) slip appear from the resist process. These patches more than likely represent a cream underslip. Tierra Mojada sherds are highly polished and have the characteristic waxy feel of later Preclassic ceramics.

Forms:

1. bowls or dishes with flaring sides, direct rims, and rounded lips; rim diameters are 20 to 25 cm and wall thicknesses 0.6 to 0.9 cm; and

2. bowls or dishes with recurving or composite sides, direct rims, and rounded lips; rim diameters are 20 to 25 cm and wall thicknesses 0.6 to 0.9 cm.

Intraregional locations and contexts: Tierra Mojada appears exclusively at contexts in Cival.

Interregional locations and contexts: Tierra Mojada Resist is another strong marker of the Late Middle Preclassic Mamom Sphere in the lowlands and can be found at Uaxactun (personal observation, IDAEH ceramoteca), Nakbe (Forsyth 1993:39), Altar de Sacrificios (personal observation, IDAEH ceramoteca), the Petxbatun region (Foias and Bishop 2013:64–65), Colha (Valdez 1987:87), K'axob (Lopez Varela 2004), and Seibal (Sabloff 1975:71–73, Figures 109–115); it is also defined as Unspecified Variety at Piedras Negras (Muñoz 2004:10).

Comment: Tierra Mojada Resist shares many similarities with paste, form, and surface modes of the established types of Joventud Group ceramics. It is possible that Tierra Mojada was part of an underrepresented second tradition of ceramic production during the Late Middle Preclassic period at Cival. This idea is discussed in Chapter 8.

Illustration: Figure 3.7e.

Pital Cream: Pital Variety

Established: Smith and Gifford at Uaxactun (1966: 161, 170).

Group: Pital
Ware: Flores Waxy
Complex: Yax Te
Sphere: Mamom
Ceramic Group Frequency: 107 rims, 124 bodies, 1 whole vessel, 232 total, 80.6 percent of group, 4.1 percent of complex.

Principal identifying attributes: (1) Thick cream slip and (2) lustrous waxy surface finish.

Paste, firing, and temper: Paste is medium to fine in texture. Primary paste inclusions are carbonate based and include crystalline calcite, sherd, and burnt organics. Paste color is a light yellow (10YR7/4), buff (10YR8/3), or even pink (5YR7/4). Darker firing cores are uncommon but present.

Surface finish and decoration: Vessel surfaces are well-smoothed and polished. Slip is thick and usually a strong white (10YR8/1) color. Crackling or crazing of slip is common. Fire clouds are also common.

Forms:
1. Dishes or bowls with flaring sides, direct rims, and rounded lips; rim diameters measure 20 to 25 cm and wall thicknesses 0.6 to 0.9 cm;
2. bowls or dishes with flaring sides, gradually everted rims, and rounded lips; rim diameters measure 25 to 36 cm and wall thicknesses 0.6 to 0.9 cm; and
3. possible mushroom stands (no form data).

Intraregional locations and contexts: With the exception of one body sherd at K'o, Pital Cream: Pital Variety had been found exclusively at Cival.

Interregional locations and contexts: Pital Cream has been found at Uaxactun (Smith and Gifford 1966:170), Barton Ramie (Gifford 1976:81), Altar de Sacrificios (Adams 1971:25), Seibal (Sabloff 1975:62, 66–67), Becan (Ball 1977:36), Cuello (Kosakowsky 1987:48–49), K'axob (Lopez Varela 2004), and the Petexbatun region (Foias and Bishop 2013:67–68). It is an Unspecified Variety at El Mirador (Forsyth 1989:18), Piedras Negras (Muñoz 2004:10), Chan (Kosakowsky 2012:62), Cahal Pech (Awe 1992:240), and Colha (Valdez 1987:91).

Comment: Production modes of Pital Cream are similar to the larger lowland modes found in the less frequent, yet established, varieties of Joventud Group ceramics. The choice of carbonate-based pastes with sherd temper and the waxy surface finish make this type a precursor to the later Flor Cream of the Itzamkanak Complex. Differences between Flor and Pital are slight and involve variations in form (Pital Cream forms are smaller flaring-sided bowls and dishes while Flor Cream forms are larger bowls often with wider everted rims and bead lips), paste (Pital is the only type to be made from a characteristic pink paste), and surface finish (Pital Cream slip is much whiter than the more yellow Flor Cream).

Illustration: Figure 3.8a.

Paso Danto Incised: Paso Danto Variety

Established: Smith and Gifford (1966:160–161, 170) at Uaxactun.

Group: Pital
Ware: Flores Waxy
Complex: Yax Te
Sphere: Mamom
Ceramic Group Frequency: 9 rims, 5 bodies, 14 total, 6.7 percent of group, 0.3 percent of complex.

Principal identifying attributes: (1) Thick white cream slip, (2) lustrous waxy finish, and (3) preslip, thin grooved-incision.

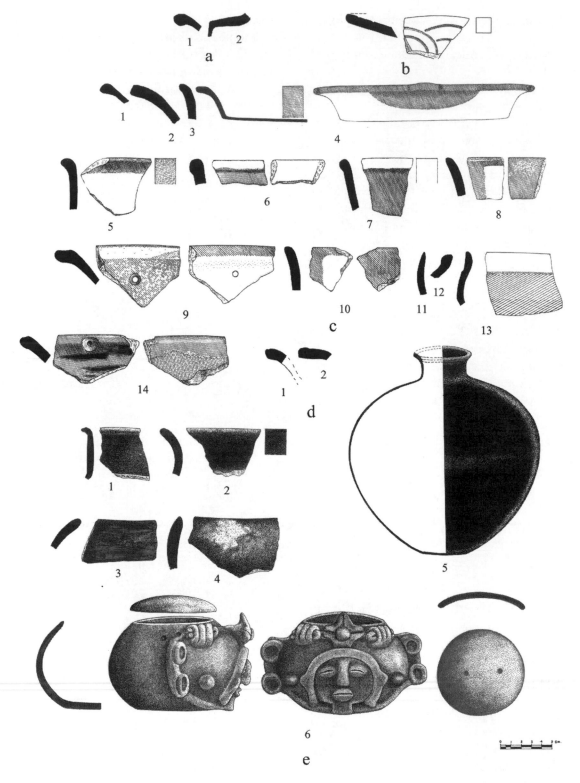

Figure 3.8. Pital Cream: Pital Variety: (a1) CIV.T.10.09 and (a2) CIV.T.01.04. Paso Danto Incised: Paso Danto Variety: (b1) CIV.L.01.01. Muxanal Red-on-cream: Muxanal Variety: (c1) CL.04.01, (c2) CIV.T.10.11, (c3) CIV.10.10, (c4) CIV.T.63.02, (c5) CL.04.01, (c6) CIV.T.28.110, (c7) CL.04.01, (c8) CIV.T.28.08, (c9) CIV.L.HGRP.14.01, (c10) CIV.T.28.08, (c11) CIV.T.11.05, (c12) CIV.T.01.04, (c13) CIV.T.10.11, and (c14) CL.04.01. Unnamed Red-on-cream Incised (Pital Group): (d1 and d2) CL.04.01. Chunhinta Black: Chunhinta Variety: (e1–e4) CL.04.01, (e5) CT.08.47.02.01.02, (e6) KOL.T.34.30(V8). Drawings by Michael G. Callaghan (a, c1–c3, d) and Fernando Alvarez (b, c4–c14, e) (Holmul Archaeological Project).

Paste, firing, and temper: Paste is identical to Pital Cream.

Surface finish and decoration: Surface decoration is identical to Pital Cream with the addition of preslip, fine-line incision on wide-everted rims. Vessel surfaces are well smoothed and polished. Slip is thick and usually a strong white color (10YR8/1). Crackling or crazing of slip is common. Fire clouds are also common. Incision takes the form of single lines or even double-line breaks and simple geometric patterns created by one or two lines.

Forms:

1. Bowls or dishes with flaring or outcurving sides and everted or wide-everted rims, rounded lips sometimes with beads; rim diameters measure 18 to 22 cm and wall thicknesses 0.6 to 0.9 cm; and

2. bowls with rounded sides; direct, 20-cm-diameter rims, rounded lips; and 0.7-cm-thick walls. Only one example of this form was identified.

Intraregional locations and contexts: Found exclusively from contexts at Cival.

Interregional locations and contexts: Paso Danto is another strong marker of the Mamom Sphere in the lowlands and has been found at Uaxactun (Smith 1955: Figures 69c 11 and 77a7), Seibal (Sabloff 1975:67), El Mirador (Forsyth 1989:19), Nakbe (Forsyth 1993), Becan (Ball 1977:83), Barton Ramie (Gifford 1976:81-82), Cuello (Kosakowsky 1987:49), the Petexbatun region (Foias and Bishop 2013:68-69), and Becan (Ball 1977:83). Paso Danto with post-slip incision occurs in the Yaxha-Sacnab area (Rice 1979:13) and as an Unspecified Variety at Colha (Valdez 1987:91-92) and Piedras Negras (Muñoz 2004:10).

Illustration: Figure 3.8b.

Muxanal Red-on-cream: Muxanal Variety

Established: Smith and Gifford at Uaxactun (1966: 160, 170).
Group: Pital
Ware: Flores Waxy
Complex: Yax Te
Sphere: Mamom
Ceramic Group Frequency: 14 rims, 4 bodies, 1 whole vessel, 19 total, 11.2 percent of group, 0.6 percent of complex.
Principal identifying attributes: (1) Red slip on vessel exteriors and cream slip on vessel interiors or vice versa and (2) dichrome effect created by single band of cream or red slip on and below lip on vessel exterior.

Paste, firing, and temper: The major paste variant is similar to Pital Cream: Pital Variety (also Joventud Red: Joventud Variety).

Surface finish and decoration: Exteriors are one color whereas interiors are another. The interior color may extend over the lip and slightly down the exterior rims. Slips are thick and waxy and polished to a high shine. The cream (10YR8/1) slip may have been applied first and the red slip then applied over it.

Forms:

1. Bowls or dishes with flaring or outcurving sides, direct or gradually everted rims, rounded lips, and flat bases; rim diameters measure 20 to 25 cm and wall thicknesses 0.6 to 0.9 cm;

2. round-sided bowls with direct rims and rounded lips; rim diameters measure 15 to 22 cm and wall thicknesses 0.6 to 0.9 cm; and

3. rare "cuspidor" forms (no form data).

Intraregional locations and contexts: Muxanal Red-on-cream is found at Cival and Holmul.

Interregional locations and contexts: Muxanal Red-on-cream occurs at Uaxacatun (Smith and Gifford 1966:170), Altar de Sacrificios (Adams 1971:27), El Mirador (Forsyth 1989:18–19), in the Yaxha-Sacnab region (Rice 1979:22), at Calakmul (Dominguez-Carrasco 1994:51), and in the Petexbatun region (Foias and Bishop 2013:70–71). It appears as an Unspecified Variety at Chan (Kosakowsky 2012:62), K'axob (Lopez Varela 2004), and as Lazaro Variety at Colha (Valdez 1987:92). It is placed in its own ceramic group at Becan where Ball (1977:48) defines a Comprimido Variety, as well as at Cuello where Kosakowsky (1987:49–51) defines a San Lazaro Variety.

Illustration: Figure 3.8c.

Unnamed Red-on-cream Incised (Pital Group)

Established: Callaghan in this study
Group: Pital
Ware: Flores Waxy
Complex: Yax Te
Sphere: Mamom
Sample: 2 rims, 0 bodies, 2 total, 1.5 percent of group, 0.1 percent of complex.
Principal identifying attributes: (1) Red slip on vessel exterior and cream-colored slip on vessel interior or vice versa, (2) dichrome effect created by single band of cream or red slip on and below lip on vessel exterior, (3) thin, preslip grooved-incision on vessel rim and lip, and (4) bowls with flaring sides and everted rim.

Paste, firing, and temper: The major paste variant is similar to Pital Cream: Pital Variety (also Joventud Red: Joventud Variety).

Surface finish and decoration: Exteriors are one color whereas interiors are another. The interior color may extend over the lip and slightly down exterior rims. Slips are thick and waxy and polished to a high shine. Cream (10YR8/1) slip may be applied first and a red slip is applied over it. Incision on this type is thin and grooved prior to slip being applied. The incision occurs in bands and can be seen in double-line-break patterns.

Form: Bowl with flaring sides, gradually everted rims, and rounded lips, with 20- to 25-cm diameter rims and 0.6- to 0.9-cm thick walls.

Intraregional locations and contexts: This Unnamed Red-on-cream Incised type is found exclusively at Cival.

Interregional locations and contexts: This type is most likely an incised variety of Muxanal Red-on-cream. This type is rare in the lowlands, but Ball (1977:48) identifies a red-on-cream incised type at Becan (Muxanal Red-on-cream: Comprimido Variety), as does Kosakowsky (1987:48–51) at Cuello (Muxanal red-on-cream: San Lazaro Variety and Other Muxanal Ceramic Group Pottery: Unspecified Variety). Foias and Bishop (2013:71–72) describe an incised Muxanal type in the Petexbatun region, but leave the variety name unclassified due to the small sample. The forms and surface modes of the ceramics from other sites are not similar to the Holmul material.

Comments: A new variety based on these examples was not created because the sample was too small. Some analysts recognize incision as a mode of decoration in type: variety descriptions of Muxanal Red-on-cream: Comprimido Variety at Becan (Ball 1977:48) and Muxanal Red-on-cream: San Lazaro Variety at Cuello (Kosakowsky 1987:49).

Illustration: Figure 3.8d.

Chunhinta Black: Chunhinta Variety

Established: Smith and Gifford at Uaxactun (1966: 156, 170).

   Group: Chunhinta
   Ware: Flores Waxy
   Complex: Yax Te
   Sphere: Mamom
   Ceramic Group Frequency: 187 rims, 683 bodies, 4 whole vessels, 874 total, 65.4 percent of group, 7.3 percent of complex.

Principal identifying attributes: (1) Black fading to gray slip and (2) carbonate temper with crystal calcite.

Paste, firing, and temper: The major paste variant is medium- to fine-textured and carbonate-based with many crystalline calcite inclusions. Color is gray (10YR4/1) to black.

Surface finish and decoration: Surfaces are well-smoothed and highly polished. Slip is thick and varies from gray to deep black.

Forms:

   1. Bowls with outcurving sides, direct rims, and rounded lips; rim diameters are 20 to 25 cm and wall thicknesses 0.6 to 0.9 cm;

   2. teardrop and globular jars with restricted short or vertical necks; 8–rim diameters measure 8 to 12 cm, wall thicknesses 0.7 to 0.8 cm, and neck heights 1.3 to 2.9 cm;

   3. bowls with incurving or insloping sides, 15- to 22-cm-diameter rims, and 0.6- to 0.9-cm-thick walls.

Intraregional locations and contexts: Chunhinta Black ceramics are most commonly found at Cival, but sherds have also been found at Holmul, La Sufricaya, and K'o (where one whole modeled vessel was excavated). Three Chunhinta vessels were found in association with the Middle Preclassic period Cache 4, located in the E-Group plaza at Cival (context number CT08.46) (Estrada-Belli 2010).

Interregional locations and contexts: Chunhinta Black occurs at Uaxactun (Smith and Gifford 1966:170), Barton Ramie (Gifford 1976:82–83), Tikal (Culbert 1993:13; 2006), Altar de Sacrificios (Adams 1971:24), Seibal (Sabloff 1975:69), Becan (Ball 1977:30), Cuello (Kosakowsky 1987:47), the Petexbatun region (Foias and Bishop 2013:72–73), Colha (Valdez 1987:87–91), Cahal Pech (Awe 1992:240), and El Mirador (Forsyth 1989:16–18). It occurs as an Unspecified Variety at K'axob (Lopez Varela 2004), Chan (Kosakowsky 2012:62) and Piedras Negras (Muñoz 2004:10).

Illustration: Figure 3.8e (note that 3.8e4 and 6 are drawn in stipple to show form contours) and Figure 3.9.

Deprecio Incised: Deprecio Variety

Established: Smith and Gifford at Uaxactun (1966: 157, 170).

   Group: Chunhinta
   Ware: Flores Waxy
   Complex: Yax Te

Figure 3.9. Chunhinta Black: Chunhinta Variety (KOL.T.34.30, Vessel 8). This is the same vessel illustrated in Figure 3.8e6. Photo by John Tomasic, courtesy of the Holmul Regional Archaeological Project.

Sphere: Mamom

Ceramic Group Frequency: 62 rims, 71 bodies, 1 whole vessel, 134 total, 21.6 percent of group, 2.4 percent of complex.

Principal identifying attributes: (1) Black fading to gray slip and (2) post-firing, fine-line incision usually occurring in horizontal parallel lines or geometric shapes on vessel exteriors,.

Paste, firing, and temper: Identical to Chunhinta Black: Chunhinta Variety.

Surface finish and decoration: Same as Chunhinta Black with fine-line, post-slip incision. The location of incision on the vessel varies with form; it can occur as simple horizontal parallel lines just below the lip on bowl exteriors or as geometric patterns on both exterior bowl walls and shoulder breaks on jars. Jars may also display vertical bands of geometric incision that run down vessel exteriors.

Forms:

1. Bowls with incurved or insloping sides, direct rims, and rounded lips; rim diameters measure 20 to 25 cm and wall thicknesses 0.6 to 0.9 cm;

2. globular jars with vertical, chamfered necks, direct rims, and round lips; rim diameters measure 8 to 12 cm, wall thicknesses 0.6 to 0.9 cm, and neck heights 1.3 to 3 cm; and

3. teardrop-shaped jars with short, outcurved necks, direct rims, and rounded lips; rim diameters measure 8 to 12 cm, wall thicknesses 0.6 to 0.9 cm, and neck heights 1.3 to 3 cm.

Intraregional locations and contexts: Found mostly at Cival, but also at Holmul; one sherd has been found at La Sufricaya. One Deprecio Incised jar was found in association with Cache 4 in the E Group Plaza at Cival (context number CT08.46) (Estrada-Belli 2010).

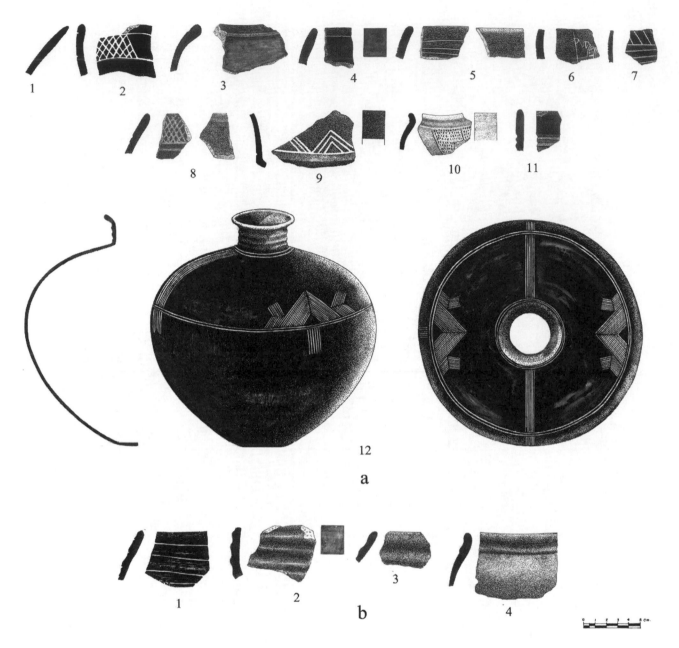

Figure 3.10. Deprecio Incised: Deprecio Variety: (a1) CIV.T.16.03, (a2) CIV.T.11.05, (a3–a8) CL.04.01, (a9) HOL.T.71.06, (a10) CIV.T.28.110, (a11) CL.04.01, and (a12) CIV.T.08.47. Centenario Fluted: Centenario Variety: (b1) CIV.T.01.04, and (b2 –b4) CL.04.01. Drawings by Fernando Alvarez (Holmul Archaeological Project).

Interregional locations and contexts: Deprecio Incised also occurs at Uaxactun (Smith and Gifford 1966:170), Barton Ramie (Gifford 1976:83), Altar de Sacrificios (Adams 1971:43), Seibal (Sabloff 1975:69–70), Becan (Ball 1977:82), Cuello (Kosakowsky 1987:47–48), El Mirador (Forsyth 1989:18), and Calakmul (Dominguez-Carrasco 1994:51 where she names it "Desprecio").

It occurs as an Unspecified Variety at Chan (Kosakowsky 2012:62) and in the Petexbatun region (Foias and Bishop 2013:73–74, where they use the name "Desprecio"); and as Grooved-incised Variety at Colha (Valdez 1987:90).

Illustration: Figure 3.10a. Note that some illustrations are drawn in stipple to show form contours.

Centenario Fluted: Centenario Variety

Established: Smith and Gifford at Uaxactun (1966: 156, 170).

Group: Chunhinta
Ware: Flores Waxy
Complex: Yax Te
Sphere: Mamom
Ceramic Group Frequency: 38 rims, 12 bodies, 50 total, 13 percent of group, 1.4 percent of complex.

Principal identifying attributes: (1) Black fading to gray slip and (2) horizontal fluting on vessel exteriors.

Paste, firing, and temper: Same as Chunhinta Black: Chunhinta Variety.

Surface finish and decoration: Same as Chunhinta Black with the inclusion of horizontal fluting and occasional fine–line, post-firing incision in the form of horizontal parallel lines immediately below each horizontal flute (Figure 3.10b1).

Forms:
1. Bowls with incurving sides, direct rims, and rounded lips; rim diameters measure 10 to 18 cm and wall thicknesses 0.5 to 0.7 cm and
2. bowls with round sides, direct rims, and rounded lips; rim diameters measure 15 to 20 cm and wall thicknesses 0.5 to 0.9 cm.

Intraregional locations and contexts: As rare as Centenario appears to be in the Holmul region, it has been found at each of the four major sites in the area—most frequently at Cival, but also at Holmul, La Sufricaya, and K'o.

Interregional locations and contexts: Centenario Fluted also appears at Uaxactun (Smith and Gifford 1966:156, 170), Altar de Sacrificios (Adams 1971:48), Seibal (Sabloff 1975:70), and as Unspecified Variety in the Petexbatun region (Foias and Bishop 2013:74–75). Centenario Fluted is another strong Middle Preclassic Mamom Sphere diagnostic.

Illustration: Figure 3.10b. Note that some illustrations are drawn in stipple to show form contours.

CHAPTER FOUR

Itzamkanak Complex

Michael G. Callaghan

The Itzamkanak Complex dates between 400 BC and AD 230. Dating was determined through a combination of radiocarbon samples (Estrada-Belli 2008:15, 144; 2006b:44) (see Table 1.2) and typological comparison to other sites. The earliest date associated with an Itzamkanak deposit comes from fill within the first phase of Building B, Group II at Holmul (400–340 BC calibrated) (Estrada-Belli 2008:15). Charcoal found in an Itzamkanak deposit associated with the fourth construction episode of Structure 1 at Cival returned a calibrated date of 260–160 BC (Estrada-Belli 2006b:65). Finally, radiocarbon dating of bone found in the Terminal Preclassic period Burial 10 within Building B, Group II at Holmul returned a date of AD 120–230 (Estrada-Belli 2006a:4).

Descriptions of Itzamkanak material included in this study come from 4,376 rim sherds, 16,108 diagnostic body sherds, and 11 whole vessels for a total of 20,492 samples. Two wares, 7 groups, and 20 type: varieties define the Itzamkanak Complex (Table 4.1). The majority of type-varieties are slipped (86%). Typologically, Itzamkanak ceramics resemble material of the Chicanel Sphere during the Late Preclassic period in the Maya lowlands and are contemporaneous with Chicanel Complex ceramics at Uaxacatun (Smith 1955); Chuen, Cauac, and Cimi Complex ceramics at Tikal (Culbert 1993, 2003, 2006), the Cascabel Complex at El Mirador (Forsyth 1989), the Plancha through early Salinas Complexes at Altar de Sacrificios (Adams 1971), the Cantutse Complex at Seibal (Sabloff 1975), the Barton Creek and Mount Hope Complexes at Barton Ramie (Gifford 1976), the Xakal Complex at Cahal Pech (Awe 1992:240–248), the Cadle and Potts Complexes at Chan (Kosakowsky 2012:50–52), the Abal Complex at Piedras Negras (Muñoz 2004:10–11), the Kaynikte Complex at Calakmul (Dominguez-Carrasco 1994:52), the K'atabche'k'ax Complex at K'axob (Lopez Varela 2004:179–185), the Onecimo Complex at Colha (Valdez 1987:114–138), the Ixtabai, C'oh, and Tulix Complexes at Cerros (Robertson-Freidel 1980), the Faisan Complex in the Petexbatun region (Foias and Bishop 2013), the Late Preclassic Complex at La Milpa (Sagebiel 2005) and Cocos Complex at Cuello (Kosakowsky 1987). Itzamkanak material has been found at every site in the Holmul region. Itzamkanak ceramics show definitive changes in paste, form, and surface technologies when compared to the majority of types from the preceding Yax Te Complex. Itzamkanak Complex material represents strong participation with other sites included in the Chicanel Sphere. Itzamkanak Complex wares are described next, followed by type descriptions. Interpretations of the complex are offered in Chapter 8.

UAXACTUN UNSLIPPED WARE

Smith and Gifford (1966:169) established this ware at Uaxactun. It is characterized by roughly smoothed unslipped surfaces. Decoration takes the form of striations on Sapote Striated: Sapote Variety or occasionally vertical scratch marks on Achiotes Unslipped: Variety Unspecified. Vessel surfaces are the color of pastes (7.5YR5/2, 4/2). Pastes are coarse- to medium-textured with primary inclusions of crystalline calcite. Type: varieties within Uaxactun Ware dating to the Itzamkanak Complex include

Achiotes Group
    Achiotes Unslipped: Achiotes Variety
    Achiotes Unslipped: Variety Unspecified
      (Itzamkanak)
    Sapote Striated: Sapote Variety

Table 4.1. Ceramic Wares, Groups, Types, and Varieties of the Late Preclassic Period (Itzamkanak Complex)

Ware	Group (% of complex)	Type: Variety	Numbers			Percentages	
			Rims	Bodies	Vessels	Group	Complex
Uaxactun Unslipped	Achiotes (14.0%)	Achiotes Unslipped: Achiotes Variety	586	3294	0	95.8	13.4
		Achiotes Unslipped: Variety Unspecified (Itzamkanak)	5	144	0	0.8	0.1
		Sapote Striated: Sapote Variety	21	1165	0	3.4	0.5
Paso Caballo Waxy	Sierra (66.4%)	Sierra Red: Sierra Variety	2475	8268	10	85.3	56.6
		Laguna Verde Incised: Laguna Verde Variety	132	59	0	4.5	3.0
		Laguna Verde Incised	43	2	0	1.5	1.0
		Altamira Fluted	33	40	0	1.1	0.8
		Repasto Black-on-red	2	3	0	0.1	0.05
		Society Hall	202	216	0	6.9	4.6
		Unnamed Punctated	1	1	0	0.0	0.02
		Unnamed Modeled	2	1	0	0.1	0.05
		Unnamed Dichrome	11	23	0	0.4	0.3
		Unnamed Red-and-unslipped	2	2	0	0.1	0.05
	Caramba (0.02%)	Unnamed Red-on-orange	1			100.0	0.02
	Zapatista (< 0.01%)	Unnamed Trickle-on-gray		2		100.0	< 0.01
	Flor (3.5%)	Flor Cream: Flor Variety	139	202	0	91.4	3.2
		Accordian Incised: Accordian Variety	13	3	0	8.6	0.3
	Polvero (13.7%)	Polvero Black: Polvero Variety	572	2624	0	95.0	13.0
		Lechugal Incised: Lechugal Variety	30	57	0	5.0	0.7
	Boxcay (2.4%)	Boxcay Brown: Boxcay Variety	106	2	1	100.0	2.4
		TOTALS	**4376**	**16,108**	**11**		

PASO CABALLO WAXY WARE

Smith and Gifford (1966:167) established Paso Caballo Waxy Ware at Uaxactun. It is the only slipped ware dating to the Itzamkanak Complex in the Holmul region. Paso Caballo Waxy Ware is characterized by highly polished or burnished surfaces that feel "greasy" or "waxy" to the touch. Slipped ceramics include red, black, cream, and black-on-red colors. Surface decoration includes incision, grooved-incision, chamfering, fluting, modeling, applique, punctation, impression, dichrome due to firing, trickling, and resist. Red slips tend toward true red

(10R4/8, 2.5YR4/6, 2.5YR4/8) and cream slips toward a more yellow (10YR8/3) or tan (7.5YR5/5) than white. Pastes are medium-textured and red-orange (7.5YR6/8), to gray (10YR5/1), to yellow-brown (10YR7/4). Primary paste inclusions are crystalline calcite, sherd temper (grog), burnt organics, and shell. Groups and type: varieties within Paso Caballo Waxy Ware include

Sierra Group
    Sierra Red: Sierra Variety
    Laguna Verde Incised: Laguna Verde Variety
    Laguna Verde Incised: Grooved-incised Variety
    Altamira Fluted: Altamira Variety
    Unnamed Punctated (Sierra Group)
    Unnamed Modeled (Sierra Group)
    Unnamed Dichrome (Sierra Group)
    Unnamed Red-and-unslipped (Sierra Group)
    Repasto Black-on-red: Variety Unspecified
    Society Hall: Society Hall Variety
Caramba Group
    Unnamed Red-on-orange (Caramba Group)
Zapatista Group
    Unnamed Trickle-on-gray (Zapatista Group)
Flor Group
    Flor Cream: Flor Variety
    Accordian Incised: Accordian Variety
Polvero Group
    Polvero Black: Polvero Variety
    Lechugal Incised: Lechugal Variety
Boxcay Group
    Boxcay Brown: Boxcay Variety

TYPE DESCRIPTIONS

Achiotes Unslipped: Achiotes Variety

Established: Smith and Gifford at Uaxactun (1966: 154, 170).
    Group: Achiotes
    Ware: Uaxactun Unslipped
    Complex: Itzamkanak
    Sphere: Chicanel
    Ceramic Group Frequency: 586 rims, 3,294 bodies, 3,880 total, 95.8 percent of group, 13.4 percent of complex.
    Principal identifying attributes: (1) Unslipped surface, (2) coarse–tempered paste, and (3) jars of varying sizes with various rim forms.
    Paste, firing, and temper: Pastes are coarse to medium in texture and yellow (10YR6/4) or gray (10YR5/1) in color. The primary and usually only inclusions are large fragments of crystalline calcite. Firing cores are also common.
    Surface finish and decoration: Surfaces are usually smoothed and always unslipped on vessel exteriors and interiors. Surface color is similar to paste color, but is generally gray (10YR5/1).
    Forms: Jars with outcurving necks and various rim forms. Rim diameters measure 14 to 30 cm, wall thicknesses 0.7 to 1.3 cm, and neck heights 1.4 to 4.4 cm.
    Intraregional locations and contexts: Achiotes Unslipped is found wherever Late Preclassic sherds are encountered. Achiotes Unslipped occurs in the largest quantities at Cival and in contexts from Building B, Group II at Holmul. As noted in Chapter 3, it is currently difficult to differentiate between Middle Preclassic Yax Te material and Late Preclassic Itzamkanak material. Two potentially significant characteristics may be related to form. Yax Te vessels appear to have smaller diameters and are shorter in height. Furthermore, rim forms are less varied, with the most common form being direct and outcurving. Finally, there appear to be more examples of handles and handle scars on Yax Te material. Ceramic group frequencies and illustrations listed in this description include sherds from stratified Itzamkanak deposits at Cival and Holtun.
    Interregional locations and contexts: Achiotes Unslipped occurs at Uaxactun (Smith and Gifford 1966:154), Barton Ramie (Gifford 1976:108), Altar de Sacrificios (Adams 1971:18), Becan (Ball 1977:8), Seibal (Sabloff 1975:46), the Valle de Dolores (Laporte et al. 1993:65–66), El Mirador (Forsyth 1989:49), Tikal (Culbert 2006), and the Petexbatun region (Foias and Bishop 2013:82–84). It is important to note that analysts working at sites in Belize have not identified Achiotes Unslipped in their collections. Unslipped ceramics belong to a different ware and tradition both in the Belize River Valley and northern Belize. At Cuello and Colha the predominant unslipped type is Richardson Peak (Kosakowsky 1987:55–56; Pring 1977b; Valdes 1987:76–77). Gifford (1976:108–111) implies that there is an Achiotes-like unslipped type at Barton Rame during the Late Preclassic through his identification of the central Petén Paila Unslipped type (he leaves the variety unspecified). Sagebiel (2005:166–168) does the same at La Milpa and Kosakowsky (2012:62) at Chan. Although Richardson Peak and Paila may resemble Achiotes, analysts do not believe the types are identical. I believe this indicates an important distinction between central Petén and Belizean pottery-making traditions. Prehistoric peoples in the Petén and Belize may have shared technologies and ideas about making ceramics,

but their unslipped utilitarian traditions are quite distinct, and, through implication, their cultural practices regarding food storage and preparation.

Illustration: Figure 3.1a1–14.

Achiotes Unslipped: Variety Unspecified (Itzamkanak)

Established: Type named by Smith and Gifford at Uaxactun (1966:154, 170), Variety named by Callaghan (2008:318–319).

Group: Achiotes
Ware: Uaxactun Unslipped
Ceramic Complex: Itzamkanak
Sphere: Chicanel
Ceramic Group Frequency: 5 rims, 144 bodies, 149 total, 0.8 percent of group, 0.1 percent of complex.

Principal identifying attributes: (1) Unslipped surface, (2) coarse-tempered paste, (3) small, globular, short-neck jars, and (4) scratched vertical lines on vessel exteriors.

Paste, firing, and temper: Paste, firing, and temper are identical to Achiotes Unslipped: Achiotes Variety.

Surface finish and decoration: Surface finish is the same as Achiotes Unslipped: Achiotes Variety with the addition of crude, long vertical scratch marks beginning at the base of the neck and extending down the vessel exteriors.

Forms: Small, short-necked jars with outcurved rims. Rim diameters measure 10 to 15 cm, wall thicknesses 0.7 to 1 cm, and neck heights 1.4 to 2.4 cm.

Intraregional locations and contexts: Achiotes Unslipped: Unspecified Variety appears in largest quantities at Cival, but a handful of sherds have been found in contexts from Building B, Group II at Holmul.

Interregional locations and contexts: I have not seen mention of this variety of Achiotes in the ceramic literature for the lowlands. Perhaps it was classified as Sapote Striated at sites and therefore overlooked. This is probably not the case, however, and the type: variety is local to the Holmul region. While scratching on Achiotes may not have been common at other sites, post-fire scratching on slipped types was not uncommon at other lowland sites like Tikal (Culbert 1993:Figures 7a–b, 10a) and Cerros (Robertson-Freidel 1980:Figure 21e, 28e).

Illustration: Figure 3.2b.

Sapote Striated: Sapote Variety

Established: Smith and Gifford at Uaxactun (1966: 162, 170).

Group: Achiotes

Ware: Uaxactun Unslipped
Complex: Itzamkanak
Sphere: Chicanel
Ceramic Group Frequency: 21 rims, 1,165 bodies, 1,186 total, 3.4 percent of group, 0.5 percent of complex.

Principal identifying attributes: (1) Unslipped surfaces and (2) fine to medium striation on vessel exteriors.

Paste, firing, and temper: Paste is coarse to medium in texture with crystalline calcite inclusions. Two colors of this variant exist: one fires to a dark gray (10YR4/1); the other is orange (7.5YR6/8). The difference in paste color is best considered a modal distinction and does not warrant the creation of another type or even variety.

Surface finish and decoration: The unslipped vessel surfaces are smoothed and are the color of pastes: gray (10YR4/1) and orange (7.5YR6/8). Striated lines occur in multiple directions and often overlap. Lines are relatively thin, shallow, and close together. This is in contrast to later Triunfo type jars with their characteristic bold, deep, and more widely separated striations.

Forms:

1. Jars with short outflaring or outcurving necks, direct rims, and rounded lips. Rim diameters measure 14 to 24 cm, wall thicknesses 0.7 to 0.9 cm, and neck heights 1.4 to 2 cm;

2. tecomates with 13- to 18-cm diameter rims and 0.7- to 0.9-cm thick walls;

3. bowls with flaring sides (extremely rare, measurements unknown); and

4. miniature vessel with 2.5-cm diameter rims, 0.5-cm thick walls, and heights of 3 cm.

Intraregional locations and contexts: Sapote Striated is found in Late Preclassic contexts at Cival, Ko, Holmul, and La Sufricaya.

Interregional locations and contexts: Sapote Striated is also found at Uaxactun (Smith and Gifford 1966:162, 170), Barton Ramie (Gifford 1976:105), Altar de Sacrificios (Adams 1971:19), Becan (Ball 1977:10, 13), Seibal (Sabloff 1975:77), El Mirador (Forsyth 1989:46), Tikal (Culbert 1993:14; 2006), the Petexbatun region where it is labeled "Zapote" (Foias and Bishop 2013:84–85), Cuello (Kosakowsky 1987:56), Colha (Valdez 1987:77–78), Calakmul (Dominguez-Carrasco 1994:52), Yaxchilan (Lopez Varela 1989:80–82), K'axob (Lopez Varela 2004), Chan (Kosakowsky 2012:62), La Milpa (Sagebiel 2005:169–174), and Cerros (Robertson-Freidel 1980:106–112). Forsyth (Forsyth 1989:46) reports the same very rare forms of Sapote Striated at El Mirador (i.e., the bowl with flaring sides—classified as a plate—and the tecomate form). Valdez (1987:77–78) also identifies a tecomate form. While Sapote Striated may be more common in areas outside of the Petén, varieties are given local names or remain unspecified.

Illustration: Figure 3.2a.

Sierra Red: Sierra Variety

Established: Smith and Gifford at Uaxactun (1966: 163, 170).

Group: Sierra
Ware: Paso Caballo Waxy
Complex: Itzamkanak
Sphere: Chicanel
Ceramic Group Frequency: 2,475 rims, 8,268 bodies, 10 whole vessels, 10,753 total, 85.3 percent of group, 56.6 percent of complex.

Principal identifying attributes: (1) Lustrous, "waxy" surface treatment and (2) red slip.

Paste, firing, and temper: Paste varies greatly across the Holmul region and could point to different production units centered on specific sites. Paste color ranges from red-orange (7.5YR6/8) (at K'o) to gray (10YR5/1), and yellow-brown (10YR7/4) (at Holmul, La Sufricaya, and Cival). Temper includes large crystalline calcite, sherd, white calcite, occasional burnt organics, shell, and large pieces of quartz.

Surface finish and decoration: Surfaces are well smoothed and polished. The slip is a thick, deep red (10R4/8; 2.5YR4/6, 4/8) and waxy. Fire-clouding is extremely common and can produce three or more colors on the same vessel (red, black, and buff). This has often led to what some scholars consider the misclassification of Sierra Red as other Late Preclassic slipped types such as Polvero Black or even Flor Cream. The most common form of fire-clouding is a cream or tan color on the base and lower walls of serving vessels. Slip crackling or crazing is also common.

Forms: Forms vary greatly in the Holmul region but constitute 8 major classes:

1. bowls or dishes with flaring or outcurving sides, direct or slightly everted rims, rounded lips, and flat bases; rim diameters measure 11 to 42 cm, wall thicknesses 0.5 to 1.1 cm, and heights 4 to 17 cm;

2. bowls with flaring sides, incurving rims, and rounded lips; rim diameters measure 9 to 33 cm, wall thicknesses 0.5 to 1.2 cm, and heights 5 to 15 cm;

3. bowls with round sides, direct rims, and rounded lips; rim diameters measure 10 to 24cm, wall thicknesses 0.5 to 1.1 cm, and heights 5 to 15 cm;

4. bowls with lateral angles, direct rims, and rounded lips; rim diameters measure 18 to 45cm, wall thicknesses 0.7 to 1.6 cm, and heights 5 to 17 cm;

5. bowls with z-angles, direct rims, and rounded lips; rim diameters measure 11 to 35 cm, wall thicknesses 0.5 to 1.1 cm, and heights 6 to 15 cm;

6. jars with short, outcurved necks; rim diameters measure 8 to 12 cm, wall thicknesses 0.5 to 1.2 cm, and neck heights 1 to 2 cm;

7. bowls with vertical sides, slightly everted rims, and rounded lips; rim diameters measure 11 to 25 cm, wall thicknesses 0.5 to 1.1 cm, and height 8 to 20 cm; and

8. mushroom composite forms (no form data available).

Intraregional locations and contexts: Sierra Red has been found at Cival, Holmul, K'o, La Sufricaya, Hamontun, T'ot, and Dos Aguadas.

Interregional locations and contexts: Sierra Red appears at Uaxactun (Smith and Gifford 1966:163), Barton Ramie (Gifford 1976:85–90), Altar de Sacrificios (Adams 1971:21), Becan (Ball 1977:18, 21), Seibal (Sabloff 1975:77–78), El Mirador (Forsyth 1989:21–27), Tikal (Culbert 1993:14; 2006), the Petexbatun region (Foias and Bishop 2013:86–89), Piedras Negras (Muñoz 2004:11), Calakmul (Dominguez-Carrasco 1994:52), La Milpa (Sagebiel 2005:178–189), Chan (Kosakowsky 2012:62), Cuello (Kosakowsky 1987:58–62), Yaxchilan (Lopez Varela 1989:82), K'axob (Berry et al. 2004; Lopez Varela 2004), Colha (Valdez 1987:127), Cerros (Robertson-Freidel 1980:67–84), and as a Sierra Red: Chon Variety at Edzná (Forsyth 1983:33–36).

Comment: Because fire-clouding is so common among Sierra Group sherds, it is possible that this surface manipulation may have been intentional on the part of Late Preclassic potters. The creation of variegated surface colors from differential firing is a tradition that began in the Middle Preclassic in the Holmul region and continued through the Terminal Classic. Differential firing was skillfully employed in the Late Preclassic and could have been a forerunner to the use of multiple slips or paint in the Classic period.

Illustration: Figures 4.1, 4.2, and 4.3. Note that color conventions on figures 4.2a5, 4.2a6, and 4.3a1–6 show the vessels as unslipped. These vessels are not unslipped, but they are almost completely eroded. Patches of red slip on the interior and exteriors, as well as context, paste, form, led me to classify the vessels as Sierra Red.

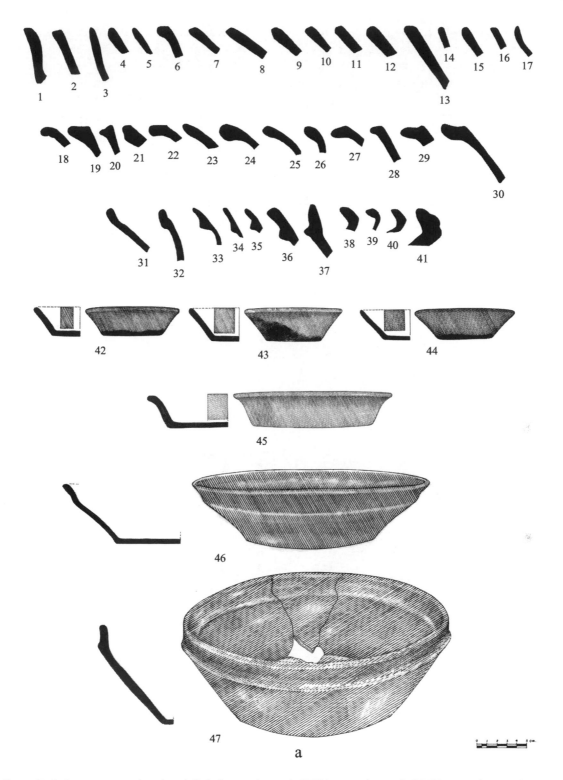

Figure 4.1. Sierra Red: Sierra Variety bowl and dish forms: (a1–a2) CIV.T.01.04, (a3–a6) CIV.T.16.03, (a7–a16) CIV.T.16.06, (a17) CIV.T.16.02, (a18) CIV.T.16.04, (a19–a21) CIV.T.15.05, (a23–a24) CIV.T.16.03, (a25–a26) CIV.T.01.04, (a 27) CIV.T.15.05, (a28) CIV.T.16.04, (a29) CIV.T.16.03, (a30) ST.08.71, (a31) CIV.T.15:02, (a32) CIV.T.18.08, (a33) CIV.T.16.03, (a34) CIV.T.16.01, (a35) CL.04.01, (a36) CIV.T.16.04, (a37) HOL.T.55.19, (a38) CIV.T.16.04, (a39) CIV.T.16.03, (a40 CIV.T.16.04, (a41) CIV.T.16.03, (a42) BLDG.B.V1.R8, (a43) BLDG.B.V6.R8, (a44) BLDG.B.V7.R8, (a45) KOL.T.34.17 V3, (a46) CAR.STR.3.LT.01, and (a47) CAR.STR.3.L1. Drawings by Michael G. Callaghan (a1–a41) and Fernando Alvarez (a42–a47) (Holmul Archaeological Project).

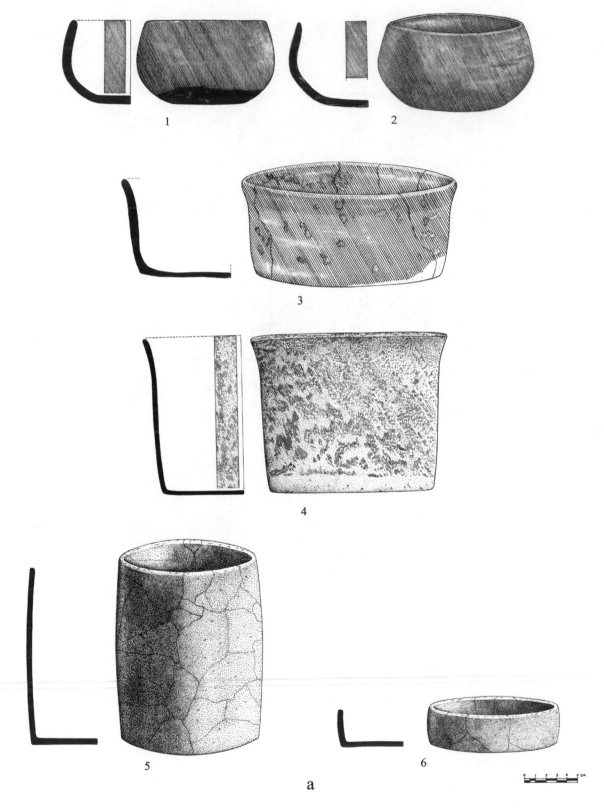

Figure 4.2. Sierra Red: Sierra Variety bowl forms: (a1) BLDG.B.V3.R8, (a2) KOL.T.34.20 V7, (a3) CIV.T.30.04, (a4) CIV.T.64.05.02.02, and (a5–a6) CT.08.52.02.01. Drawings by Fernando Alvarez (Holmul Archaeological Project).

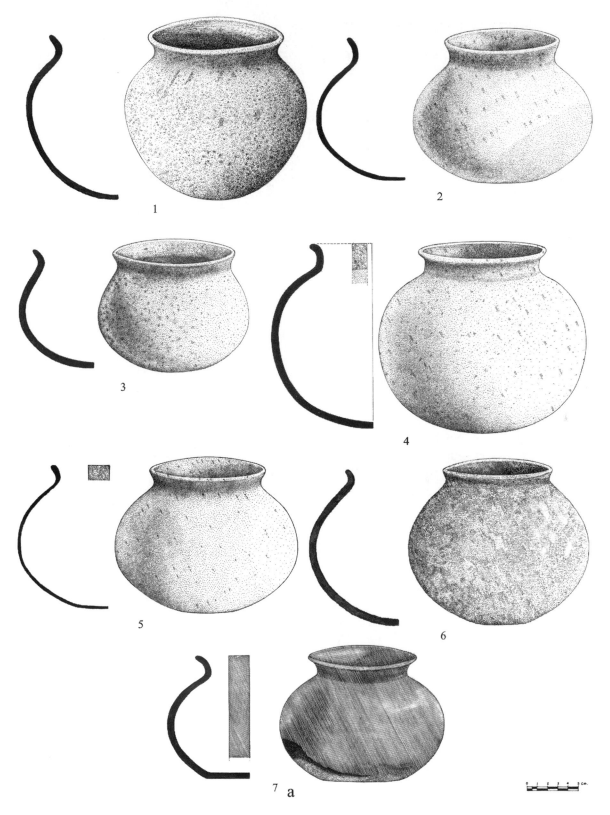

Figure 4.3. Sierra Red: Sierra Variety jar forms: (a1) CIV.T.64.05.02.08, (a2) CIV.T.64.05.05.03, (a3) CIV.T.05.02.04, (a4) CIV.T.64.06.02.01, (a5) CIV.T.64.05.02.06, (a6) CIV.T.64.05.02.07, (a7) KOL.T.34.28 V1. Drawings by Fernando Alvarez (Holmul Archaeological Project).

Laguna Verde Incised: Laguna Verde Variety

Established: Smith and Gifford at Uaxactun (1966: 159, 170).
    Group: Sierra
    Ware: Paso Caballo Waxy
    Complex: Itzamkanak
    Sphere: Chicanel
    Ceramic Group Frequency: 132 rims, 59 bodies, 191 total, 4.5 percent of group, 3 percent of complex.
    Principal identifying attributes: (1) Lustrous, waxy surface treatment, (2) red slip, and (3) post-slip or preslip incision on vessel surfaces.
    Paste, firing, and temper: Paste, firing, and temper is similar to Sierra Red: Sierra Variety.
    Surface finish and decoration: Well-smoothed and burnished surfaces are covered in a lustrous, waxy deep red (10R4/8; 2.5YR4/6, 4/8) slip. Preslip or post-slip incision is found on walls or medial flanges of vessel exteriors. Incision can be present in the form of bands of lines, simple geometric designs, or abstract symbols (e.g., Figure 4.4a13). Slip crackling or crazing is common.
    Forms:
    1. Bowls with flaring sides, medial flanges, direct rims, and round lips; rim diameters measure 13 to 35 cm, wall thicknesses 0.8 to 1 cm, and heights 5 to 17 cm;
    2. bowls with flaring or outcurving sides, everted rims, and rounded lips; rim diameters measure 15 to 32 cm, wall thicknesses 0.7 to 1.1 cm, and heights 4 to 12 cm; and
    3. bowls with flaring sides, z-angles, direct rims, and rounded lips; rim diameters measure 11 to 25 cm, wall thicknesses 0.5 to 1.1 cm, and heights 5 to 13 cm.

Intraregional locations and contexts: While Laguna Verde is relatively rare in the Holmul region, it has been found at every major site including Cival, Holmul, La Sufricaya, and K'o.
Interregional locations and contexts: Laguna Verde Incised: Laguna Verde Variety also appears at Uaxactun (Smith and Gifford 1966:170), Barton Ramie (Gifford 1976:91), Altar de Sacrificios (Adams 1971:43), Becan (Ball 1977:83), Seibal (Sabloff 1975:78), El Mirador (Forsyth 1989:27–29), Tikal (Culbert 1993:14, 2006), and the Petexbatun region (Foias and Bishop 2012:90–92). It appears as an Unspecified Variety at Edzná (Forsyth 1983:37–38), Colha (Valdez 1987:127), K'axob (Lopez Varela 2004), La Milpa (Sagebiel 2005:193–194), Calakmul (Dominguez-Carrasco 1994:52), Piedras Negras (Muñoz 2004:11), and Cuello (Kosakowsky 1987:70).

Illustration: Figure 4.4a. Note that color conventions for some sherds indicate red-and-unslipped—these vessels are not red-and-unslipped; they are eroded.

Laguna Verde Incised: Grooved-incised Variety

Established: Sabloff at Seibal (1975:80).
    Group: Sierra
    Ware: Paso Caballo Waxy
    Complex: Itzamkanak
    Sphere: Chicanel
    Ceramic Group Frequency: 43 rims, 2 bodies, 45 total, 1.5 percent of group, 1 percent of complex.
    Principal identifying attributes: (1) Lustrous, waxy surface finish, (2) red slip, (3) rounded bands of grooved-incision on everted rims or exterior vessel surfaces, and (4) bowls with everted rims.
    Paste, firing, and temper: Paste, firing, and temper is similar to Sierra Red: Sierra Variety.
    Surface finish and decoration: Same deep red (10R4/8; 2.5YR4/6, 4/8) waxy slip and burnished surfaces similar to Sierra Red. Incision takes the form of preslip circumferential deep, rounded, grooved-incision on vessel exteriors just below the lip and on wide, everted rims. Slip crackling or crazing is common.
    Forms:
    1. Bowls with flaring sides, everted rim, and rounded lips; rim diameters measure 14 to 25 cm, wall thicknesses 0.5 to 1.2 cm, and heights 5 to 9 cm; and
    2. bowls with flaring or outcurving sides, wide-everted rims, and rounded lips; rim diameters measure 15 to 30 cm, wall thicknesses 0.5 to 1.2 cm, and heights 6 to 9 cm.

Intraregional locations and contexts: Like Laguna Verde Incised: Laguna Verde Variety. Although this type is relatively rare in the Holmul region it occurs in Late Preclassic contexts at Cival, Holmul, La Sufricaya, and K'o.
Interregional locations and contexts: Laguna Verde Incised: Groove-Incised Variety can be found at Seibal (Sabloff 1975:80–84), in the Petexbatun region (Foias and Bishop 2013:92–93), at Cuello (Kosakowsky 1987:69–70), La Milpa (Sagebiel 2005:194–200), Chan (Kosakowsky 2012:62), K'axob (Lopez Varela 2004), and Cerros (Robertson-Freidel 1980:79).
Illustration: Figure 4.4b. Note that color conventions on some sherds appear unslipped—these sherds are not unslipped, but are eroded, as indicated by the stippled drawing.

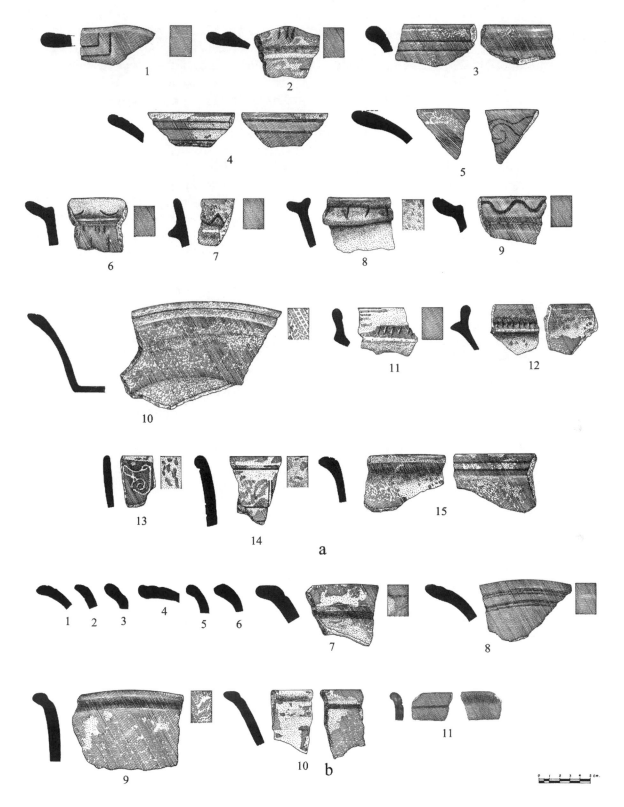

Figure 4.4. Laguna Verde Incised: Laguna Verde Variety: (a1) CIV.T.22.02, (a2) CIV.T.22.03, (a3–a5) CIV.T.22.06, (a6) KOL.04.07, (a7) CT.07.03, (a8) ST.17.12, (a9) CIV.T.22.03, (a10) ST.19.07, (a11) KOL.T.11.03, (a12) SUF.28.06, (a13) CIV.T.08.88.03.01, (a14) CIV.T.22.01, and (a15) Unknown provenance. Laguna Verde Incised: Grooved-incised Variety: (b1–b2) CIV.T.10.04, (b3–b4) ST.08.08, (b5–b6) CIV.T.01.04, (b7–b8) CIV.1.06.00, (b9) CIV.T.22.00, (b10) CIV.T.22.02, and (b11) HOL.T.75.08. Drawings by Fernando Alvarez (Holmul Archaeological Project).

Altamira Fluted: Altamira Variety

Established: Smith and Gifford at Uaxactun (1966: 154, 170).
Group: Sierra
Ware: Paso Caballo Waxy
Complex: Itzamkanak
Sphere: Chicanel
Ceramic Group Frequency: 33 rims, 40 bodies, 73 total, 1.1 percent of group, 0.8 percent of complex.
Principal identifying attributes: (1) Lustrous, waxy vessel surfaces, (2) deep red slip, (3) horizontal fluting, and (4) vertical fluting.
Paste, firing, and temper: Paste, firing, and temper are similar to Sierra Red: Sierra Variety.
Surface finish and decoration: Paso Caballo Waxy has the same deep red (10R4/8; 2.5YR4/6, 4/8) waxy slip and burnished surfaces as Sierra Red. Decoration takes the form of (1) wide preslip vertical fluting, (2) wide preslip horizontal fluting, or (3) incised preslip vertical incision that resembles fluting—on these forms a horizontal chamfer appears at the rim of the vessel on the exterior. Slip crackling or crazing is common.
Forms:

1. Bowls with flaring or recurving sides, direct rims, and rounded lips; rim diameters measure 14 to 30 cm, wall thicknesses 0.5 to 1.1 cm and

2. one possible vase or "funerary urn" form (not shown in illustrations; see Forsyth 1989:30–31 and Culbert 1993:Figure 5a–b, Figure 9b4). Rim diameters measure 26 cm and wall thicknesses 0.8 cm.

Intraregional locations and contexts: Altamira Fluted is found at Cival, but also occurs at Holmul, and La Sufricaya.
Interregional locations and contexts: Alta Mira Fluted: Altamira Variety has been found at Uaxactun (Smith and Gifford 1966:170), Barton Ramie (Gifford 1976:90–91), Altar de Sacrificios (Adams 1971:48), Seibal (Sabloff 1975:84), El Mirador (Forsyth 1989:31), Tikal (Culbert 1993: Figures 5a–b, 6c, 9b2–4), and Edzná (Forsyth 1983:39–40). It appears at La Milpa as a Variety Unspecified (Sagebiel 2005:190–192), as well as Calakmul (Dominguez-Carrasco 1994:52), Piedras Negras (Muñoz 2004:11), and the Petexbatun region (Foias and Bishop 2013:93).
Illustration: Figure 4.5a.

Society Hall: Society Hall Variety

Established: Elevated to a type at Cuello by Kosakowsky (1987: 64–68), originally named as a variety of Sierra Red by Gifford (1976:90) at Barton Ramie.
Group: Sierra
Ware: Paso Caballo Waxy
Complex: Itzamkanak
Sphere: Chicanel
Ceramic Group Frequency: 202 rims, 216 bodies, 418 total, 6.9 percent of group, 4.6 percent of complex.
Principal identifying attributes: (1) Streaky red slip, (2) waxy surface finish, and (3) everted rim bowls or dishes.
Paste, firing, and temper: Paste, firing, and temper are similar to Sierra Red: Sierra Variety.
Surface finish and decoration: Slip color is identical to Sierra Red (10R4/8; 2.5YR4/6, 4/8), but Society Hall slips are much thinner and were brushed onto vessel exteriors, which created a "streaky" effect. This effect could be achieved by the application of one layer of thin red slip or two applications of slip, one thicker than the other. Slip crackling or crazing is common.
Forms: Forms are similar to Sierra Red: Sierra Variety; they vary greatly in the Holmul region but constitute five major classes:

1. bowls or dishes with flaring or outcurving sides, direct or slightly everted rims, rounded lips, and flat bases; rim diameters measure 11 to 42cm, wall thicknesses 0.5 to 1.1 cm, and heights 4 to 17 cm;

2. bowls with flaring sides, incurving rims, and rounded lips; rim diameters measure 9 to 33 cm, wall thicknesses 0.5 to 1.2 cm, and heights 5 to 15 cm;

3. bowls with round sides, direct rims, and rounded lips; rim diameters measure 10 to 24 cm, wall thicknesses 0.5 to 1.1 cm, and heights 5 to 15 cm;

4. bowls with vertical sides, slightly everted rims, and rounded lips; rim diameters measure 11 to 25 cm, wall thicknesses 0.5 to 1.1 cm, and heights 8 to 20 cm; and

5. jars with outcurved short necks; rim diameters measure 8 to 12 cm, wall thicknesses 0.5 to 1.2 cm, and neck heights 1 to 2 cm.

Intraregional locations and contexts: Society Hall: Society Variety is fairly common and appears in Late Preclassic deposits from Cival, Holmul, and K'o.
Interregional locations and contexts: Society Hall is found mostly at Belizean sites. It appears at Barton Ramie

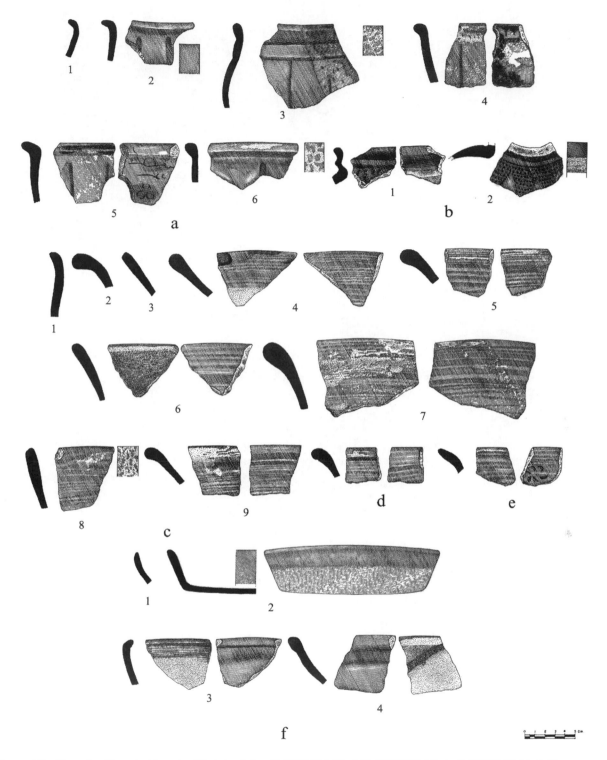

Figure 4.5. Altamira Fluted: Altamira Variety: (a1–a2) CIV.T.16.02, (a3) CIV.T.22.00, (a4) CIV.T.22.01, (a5) CIV.T.22.04, and (a6) CIV.T.22.01. Unnamed Punctated (Sierra Group): (b1) HOL.T.75.09 and (b2) HOL.T.76.12A. Society Hall: Society Hall Variety: (c1) CIV.T.11.04, (c2) CIV.T.16.03, (c3) CIV.T.16.04, (c4–c6) CIV.L.06.00, (c7) CIV.T.08.00, (c8) CIV.T.16.04, and (c9) CIV.T.22.02.E. Society Hall (Incised): (d) CIV.L.06.00. Society Hall (Impressed): (e) CIV.L.06.00. Unnamed Dichrome (Sierra Group): (f1) CIV.T.16.02 and (f2) CIV.22.01. Unnamed Red-and-unslipped (Sierra Group): (f3) CIV.L.6.00 and (f4) KOL.34.18.v4. Drawings by Fernando Alvarez (a1, a3–a6, b, c4–c9, d, e, f2–f4) and Michael G. Callaghan (a2, c1–c3, f1) (Holmul Archaeological Project).

(Gifford 1976:90), Cerros (Robertson-Freidel 1980:74), Cuello (Kosakowsky 1987:64–68), La Milpa (Sagebiel 2005:206–210), Chan (Kosakowsky 2012:62), K'axob (Lopez Varela 2004), and Colha (Valdez 1987:115–116). But it is also reported at Tikal (Culbert 2006).

Comment: The streaky slip on sherds appears to be intentional, which led Kosakowsky (1987:64–68) to classify Society Hall as its own type. Note that two sherds are incised (Figure 4.5d) and impressed (Figure 4.5e). I thought these variations were worth noting in the description and illustrations, but I have not created new type-varieties for these samples because their numbers are currently so low.

Illustration: Figure 4.5c.

Repasto Black-on-red: Variety Unspecified

Established: Smith and Gifford (1966:161, 170) at Uaxactun.
> *Group:* Sierra
> *Ware:* Paso Caballo Waxy
> *Complex:* Itzamkanak
> *Sphere:* Chicanel
> *Ceramic Group Frequency:* 2 rims, 3 bodies, 5 total, 0.1 percent of group, 0.05 percent of complex.
> *Principal identifying attributes:* (1) Lustrous, waxy surface treatment, (2) red slip, and (3) black resist-like decoration over red slip on vessel exteriors.
> *Paste, firing, and temper:* Paste, firing, and temper are the same as Sierra Red: Sierra Variety.
> *Surface finish and decoration:* Slip color is identical to Sierra Red (10R4/8; 2.5YR4/6, 4/8). Black resist paint creates red negative space (simple geometric designs like circles and bars) on the exterior of sherds.
> *Forms:* Bowls with flaring sides, direct rims, and rounded lips (no form data available).
> *Intraregional locations and contexts:* Repasto Black-on-red has only been found at the site of Cival.
> *Interregional locations and contexts:* Repasto Black-on-red: Repasto Variety is found at Uaxactun (Smith and Gifford 1966:161,170), Altar de Sacrificios (Adams 1971:28), Tikal (Culbert 1993:Figure 2d1, 3a, 14-1b2; Laporte and Valdes 1993:40), El Mirador (Forsyth 1989:33), La Milpa (Sagebiel 2005:210-211), Becan (Ball 1977:50), and Edzná (Forsyth 1983:41). Robertson-Freidel (1980:138–142) defines a black-on-red type at Cerros (i.e., Zorra Black-on-red), but its principal identifying attributes are not identical to the Repasto type Holmul.
> *Illustration:* Figure 4.6.

Figure 4.6. Repasto Black-on-red: Variety Unspecified. Photo by Michael. G. Callaghan.

Unnamed Modeled (Sierra Group)

Established: Callaghan in this study.
> *Group:* Sierra
> *Ware:* Paso Caballo Waxy
> *Complex:* Itzamkanak
> *Sphere:* Chicanel
> *Ceramic Group Frequency:* 2 rims, 1 body, 3 total, 0.1 percent of group, 0.05 percent of complex.
> *Principal identifying attributes:* (1) Lustrous, waxy surface treatment, (2) red slip, and (3) modeling on exterior surfaces.
> *Paste, firing, and temper:* Paste, firing, and temper are same as Sierra Red: Sierra Variety.
> *Surface finish and decoration:* Slip color is identical to Sierra Red (10R4/8; 2.5YR4/6, 4/8). Exterior surfaces on the two sherds in the collection are modeled, but the design cannot be deciphered at this point.
> *Forms:* Not determined.
> *Intraregional locations and contexts:* The only three sherds of this unnamed modeled type of Sierra Red were found in substructure excavations of Building B, Group II at Holmul.
> *Interregional locations and contexts:* Modeling on Sierra Red vessels is present in small frequencies at sites in Belize. Kosakowsky (1987:74–76) reports an unnamed modeled type belonging to the Sierra Group at Cuello. Berry and colleagues (2004:208–9, 216–17) describe Sierra Red spouted jars with modeled decoration at K'axob and leave the variety unspecified. Unfortunately, the Holmul sherds are not diagnostic as to forms, so I cannot positively state these sherds belonged to spouted jars.
> *Illustration:* Figure 4.7b1–3.

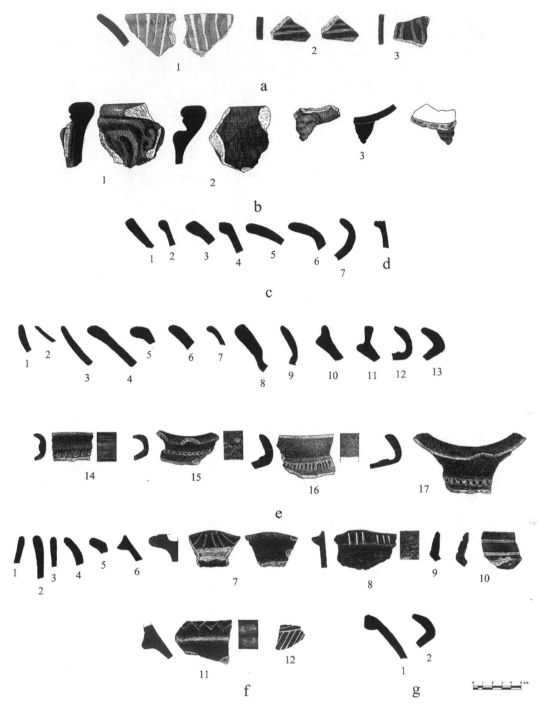

Figure 4.7. Unnamed Red-on-orange (Caramba Group): (a1) HOL.T.75.08. Unnamed Trickle-on-gray (Zapatista Group): (a2–a3) Unknown provenance. Unnamed Modeled (Sierra Group): (b1–b2) HOL.T.75.10 and (b3) HOL.T.75.08. Flor Cream: Flor Variety: (c1) CIV.T.10.15, (c2) CIV.T.10.11, (c3–c4) CIV.T.10.15, (c5) CIV.T.10.11, (c6) CIV.T.10.10, (c7) CIV.T.10.11. Accordian Incised: Accordian Variety: (d) CIV.T.01.04. Polvero Black: Polvero Variety: (e1) CIV.T.16.03, (e2) CIV.T.16.04, (e3) CIV.T.18.08, (e4) CIV.T.12.15, (e5) CIV.T.15.02, (e6–e7) CIV.T.10.04, (e8) CIV.T.01.04, (e9) HOL.T.56.01, (e10) HOL.T.49.13, (e11) HOL.T.16.01, (e12) (CIV.T.16.01), (e13) CIV.T.10.04, (e14) SUF.T.23.06, (e15) HOL.T.71.03, and (e16–e17) CIV.T.01.04. Lechugal Incised: Lechugal Variety: (f1–f5) CIV.T.01.04, (f6) CIV.T.18.08, (f7) HOL.T.BLDG.B.R1, (f8) CIV.T.18.08, (f9–f10) CIV.T.16.03, (f11) CIV.T.22.03, and (f12) ST.08.02. Boxcay Brown: Boxcay Variety: (g1) HOL.T.49.13 and (g2) CIV.T.16.01. Drawings by Fernando Alvarez (a, b, e14–e17, f7–f8, f10–f12) and Michael G. Callaghan (c, d, e1–e13, f1–f6, f9, g) (Holmul Archaeological Project).

Figure 4.8. Unnamed Dichrome (Sierra Group). Photo by Michael G. Callaghan.

Unnamed Dichrome (Sierra Group)

Established: Callaghan in this study.
Group: Sierra
Ware: Paso Caballo Waxy
Ceramic Complex: Itzamkanak
Sphere: Chicanel
Ceramic Group Frequency: 11 rims, 23 bodies, 34 total, 0.4 percent of group, 0.3 percent of complex.
Principal identifying attributes: (1) Lustrous, waxy surface treatment, (2) red slip, and (3) yellow or tan coloration on the base of exterior vessel walls.
Paste, firing, and temper: Paste, firing, and temper are the same as Sierra Red: Sierra Variety.
Surface finish and decoration: Slip color is identical to Sierra Red (10R4/8; 2.5YR4/6, 4/8). What appears to be cream, yellow, or buff fire-clouding appears on the exterior base and lower portions of vessel walls. The yellow to tan color is within the range of Flor Cream (10YR8/3 or 7.5YR5/5). It is also important to note that exterior red surfaces can also appear streaky, similar to Society Hall.
Forms:

1. Bowls with outcurving sides, direct rims, and rounded lips; rim diameters measure 11 to 25 cm, wall thicknesses 0.5 to 0.7 cm, and heights 4 to 17 cm and

2. bowls with rounded sides, direct rims, and rounded lips; rim diameters measure 10 to 24 cm, wall thicknesses 0.5 to 0.7 cm, and height 5 to 15 cm.

Intraregional locations and contexts: The small sample of this dichrome material has been found in Structure 1 at Cival.
Interregional locations and contexts: At first glance, the Sierra Red dichrome at Holmul may appear similar to Matamore Dichrome: Shipyard Variety originally defined by Pring (1977b) at Cuello (see also Kosakowsky 1987:79–80 for Matamore Dichrome: Matamore Variety), and also found at Cerros (Robertson-Freidel 1980:223–228), La Milpa (Sagebiel 2005:212–217), and Colha (Valdez 1987:145–146). Note that these are Terminal Preclassic period types in Belize. The Holmul material may also appear similar to Mateo Red-on-cream defined by Adams (1971:28) at Altar de Sacrificios. These Belizean and Pasión types are, however, quite dissimilar to the Holmul examples. Usually, these type: varieties involve the differential slipping of vessel interiors and exteriors, with one side being one color and the other another. Furthermore, the color and surface finish of Matamore type: varieties are distinct enough from Sierra Red at Belizean sites that researchers place the type outside of the Sierra Group. Finally, in the case of Matamore Dichrome: Shipyard Variety, Robertson-Freidel (1980:223–228) notes the presence of two separate cream and red slips on vessel surfaces. This is not the case with the Holmul samples. It appears that Holmul samples display different colors on vessel exteriors due to fire clouds, not double-slipping.
Illustration: Figures 4.5f1–2 and 4.8.

Unnamed Punctated (Sierra Group)

Established: Callaghan in this study.
Group: Sierra
Ware: Paso Caballo Waxy
Complex: Itzamkanak
Sphere: Chicanel
Ceramic Group Frequency: 1 rim, 1 body, 2 total, 0.03 percent of group, 0.02 percent of complex.
Principal identifying modes: (1) Lustrous, waxy surface treatment, (2) red slip, (3) punctations on vessel exteriors, and (4) jar forms.
Paste, firing, and temper: Paste, temper, and firing are same as Sierra Red: Sierra Variety.
Surface finish and decoration: Well-smoothed and burnished surfaces are covered in a lustrous, waxy deep red (10R4/8; 2.5YR4/6, 4/8) slip. Punctation is found on exterior walls of jars at the shoulder break. Slip crackling or crazing is common.
Forms: Small jars with outcurving rims and round lips (no measurement data available).
Intraregional locations and contexts: This type is extremely rare; one sherd has been found at Holmul and one at Cival.
Interregional locations and contexts: These samples are similar to the type Lagartos Punctated: Lagartos Variety, which was originally defined at Uaxactun (Smith and Gifford 1966:170). The type also occurs at Altar de Sacrificios (Adams 1971:46), Seibal (Sabloff 1975:84), El Mirador (Forsyth 1989:31, 33), and Calakmul (Dominguez-Carrasco 1994:52). It appears as an Unspecified Variety at Chan (Kosakowsky 2012:62), Yaxchilan (Lopez Varela 1989:83–84), K'axob (Lopez Varela 2004), Colha (Valdez 1987:132–133), and Cuello (Kosakowsky 1987:70–71). Due to the extremely small sample size, however, I hesitate to positively identify these samples as Lagartos Punctated, but I did think it important to record them in this study.
Illustration: Figure 4.5b.

Unnamed Red-and-unslipped (Sierra Group)

Established: Callaghan in this study.
Group: Sierra
Ware: Paso Caballo Waxy
Complex: Itzamkanak
Sphere: Chicanel
Ceramic Group Frequency: 2 rims, 2 bodies, 4 total, 0.1 percent of group, 0.05 percent of complex.
Principal identifying modes: (1) Lustrous, waxy surface treatment and (2) combinations of red slipped and unslipped vessel surfaces.

Paste, firing, and temper: Paste, temper, and firing are same as Sierra Red: Sierra Variety.
Surface finish and decoration: Well-smoothed and burnished surfaces are partially covered in a lustrous, waxy deep red (10R4/8; 2.5YR4/6, 4/8) slip. On the two samples in the present collection, the red slip is found on the exterior of one and on the interior and partially on the exterior (over the rim and slightly down the exterior wall) of the other.
Forms:
  1. Bowls with flaring sides, incurving rims, and rounded lips, (no measurement data available) and
  2. bowls with flaring sides, bolstered rim, and rounded lip (no measurement data available).

Intraregional locations and contexts: This type of ceramic is extremely rare in the Holmul region; it has been found at Cival.
Interregional locations and contexts: At first glance, these samples appear similar to Puletan Red-and-unslipped: Puletan Variety, which was originally defined by Pring (1977b) at Cuello, as well as Puletan Red-and-unslipped: Unnamed Variety originally defined by Kosakowsky (1987:74) at Cuello. The Holmul region samples differ from the Cuello material, however, in that they do not display the same slip patterns as the two Puletan varieties. They also do not display any other sign of secondary decoration as the Cuello material does. Due to the extremely small sample size, I hesitate to positively identify these samples as yet another variety of Puletan Red-and-unslipped, but I did think it important to record them for this report.
Illustration: Figure 4.5f3–4.

Unnamed Red-on-orange (Caramba Group)

Established: Callaghan in this study.
Group: Caramba
Ware: Paso Caballo Waxy
Complex: Itzamkanak
Sphere: Chicanel
Ceramic Group Frequency: 1 rim, 1 total, 100 percent of group, 0.02 percent of complex.
Principal identifying attributes: (1) Lustrous, waxy surface treatment and 2. multiple vertical squiggly lines over red-orange slip.
Paste, firing, and temper: Paste, firing, and temper are similar to Sierra Red: Sierra Variety, despite this sherd belonging to an entirely different group.
Surface finish and decoration: Red and red-orange slip colors are similar to Sierra Red (10R4/8; 2.5YR4/6, 4/8).

Parallel squiggly red lines appear over a lighter red-orange slip on both interior and exterior of this one sherd.

Forms: Bowl with outcurving slightly everted sides, direct rim, and rounded lip (no measurements available).

Intraregional locations and contexts: The single sample of this material comes from HOL.T.75, which is in the substructure of Building B, Group II.

Interregional locations and contexts: It is entirely possible this sample belongs to Caramba Red-on-orange: Caramba Variety, which was established at Altar de Sacrificios (Adams 1971:28) and also appears at Becan (Ball 1977:50), Edzná (Forsyth 1983:53–54), and Tikal (Culbert 2006; 1993:Figure 4a, 9b5, 10d, 11a6–7, 12a, 13c), and the Petexbatun region (Foias and Bishop 2013:106). Forsyth (1989:43–44) also reports the type at Mirador, where he remarks that both the slip color and paste are markedly similar to Sierra Red. This is the case with the Holmul sample as well. Without a larger sample and more direct experience with this type, however, I hesitate to classify this one sherd as Caramba Red-on-orange: Caramba Variety.

Illustration: Figure 4.7a1.

Unnamed Trickle-on-gray (Zapatista Group)

Established: Callaghan in this study.
Group: Zapatista
Ware: Unspecified
Complex: Itzamkanak
Sphere: Chicanel
Ceramic Group Frequency: 0 rims, 2 bodies, 2 total, 100 percent of group, less than 0.01 percent of complex.

Principal identifying attributes: (1) Light cream wash and (2) black trickle decoration.

Paste, firing, and temper: The paste is medium in texture, dull gray (10YR5/1) in color, and contains crystalline calcite inclusions. One sample has a firing core while the other does not.

Surface finish and decoration: Interior and exterior surfaces are well-smoothed. On both examples, a thin cream wash was applied to the exterior surfaces and then a light black paint or slip was trickled over the exterior surface. On one example the trickle decoration appears on the interior and exterior.

Forms: Accurate form data are not available because these are body sherds. Based on the interior and exterior decoration on one sherd, and exclusive exterior decoration on the other, this type may have been present in both bowl and jar forms.

Intraregional locations and contexts: Unfortunately, these two samples lack provenience.

Interregional locations and contexts: Ball (1977:50) established the Zapatista Group at Becan. Zapatista Trickled Dichrome has also been found in El Mirador (Forsyth 1989:45–46) as well as Cerros (Robertson-Freidel 1980:245–249). Without a larger sample, rim sherds, and more direct experience with this type, however, I hesitate to classify these two unprovenanced sherds as Zapatista.

Illustration: Figure 4.7a2–3.

Flor Cream: Flor Variety

Established: Smith and Gifford at Uaxactun (1966: 158, 170).
Group: Flor
Ware: Paso Caballo Waxy
Complex: Itzamkanak
Sphere: Chicanel
Ceramic Group Frequency: 139 rims, 202 bodies, 341 total, 91.4 percent of group, and 3.2 percent of complex.

Principal identifying attributes: (1) Lustrous, waxy highly burnished vessel surfaces, (2) thick cream slip, and (3) buff-colored paste.

Paste, firing, and temper: The paste is medium in texture and is carbonate based with crystalline calcite, sherd, and burnt organic inclusions. The color is buff (10YR7/3) or yellow (10YR7/4). Firing cores are infrequent, but present in some samples.

Surface finish and decoration: Vessel surfaces are smoothed and highly polished. The slip is waxy, evenly applied, and thick. The creamy color of the slip can vary from white (10YR8/1) to yellow (10YR8/3) to tan (7.5YR5/5). Fire clouds are frequent on vessel exteriors.

Forms:

1. Bowls with outflaring sides, everted rims, and rounded lips sometimes with beads; rim diameters measure 12 to 33 cm, and wall thicknesses 0.5 to 1 cm;

2. bowls with outflaring sides, wide-everted rims, and rounded lips; rim diameters measure 13 to 35 cm and wall thicknesses 0.5 to 0.9 cm; and

3. jars with short, outcurving necks, direct rims, and rounded lips; rim diameters measure 8 to12 cm, wall thicknesses 0.5 to 1.2 cm, and neck heights 1 to 2 cm.

Intraregional locations and contexts: Flor Cream is relatively rare in the Holmul region compared to Sierra Red and Polvero Black, but can be found at Holmul, Cival, K'o, and La Sufricaya.

Interregional locations and contexts: Flor Cream: Flor Variety appears at Uaxactun (Smith and Gifford

1966: 170), Barton Ramie (Gifford 1976:95–96), Altar de Sacrificios (Adams 1971:28), Seibal (Sabloff 1975:94, 96), Cuello (Kosakowsky 1987:78–79), El Mirador (Forsyth 1989:39–43), Tikal (Culbert 1993:13, 2006), La Milpa (Sagebiel 2005:227–230), and Piedras Negras (Muñoz 2004:11). It appears as an Unspecified Variety at K'axob (Lopez Varela 2004), Yaxchilan (Lopez Varela 1989:79–80), Chan (Kosakowsky 2012:62), Edzná (Forsyth 1983:49–50), and the Petexbatun region (Foias and Bishop 2013:96–99).

Illustration: Figure 4.7c.

Accordian Incised: Accordian Variety

Established: Smith and Gifford at Uaxactun (1966: 154, 170).
Group: Flor
Ware: Paso Caballo Waxy
Complex: Itzamkanak
Sphere: Chicanel
Ceramic Group Frequency: 13 rims, 3 bodies, 16 total, 8.6 percent of group, 0.3 percent of complex.
Principal identifying attributes: (1) Lustrous, waxy highly burnished vessel surfaces, (2) thick cream slip, (3) preslip or post-slip incision, (4) buff-colored paste, and (5) bowls with flaring sides and everted rims.
Paste, firing, and temper: Paste, temper, and firing are the same as Flor Cream.
Surface finish and decoration: Lustrous, highly burnished vessel surfaces with thick cream (10YR8/1), yellow (10YR8/3), or tan (7.5YR5/5) slips. Incised lines can be pre- or post-slip. If incision is executed after slipping, the buff-colored paste shows through. Incision occurs in circumferential bands on wide-everted rim bowls or dishes.
Forms: Bowls or dishes with flaring sides, everted or wide-everted rims, and rounded lips. Rim diameters measure 11 to 30 cm and wall thickness 0.5 to 0.9 cm.
Intraregional locations and contexts: Accordian Incised is extremely rare in the Holmul region, but does occur in small quantities at Cival, Holmul, K'o, and La Sufricaya.
Interregional locations and contexts: Accordian Incised: Accordian Variety is also rare throughout the lowlands in the Late Preclassic, but it can be found at Uaxactun (Smith and Gifford 1966:170), Barton Ramie (Gifford 1976:84–95), and as Unspecified Variety at Edzná (Forsyth 1983:51), and the Petexbatun region where it is named "Acordeon Incised" (Foias and Bishop 2013:99–100).
Illustration: Figure 4.7d.

Polvero Black: Polvero Variety

Established: Smith and Gifford at Uaxactun (1966: 162, 170).
Group: Polvero
Ware: Paso Caballo Waxy
Complex: Itzamkanak
Sphere: Chicanel
Ceramic Group Frequency: 572 rims, 2,624 bodies, 3,196 total, 95 percent of group, 13 percent of complex.
Principal identifying attributes: (1) Lustrous, waxy vessel surfaces and (2) deep black slip.
Paste, firing, and temper: The paste is medium in texture and usually has many crystalline calcite inclusions. Sherd temper was occasionally added to the paste, but this is rare. Color is gray (10YR4/1) or black.
Surface finish and decoration: On unrestricted forms, vessel interiors and exteriors are highly polished with a deep waxy black slip. Color is usually quite consistent and slip crackling or crazing is common.
Forms:
    1. Bowls with round or slightly flaring sides, direct rims, and either rounded or pinched lips; rim diameter measure 10 to 24 cm and wall thicknesses 0.5 to 0.8 cm;
    2. bowls with z-angles, direct rims, and rounded lips; rim diameters measure 11 to 35 cm and wall thicknesses 0.5 to 1.1 cm; and
    3. jars with short, outcurved necks, direct rims, and rounded lips; rim diameters measure 8 to 12 cm, wall thicknesses 0.5 to 1.2 cm, and neck heights 1 to 2 cm.

Intraregional locations and contexts: Polvero Black ceramics occur at Cival, Holmul, K'o and La Sufricaya.
Interregional locations and contexts: Polvero Black: Polvero Variety occurs at Uaxactun (Smith and Gifford 1966:161,170), Barton Ramie (Gifford 1976:96–99), Altar de Sacrificios (Adams 1971:24), Seibal (Sabloff 1975:87), El Mirador (Forsyth 1989:36–38), Edzná (Forsyth 1983:45–48), Tikal (Culbert 1993:14, 2006), Cuello (Kosakowsky 1987:76–78), the Petexbatun region (Foias and Bishop 2013:102–105), La Milpa (Sagebiel 2005:217–222), and Piedras Negras (Muñoz 2004:11). It appears as an Unspecified Variety at Colha (Valdez 1987:117), Yaxchilan (Lopez Varela 1989:79–80), and Chan (Kosakowsky 2012:62).
Illustration: Figure 4.7e.

Lechugal Incised: Lechugal Variety

Established: Smith and Gifford at Uaxactun (1966: 159, 170).
Group: Polvero

Ware: Paso Caballo Waxy
Complex: Itzamkanak
Sphere: Chicanel
Ceramic Group Frequency: 30 rims, 57 bodies, 87 total, 5 percent of group, 0.7 percent of complex.

Principal identifying attributes: (1) Lustrous, waxy vessel surfaces, (2) deep black slip, and (3) preslip incision, sometimes very deep.

Paste, firing, and temper: Paste, temper, and firing are the same as Polvero Black.

Surface finish and decoration: Surfaces are highly burnished. The waxy black slip was applied to vessel interiors and exteriors on unrestricted forms. Incision was executed both preslip and post-slip. Incision usually appears as vertical slashes on medial flanges, but can take the form of deeply incised bands of zig-zags or other geometric designs on vessel exteriors.

Forms:

1. Bowls with flaring sides, medial flanges, direct rims, and rounded lips; rim diameters measure 9 to 33 cm and wall thicknesses 0.5 to 0.7 cm and

2. bowls with flaring sides, z-angles, direct rims, and rounded lips; rim diameters measure 11 to 35 cm and wall thicknesses 0.5 to 1.1 cm.

Intraregional locations and contexts: Lechugal Incised is relatively rare in the Holmul region, but it does occur in largest quantities at Cival and in lesser numbers in Holmul, K'o, and La Sufricaya.

Interregional locations and contexts: Lechugal Incised: Lechugal Variety is also found at Uaxactun (Smith and Gifford 1966:159, 170), Barton Ramie (Gifford 1976:99), Altar de Sacrificios (Adams 1971:43), Cuello (Kosakowsky 1987:78), El Mirador (Forsyth 1989:38–39), Tikal (Culbert 1993:14, 2006), Calakmul (Dominguez-Carrasco 1994:52), an La Milpa (Sagebiel 2005:223–224). It is similar to Macaw Bank Variety at Colha (Valdez 1987:117–118), and may be similar to Gouged-incised Variety at Edzná (Forsyth 1983:48–49). It appears as an Unspecified Variety at Chan (Kosakowsky 2012:62) and in the Petexbatun region (Foias and Bishop 2013:104–105).

Illustration: Figure 4.7f.

Boxcay Brown: Boxcay Variety

Established: Culbert (1993:13, 2006) at Tikal.
Group: Boxcay
Ware: Paso Caballo Waxy
Complex: Itzamkanak
Sphere: Chicanel
Ceramic Group Frequency: 106 rims, 2 bodies, 1 whole vessel, 109 total, 100 percent of group, 2.4 percent of complex.

Principal identifying attributes: (1) Lustrous, waxy vessel surfaces and (2) consistent brown slip.

Paste, firing, and temper: The paste is medium in texture and carbonate-based with crystalline calcite, sherd, and burnt organic inclusions. Paste color is yellow (10YR7/4). Firing cores are not present in this sample.

Surface finish and decoration: Vessel surfaces are smoothed and well-polished. Slip color is a consistent light brown (7.5YR4/4) and not an uneven mottled or variegated. Crackling or slip crazing is common.

Forms:

1. Bowls with composite recurving sides, outcurving necks, direct rims, and rounded lips; rim diameters measure 11 to 25 cm and wall thicknesses 0.5 to 0.9 cm;

2. bowls with 11- to 32–cm-diameter rims and 0.5- to 0.9-cm-thick walls; and

3. jars with outcurving necks, direct rims, and rounded lips; rim diameters measure 8 to 12 cm, wall thicknesses 0.5 to 1.2 cm, and neck heights 1 to 2 cm.

Intraregional locations and contexts: Boxcay Brown is rare in the Holmul region, but does occur at Cival.

Interregional locations and contexts: Boxcay Brown: Boxcay Variety appears at Tikal (Culbert 1993:13, 2006), in the Valle de Dolores (Laporte et al. 1993:74), and at Piedras Negras (Muñoz 2004:52). There is a Belizean brown group named San Felipe Golden Brown that was defined by Gifford (1976:113–116) at Barton Ramie and later identified at La Milpa (Sagebiel 2005:224–227), Chan (Kosakowsky 2012:62), and also at Colha (Valdez 1987:143–144) during the Terminal Preclassic. But these Belizean brown ceramics are different from Boxcay in terms of form and surface finish. (San Felipe Brown has unevenly applied slip.)

Comment: It could be argued that Boxcay is simply a residual type category. Sherds placed in the Boxcay type could be "misfired" or fire-clouded sherds from Sierra, Polvero, or Flor vessels. With the discovery of an even-fired brown Boxcay vessel from a Late Preclassic burial at Cival in 2005, however, it is more likely that Holmul region potters intentionally created brown vessels.

Illustration: Figure 4.7g.

CHAPTER FIVE

Wayab Subcomplex

Michael G. Callaghan

The Wayab ceramic Subcomplex dates between AD 120 and 230. The subcomplex dates were determined through a combination of radiocarbon samples (Table 1.2; Estrada-Belli 2008:15, 144; 2006b:44) and typological comparisons to other sites. The main radiocarbon date comes from a bone found in Burial 10 within Building B, Group II at Holmul. The bone returned a calibrated date of AD 120 to 230 (Estrada-Belli 2006a:4).

The Wayab Subcomplex is not a complete ceramic assemblage and does not represent a full ceramic complex. It is best described as a collection of serving vessels of types and modes that crosscut the Late Preclassic and Early Classic periods (see also Brady et al. 1998). Whole vessels of this subcomplex are restricted to ritual contexts at Holmul. Significant contexts include Room 8, the Room 8 vault, and Room 9 in Building B, Group II as well as Burial 10 (Callaghan 2013; Merwin and Vaillant 1932; Neivens 2005). The descriptions of Wayab material included in this study come from an examination of 14 whole vessels, 11 rim sherds, and 4 diagnostic body sherds for a total of 29 representative samples. Two wares, 5 groups, and 8 type-varieties define the Wayab Subcomplex (Table 5.1). All type: varieties are slipped. Wayab ceramics resemble a combination of types and modes from both the Itzamkanak Late Preclassic Complex and the K'ak Early Classic Complex. Wares include the Late Preclassic Paso Caballo Waxy Ware with its Sierra and Flor Groups, and the Classic Period Petén Gloss Ware with its Aguila, Ixcanrio, and Actuncan Groups. Wayab Subcomplex material dates to what has often been referred to as the Protoclassic period (Brady et al. 1998; Pring 1977a, 2000; Willey 1977) and is contemporaneous with the proposed Matzanel Complex at Uaxactun (Smith 1955:22), the Cimi Complex at Tikal (Culbert 1993, 2003, 2006), the Paixbancito Subcomplex at El Mirador (Forsyth 1989:51–60), the early Salinas Complex at Altar de Sacrificios (Adams 1971:93–94), the Poderes Complex (Sepos Subcomplex) at Edzná (Forsyth 1983:62–65), and the Floral Park Complex at Barton Ramie (Gifford 1976:127–153). Wayab Subcomplex material represents diagnostic ceramics from the second phase of Brady and colleagues' (1998) proposed Terminal Preclassic ceramic period, which dates from AD 250 to 400. Although Holmul is traditionally known for its Terminal Preclassic period ceramic material, Wayab Subcomplex ceramics are extremely rare in the region. It is also important to note that no phase 2 Aguacate Orange types or phase 1 diagnostic ceramics have been found in the Holmul region to date. Phase 1 ceramics would include, among others, Iberia Orange, Ixobel Orange, and ceramics displaying the Usulutan mode of decoration (Brady et al. 1998). Brief descriptions of the wares within the Wayab Subcomplex are presented next, followed by type descriptions. I offer interpretations in the summary chapter (see also Callaghan 2008, 2013; Callaghan et al. 2013).

PASO CABALLO WAXY WARE

Smith and Gifford (1966:167) established Paso Caballo Waxy Ware at Uaxactun. It is the primary slipped ware of the Late Preclassic period. Paso Caballo Waxy Ware is characterized by highly polished or burnished surfaces that feel greasy or waxy to the touch. Slipped ceramics in the Wayab Subcomplex include red and cream colors.

Table 5.1. Ceramic Wares, Groups, Types, and Varieties of the Terminal Preclassic Period (Wayab Subcomplex)

Ware	Group (% of subcomplex)	Type: Variety	Numbers			Percentages	
			Rims	Bodies	Vessels	Group	Subcomplex
Petén Gloss	Aguila (24%)	Aguila Orange: Variety Unspecified (Wayab)	3	0	3	100.0	20.7
	Ixcanrio (56%)	Ixcanrio Orange Polychrome: Ixcanrio Variety	6	4	2	57.1	27.6
		Ixcanrio Orange Polychrome: Turnbull Variety	1	0	1	14.3	6.9
		Ixcanrio Orange Polychrome: Variety Unspecified (Wayab)	1	0	3	28.6	13.8
	Actuncan (4%)	Actuncan Orange Polychrome: Variety Unspecified (Wayab)	0	0	1	100.0	3.4
Paso Caballo Waxy	Sierra (8%)	Sierra Red: Variety Unspecified (Wayab)	0	0	2	100.0	6.9
	Flor (4%)	Flor Cream: Variety Unspecified (Wayab)	0	0	1	50.0	3.4
		Accordian Incised: Variety Unspecified (Wayab)	0	0	1	50.0	3.4
		TOTALS	**11**	**4**	**14**		

Surface decoration includes incision and modeling of vessel supports. Red slips tend toward true red (10R4/8; 2.5YR4/6, 4/8) and cream slips toward a more yellow (10YR8/3) or tan (7.5YR5/5) than white. Pastes are medium-textured and red-orange (7.5YR6/8), to gray (10YR5/1), to yellow-brown (10YR7/4). Primary paste inclusions are crystalline calcite, sherd temper (grog), burnt organics, and even shell. Groups and type: varieties within Paso Caballo Waxy Ware include

Sierra Group
    Sierra Red: Variety Unspecified (Wayab)
Flor Group
    Flor Cream: Variety Unspecified (Wayab)
    Accordian Incised: Variety Unspecified (Wayab)

PETÉN GLOSS WARE

Smith and Gifford (1966:167–168) defined Petén Gloss Ware at Uaxactun. Surfaces are well-smoothed and polished to a shine. Slip color is predominantly orange (2.5YR5/8; 5YR5/8, 6/8). Decoration includes incision, polychrome painting (red-and-black-on-orange), black-on-orange painting, and modeling of vessel supports. Pastes are light colored and range from yellow (10YR7/4, 7/3) to buff (10YR8/2). Common inclusions are volcanic ash, crystalline calcite, and spherical gray calcite. Groups and type: varieties within Petén Gloss Ware of the Wayab Subcomplex include

Aguila Group
    Aguila Orange: Variety Unspecified (Wayab)
Ixcanrio Group
    Ixcanrio Orange Polychrome: Ixcanrio Variety
    Ixcanrio Orange Polychrome: Turnbull Variety
    Ixcanrio Orange Polychrome: Variety Unspecified (Wayab)
Actuncan Group
    Actuncan Orange Polychrome: Variety Unspecified (Wayab)

TYPE DESCRIPTIONS

Sierra Red: Variety Unspecified (Wayab)

Established: Type named Smith by and Gifford (1966:163,170), Variety named by Pring (2000:47).

Group: Sierra
Ware: Paso Caballo Waxy
Subcomplex: Wayab
Sphere: Floral Park
Ceramic Group Frequency: 2 whole vessels (Vessel 2, Room 8, Building B and Vessel 5, Room 8, Building B, see Appendix 4), 2 total, 100 percent of group, 6.9 percent of subcomplex.

Principal identifying attributes: (1) Slightly waxy surface treatment, (2) red slip, (3) vase with tetrapod mammiform supports, and (4) "cotton reel" pot stand.

Paste, firing, and temper: Paste, firing, and temper were difficult to identify for this type: variety. The only examples of this variety of Sierra Red are two whole vessels: one is currently housed at the American Museum of Natural History in New York, and the other at the Peabody Museum in Cambridge, Massachusetts. Paste color for both vessels appears to be within the normal range for Sierra Red (10YR5/1, 7/4), but texture and inclusions could not be verified.

Surface finish and decoration: The surface of these vessels varies. The vase (Vessel 2, Room 8, Building B) is smoothed and roughly burnished. Its slip color is red (10R4/8), but the texture of the surface is not nearly as waxy or greasy as other Itzamkanak Sierra Variety vessels. The bottoms of the tetrapod supports remain unslipped. The pot stand (Vessel 5 from Room 8, Building B) is heavily fire-clouded making the surface appear almost black, but the characteristic Sierra Red slip is unmistakable.

Forms: The only two forms of this unspecified variety are

1. a vase with vertical yet slightly outflaring sides, a direct rim, rounded lip, and four hollow mammiform supports with vertical vents and nubbin tips; rim diameter is 11.5 cm, wall thickness 0.8 cm, and height 15 cm and

2. a "cotton reel" pot stand with flaring ends and cylindrical central section with small holes cut into the body; rim diameter is 9.5 cm, wall thickness 0.6 cm, and height 1.7 cm.

Intraregional locations and contexts: This type: variety is only found in Room 8 of Building B, Group II at Holmul.

Interregional locations and contexts: Sierra Red with mammiform supports dating to the Terminal Preclassic period also occurs at Chan Chich, Belize, in Tomb 2 (Houk et al. 2010:Figure 8a–d) and Buena Vista del Cayo, Belize (Brady et al. 1998:Figure 3f). Pring (2000:63) identified Vessel 1 in Chultun B at Tzimin Kax as Sierra Red as well as Vessel 1 at Cahal Cunil in Vaulted Chamber 1 (Pring 2000:67). Incised and dichrome types with mammiform supports belonging to the Sierra Group are also found in Terminal Preclassic period deposits. At Nohmul, Pring (2000:85 and Figure 45) identified Vessel 13 as Laguna Verde Incised: Grooved Incised Variety. At Chan Chich in Tomb 2, Houk and colleagues (2010: Figure 8i) identified Vessel 11 as Matamore Dichrome: Variety Unspecified. Examples also come from Buena Vista del Cayo, Belize (Brady et al. 1998:Figure 3a). Sierra Red pot stands are not reported elsewhere, but red-on-orange, polychrome, and monochrome red examples are also noted at Tzimin Kax and Nohmul (see Pring 2000:61, 66, 80).

Comment: While the Sierra Red type of ceramic is not new to the Terminal Classic subcomplex, the specific vase with mammiform tetrapod supports and pot stand forms are new to the ceramic inventory. Like the other types listed in this subcomplex, these Sierra Red forms represent a unique Terminal Preclassic period combination of form and surface modes. I identified these two vessels as Variety Unspecified not because I think they resemble Unspecified Varieties of Sierra Red previously defined at any other site, but because their attributes do not allow me to place them in any other established variety of Sierra Red. Furthermore, the sample is so small that it does not meet my threshold of 50 rim sherds to establish a new variety. Pring (2000:48–49) suggested this vessel could be Puletan Red-and-unslipped. Although there are a handful of Sierra red-and-unslipped sherds in the region, I hesitate to identify Vessel 5 as Puletan. As mentioned in Chapter 4, the sample of red-and-unslipped ceramics in the region is small and not identifiable as Puletan, so I am not comfortable placing these sherds in the Puletan type. Furthermore, while Vessel 5 is red-and-unslipped, I do not think this is decorative, as is the case with true Puletan types (see Kosakowsky 1987:73–75; Pring 1977b). The unslipped portions of the vessel would not be visible because they occur within the body of the cotton reel and on the base. I think that Vessel 5 is better left as an Unspecified Variety of Sierra Red.

Illustration: Figure 5.1a.

Figure 5.1. Sierra Red: Variety Unspecified (Wayab): (a1) HOL.TGRP.2.BLDG B.V2.R.8 and (a2) HOL. TGRP.2.BLDG B.V5.R8. Flor Cream: Variety Unspecified (Wayab): (b1) HOL.TGRP.2.BLDG B. V9.R8V. Accordian Incised: Variety Unspecified (Wayab): (c1) HOL.TGRP.2.BLDG B.V5.R.9. Aguila Orange: Variety Unspecified (Wayab): (d1) HOL.TGRP.2.BLDG B.V3.R9, (d2) HOL.TGRP.2.BLDG B.V7.R9, (d3) HOL.L.63.01, and (d4) HOL.T.GRP.2.BLDG B.V8.R.8. Drawings by Fernando Alvarez (Holmul Archaeological Project).

Flor Cream: Variety Unspecified (Wayab)

Established: Type named by Smith & Gifford (1966:158,170), Variety named by Callaghan in this study.
Group: Flor
Ware: Paso Caballo Waxy
Subcomplex: Wayab
Sphere: Floral Park
Ceramic Group Frequency: 1 whole vessel (Vessel 9, Room 8 Vault, Building B; see Appendix A), 1 total, 50 percent of group, 3.4 percent of subcomplex.
Principal identifying attributes: (1) Thick cream slip, (2) pink and blue painted stucco exterior, (3) buff colored paste, and (4) jar with bridge spout.
Paste, firing, and temper: Because this was a whole vessel, paste composition and texture were difficult to identify. Paste that was showing through on the eroded surface appears medium in texture with crystalline calcite inclusions. The color is buff (10YR7/3) or yellow (10YR7/4).
Surface finish and decoration: The vessel surface was well-smoothed then covered with a white cream slip (10YR8/1). Sometime after the vessel was slipped, stucco was applied to the exterior surface. The stucco was then painted with pink and blue pigments. Designs are geometric and consist of step motifs and one crossed "x" pattern.
Forms: Pitcher (jar) with bridge spout. The rim diameter is 11cm, wall thickness 0.6 cm, neck height 3.7 cm, and height 14.5 cm.
Intraregional locations and contexts: The vessel representing this type: variety was discovered in the Room 8 Vault of Building B, Group II at Holmul.
Interregional locations and contexts: Incised cream or red-and-buff pitchers appear in Tomb 2 at Chan Chich (Houk et al. 2010:Figure 7) as well as burial contexts at Colha and Lamanai (Powis et al. 2002). Pitchers, in the Sierra Red type, appear in burial contexts and ritual deposits at K'axob (Berry et al. 2004) and Cuello (Kosakowsky 1987:83-85). This shows there might be a positive correlation between pitcher forms and special deposits.
Comment: The combination of surface and form modes on this vessel represents a mixture of Late Preclassic and Early Classic characteristics. The bridge-spout pitcher form is a strong Late Preclassic period mode, as is the waxy cream slip. The painted stucco decoration is more common in Early Classic types—specifically Balanza Black (described in Chapter 6). Pring (2000:50–51) identified this vessel as Unnamed Early Classic Buff: Variety Unspecified (stucco added). I am more comfortable placing this vessel in the Flor Group because its form, surface, finish, and paste composition seem quite similar to Flor examples found elsewhere in the Holmul region during the Late Preclassic period. Vessel 9 displays no slip, polishing, form, or paste attributes that resemble Early Classic pottery. An Early Classic mode present on the vessel, however, is the application of stucco with polychrome painting. It is quite possible that this vessel was first produced in the tradition of Flor Cream ceramics, then covered in stucco and painted in a decorative tradition of the Early Classic period. That is why Vessel 9 is such an excellent of Terminal Preclassic pottery—it displays a combination of Late Preclassic and Early Classic modes. As is the case with the Sierra Group ceramics previously described, this vessel is classified as Variety Unspecified because its attributes do not allow me to place it in any established variety of Flor Cream. Furthermore, the sample is so small that it does not meet my threshold of 50 rim sherds to establish a new variety.
Illustration: Figure 5.1b.

Accordian Incised: Variety Unspecified (Wayab)

Established: Type named Smith & Gifford (1966:154, 170), Variety by Callaghan in this study.
Group: Flor
Ware: Paso Caballo Waxy
Subcomplex: Wayab
Sphere: Floral Park
Ceramic Group Frequency: 1 whole vessel (Vessel 5, Room 9, Building B, see Appendix 4), 1 total, 50 percent of group, 3.4 percent of subcomplex.
Principal identifying attributes: (1) Waxy polished vessel surfaces, (2) thick cream slip, (3) post-slip incision, (4) buff colored paste, and (5) jar with bridge spout.
Paste, firing, and temper: Paste, temper, and firing were difficult to identify on this sample because the vessel was on display behind glass at the Peabody Museum in Cambridge, Massachusetts. It appeared to be similar to Flor Cream. Paste color was buff to pink and appeared to be medium in texture.
Surface finish and decoration: The vessel surface was highly burnished with a thick yellow-cream slip. Incised lines were created after the slip was applied because the buff-colored paste shows through to the surface. The incision occurs in double-line circumferential bands below the rim at the shoulder break and as partial circular "wave" patterns around the body of the vessel exterior.
Forms: Jar (pitcher) with bridge-spout. The rim diameter is 11 cm, wall thickness 0.7 cm, neck height 3.2 cm, and height 13 cm (measurements from Pring 2000:55).

Intraregional locations and contexts: The vessel representing this type: variety of Accordian Incised was found in Room 9 of Building B, in Group II at Holmul.

Interregional locations and contexts: Cream or red-and-buff incised pitchers appear in Tomb 2 at Chan Chich (Houk et al. 2010:Figure 7) as well as in burial contexts at Colha and Lamanai (Powis et al. 2002). Remember, pitcher forms of Sierra Red types were found in burial and special deposits at K'axob (Berry et al. 2004) and Cuello (Kosakowsky 1987-83-85), suggesting pitchers may be positively correlated with ritual deposits.

Comments: Pring (2000:55) identifies Vessel 5, Room 9, as Preclassic Buff: Unnamed Incised. After viewing the material myself, and having the benefit of studying the present corpus Holmul region ceramics, I am comfortable identifying this vessel as Accordian Incised: Variety Unspecified. Like Vessel 9, Room 8, this vessel displays a combination of unmistakable Late Preclassic modes combined with an Early Classic mode. The Late Preclassic modes include form (i.e., jar with spout), surface finish (a waxy cream slip with post-slip incision), and paste (buff-colored and possibly containing crystalline calcite). The Early Classic mode is related to form, namely the ring base. This vessel does not resemble any Unspecified Variety of Accordian Incised previously defined at other sites and its attributes do not allow me to place it in any other established variety of Accordian Incised. The sample of one does not meet my threshold of 50 rim sherds to establish a new variety.

Illustration: Figure 5.1c.

Aguila Orange: Variety Unspecified (Wayab)

Established: Type named by Smith and Gifford (1966:151, 170), Variety named by Pring (2000:50).
   Group: Aguila
   Ware: Petén Gloss
   Ceramic Subcomplex: Wayab
   Sphere: Floral Park
Ceramic Group Frequency: 3 whole vessels (Vessel 8, Room 8 Vault; Vessels 3 and 7, Room 9 all from Building B, Group 2 at Holmul, see Appendix 4), 3 rims, 6 total, 100 percent of group, 20.7 percent of subcomplex.
Principal identifying attributes: (1) Orange slip, (2) highly polished surface, (3) bowls with z-angles and tetrapod supports, and (4) bowls with round sides and annular bases.
Paste, firing, and temper: The paste is medium to fine in texture. Aplastics can include crushed volcanic glass with slivers of mica, or even sherd temper, but are more

generally carbonate-based with well rounded, medium-fine, gray calcite inclusions. Paste color is relatively consistent and remains buff (10YR8/3; 2.5YR7/3) or light brown (10YR6/3) throughout the sample.

Surface finish and decoration: Surfaces are well-smoothed and polished. Surface color is a rather brilliant orange (5YR5/8, 6/8; 2.5YR5/8)

Forms:
   1. Plate with flaring sides, slightly everted rim, rounded lip, flat base, and four large supports; rim diameter is 36 cm, wall thickness 1 cm, and height 14 cm;
   2. bowl with outcurving sides, direct rim, rounded lip, convex base, and four large hollow supports; rim diameter is 25 cm, wall thickness 0.9 cm, and height 14 cm; and
   3. bowl with rounded sides and annular base; rim diameter is 23.5 cm, wall thickness 0.7 cm, and height 11 cm.

   Some hollow mammiform supports have been found mixed in fill contexts, but whether these sherds belong to Aguila monochrome types or Ixcanrio Polychromes is impossible to tell.

Intraregional locations and contexts: Aguila Orange pottery of the Terminal Preclassic subcomplex has been found almost exclusively in fill contexts of Building B Group II. The whole vessels came from Building B, Room 8 Vault (Vessel 8) and Building B, Room 9 (Vessels 3 and 7) at Holmul.

Interregional locations and contexts: Aguila Orange material dating to the Terminal Preclassic period can be found at Naj Tunich Cave in Guatemala where Brady (1989) classified it as Aguila Orange: La Compuerta Variety. At Edzná, Forsyth (1983:63–64) also defined an Aguila Orange: Variety Unspecified with a cream under-slip that occurs in a bowl form with flaring sides. This is not, however, the same as the Variety Unspecified in the Holmul region.

Comment: It is important to note that the type: variety described here fits well within the definition of Aguila Group ceramics. Noted in the introduction to this chapter, no samples of Aguacate Orange material have been found in the Holmul region. It is worth noting the difference between the two groups here. Because of the excellent preservation of cave ceramics, Brady (1989) was able to distinguish Aguila Orange material from orange ceramics belonging to the dull or matte finish Aguacate Group of Holmul Orange Ware previously established by Gifford (1976:129–137) at Barton Ramie and belonging to the Floral Park Ceramic Sphere. Brady and colleagues (1998) distinguished Aguila Orange of the Terminal Preclassic period from Aguacate Orange through the presence of a thin cream underslip or light colored paste which has been polished to a high shine. Brady and colleagues (1998) also note specific form modes (e.g., large bulbous mammiform supports in Aguila material and smaller supports in Aguacate) and surface modes (Aguila Orange material has a thick orange slip that is highly polished while Aguacate displays a thin slip and remains dull) that distinguish the two types of material. In his previous analysis of pottery from Room 8, the Room 8 Vault, and Room 9 of Building B, Group II at Holmul, Pring (2000:50, 53, 56) classifies the orange pottery as Aguila Orange: Variety Unspecified material. He notes that the combination of high polish and lack of distinct pink Aguacate paste on these vessels factored greatly into his classification. I agree with Pring. I identify these samples as Variety Unspecified not because they resemble an Unspecified Variety of Aguila Orange previously defined at any other site, but because their attributes do not allow me to place them in any other established variety of Aguila Orange. The sample t does not meet my threshold of 50 rim sherds to establish a new variety.

Illustration: Figure 5.1d.

Ixcanrio Orange Polychrome: Ixcanrio Variety

Established: Willey and Gifford 1961.
Group: Ixcanrio
Ware: Petén Gloss
Subcomplex: Wayab
Sphere: Floral Park
Ceramic Group Frequency: 6 rims, 4 bodies, 2 whole vessels (Vessel 4, Room 9, and Vessel 6 Room 9 both from Building B, Group 2 at Holmul, see Appendix 4), 12 total, 57.1 percent of group, 27.6 percent of subcomplex.
Principal identifying attributes: (1) Glossy surface treatment resulting from cream underslip or highly polished preslip vessel surfaces; (2) polychrome painting over orange slip; (3) design motifs include dotted lines, step frets, circumferential bands and other geometric patterns; and (4) bowls with tetrapod supports.
Paste, firing, and temper: Paste color varies from buff (10YR8/3) to yellow (10YR7/3). Primary inclusions also vary, with the majority of pastes being carbonate-based with medium- to fine-grained inclusions, primarily calcite. Three major paste variants have been identified including (1) yellow (10YR7/3), medium-fine, with well-rounded gray calcite inclusions; (2) yellow (10YR7/3),

medium-fine, with sherd and crystal calcite inclusions (this paste is more similar to Late Preclassic pastes of Sierra Red material); and (3) yellow (10YR7/3), fine, with volcanic glass and muscovite inclusions.

Surface finish and decoration: Vessel surfaces are highly polished. No evidence of cream underslip was found on the sherds used in this study. However, signs of underslip appeared on the surface of vessels in the Peabody Museum. Polychrome painting is executed over an orange slip surface with color within the range of 5YR5/8, 6/8, and 2.5YR5/8. Designs include red (10R4/8) or black horizontal circumferential bands, dotted lines, step frets, mat patterns, and other geometric shapes.
Forms:
  1. Bowl with outcurving walls, direct rim, rounded lip, convex base, and hollow tetrapod supports (mammiform, cylindrical, or bulbous); rim diameter is 26.5 cm, wall thickness 0.7 cm, and height 12.5 cm; and
  2. vase with flaring sides and chamfer, everted rim with rounded lip, and bulbous supports; rim diameter is 10 cm, wall thickness 0.6 cm, and height 19.5 cm.

Intraregional locations and contexts: The whole Ixcanrio vessels were found in vaulted tombs of Building B, Group 2 at Holmul (Merwin and Vaillant 1932; Neivens 2005). Only a handful of sherds were found in fill within the earlier phases of Building B.

Interregional locations and contexts: Ixcanrio Orange Polychrome has been identified at Barton Ramie (Gifford 1976:143–145), Naj Tunich (Brady 1989), Nohmul, Mountain Cow, and Chetumal (Pring 2000), the Valle de Dolores (Laporte et al. 1993:87), Uaxactun (Smith and Gifford 1966:158), Tikal (Laporte et al. 1992:Figure 22), Altar de Sacrificios (Adams 1971:36), Colha (Valdes 1987:152–154), and K'axob (Berry et al. 2004:250–251). It appears as an Unnamed Orange Polychrome: Ixcanrio Orange Polychrome at El Mirador (Forsyth 1989:57), and as an Unspecified Variety at Edzná (Forsyth 1983:65). See Pring 2000 for a comprehensive listing of the distributions of Ixcanrio and other Terminal Preclassic markers.

Comment: Smith and Gifford (1966:158) place Ixcanrio within Holmul Orange Ware and the Aguacate Orange Ceramic Group, but Ixcanrio clearly displays the glossy surface treatment characteristic of Petén Gloss Ware. At El Mirador Forsyth (1989:57) places Ixcanrio in the Aguila Ceramic Group of Petén Gloss Ware as does Laporte and colleagues (Laporte et al. 1993:87) in the Valle de Dolores. Pring (2000:54–56) identified Vessels

4 and 6 from Building B, Group 2 as Ixcanrio Orange Polychrome: Variety Unspecified, but also suggests they are probably Ixcanrio Variety. I agree with Pring, and feel quite comfortable identifying these vessels and sherds as Ixcanrio Orange Polychrome: Ixcanrio Variety. What I think defines them as Ixcanrio Variety is their telltale geometric designs. As I explain in the following descriptions other type: varieties of Ixcanrio Orange Polychrome can be distinguished by the design elements.

Illustration: Figure 5.2a.

Ixcanrio Orange Polychrome: Turnbull Variety

Established: Type named by Willey and Gifford 1961; Variety named by Pring (1977b) for northern Belize.

Group: Ixcanrio
Ware: Petén Gloss
Subcomplex: Wayab
Sphere: Floral Park
Ceramic Group Frequency: 1 rim, 1 whole vessel (Vessel 1, Room 9, Building B, Group 2 at Holmul, see Appendix 4), 2 total, 14.3 percent of group, 6.9 percent of subcomplex

Principal identifying attributes: (1) Glossy surface treatment, (2) polychrome painting over orange slip, (3) design motifs include vertical parallel squiggly lines, and (4) bowl with annular base.

Paste, firing, and temper: Paste, temper, and firing are similar to Ixcanrio Orange Polychrome: Ixcanrio Variety.

Surface finish and decoration: Vessel surfaces are highly polished. The glossy surface treatment could have resulted from the application of a cream underslip or a highly polished preslip surface. Polychrome painting was executed over an orange slip surface with color within the range of variation for other Terminal Preclassic orange gloss ware (5YR5/8, 6/8; 2.5YR5/8). Designs include red (10R4/8) or black horizontal circumferential rim bands and characteristic groups of vertical parallel squiggly black lines.

Forms: Bowl with round sides, direct rim, rounded lip, and annular base. Rim diameter is 26 cm, wall thickness 0.6 cm, and height 12 cm.

Intraregional locations and contexts: Only one whole Ixcanrio Orange Polychrome: Turnbull Variety vessel has been found at Holmul. This is Vessel 1 of Room 9 in Building B, Group II (Merwin and Vaillant 1932). One sherd has been found at La Sufricaya.

Interregional locations and contexts: Ixcanrio Orange Polychrome: Turnbull Variety has been found at Nohmul

(Pring 2000:82–84, 87). At Tikal, Culbert (1993: Figure 139, b1) classified a similar looking tetrapod bowl with black-on-orange design as Sacluc Black-on-orange: Xux Variety.

Comment: Because of its extreme scarcity in the Holmul region and more common occurrence at sites in northern Belize (Pring 1977b), it is probable that this variety of Ixcanrio is an import into the area, possibly from Belize.

Illustration: Figure 5.2b.

Ixcanrio Orange Polychrome: Variety Unspecified (Wayab)

Established: Type named by Willey and Gifford 1961, Variety named by Callaghan (2008) at Holmul.

Group: Ixcanrio
Ware: Petén Gloss
Subcomplex: Wayab
Sphere: Floral Park
Ceramic Group Frequency: 1 rim, 3 whole vessels (Vessel 10, Room 8 Vault; Vessel 2, Room 9, and SF# HOL.T.41.10.02.01 all from Building B, Group 2 at Holmul, see Appendix 4), 4 total, 28.6 percent of group, 13.8 percent of subcomplex.

Principal identifying attributes: (1) Glossy surface, (2) polychrome painting over orange slip, (3) design motifs include complicated abstract or conventionalized objects, and (4) bowls with tetrapod supports.

Paste, firing, and temper: Paste color varies from buff (10YR8/3) to yellow (10YR7/3). Two samples were whole vessels currently housed at the Peabody Museum in Cambridge, Massachusetts and no paste sections could be studied. The other sample was a whole vessel found in Burial 10 in Building B, Group II at Holmul (Neivens 2005). From the surface, pastes appear to have medium to fine textures and are buff to yellow in color. Hammond (1984:10), Pring (2000:51–52), and I (2008:134) have noted the presence of sherd temper, which is visible in the surface of Peabody vessel c5650 (Vessel 10 from the Room 8 Vault of Building B, Group II). It is possible these vessels are as varied in paste composition as Ixcanrio Orange Polychrome: Ixcanrio Variety.

Surface finish and decoration: Vessel surfaces are highly polished and orange (5YR5/8, 6/8; 2.5YR5/8). The glossy surfaces could be the result of a cream underslip or highly polished preslip, as exemplified in the other Aguila Group ceramics. One of the characteristics that distinguish these unspecified vessels from Ixcanrio

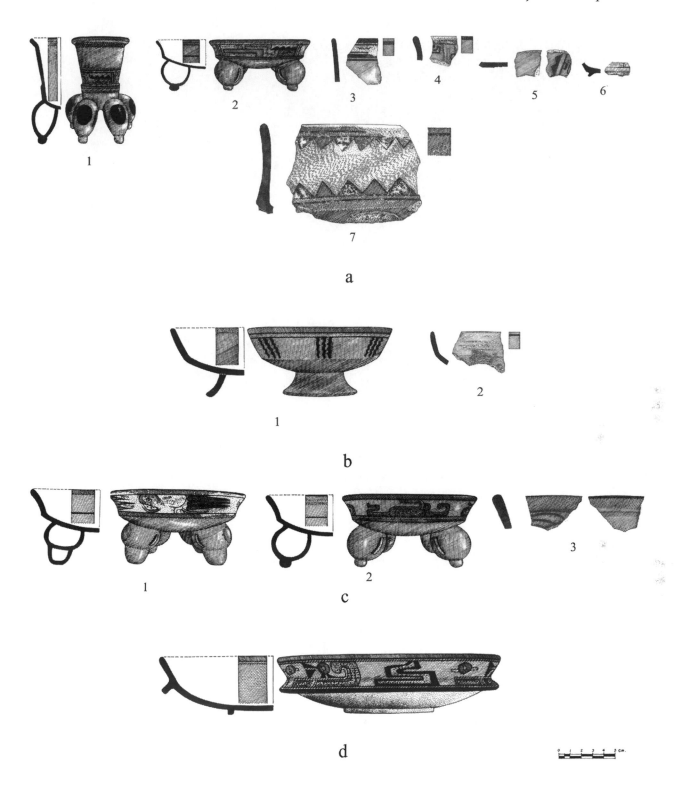

Figure 5.2. Ixcanrio Orange Polychrome: Ixcanrio Variety: (a1) HOL.T.GRP.2.BLDG B.V6.R9, (a2) HOL. TGRP.2.BLDG B.V4.R9, (a3) KOL.T.13.05, (a4) HOL.T.41.06, (a5) BLDG.B.R1, (a6) HOL.T.49.04, and (a7) Unknown provenance. Ixcanrio Orange Polychrome: Turnbull Variety: (b1) HOL.TGRP.2.BLDG B.V1.R9 and (b2) SUF.L.08.00. Ixcanrio Orange Polychrome: Variety Unspecified (Wayab): (c1) HOL.TGRP.2.BLDG B.V10. R8V, (c2) HOL.TGRP.2.BLDG B.V2.R9, and (c3) N/A. Actuncan Orange Polychrome: Variety Unspecified (Wayab): (d1) HOL.T.GRP.2.BLDG B.V4.R8. Drawings by Fernando Alvarez (Holmul Archaeological Project).

Figure 5.3 Ixcanrio Orange Polychrome: Variety Unspecified (Wayab)
(Pot 1 Burial 10 from Holmul). Photo by Michael G. Callaghan.

Variety is the cream or buff (10YR8/2) background panels on which the main design is applied. Also, the main designs consist of more complex conventionalized themes such as the macaw on Vessel 10 (Figure 5.2c1), the serpent motif on Vessel 2 (Figure 5.2c2), and the weave or mat pattern on SF# HOL.T.41.10.02.01 (Figure 5.3). These are not like the simple geometric patterns of Ixcanrio Orange Polychrome: Ixcanrio Variety.

Forms: Bowls with outcurving sides, direct rims, rounded lips, convex bases, and hollow tetrapod supports (mammiform, cylindrical, or bulbous).Rim diameters measure 22.5 to 24 cm, wall thicknesses 0.7 to .95 cm, and heights 13 cm.

Intraregional locations and contexts: Whole Ixcanrio: Variety Unspecified (Wayab) vessels are only found in vaulted tombs of Building B, Group II (Merwin and Vaillant 1932) and in a burial cist also found in Building B, Group II (Neivens 2005) at Holmul. A single sherd was found associated within this same excavation.

Interregional locations and contexts: Similar varieties appear at Naj Tunich (Brady 1989) and Chetumal (Pring 2000).

Comment: These varieties of Ixcanrio appear to be better executed than the Ixcanrio Orange Polychrome: Ixcanrio Variety examples. Forms are tighter, with straighter lines and designs that are more complex, both in composition and execution. Because these are all whole vessels, it is impossible to get a better look at paste characteristics without partially destroying them, but they appear to represent a range of different paste types. I classify these samples as Variety Unspecified not because I believe they resemble an Unspecified Variety of Ixcanrio Orange Polychrome previously defined at any other site, but because their attributes do not allow me to place them in any other established variety of Ixcanrio Orange Polychrome. The sample does not meet my threshold of 50 rim sherds to establish a new variety.

Illustration: Figures 5.2c and 5.3.

Actuncan Orange Polychrome: Variety Unspecified (Wayab)

Established: Type named Smith and Gifford (1966:154, 171); Variety named by Pring 2000.

Group: Actuncan

Ware: Petén Gloss

Subcomplex: Wayab

Sphere: Floral Park

Ceramic Group Frequency: 1 whole vessel (Vessel 4, Room 8 of Building B, Group II, see Appendix 4), 1 total, 100 percent of group, 3.4 percent of subcomplex

Principal identifying attributes: (1) Orange slip, (2) highly polished vessel surfaces, (3) red and black paint on orange background, (4) design includes simple geometric patterns and dotted lines, and (5) bowl with composite sides, basal flange, and ring base.

Paste, firing, and temper: The only example of this type-variety is Vessel 4 from Room 8, Building B, Group II at Holmul. The vessel was on display behind glass at the Peabody Museum in Cambridge, Massachusetts. Paste characteristics were difficult to identify firsthand.

Surface finish and decoration: The interior and exterior surfaces are well-smoothed and highly polished. A cream underslip may have been applied before the application of an orange (5YR 6/6) slip, which acts as a background for painting. Red (10R4/8) and black horizontal circumferential bands are painted on or just below the lip of the vessel interior and exterior. The exterior design motifs include complex geometric patterns executed with the use of dotted lines.

Forms: Bowl with composite sides, basal flange, direct rim, and rounded lip. Rim diameter measures 32 cm, wall thicknesses 0.7 to 0.9 cm, and height 8 cm (measurements from Pring 2000:48).

Intraregional locations and contexts: Actuncan Orange Polychrome: Actuncan Variety can be found at La Sufricaya, K'o, Holmul, Hamontun, and Cival.

Interregional locations and contexts: Actuncan Orange Polychrome: Actuncan Variety appears at Uaxactun (Smith and Gifford 1966:154), Barton Ramie (Gifford 1976:170–173), Altar de Sacrificios (Adams 1971:36–37), Yaxchilan (Lopez Varela 1989:85), K'axob (Berry et al. 252–253, 256–259), Colha (Valdes 1987:169–172), and is subsumed under Actuncan/Dos Arroyos at Seibal because of poor preservation (Sabloff 1975:105). None of these are the Unspecified Variety described here.

Comment: This is undoubtedly an early facet Early Classic type: variety, but like the other type-varieties in this subcomplex, Actuncan Orange Polychrome crosscuts the end of the Late Preclassic and beginning of the Early Classic periods. It is found associated with other Terminal Preclassic subcomplex type: varieties in ritual deposits and that is why I include it in this subcomplex. I identify this sample as Variety Unspecified not because I believe it resembles an Unspecified Variety of Actuncan Orange Polychrome previously defined at any other site, but because its attributes do not allow me to place it in any other established variety of Actuncan Orange Polychrome. Furthermore, the sample does not meet my threshold of 50 rim sherds to establish a new variety.

Illustration: Figure 5.2d.

CHAPTER SIX

K'ak Complex

Michael G. Callaghan

The K'ak Complex dates between AD 230 and 550. Dates were determined through a combination of radiocarbon samples (Estrada-Belli 2006b:65) (see Table 1.2) and typological comparison to other sites. While there is no radiocarbon date associated with the beginning of the K'ak Complex, the complex began sometime after AD 230. This date comes from bone found in Terminal Preclassic period Burial 10 within Building B, Group II at Holmul, which returned a date of AD 120 to 230 (Estrada-Belli 2006a:4). There is no radiocarbon date associated with the end of the complex, but using typological comparison to ceramics from other lowland complexes, as well as contextual data from deposits related to inscriptions in Building A, Group II at Holmul (see Chapter 1), it is reasonable to propose an end date of approximately AD 550.

Descriptions of K'ak material included in this study come from 2,098 rim sherds, 10,984 diagnostic body sherds, and 64 whole vessels for a total of 13,145 samples. Three wares (1 Unspecified), 8 groups, and 25 type: varieties define the K'ak Complex (Table 6.1). The majority of type-varieties are slipped (79 percent). There is a noticeable increase in unslipped type: varieties from the preceding Preclassic periods, although this might be a function of Middle and Late Preclassic mixed deposits. Typologically, K'ak ceramics resemble material of the Tzakol sphere during the Early Classic period in the Maya lowlands. Here I separate the K'ak Complex into three facets: K'ak 1 (early), K'ak 2 (middle), and K'ak 3 (late). It is important to note that these facets do not represent distinct and separate ceramic complexes. Instead, these facets are distinguished from one another based on the appearance and disappearance of diagnostic types, as well as changes in modes of established Early Classic type: varieties.

K'ak 1 facet ceramics belong to the larger Tzakol Sphere (Tzakol 1 facet), first defined by Smith (1955:23–24; see also Willey et al. 1967:298–299) and Smith and Gifford (1966:171) for Uaxactun; they date between AD 230 and 300. During K'ak 1, the ceramics from the Aguila, Balanza, Dos Hermanos, and Quintal Groups make an appearance. Diagnostic types of the K'ak 1 facet include Actuncan Orange Polychrome and Boleto Black-on-orange. Modal differences distinguish K'ak 1 types from later K'ak 2 and 3 types. Most important are paste and form modes within the Aguila Group. K'ak 1 Aguila pastes are buff-colored and loaded with small spheres of gray calcite (i.e., peloid calcite). Form modes of K'ak 1 Aguila Orange include rounded-z angles on bowl forms and rounded lip treatments. Basal flanges occur on Aguila and Actuncan Group ceramics, but are small in size. Ring bases become frequent. Composite bowl forms are not as tall as later K'ak 2 forms. Significant deposits of K'ak 1 ceramics include the Room 8 Vault and Room 7 in Building B, Group II at Holmul, as well as contexts at the site of Hamontun. K'ak 2 facet ceramics are contemporaneous with Tzakol sphere (Tzakol 2 facet) ceramics as defined by Smith (1955:23–24; see also Willey et al. 1967:298–299) and Smith and Gifford (1966:171) for Uaxactun and may date between AD 300 and 450. They are also contemporaneous with Manik 2 Complex ceramics at Tikal (Culbert 1993, 2003, 2006). During the K'ak 2 facet, Actuncan Orange Polychrome and Boleto Black-on-orange disappeared. Dos Arroyos Orange Polychrome

Table 6.1. Ceramic Wares, Groups, Types, and Varieties of the Early Classic Period (K'ak Complex)

Ware	Group (% of complex)	Type: Variety	Numbers			Percentages	
			Rims	Bodies	Vessels	Group	Complex
Uaxactun Unslipped	Quintal (18%)	Quintal Unslipped: Quintal Variety	346	1982	0	88.9	16.0
		Quintal Unslipped: Variety Unspecified	0	0	2	0.5	0.1
		Triunfo Striated: Triunfo Variety	38	2474	1	10.0	1.8
		Triunfo Striated: Variety Unspecified	0	0	1	0.3	0.05
	Unnamed (0.0%)	Unnamed Unslipped and Modeled (K'ak)	0	0	1	0.3	0.05
Unspecified	Paxbán (3.0%)	Paxbán Unslipped: Paxbán Variety	64	127	0	100.0	3.0
Petén Gloss	Aguila (54.9%)	Aguila Orange: Aguila Variety	919	4460	9	78.2	42.9
		Pita Incised: Pita Variety	76	80	1	6.5	3.6
		Nitan Composite: Nitan Variety	119	28	4	10.4	5.7
		Bocul Orange-on-cream: Bocul Variety	49	96	1	4.2	2.3
		Bocul Orange-on-cream: Variety Unspecified	7	5	0	0.6	0.3
		Unnamed Modeled			1	0.1	0.05
	Dos Hermanos (0.3%)	Dos Hermanos Red: Dos Hermanos Variety	4	10	2	100.0	0.3
	Balanza (17.6%)	Balanza Black: Balanza Variety	246	1479	9	66.9	11.8
		Lucha Incised: Lucha Variety	101	105	11	29.4	5.2
		Lucha Incised: Variety Unspecified	0	0	2	0.5	0.1
		Urita Gouged-incised: Urita Variety	10	22	2	3.1	0.6
		Positas Modeled: Positas Variety	0	10	0	0.0	<0.01
	Actuncan (2.1%)	Actuncan Orange Polychrome: Actuncan Variety	21	4	1	48.9	1.0
		Boleto Black-on-orange: Boleto Variety	20	2	3	51.1	1.1
	Dos Arroyos (3.9%)	Dos Arroyos Orange Polychrome: Dos Arroyos Variety	59	72	4	75.0	2.9
		Caldero Buff Polychrome: Caldero Variety	19	28	2	25.0	1.0
	Japon (0.1%)	Japon Resist: Japon Variety	0	0	2	100.0	0.1
	Unnamed (0.2%)	Unnamed Polychrome (K'ak)	0	0	2		0.1
		Unnamed Red Slipped (K'ak 2-3)	0	0	3		0.1
		TOTALS	2098	10,984	64		

and Caldero Buff Polychrome appeared. Polychrome painting design on these two types is more complex than previous polychrome types. Composite bowl forms with basal flanges are wider and taller, and flanges become much larger. Lids appear at this time, often with modeled handles. Rounded z-angle and z-angle forms diminish in frequency. Incision on Balanza Group vessels becomes more ornate and complex—specifically within the Lucha Incised and Urita Gouged-incised types. Significant deposits of K'ak 2 material include Rooms 1 and 2 in Building B, Group II at Holmul, as well as some deposits at La Sufricaya and Cival.

K'ak 3 facet material is part of the Tzakol ceramic sphere (Tzakol 3 facet) as defined by Smith (1955:23–24; Willey et al. 1967:298–199) and Smith and Gifford (1966:171) at Uaxactun and may date between AD 450 and 550. They are also contemporaneous with Manik 3 ceramics at Tikal (Culbert 1993, 2003, 2006; Laporte et al. 1992). The K'ak 3 facet is characterized by the addition of one new Unspecified Ware, new type-varieties, and modal changes within existing types. The new Unspecified Ware is defined by light-colored volcanic ash-tempered paste. This ware is comprised of unslipped small, flaring bowl forms and unconventional modeled and applique forms. All of these vessels appear to be censers. New type: varieties in the established Petén Gloss Ware include Bocul Orange-on-cream: Bocul Variety and Bocul Orange-on-cream: Unspecified Variety. Modal changes in Aguila Orange include the increased use of pastes with volcanic ash inclusions, wider open plate and bowl forms with shorter sides, and smaller flanges. Form modes indicative of K'ak 3 facet ceramics include large bucket shapes with everted rims (both in the Aguila and Balanza Groups) as well as cylinders with solid (sometimes slab) tripod supports. The most significant K'ak 3 deposits are found in Structure 1 at La Sufricaya. The wares are described briefly, followed by type descriptions for the larger K'ak Complex. I make note of specific facet markers within the "comments" sections. Interpretations of the K'ak Complex and changes during its three phases can be found in Chapter 8.

UAXCATUN UNSLIPPED WARE

Smith and Gifford (1966:169) established this ware at Uaxactun. It is characterized by roughly smoothed unslipped surfaces. Decoration includes striation, applique, and modeling. Vessel surfaces are the color of pastes (7.5YR5/2, 4/2). Pastes are coarse to medium in texture with primary inclusions of crystalline calcite. Type: varieties within Uaxactun Unslipped Ware dating to the K'ak Complex include

> Quintal Group
> Quintal Unslipped: Quintal Variety
> Quintal Unslipped: Variety Unspecified
> Triunfo Striated: Triunfo Variety
> Triunfo Striated: Variety Unspecified
> Unnamed Group
> Unnamed Unslipped and Modeled (K'ak)

PETÉN GLOSS WARE

Smith and Gifford (1966:167–168) defined Petén Gloss Ware at Uaxactun. Surfaces are well smoothed and polished to a shine. No polish or burnish marks are visible. Slip color in the Early Classic is predominantly orange (2.5YR5/8; 5YR5/8, 6/8), black, and red (10R4/8). Decoration includes incision, gouged-incision, scratching, punctation, impressing, polychrome painting (red-and-black-on-orange, red-and-black-on-buff), black-on-orange painting, resist, modeling, and applique. Pastes are light-colored and range from yellow (10YR7/4, 7/3) to buff (10YR8/2). Common inclusions are volcanic ash, crystalline calcite, and spherical gray calcite. Groups and type: varieties within Petén Gloss Ware of the K'ak Complex include

> Aguila Group
> Aguila Orange: Aguila Variety
> Pita Incised: Pita Variety
> Nitan Composite: Nitan Variety
> Bocul Orange-on-cream: Bocul Variety
> Bocul Orange-on-cream: Variety Unspecified
> Unnamed Modeled (Aguila Group)
> Dos Hermanos Group
> Dos Hermanos Red: Dos Hermanos Variety
> Balanza Group
> Balanza Black: Balanza Variety
> Lucha Incised: Lucha Variety
> Lucha Incised: Variety Unspecified
> Urita Gouged-incised: Urita Variety
> Positas Modeled: Positas Variety
> Actuncan Group
> Actuncan Orange Polychrome: Actuncan Variety
> Boleto Black-on-orange: Boleto Variety
> Dos Arroyos Group
> Dos Arroyos Orange Polychrome: Dos Arroyos Variety

Caldero Buff Polychrome: Caldero Variety
Japon Group
    Japon Resist: Japon Variety
Unnamed Group
    Unnamed Polychrome (K'ak)
    Unnamed Red Slipped (K'ak 2-3)

UNSPECIFIED WARE

This Unspecified Ware of the K'ak 3 facet has not been previously defined. Surfaces are very well-smoothed and left unslipped. The surfaces are the color of pastes, either light gray or white (10YR8/2). Decoration, when present, takes the form of appliquéd objects including winding impressed filets, buttons, and hollow cylinders. Impression appears on cone-shaped forms, possibly applied to make the vessel look like a corncob. The pastes are fine-textured, extremely light gray in color (10YR8/2), with volcanic ash inclusions. Most Unspecified Ware forms are censers. These ceramics were placed in their own ware because pastes, surface finishes, and forms do not resemble ceramics in the Uaxactun Unslipped Ware. The group and type: variety defined for this ware is

Paxbán Group
    Paxbán Unslipped: Paxbán Variety

TYPE DESCRIPTIONS

Quintal Unslipped: Quintal Variety

Established: Smith and Gifford at Uaxactun (1966: 161, 171).
Group: Quintal
Ware: Uaxactun Unslipped
Complex: K'ak 1-3
Sphere: Tzakol 1-3
Ceramic Group Frequency: 346 rims, 1,982 bodies, 2,328 total, 88.9 percent of group, 16 percent of complex.
Principal identifying attributes: (1) Smoothed unslipped vessel surfaces, (2) large jar forms with vertical necks and bolstered rim.
Paste, firing, and temper: Paste texture is coarse with large crystalline calcite inclusions. Paste color is gray (10YR5/1) to buff/pink (5YR6/4) with no examples of firing cores.
Surface finish and decoration: Surfaces are smoothed and left unslipped. Paste color is gray (10YR5/1) to buff/pink (5YR6/4).

Forms:
1. Large jars with vertical necks, direct or exterior bolstered rims; rim diameters measure 20 to 33 cm, wall thicknesses 0.7 to 1.2 cm, and neck heights 8 to 11 cm; and
2. large flaring sided forms with direct rims and squared lips (very rare); these forms might be very large bowls, comales, or possibly lids (no measurements available).

Intraregional locations and contexts: Quintal Unslipped: Quintal Variety is found in Early Classic contexts at La Sufricaya, K'o, Holmul, and Cival.
Interregional locations and contexts: Quintal Unslipped can be found at Uaxactun (Smith and Gifford 1966:161), El Mirador (Forsyth 1989:73-75), Tikal (Culbert 1993:14, 2006), Calakmul (Dominguez-Carrasco 1994:52), and the Petexbatun region (Foias and Bishop 2013:116–118). It appears as an Unspecified Variety at Seibal (Sabloff 1975:101), Yaxchilan (Lopez Varela 1989:98), La Milpa (Sagebiel 2005:234–239), Chan (Kosakowsky 2012:62), and Edzná (Forsyth 1983:78–79. Gifford (1976:190) identified an unslipped type at Barton Ramie (Hewlett Bank Unslipped), but it is not equivalent to Quintal Unslipped. The absence of a Guatemalan or Petén unslipped type: variety in Belize continued a pattern established in the Preclassic periods. Furthermore, type: varieties in general between the Petén and Belize continued to diverge throughout the Early and Late Classic periods.
Comments: Quintal Unslipped is present throughout facets 1-3 of the K'ak Complex.
Illustration: Figure 6.1a.

Quintal Unslipped: Variety Unspecified

Established: Type by Smith and Gifford (1966:161, 171) at Uaxactun, Variety by Callaghan in this study.
Group: Quintal
Ware: Uaxactun Unslipped
Complex: K'ak 2-3
Sphere: Tzakol 2-3
Ceramic Group Frequency: 2 whole vessels (Vessel 5, Room 2 and Vessel 15, Room 1 both from Building B, Group II at Holmul; see Appendix A), 2 total, 0.5 percent of group, 0.1 percent of complex.
Principal identifying attributes: (1) Smoothed unslipped vessel surfaces and (2) secondary decoration such as applique fillet, modeling, and/or black slip.

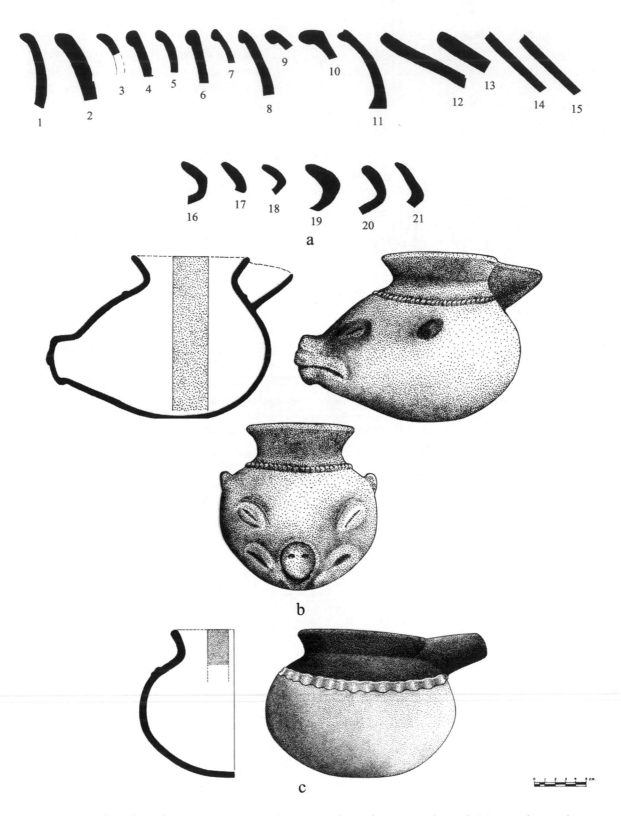

Figure 6.1. Quintal Unslipped: Quintal Variety: (a1) ST.08.55, (a2–a3) ST.08.08, (a4–a6) ST.08.80, (a7–a10) ST.08.08, (a11) ST.08.55, (a12) ST.08.34, (a13) ST.08.05, (a14–a15) ST.08.02, (a16–a18) ST.08.08, (a19) ST.08.34, and (a20–a21) ST.08.08. Quintal Unslipped: Variety Unspecified: (b) BLDG.B.V5.R2.S13-14 and (c) BLDG.B.V15. R1.S1. Drawings by Michael G. Callaghan (a) and Fernando Alvarez (b, c) (Holmul Archaeological Project).

Paste, firing, and temper: Paste, temper, and firing are the same as Quintal Unslipped: Quintal Variety. Paste texture is coarse with large crystalline calcite inclusions. Paste color is gray (10YR5/1).

Surface finish and decoration: Surfaces are smoothed and left unslipped. Paste color is gray (10YR5/1). This type differs from the established named variety of Quintal Unslipped due to its secondary decoration. These vessels display an applique fillet encircling the base of the neck at the shoulder break, as well as other secondary decoration such as a modeling (e.g., in the form of a peccary snout, eyes, and small ears) or even black slip around the rim and down the neck to applique fillet.

Forms: Jars with gutter spouts, outcurving necks, direct rims, rounded lips, and spouts. Rim diameters measure 10 to 16 cm, wall thicknesses 0.9 cm, and heights range from 12 to 21 cm.

Intraregional locations and contexts: Quintal Unslipped: Variety Unspecified has been found only found in Rooms 1 and 2 of Building, Group II at Holmul.

Interregional locations and contexts: This Unspecified Variety of modeled and appliqued Quintal Unslipped has not been identified at any other sites. The "shoepot" form of Vessel 5 from room 2 is, however, usually considered a Late or Terminal Preclassic form mode (see Brady 1989, 1992). The form may be more common in the Preclassic period, but the surface finish and decoration, as well as the paste place it more firmly in the Quintal Group. This variety does not resemble any other Unspecified Variety of Quintal Unslipped described from other sites. I have chosen to leave the varietal name unspecified because the sample small and does not meet the 50-rim-sherd threshold outlined in Chapter 1.

Illustration: Figure 6.1b–c.

Triunfo Striated: Triunfo Variety

Established: Smith and Gifford at Uaxactun (1966: 163, 171).

Group: Quintal
Ware: Uaxactun Unslipped
Complex: K'ak 1-3
Sphere: Tzakol 1-3
Ceramic Group Frequency: 38 rims, 2,474 bodies, 1 whole vessel, 2,513 total, 10 percent of group, 1.8 percent of complex.

Principal identifying attributes: (1) Unslipped and smoothed vessel surfaces, (2) deep to medium striations on vessel exteriors often continuing up to the lip on exterior rim, and (3) large jar forms with vertical neck and notched lip.

Paste, firing, and temper: Paste is medium to coarse in texture with large crystalline calcite inclusions. It is very similar to Quintal Unslipped. Paste color is gray (10YR5/1) to buff/pink (5YR6/4).

Surface finish and decoration: Smoothed vessel exteriors with medium to deep striations. Striations often continue all the way up the neck to the lip on vessel exteriors and interiors. Striations on the body are applied diagonally and frequently cross one another. Striations on the neck are strictly horizontal. Paste color is gray (10YR5/1) to buff/pink (5YR6/4).

Forms: Jars with vertical necks, direct rims, and notched or interior beveled lips. Rim diameters measure 10 to 16 cm, wall thicknesses 0.9 cm, and heights 12 to 21 cm.

Intraregional locations and contexts: Triunfo Striated: Triunfo Variety has been found in the largest quantities at La Sufricaya, but has also been found in smaller quantities at K'o and in very small quantities at Holmul.

Interregional locations and contexts: Triunfo Striated: Triunfo Variety can also be found at Uaxactun (Smith and Gifford 1966:163), El Mirador (Forsyth 1989: 73), Tikal (Culbert 1993:15, 2006), and Calakmul (Dominguez-Carrasco 1994:52). It occurs as an Unspecified Variety in Seibal (Sabloff 1975:101–102), the Petexbatun region (Foias and Bishop 2013:119–120) Yaxchilan (Lopez Varela 1989:99), Chan (Kosakowsky 2012:62), and K'axob (Lopez Varela 2004). It occurs as local varieties at Edzná (Forsyth 1983:77), Altar de Sacrificios (Adams 1971:19), La Milpa (Sagebiel 2005:243–246), and Becan (Ball 1977:14). At Barton Ramie Gifford (1976:183–190) identified an unslipped striated equivalent, but named it Mopan Striated. The Holmul type of Triunfo Striated is very similar to Mopan Striated. Both types have distinct notched lips and striations that continue up the exterior rim of the vessel.

Comment: Smith and Gifford (1966:163, 171) originally placed Triunfo within its own group at Uaxactun. In the Holmul region, Triunfo paste and form attributes are so consistent with Quintal Unslipped ceramics that I have chosen to place Triunfo in the Quintal Group. It is likely these two types of pottery were produced within the same larger, unslipped ceramic tradition. Triunfo Striated is present throughout facets 1-3 of the K'ak Complex.

Illustration: Figure 6.2a1–7.

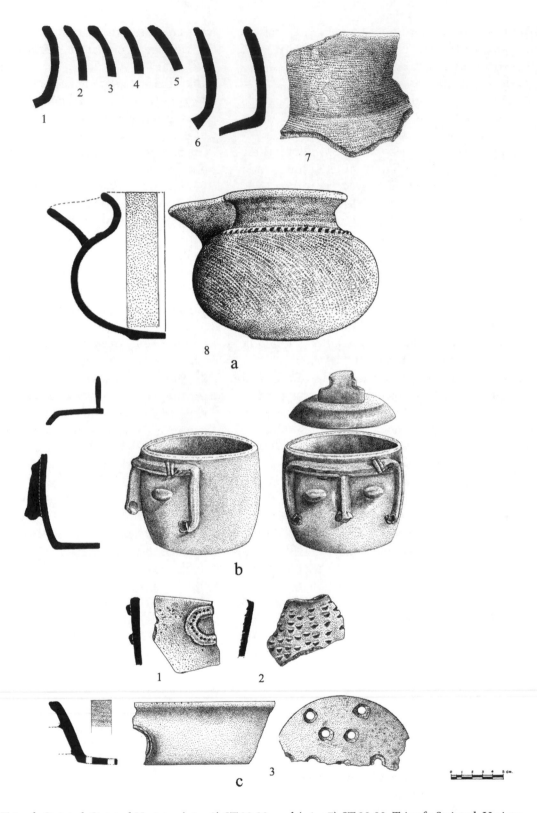

Figure 6.2. Triunfo Striated: Striated Variety: (a1–a3) ST.08.02, and (a4–a7) ST.08.80. Triunfo Striated: Variety Unspecified: (a8) BLDG.B.V4.R2.S13-14. Unnamed Unslipped and Modeled (K'ak): (b) KOL.L.02.08.02.01. Paxbán Unslipped: Paxbán Variety: (c1) ST.08.80, (c2) ST.08.55, and (c3) ST.08.80.01.05. Drawings by Michael G. Callaghan (a1–a6) and Fernando Alvarez (a7–a8, b, c) (Holmul Archaeological Project).

Triunfo Striated: Variety Unspecified

Established: Type established by Smith and Gifford (1966:163, 171) at Uaxactun, Variety by Callaghan in this study.
  Group: Quintal
  Ware: Uaxactun Unslipped
  Complex: K'ak 2-3
  Sphere: Tzakol 2-3
  Ceramic Group Frequency: 1 whole vessel (Vessel 4, Room 2, Building B, Group II, Holmul), 1 total, 0.3 percent of group, 0.05 percent of complex.
  Principal identifying attributes: (1) Unslipped and vessel surfaces, (2) deep to medium striations on vessel exterior, and (3) fingernail impressions on shoulder break around the neck.
  Paste, firing, and temper: Paste is medium to coarse in texture with large crystalline calcite inclusions, the same as Triunfo Striated: Triunfo Variety. Paste color is gray (10YR5/1).
  Surface finish and decoration: Smoothed vessel exteriors with medium to deep striations, which stop at the shoulder break. There is a single row of fingernail impressions at the shoulder break. Surface color is gray (10YR5/1).
  Forms: Jar with gutter spouts, outcurving necks, direct rims, and rounded lips. The rim diameter is 13 cm, wall thickness 0.9 cm, and height 20 cm.
  Intraregional locations and contexts: The only example of this Unspecified Variety is found in Room 2 of Building B at Holmul.
  Interregional locations and contexts: I have no knowledge of a variety of Triunfo Striated like this one at any other site.
  Illustration: Figure 6.2a8.

Unnamed Unslipped and Modeled (K'ak)

Established: Callaghan in this study.
  Group: Unnamed
  Ware: Unspecified
  Complex: K'ak
  Sphere: Tzakol
  Ceramic Group Frequency: 1 whole vessel, 1 total, 0.3 percent of group, 0.05 percent of complex.
  Principal identifying modes: (1) Vase with barrel shape sides and (2) modeled and appliquéd design elements.
  Paste, firing, and temper: Paste is coarse-textured with crystalline calcite inclusions. The paste is more coarse

than Quintal Unslipped and includes large pieces of angular crystalline calcite. Paste color is gray (10YR5/1).
  Surface finish and decoration: The interior and exterior of the vessel are heavily eroded. A crude face was created by modeled and appliquéd design. The vessel has a lid. Surface decoration (as well as paste and form) are not the principal identifying attributes of the Quintal Group, making it difficult for me to justify placing this vessel within that group.
  Forms: Bowl with barrel-shaped sides, direct rim, and squared lip. Rim diameter is 12 cm, wall thickness 0.9 cm, and height 11 cm.
  Intraregional locations and contexts: The only example of this type was found at K'o in the sidewall of a looter's trench in Structure 39. The vessel was part of a cache found in the western stairway of the structure that was deposited during the Early Classic period (Tomasic 2009:272–277).
  Interregional locations and contexts: This vessel resembles an "image censer" (Rice 1999), which often served as a "face cache" (Chase and Chase 1994) in Early Classic eastern shrine structures at Caracol, Belize. A similar face cache was found at Blue Creek in northern Belize and contained jade, marine, shell, coral, stingray spines, and sponge spicules (Driver 2008:213–214, Figure 6.23).
  Comment: According to Tomasic (2009:272), this image censer contained, "a number of artifacts, including two types of coral, three "Charlie Chaplin" figurines, as well as disk-like objects of jade and shell, hook-shaped jade and shell objects, greenstone microdebitage, a broken jade bead, a chert flake, charred seeds, pyrite fragments, wedge-shaped pieces of Spondylus, and two unidentified species of shells." The style of the vessel and "Charlie Chaplin" (Moholy-Nagy and Coe 2008) figurines place the vessel within the Early Classic period, although the phase is unknown.
  Illustration: Figure 6.2b.

Paxbán Unslipped: Paxbán Variety

Established: Callaghan in this study.
  Group: Paxbán
  Ware: Unspecified
  Complex: K'ak 3
  Sphere: Tzakol 3
  Ceramic Group Frequency: 64 rims, 127 bodies, 191 total, 100 percent of group, 3 percent of complex.
  Principal identifying attributes: (1) Smoothed unslipped vessel surfaces, (2) white volcanic ash-tempered paste,

(3) appliqué objects and impression, (4) small bowls with flaring walls, and (5) unconventional forms.

Paste, firing, and temper: Paste, along with vessel forms, is what sets this type of pottery apart from pottery of the Quintal group. The paste is fine-textured with volcanic ash inclusions. The color is extremely light, almost white (10YR8/2). Firing cores are not present.

Surface finish and decoration: Surfaces are very well-smoothed and left unslipped. Appliqué objects were applied to create various designs including winding impressed filets, buttons, and hollow cylinders. Impression appears on cone-shaped forms, possibly applied to make the vessel look like a corncob. Surface color is light gray or white (10YR8/2).

Forms: Vessels are generally fragmented, but two forms can be distinguished:

1. small bowls with flaring sides, direct rim, squared lips, and flat bases; rim diameters measure 9 to 12 cm and wall thicknesses 0.7 to 0.9 cm; and

2. unconventional composite forms such as tall hollow cylinders (e.g., lacking a base), which sometimes have braided handles (no measurements available).

Intraregional locations and contexts: Paxbán Unslipped has been found almost exclusively at La Sufricaya, but has been found in the form of single sherds at Holmul and Cival.

Interregional locations and contexts: This specific type of Early Classic censerware has not been well-documented at other lowland sites, but resembles Candelario Appliqué from Uaxactun (Smith and Gifford 1966:155, 171) and even Hoya Punctated, which has also been found at Uaxactun (Smith and Gifford 1966:158, 171). These types, however, are placed within the Uaxactun Unslipped Ware owing to their paste and form characteristics.

Comment: Paxbán censerware was placed in its own ware because pastes, forms, and surface finishes resemble none of the ceramics in the Quintal group, much less Uaxactun Unslipped Ware. What truly sets the Paxbán Group apart is the consistent use of volcanic ash temper as well as its creamy white or gray paste. This leads me to believe that censerware ceramic production comprised a separate tradition of unslipped pottery manufacture. Design is also very interesting and leads to stylistic similarities of ceramics at La Sufricaya and Uaxactun. One piece in particular could indicate some kind of Mexican ideological influence. Pieces of a corncob censer were discovered in excavations of Structure 1 at La Sufricaya.

Corncob censers have been found at other lowland sites (Smith 1955:Figure 17b9), but they are quite rare. Censers of this shape were also found in Teotihuacan (Rattray 2001:Figures 100, 134, 135). Paxbán Unslipped is a K'ak 3 facet diagnostic marker.

Illustration: Figures 6.2c and 6.3. Note that 6.2c1-2 also appear in Figure 6.3.

Aguila Orange: Aguila Variety

Established: Smith and Gifford at Uaxactun (1966: 154, 171).

> *Group:* Aguila
> *Ware:* Petén Gloss
> *Complex:* K'ak 1-3
> *Sphere:* Tzakol 1-3

Ceramic Group Frequency: 919 rims, 4,460 bodies, 9 whole vessels, 5388 total, 78.2 percent of group, 42.9 percent of complex.

Principal identifying attributes: (1) Orange slip and (2) glossy surface finish.

Paste, firing, and temper: There are three paste variants in the Aguila Orange group; two correlate to the K'ak 1-2 and K'ak 3 facets and the third cross-cuts those facets. The K'ak 1-2 facet variant is medium-textured and exclusively loaded with well-rounded gray calcite grains. Color is buff (10YR8/3). The K'ak 3 variant is fine-textured with volcanic glass temper, sometimes including mica. Paste color is also yellow (10YR7/4, 7/3). The third paste variant is medium-textured with crystalline calcite inclusions and also yellow in color. This variant is found mostly in jar forms and crosscuts K'ak 1-3 facets.

Surface finish and decoration: Like paste composition, surface finish can also be separated into a number of variants. The first appears in the K'ak 1-2 facet. Surfaces were well smoothed before a thick orange (2.5YR5/8; 5YR5/8, 6/8) slip was applied. Vessel surfaces are highly polished and often show signs of polishing marks. The second variant appears in Aguila Orange of the K'ak 3 facet. Vessel surfaces are well-smoothed and have a thin coat of orange-red (10R4/8; 2.5YR4/8) slip. Polish is less brilliant and dull. Fire-clouding on Aguila ceramics with this type of finish is very common. Surfaces can be extremely mottled, in some cases, almost brown. Rootlet marks are also very characteristic of this type of surface treatment.

Forms: Some forms can be associated with K'ak 1-2 and K'ak 3 facets, but jars with short vertical necks, direct rims, and rounded lips occur in facets 1–3. Rim diameters

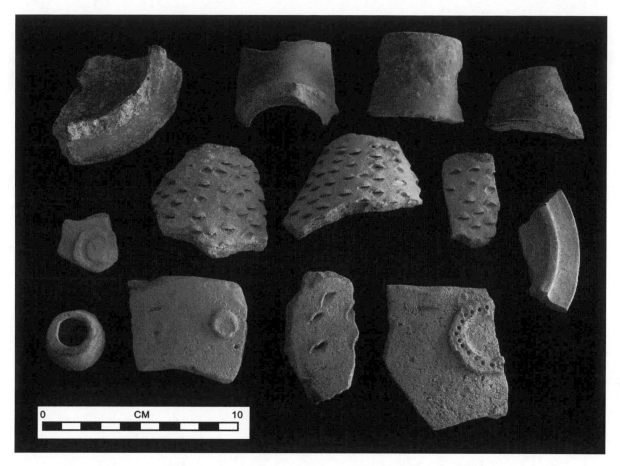

Figure 6.3. Paxbán Unslipped: Paxbán Variety. Photo by Michael G. Callaghan.

for these jars measure 8 to 10 cm and wall thicknesses 0.6 to 1.2 cm.

K'ak 1-2 forms include

1. thick-walled bowls with flaring sides, direct rims, rounded lips, and flat bases; rim diameters measure 13 to 33 cm, wall thicknesses 0.6 to 1.2 cm, and heights 5 to 10 cm and

2. thick-walled bowls with composite sides, z-angles, rounded z-angles, small basal flanges, direct rims, and rounded lips; rim diameters measure 21 to 44 cm, wall thicknesses 0.8 to 1.3 cm, and heights 6 to 10 cm.

K'ak 3 forms include

1. bowls with composite sides, basal flanges, direct rims, and squared lips; rim diameters measure 20 to 35 cm, wall thicknesses 0.8 to 1.3 cm, and heights 6 to 10 cm;

2. bowls with round sides, direct rims, and squared or rounded lips; rim diameters measure 22 to 28 cm,

wall thicknesses 0.6 to 0.9 cm, and heights 6 to 10 cm; and

3. large buckets with vertical sides, wide everted rims, and rounded lips; rim diameters measure 28 to 33 cm, wall thicknesses 0.8 to 1 cm, and heights 16 to 20 cm.

Intraregional locations and contexts: Aguila Orange: Aguila Variety has been found in varying quantities at different sites. The greatest quantity of K'ak 1-2 Aguila Orange has been found in Building B, Group II at Holmul, with a handful of sherds appearing in Cival, K'o, and La Sufricaya. The K'ak 3 variant with volcanic ash paste is found in largest quantities at La Sufricaya Structure 1 and in much smaller quantities at Cival.

Interregional locations and contexts: Aguila Orange: Aguila Variety has been found at Uaxactun (Smith and Gifford 1966:154, 171), El Mirador (Forsyth 1989:61–66), Tikal (Culbert 1993:13, 2006), Altar de Sacrificios

(Adams 1971:26–27), Yaxchilan (Lopez Varela 1989:87), Becan (Ball 1977:41), K'axob (Lopez Varela 2004), La Milpa (Sagebiel 2005:253–264), Chan (Kosakowsky 2012:62), Calakmul (Dominguez-Carrasco 1994:52), and the Petexbatun region (Foias and Bishop 2013:121–127). Gifford reports an Unspecified Variety at Barton Ramie (Gifford 1976:182) as well as Valdez (1987:166) at Colha. Forsyth (1983:67) defines a local variety at Edzná, as well as Muñoz (2004:14–17) at Piedras Negras.

Comment: It may eventually be possible to separate Aguila Orange into two varieties— one early and one late—based on paste, form, and surface modes.

Also of note is that some sherds have secondary decoration that has not been defined in other type: varieties of the Aguila Group. For example, Figure 6.5d is fluted and Figure 6.5c5 shows a streaky orange slip. Although secondary decoration not defined in other type: varieties (e.g. incising) can occur, I have not created new varieties because the sample size in each instance was only one sherd.

Illustration: Figures 6.4 and 6.5a–d.

Pita Incised: Pita Variety

Established: Smith and Gifford at Uaxactun (1966: 161, 171).
Group: Aguila
Ware: Petén Gloss
Complex: K'ak 1-3
Sphere: Tzakol 1-3
Ceramic Group Frequency: 76 rims, 80 bodies, 1 vessel, 157 total, 6.5 percent of group, 3.6 percent of complex.
Principal identifying attributes: (1) Orange slip identical to Aguila and (2) post–slip, and in some cases, post-firing incision.
Paste, firing, and temper: Paste variants are the same as described for Aguila Orange and also correlate to K'ak 1-2 and K'ak 3 facets.
Surface finish and decoration: Variants are the same as Aguila Orange and can be separated into two variants. The first appears in K'ak 1-2 facet material. Surfaces were smoothed well before a thick orange (2.5YR5/8; 5YR5/8, 6/8) slip was applied. Vessel surfaces are highly polished and often show signs of polishing marks. The second variant appears in Aguila Orange of the K'ak 3 facet. Vessel surfaces were well-smoothed and a thin coat of orange-red (10R4/8; 2.5YR4/8) slip was applied. Polish is less brilliant and duller. Fire-clouding on Aguila ceramics with this type of finish is very common. Surfaces can be extremely mottled in some cases. Rootlet

marks are also very characteristic of this type of surface treatment. Pita is different from Aguila because of the addition of post-slip and sometimes post-firing incision on flanges and rims. Designs are simple circumferential bands sometimes in pairs just below the lip on rims. Incising often takes the form of bands and vertical slash marks on basal flanges. Incision can be relatively fine or quite crude.

Forms: Forms include
1. bowls with composite sides, z-angles, rounded z-angles, small basal flanges, direct rims, and rounded lips; rim diameters measure 21 to 44 cm, wall thicknesses 0.8 to 1.3 cm, and heights 6 to 10 cm;
2. bowls with round sides, direct rims, and squared or rounded lips; rim diameters measure 22 to 28 cm, wall thicknesses 0.6 to 0.9 cm, and heights 6 to 10 cm;
3. large buckets with vertical sides, wide everted rims, and rounded lips; rim diameters measure 28 to 33 cm, wall thicknesses 0.8 to 1 cm, and heights 16 to 20 cm; and
4. scutate lids (no measurements available).

Intraregional locations and contexts: Pita Incised has been found at Holmul, La Sufricaya, and a small housemound excavated in 2005 at Cival.
Interregional locations and contexts: Pita Incised: Pita Variety has been found at Uaxactun (Smith and Gifford 1966:161, 171), and Tikal (Culbert 1993:14, 2006). It appears as an Unspecified Variety at El Mirador (Forsyth 1989:66–67), Barton Ramie (Gifford 1976:182–183), Calakmul (Dominguez-Carrasco 1994:52), Chan (Kosakowsky 2012:62), La Milpa (Sagebiel 2005:265–266), K'axob (Lopez Varela 2004), Yaxchilan (Lopez Varela 1989:98), and Becan (Ball 1977:85). Adams (1971:43–44) identified an orange-slipped incised type at Altar de Sacrificios that he names Buj Incised, but surface color and decoration are the same as Pita incised. Muñoz (2004:16) identifies Buj Incised at Piedras Negras, as do Foias and Bishop (2013:127–129) in the Petexbatun region.
Illustration: Figures 6.5e and 6.6a.

Nitan Composite: Nitan Variety

Established: Forsyth (1983:73) at Edzná.
Group: Aguila
Ware: Petén Gloss
Complex: K'ak 2-3
Sphere: Tzakol 2-3
Ceramic Group Frequency: 119 rims, 28 bodies, 4 vessels, 151 total, 10.4 percent of group, 5.7 percent of complex.

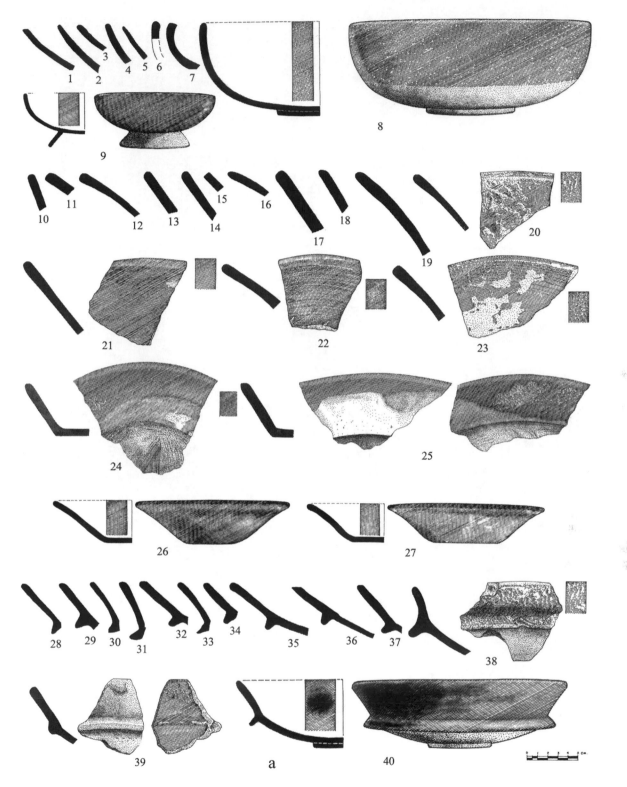

Figure. 6.4. Aguila Orange: Aguila Variety: (a1) HOL.T.63.01, (a2) ST.08.34, (a3–a4) ST.08.34, (a5) ST.08.02, (a6) HOL.T.49.23, (a7) ST.08.34, (a8) BLDG.B.V3.R1.S1, (a9) BLDG.B.V8.R8.V, (a10–a12) HOL.T.49.10, (a13–a16) HOL.T.49.16, (a17–a18) ST.08.07, (a19) ST.08.05.01, (a20) HOL.T.49.10, (a21) HOL.L.63.07, (a22) BLDG.B.L, (a23) HOL.T.49.11, (a24–a25) Unknown provenance, (a26–a27) BLDG.B.R3, (a28–a29) ST.08.80, (a30) ST.08.08, (a31) ST.08.34, (a32) ST.08.02, (a33) ST.08.05, (a34) ST.08.08, (a35–a37) ST.08.02, (a38) ST.19.04, (a39) KOL.T.03.04, and (a40) BLDG.B.V10.R1.S1. Drawings by Michael G. Callaghan (a1–a7, a10-a19, a28–37) and Fernando Alvarez (a8-a9, a20–a27, a38–a40) (Holmul Archaeological Project).

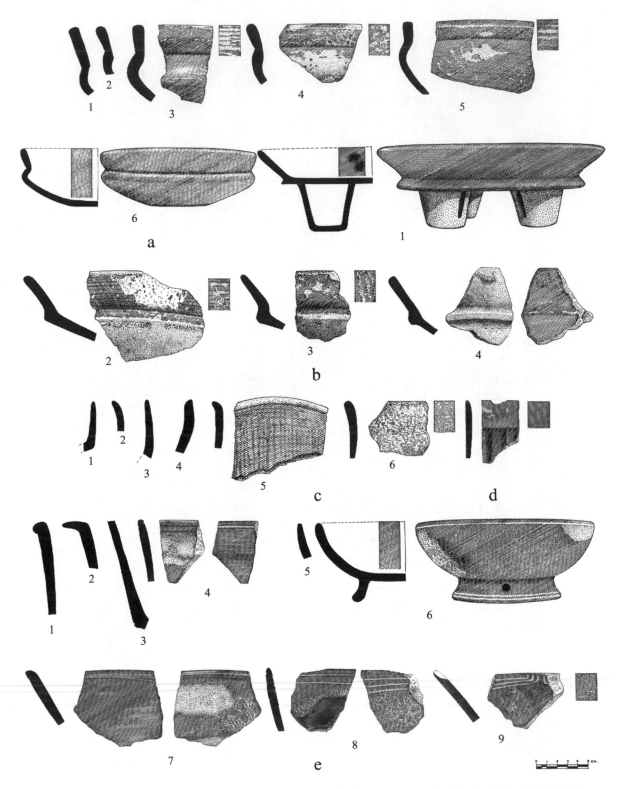

Figure 6.5. Aguila Orange: Aguila Variety: (a1) HOL.T.49.16, (a2) HOL.T.49.11, (a3) BLDG.B.L, (a4) HOL.T.49.23, (a5) BLDG.B.L, (a6) BLDG.B.V3.R7, (b1) BLDG.B.R2.POTB.S5-12, (b2) KOL.T.03.05, (b3) HOL.T.49.11, (b4) KOL.T.03.04, (c1) ST.08.80, (c2–c4) ST.08.02, (c5) ST.08.08, (c6) HOL.T.63.01, and (d1) ST.08.08. Pita Incised: Pita Variety: (e1) ST.08.57, (e2) ST.08.08.01, (e3) ST.08.08, (e4) ST.08.05, (e5) ST.08.55, (e6) BLDG.B.V8.R1.S1, (e7) ST.08.05, (e8) SUF.T.29.06, and (e9) SUF.T.37.3. Drawings by Michael G. Callaghan (a1–a2, c1–c4, e1–e3, e5) and Fernando Alvarez (a3–a6, b, c5–c6, d, e4, e6–e9) (Holmul Archaeological Project).

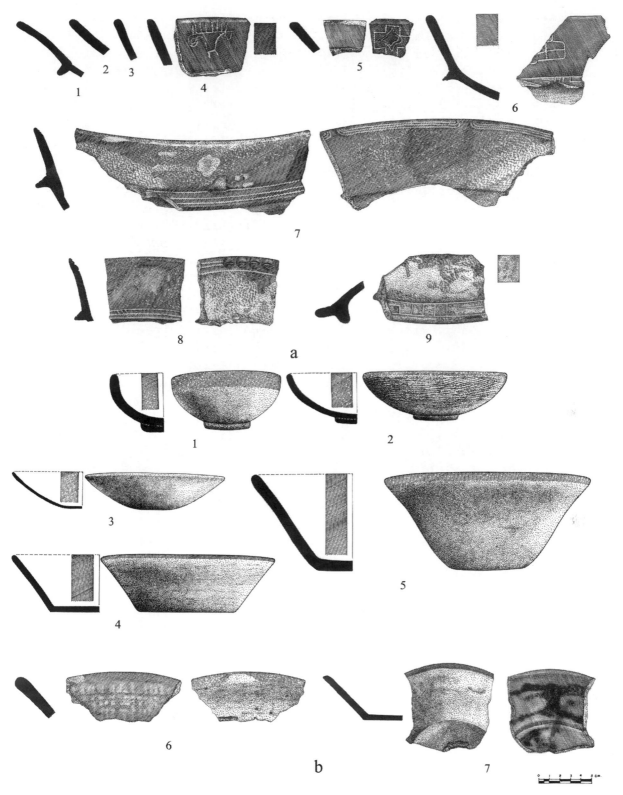

Figure 6.6. Pita Incised: Pita Variety: (a1) ST.08.55, (a2–a3) ST.08.80, (a4) ST.08.80.01, (a5) SUF.L.12.06.03.01, (a6) HOL.T.74.01, (a7) SUF.L.36.03, (a8) CIV.T.32.452, and (a9) ST.18.22. Nitan Composite: Nitan Variety: (b1) BLDG.B.V7.R1.S1, (b2) BLDG.B.V5.R1.Sa, (b3) BLDG.F.POT.B, (b4) BLDG.B.V2.R1.S6, (b5) BLDG.B.V1.R1.S6, (b6) Unknown provenance, and (b7) CIV.T.32.04. Drawings by Michael G. Callaghan (a1–a3) and Fernando Alvarez (a4–a9, b) (Holmul Archaeological Project).

Principal identifying attributes: (1) Orange slip on interior and partially on exterior, (2) dull or low gloss surface finish, (3) volcanic ash-based paste, and (4) bowls with flaring or round sides.

Paste, firing, and temper: Paste is similar to the later variant of Aguila Orange. Paste is fine-textured and yellow (10YR7/3, 7/4; 2.5Y7/2) with volcanic ash inclusions. Firing cores were not seen in the present sample.

Surface finish and decoration: Slip on the interiors of vessels are a thin, flaky orange-red (2.5YR5/8). The slip continues up to the lips of vessel interiors and may continue over the rim and down the exterior wall. The remainder of the vessel exterior is left unslipped. The unslipped portion of vessel exteriors can display a rough smoothing technique, or even raking marks. These marks can sometimes look like formal striations, but more often than not they are quite light.

Forms: Vessel forms are relatively consistent and include

1. bowls of varying size with flaring sides, direct rims, and squared lips; rim diameters measure 12 to 42 cm, wall thicknesses 0.6 to 0.9 cm, and heights 5 to 15 cm; and

2. bowls with round sides, direct rims, and rounded lips; rim diameters measure 15 to 26 cm, wall thicknesses 0.6 to 1.2 cm, and heights 5 to 10 cm.

Intraregional locations and contexts: Nitan Composite is relatively common in the Holmul region and appears in Early Classic contexts at all the major sites including Holmul, Cival, La Sufricaya, and K'o.

Interregional locations and contexts: Nitan Composite: Nitan Variety appears at Edzná (Forsyth 1983:73), El Mirador (Forsyth 1989:67), Calakmul (Dominguez-Carrasco 1994:57), and in the Petexbatun region (Foias and Bishop: 2013:127). Sagebiel (2005:266–268) has identified an Unspecified Variety at La Milpa.

Comment: Nitan Composite may appear during the end of the K'ak 2 facet. It is found as whole vessels in Rooms 1 and 2 in Building B, Group II at Holmul as well as in K'ak 3 contexts at La Sufricaya.

Illustration: Figures 6.6b, 6.7, and 7.7 (pot in center top).

Bocul Orange-on-cream: Bocul Variety

Established: Callaghan in this study.
Group: Aguila
Ware: Petén Gloss
Complex: K'ak 2-3

Sphere: Tzakol 2-3

Ceramic Group Frequency: 49 rims, 96 bodies, 1 vessel, 146 bodies, 4.2 percent of group, 2.3 percent of complex.

Principal identifying attributes: (1) Cream underslip and orange slip, (2) alternate cream and orange on exterior and interior, and (3) volcanic ash tempered paste.

Paste, firing, and temper: Paste is similar to the late variant of Aguila Orange. Paste is fine–textured and yellow in color (10R7/3, 7/4; 2.5Y7/2) with volcanic ash inclusions.

Surface finish and decoration: Surfaces were well-smoothed, then a cream underslip was applied to interiors and exteriors. Next an orange-red (2.5YR5/8) slip was applied to vessel interiors, vessel exteriors, or the lips and rims only. Surfaces were then highly polished. Fire-clouding is common, as are rootlet marks.

Forms:

1. Bowls with composite sides, basal flanges, direct rims, rounded or squared lips, and ring bases; rim diameters measure 21 to 44 cm, wall thicknesses 0.7 to 0.9 cm, and heights 6 to 10 cm; and

2. bowls with round sides, direct rim, and rounded or squared lips; rim diameters measure 22 to 28 cm, wall thickness 0.6 to 0.9 cm, and heights 6 to 10 cm.

Intraregional locations and contexts: One whole vessel of Bocul Orange-on-cream: Bocul Variety was found in Room 1, Building B, Group II at Holmul. It occurs in the largest frequencies at La Sufricaya in Structure 1, Group 1.

Interregional locations and contexts: This type has not been defined at other well-investigated lowland Maya sites to date.

Comment: Like Nitan Composite, Bocul Orange-on-cream may appear at the end of the K'ak 2 facet. It occurs in Room 1 Building B, Group II at Holmul as well as in K'ak 3 contexts at La Sufricaya. In previously publications (Callaghan 2008:379–380, 2013), I identified this type: variety preliminarily as Aguila Orange: Polished and Buff Variety.

Illustration: Figure 6.8a. Note the color convention on 6.8a7 appears to be unslipped—the exterior of this vessel is not unslipped, but slipped a light cream or buff color.

Bocul Orange-on-cream: Variety Unspecified

Established: Callaghan in this study.
Group: Aguila
Ware: Petén Gloss
Complex: K'ak 2-3
Sphere: Tzakol 2-3

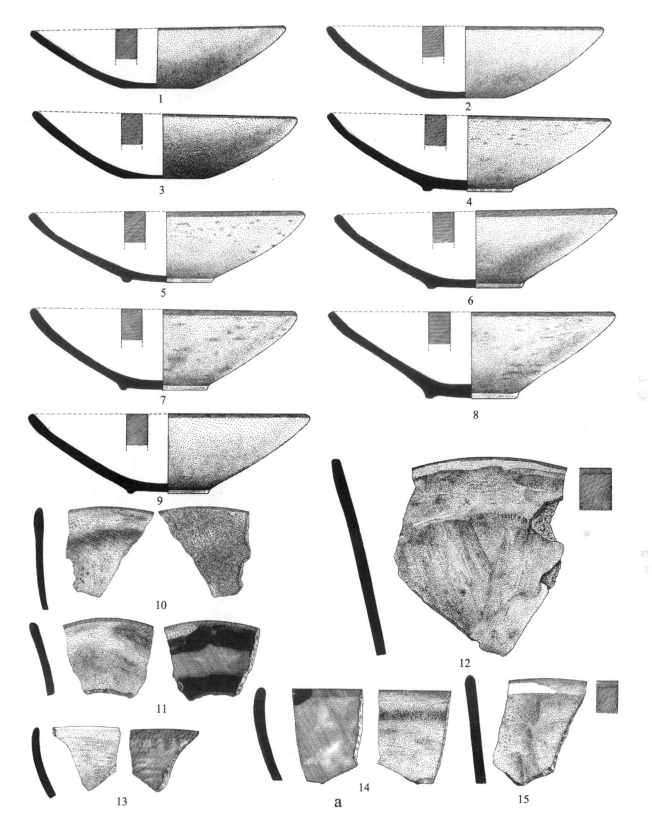

Figure 6.7. Nitan Composite: Nitan Variety: (a1) HOL.L.20.21.02.22, (a2) HOL.L.20.21.02.19, (a3) HOL.L.20.21.02.20, (a4) HOL.L.20.21.02.21, (a5) HOL.L.20.21.02.23, (a6) HOL.L.20.21.02.25, (a7–a8) HOL.L.20.21.02.27, (a9) HOL.L.20.21.02.28, (a10) HOL.T.56.01, (a11) KOL.L.2.00, (a12) SUF.L.08.02, (a13) ST.17.12, (a14) ST.08.55, (a15) SUT.L.08.00. Drawings by Fernando Alvarez (Holmul Archaeological Project).

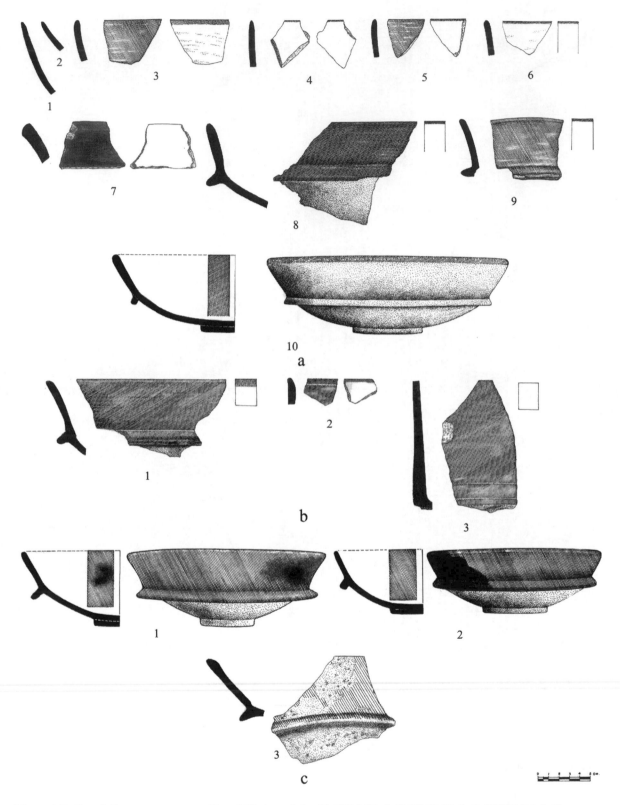

Figure 6.8. Bocul Orange-on-cream: Bocul Variety: (a1–a2) ST.08.02, (a3) ST.20.22, (a4) SLT.05.26, (a5) ST.08.34, (a6) Unknown provenance, (a7) ST.0.08, (a8) ST.08.08.01, (a9) ST.0.08, and (a10) BLDG.B.V2.R1.S1. Bocul Orange-on-cream: Variety Unspecified: (b1) ST.39.17, (b2) ST.20.29, and (b3) ST.08.08. Dos Hermanos Red: Dos Hermanos Variety: (c1) BLDG.B.V17.R1.S1, (c2) BLDG.B.V3.R2.S13-14, and (c3) HOL.T.49.03. Drawings by Michael G. Callaghan (a1–a2) and Fernando Alvarez (a3–a10, b, c) (Holmul Archaeological Project).

Ceramic Group Frequency: 7 rims, 5 bodies, 12 total, less than 0.6 percent of group, 0.3 percent of complex.

Principal identifying attributes: (1) Cream underslip and orange slip, (2) alternate cream and orange on exterior and interior, (3) volcanic ash-tempered paste, and (4) post-slip incision.

Paste, firing, and temper: Paste is identical to Bocul Orange-on-cream: Bocul Variety and similar to the late variant of Aguila Orange. Paste is fine–textured, yellow or buff in color (10R7/3, 7/4; 2.5Y7/2), with volcanic glass inclusions.

Surface finish and decoration: Surfaces are very well-smoothed. A cream underslip was applied to interiors and exteriors. Next an orange-red (2.5YR5/8) slip was applied to vessel interiors, vessel exteriors, or only the lip and rim. Surfaces were then highly polished. Fire-clouding is common, as are rootlet marks. Post-slip incision appears on the rim or basal flange in the form of simple horizontal bands or vertical slash marks.

Forms:

1. Bowls with composite sides, basal flanges, direct rims, rounded or squared lips, and ring bases; rim diameters measure 21 to 44 cm, wall thicknesses 0.7 to 0.9 cm, and heights 6 to 10 cm;

2. bowls with round sides, direct rims, and rounded or squared lips, rim diameters measure 22 to 28 cm, wall thicknesses 0.6 to 0.9 cm, and heights 6 to 10 cm; and

3. a large bucket with vertical sides, wide everted rims, and rounded lips; rim diameters measure 30 cm, wall thicknesses 1 cm, and heights 20 cm.

Intraregional locations and contexts: Bocul Orange-on-cream: Variety Unspecified has been found at La Sufricaya.

Interregional locations and contexts: To date, this type has not been defined at other lowland Maya sites.

Comment: Like Nitan Composite, this type may appear at the end of K'ak 2 facet. It appears in K'ak 3 contexts at La Sufricaya. In a previous publication (Callaghan 2008:380–381), I identified this type: variety preliminarily as Aguila Orange: Polished and Buff Incised Variety.

Illustration: Figure 6.8b.

Unnamed Modeled (Aguila Group)

Ceramic Group Frequency: 1 whole vessel, 1 total, 0.1 percent of group, 0.05 percent of complex.

Ware: Petén Gloss
Complex: K'ak 2-3

Sphere: Tzakol 2-3
Principal identifying attributes: (1) Orange slip, (2) glossy surface finish, and (3) modeling and applique.

Paste, firing, and temper: Paste is medium–textured with crystalline calcite inclusions; it is buff (10YR8/3) in color. This is the variant that crosscuts all three K'ak facets.

Surface finish and decoration: The surface is roughly smoothed. The vessel is eroded, but a thin orange-red (10R4/8; 2.5YR4/8) slip appears over most of the exterior. Polish is less brilliant and duller than other Aguila Group ceramics. Applique and modeled designs create a face on the lower vessel and possible headdress with trefoil jewel on the upper vessel.

Forms: The single urn is composed of two bowls with slightly outcurving sides, exterior thickened rims, and flat lips. Rim diameters are 20 to 21 cm, wall thicknesses 0.9 cm, and heights 11 and 12 cm for a total height of 23 cm.

Intraregional locations and contexts: This vessel comes from HOL.T.84.11.02.02, a cache outside of a tomb in the substructure of the North Pyramid in Group 1 at Holmul (Shetler 2013). No other examples of this type of Aguila Orange have been found in the Holmul region.

Interregional locations and contexts: Vessels with similar shape and applique have been found at Tikal and date to the Manik Complex (Burial 35 in Culbert 1993:Figures 28a1 and 36b). These vessels are slipped red, not orange. Culbert names them "Unnamed red appliqued type urn." While the color of these vessels is different, the form and decorative treatments are similar, so I believe it safe to assume the Holmul vessel dates to the middle or late K'ak Complex.

Illustration: Figures 6.9 and 6.10a.

Dos Hermanos Red: Dos Hermanos Variety

Established: Smith and Gifford (1966:154) at Uaxactun.
Group: Dos Hermanos
Ware: Petén Gloss
Complex: K'ak 1-3
Sphere: Tzakol 1-3
Ceramic Group Frequency: 4 rims, 10 bodies, 2 vessels, 16 total, 100 percent of group, 0.3 percent of complex.

Principal identifying attributes: (1) Red slip and (2) bowls with composite sides, basal flanges, and ring bases.

Paste, firing, and temper: Pastes can be one of two variants. The first is a medium- to fine-textured paste with crystalline calcite inclusions. This paste color is yellow (10YR7/4) or buff (10YR8/2). The second paste variant is similar to Aguila Group ceramics with volcanic

Figure 6.9. Unnamed Modeled (Aguila Group) (HOL.T.84. 11.02.02). This vessel is also illustrated in Figure 6.10a1 and on cover (foreground). Photo by Michael G. Callaghan.

ash inclusions. This paste is fine–textured and yellow (10R7/3, 7/4; 2.5Y7/2) in color.

Surface finish and decoration: Surfaces are well–smoothed and slipped red (10R4/8). Surfaces can be highly polished or remain slightly dull. Black fire-clouding is frequent.

Forms: Forms are restricted to bowls with composite sides, basal flanges, direct rims, rounded or squared lips, and ring bases. Rim diameters measure 20 to 35 cm, wall thicknesses 0.7 to 0.9 cm, and heights 6 to 10 cm.

Intraregional locations and contexts: One whole vessel of Dos Hermanos Red was found in Building B, Group II at Holmul (Vessel 2, Room 1) (see Appendix A). Sherds have also been found in Structure 1, Group 1, at La Sufricaya.

Interregional locations and contexts: Dos Hermanos Red: Dos Hermanos Variety appears at Uaxactun (Smith and Gifford 1966:154) and Calakmul (Dominguez-Carrasco 1994:52), and as an Unspecified Variety at Barton Ramie (Gifford 1976:160–161). At El Mirador

Forsyth describes it as a variety of Aguila Orange (Forsyth 1989:66), as does Kosakowsky (2012:62) at Chan.

Comment: Like Aguila Orange, it is possible that Dos Hermanos Red has a K'ak 1-2 and a K'ak 3 variant. The earlier variant has paste and surface modes more similar to Aguila Orange of K'ak 1-2, while the later variant is more similar to K'ak 3 Aguila Orange.

Illustration: Figure 6.8c.

Actuncan Orange Polychrome: Actuncan Variety

Established: Smith and Gifford (1966:154, 171) at Uaxactun.

    Group: Actuncan
    Ware: Petén Gloss
    Complex: K'ak 1
    Sphere: Tzakol 1
    Ceramic Group Frequency: 21 rims, 4 bodies, 1 vessel, 26 total, 48.9 percent of group, 1 percent of complex.

Principal identifying attributes: (1) Orange slip, (2) highly polished vessel surfaces, (3) red and black paint on an orange background, (4) simple geometric patterns and dotted lines, (5) bowls with composite sides, basal flanges, and ring bases.

Paste, firing, and temper: The paste varies greatly but is usually fine to medium in texture. Inclusions can include crystalline calcite, volcanic ash temper, or both. Paste color ranges from yellow (7.5YR6/4; 10YR7/3) to buff (10YR8/3).

Surface finish and decoration: Interior and exterior surfaces are well-smoothed and highly polished. A cream underslip may have been applied before the application of orange (5YR5/8; 2.5YR5/8) slip, which acted as a background for painting. Red (10R4/8) and black horizontal circumferential bands are painted on or just below the lip of vessel interiors and exteriors. Exterior design motifs include step-frets and other geometric patterns executed with the use of dotted lines.

Forms: Bowls with composite sides, basal flanges, direct rims, and rounded lips. Rim diameters measure 21 to 38 cm, wall thicknesses 0.7 to 0.9 cm, and heights 6 to 10 cm.

Intraregional locations and contexts: Actuncan polychromes have been found at La Sufricaya, K'o, Holmul, Hamontun, and Cival.

Interregional locations and contexts: Actuncan Orange Polychrome: Actuncan Variety appears at Uaxactun (Smith and Gifford 1966:154), Barton Ramie (Gifford 1976:170–173), Yaxchilan (Lopez Varela 1989:85), Colha (Valdez 1987:169–173), and K'axob (Lopez Varela 2004).

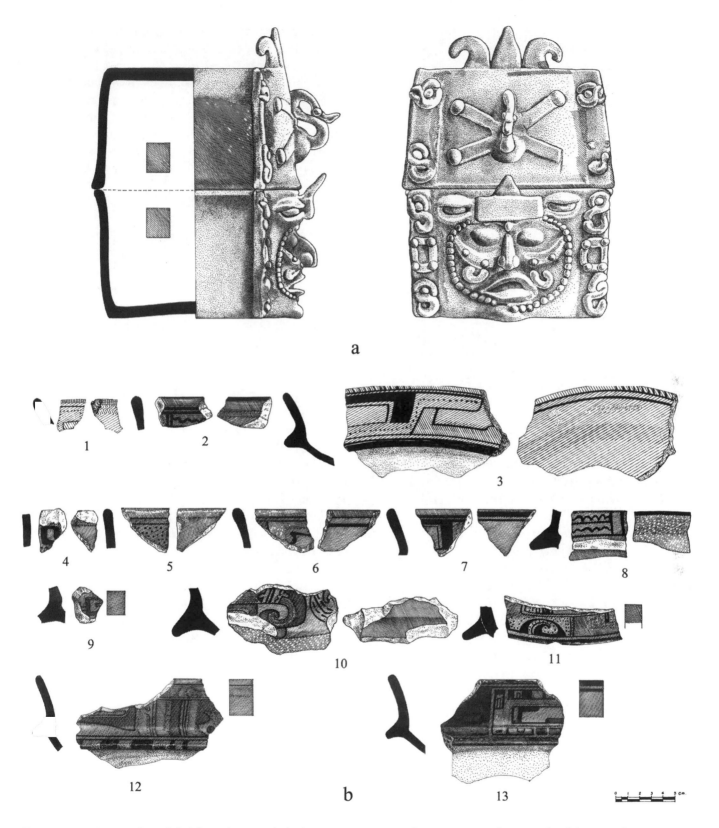

Figure 6.10. Unnamed Modeled (Aguila Group): (a1) HOL.T.84.11.02.02 (Figure 6.9 is a photograph of this vessel). Actuntcan Orange Polychrome: Actuncan Variety: (b1) HOL.T.05.49.17, (b2 –b3) HOL.T.56.01, (b4) HOL.T.42.07, (b5) HOL.T.49.16, (b6–b7) HOL.T.56.01, (b8) HOL.T.74.17.3.01, (b9) HOL.T.41.04, (b10) HOL.T.74.17.3.01, (b11) HOL.L.SURFACE, (b12) SUF.T.26.00, and (b13) ST.19.04. Drawings by Fernando Alvarez (Holmul Archaeological Project).

At Altar de Sacrificios Adams (1971:36–37) defines two local varieties Caal and Carmonate. Actuncan Orange Polychrome is subsumed under Actuncan/Dos Arroyos at Seibal because of poor preservation (Sabloff 1975:105).

Comment: In the Holmul region Actuncan Orange Polychrome is distinguished from Dos Arroyos polychrome through (1) use of dotted line motifs in exterior vessel painting, (2) slight variations in vessel form (Actuncan lip to flange distances are smaller than Dos Arroyos), and (3) archaeological context (Actuncan appears earlier than Dos Arroyos in the Holmul region). Actuncan Orange Polychrome only occurs in association with K'ak 1 facet ceramics.

Illustration: Figures 6.10b and 6.11a.

Boleto Black-on-orange: Boleto Variety

Established: Smith and Gifford (1966:155, 171).
Group: Actuncan
Ware: Petén Gloss
Complex: K'ak 1
Sphere: Tzakol 1
Ceramic Group Frequency: 20 rims, 2 bodies, 3 vessels, 25 total, 51.1 percent of group, 1.1 percent of complex.

Principal identifying attributes: (1) Orange slip, (2) black painted design in the form of horizontal bands or semi-circles, and (3) bowls with composite sides, basal flange, direct rim, rounded lip, and ring base.

Paste, firing, and temper: Paste, firing, and temper are identical to early Aguila group material. The paste is medium-textured with many well-rounded gray calcite inclusions. Paste color is buff (10YR8/3).

Surface finish and decoration: The surface finish is very similar to K'ak 1 and 2 Aguila Orange: Aguila Variety. Vessels are well-smoothed. The orange slip is thick and a true orange (5YR5/8, 2.5YR5/8), not red-orange like K'ak 3 Aguila Orange slips. Designs appear as simple horizontal bands on the lip, rim, and basal flanges. Solid black semi-circles often decorate the flanges. On bowl forms, black designs can take the form of squiggly black lines or dotted black lines on the exterior rim of vessel surfaces. Surfaces are highly polished.

Forms:

1. Bowls with composite sides, basal flanges, direct rims, rounded lips, and ring bases; rim diameters measure 18 to 31 cm, wall thicknesses 0.7 to 0.9 cm, and heights 7 to 11 cm; and

2. possible bowl with round side, direct rim, and rounded lip (no measurements available).

Intraregional locations and contexts: Boleto Black-on-orange is found at Holmul, Hamontun, La Sufricaya, and K'o.

Interregional locations and contexts: Boleto Black-on-orange: Boleto Variety has been found at Uaxactun (Smith and Gifford 1966:155) and Tikal (Culbert 2006). Gifford (1976:173) identified an Unspecified Variety at Barton Ramie. Forsyth (1989:71) identified a possible Boleto Black-on-orange type at El Mirador and names it as an Aguila Orange variety.

Comments: Boleto Black-on-orange is a K'ak 1 facet marker.

Illustration: Figures 6.11b and 6.12a.

Dos Arroyos Orange Polychrome: Dos Arroyos Variety

Established: Smith and Gifford at Uaxactun (1966: 157, 171).
Group: Dos Arroyos
Ware: Petén Gloss
Complex: K'ak 2-3
Sphere: Tzakol 2-3
Ceramic Group Frequency: 59 rims, 72 bodies, 4 vessels, 135 total, 75 percent of group, 2.9 percent of complex.

Principal identifying attributes: (1) Orange slip, (2) highly polished glossy surface, and (3) polychrome red and black painting.

Paste, firing, and temper: Dos Arroyos exhibits two paste modes that may be chronologically sensitive. The earlier K'ak 2-3 mode paste is fine or medium in texture and carbonate based with many small crystalline calcite inclusions. This paste color is yellow (7.5YR4/6) and cores can be present. The later K'ak 3 variant is fine-textured and contains volcanic ash inclusions. This paste color is yellow to buff (10YR6/4). Cores are not present in this paste variant.

Surface finish and decoration: Vessel interior and exterior surfaces are well-smoothed and polished. Orange slip (7.5YR5/8, 6/8) serves as a painting surface or background color. Black and red (10R4/8) bands, geometric patterns, and sometimes conventionalized and abstract patterns are painted on the exterior of vessel walls and basal flanges. The interiors of vessels occasionally have a band of red or black slip on or below the rim.

Forms:

1. Bowls with composite sides, basal flanges, direct rims, rounded lips, and ring bases; rim diameters measure 25 to 38 cm, wall thicknesses 0.7 to 0.9 cm, and heights 6 to 10 cm; and

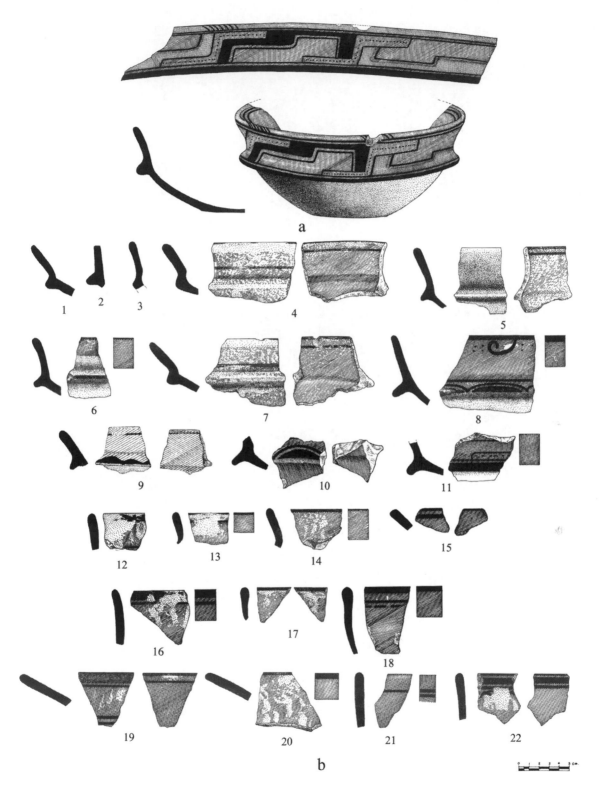

Figure 6.11. Actuntcan Orange Polychrome: Actuncan Variety: (a1) HM.LT.01.00.02.05. Boleto Black-on-orange: Boleto Variety: (b1) HOL.T.49.04, (b2) HOL.T.49.02, (b3) HOL.T.49.03, (b4) HOL.T.49.04, (b5) SUF.T.37.03, (b6) HOL. LT.63.01, (b7) HOL.T.49.04, (b8) SUF.L.08.00, (b9) HOL.T.49.02, (b10) HOL.T.74.17.3.01, (b11) HOL.BLDG.02.L, (b12–b13) HOL.LT.63.01, (b14) HOL.T.49.12, (b15) HOL.T.00.02, (b16) KOL.T.10.07, (b17) HOL.T.49.13, (b18) HOL. GIISTRF.1.6, (b19) SUF.T.26.03, (b20) SUF.L.17.00, (b21) HOL.T.49.23, and (b22) SUF.L.G. Drawings by Fernando Alvarez (a, b4–b22) and Michael G. Callaghan (b1–b3) (Holmul Archaeological Project).

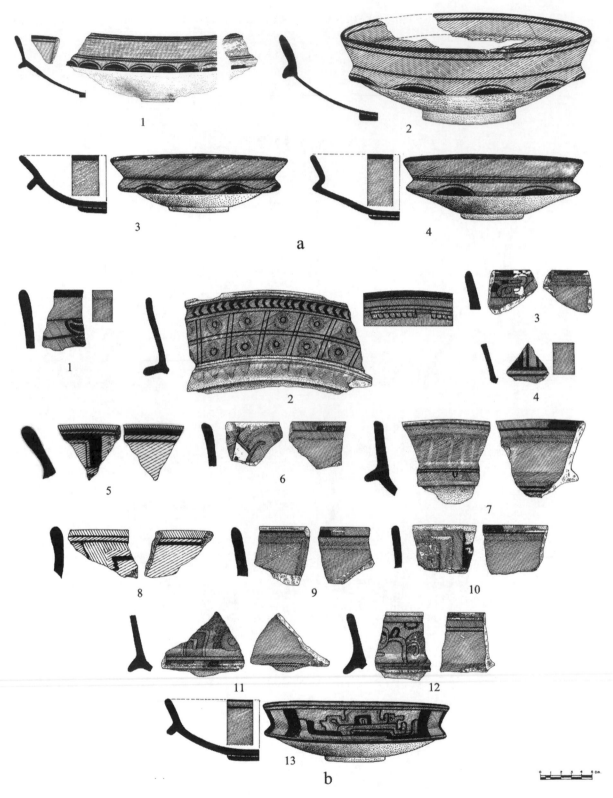

Figure 6.12. Boleto Black-on-orange: Boleto Variety: (a1) HM.LT.01.00.02.01, (a2) HM.LT.00.02.02, (a3) BLDG B.V4.R10, and (a4) BLDG B.V3.R10. Dos Arroyos Orange Polychrome: Dos Arroyos Variety: (b1) ST.07.07.01, (b2) CIV.T.32.04, (b3) KOL.T.13.03, (b4) HOL.T.41.06, (b5) HOL.T.56.01, (b6) KOL.T.07.03, (b7) ST.08.71.01.01, (b8) HOL.T.56.01, (b9) ST.08.55, (b10) SUF.L.17.00, (b11) ST.08.55, (b12) SUF.T.37.03, and (b13) BLDG.B.GRP.2.V1.R10. Drawings by Fernando Alvarez (Holmul Archaeological Project).

2. lids with 25- to 38-cm diameter rims and 0.7- to .09-cm thick walls.

Intraregional locations and contexts: Dos Arroyos Orange Polychromes are relatively rare in the Holmul region, but have been found in La Sufricaya, the burial vaults of Building B, Group II at Holmul (see Appendix A; also Merwin and Vaillant 1932), and in some fill contexts at Cival

Interregional locations and contexts: Dos Arroyos Orange: Dos Arroyos Variety is found at Uaxactun (Smith and Gifford 1966:152), Tikal (Culbert 1993:13, 2006), Colha (Valdez 1987:169), El Mirador (Forsyth 1989:68–71), La Milpa (Sagebiel 2005:311-317), Chan (Kosakowsky 2012:62), Calakmul (Dominguez-Carrasco 1994:52), and K'axob (Lopez Varela 2004). At Barton Ramie (Gifford 1976:173–182) it occurs as the established, named variety and an Unspecified Variety. It is treated as an Unspecified Variety at Altar de Sacrificios (Adams 1971:37). It occurs at Becan (Ball 1977:67–68), where it has been described as the established named variety as well a local Opuesto Variety and an Unspecified Variety. In the Petexbatun region Foias and Bishop (2013:138–140) define it at the level of the group due to poor preservation. At Edzná Forsyth (1983:71–72) identifies an Unspecified Variety, as does Lopez Varela (1989:93) at Yaxchilan, and Muñoz (2004:16) at Piedras Negras. At Seibal, Sabloff (1975:105–107) combines Dos Arroyos Group Ceramics with Actuncan Group ceramics due to poor preservation.

Comments: Dos Arroyos Orange Polychrome appears during the K'ak 2 facet and continues into the K'ak 3 facet.

Illustration: Figures 6.12b, 6.13.

Caldero Buff Polychrome: Caldero Variety

Established: Smith and Gifford at Uaxactun (1966: 155, 171).

Group: Dos Arroyos
Ware: Petén Gloss
Complex: K'ak 2-3
Sphere: Tzakol 2-3
Ceramic Group Frequency: 19 rims, 28 bodies, 2 vessels, 49 total, 25 percent of group, 1 percent of complex.
Principal identifying attributes: (1) Highly polished buff vessel exteriors and interiors, (2) red and black painted designs, and (3) bowls with composite sides and basal flanges.

Paste, firing, and temper: Paste is fine to medium in texture with crystalline calcite inclusions. Paste color is buff (10YR8/2) to yellow (2.5Y7/3, 7/4).

Surface finish and decoration: Vessel surfaces are highly polished, creating what looks like a cream underslip (10YR8/3), but it does not appear that there is one. Circumferential bands and other geometric designs were applied in red (7.5YR5/8) and black paint to vessel exteriors. Designs can also be abstract, conventionalized, or consist of natural-looking elements.

Forms:
1. Bowls with composite sides, basal flanges, direct rims, rounded lips, and ring bases. Rim diameters measure 21 to 38 cm, wall thicknesses 0.7 to 0.9 cm, and heights 6 to 10 cm; and
2. one example of an open lateral ridge plate form (measurements not available).

Intraregional locations and contexts: Caldero Buff sherds have been found at La Sufricaya and whole vessels from Merwin's original excavations were found in Building B, Group II at Holmul.

Interregional locations and contexts: Caldero Buff Polychrome: Caldero Variety has been identified at Uaxactun (Smith and Gifford 1966:155, 171), Tikal (Culbert 1993:13, 2006), and Altar de Sacrificios (Adams 1971:37). Gifford (1976:179) identified an Unspecified Variety at Barton Ramie, as well as Forsyth (1983:75) at Edzná.

Comment: Caldero Buff appears first during the K'ak 2 facet and continues into K'ak 3.

Illustration: Figure 6.14.

Japon Resist: Japon Variety

Established: Smith and Gifford at Uaxactun (1966: 158, 171).

Group: Japon
Ware: Petén Gloss
Complex: K'ak 2-3
Sphere: Tzakol 2-3
Ceramic Group Frequency: 2 vessels, 2 total, 100 percent of group, 0.1 percent of complex.
Principal identifying attributes: (1) Black resist designs on red slip and (2) cylinder vases with vertical sides and lids with modeled handles.

Paste, firing, and temper: Currently unknown. The only examples of Japon Resist in the Holmul region come from Room 2 in Building B, Group II, at Holmul. These vessels are stored in the Peabody Museum and paste samples could not be taken.

Surface finish and decoration: Vessel surfaces are well-smoothed. A red slip (2.5YR4/8) serves as the background color for a resist design. Wax or another substance that

Figure 6.13. Dos Arroyos Orange Polychrome: Dos Arroyos Variety: (a1) BLDG.B.GRP.2.V3-4.R2.S5-12, (a2) BLDG.B.GRP.SS.V6-7.Rs.S13-14, (a3) BLDG.B.GRP.2.POT.A.R2.S5-12, (a4) DAG.T.11.03.02.01, and (a5) DAG.T.11.03.02.02. Drawings by Fernando Alvarez (Holmul Archaeological Project).

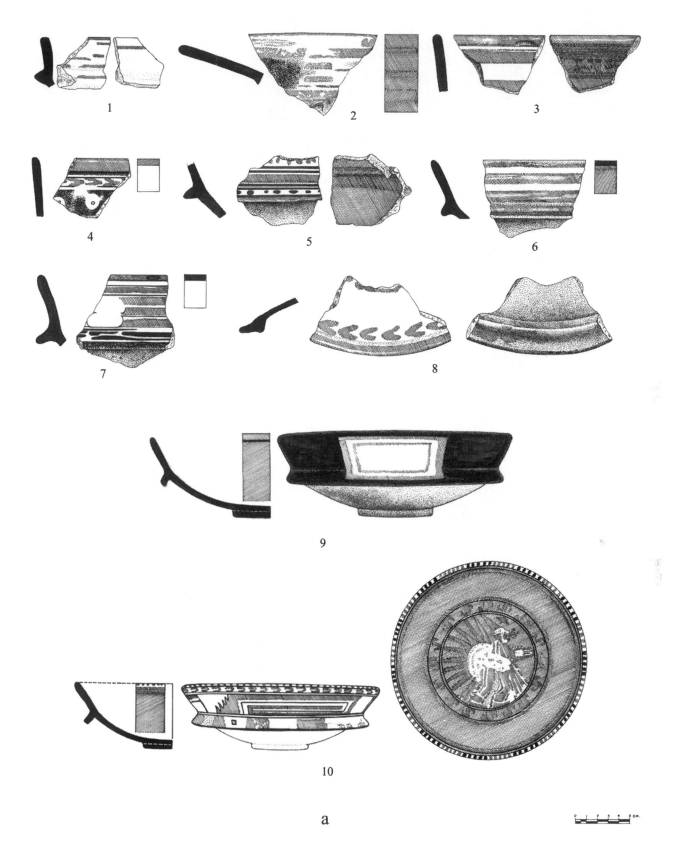

Figure 6.14. Caldero Buff Polychrome: Caldero Variety: (a1) HOL.T.71.30, (a2) ST.08.57, (a3) ST.08.80.01, (a4) ST.08.112.01.02, (a5) ST.08.80, (a6–a7) SUF.L.08.00, (a8) SUF.T.37.03, (a9) BLDG.B.GRP.2.V1.R1.S1, and (a10) BLDG.B.GRP.2.V7.R1.S6. Drawings by Fernando Alvarez (Holmul Archaeological Project).

stood up to firing was applied to create abstract and conventionalized designs. The vessels may have been fired in a reducing atmosphere to create black smudge-like areas of design where the resist material was absent. Vessel surfaces are relatively well-polished. Lids are small and trapezoidal, with modeled effigy handles.

Form: Vases with vertical sides, direct rims, rounded lips, and flat bases; rim diameters measure 13 to 14 cm, wall thicknesses 0.7 to 0.9 cm, and heights 22 to 24 cm.

Intraregional locations and contexts: Room 2, Building B, Group II, Holmul.

Interregional locations and contexts: Japon Resist: Japon Variety is very rare and is found at Uaxactun (Smith and Gifford 1966:158), Tikal (Culbert 1993:13, 2006; Laporte et al. 1992: Figure 25), and as an Unspecified Variety at Altar de Sacrificios (Adams 1971:58).

Comments: Concerning Japon Resist at Tikal, Culbert (2006) notes that "The type is so rare and so unusual that it seems almost certain that it must have been imported from an unknown source." Culbert's (2006) description is also extremely similar to the Japon Resist examples from Building B, Group II at Holmul. Vessel forms are slightly different between the two sites. At Tikal forms are cylindrical tripods while at Holmul they lack supports. Also, resist on the Holmul examples seems to be produced by a smudging effect and not necessarily the application of two slips. Similar to what Culbert notes at Tikal, because the examples of Japon Resist at Holmul are whole pots, it will be difficult if not impossible to remove a piece for INAA. This may prevent chemical sourcing using that kind of technique, which will impede our understanding of where these pots may have been produced. Japon Resist is a K'ak 2-3 facet marker.

Illustration: Figure 6.15a.

Unnamed Polychrome (K'ak)

Established: Callaghan in this study.
Group: Unnamed
Sample: 2 vessels, 2 total, 0.1 percent of complex.
Ware: Petén Gloss
Complex: K'ak 1-3
Sphere: Tzakol 1-3
Principal identifying attributes: (1) Orange slip, (2) highly polished glossy surface finish, (3) polychrome red and black painting, (4) bowls with composite sides, basal flanges, and ring bases, and (5) bowls fused to pot stand.

Paste, firing, and temper: Because these two vessels were museum pieces, I was not able to perform a paste analysis.

Surface finish and decoration: Vessel interior and exterior surfaces are well-smoothed and polished. The upper bowl of one vessel (Vessel 11, Building B, Group II, Holmul) has a cream slip; the lower pot stand has an orange slip (7.5 YR/58, 6/8) incised with a cross. The other vessel (Vessel 2, Room 10, Building B, Group II, Holmul) has black and red (10R4/8) designs on an orange slip. The designs include bands and geometric patterns painted on exterior vessel walls and the basal z-angle. The interior of Vessel 2 has a band of red and black slip on and below the rim. The style does not resemble established type: varieties in the Actuncan or Dos Arroyos Groups.

Forms: These are both rare pieces.

Vessel 11, from Room 1, Building B, Group II, Holmul is a special form with incurving, cream-slipped bowl fused atop an orange incised cotton reel pot stand. Rim diameter is 5 cm, wall thickness 0.6 cm, and height 14 cm. up II, at Holmul. The entire vessel composition is extremely rare for the Holmul region, but the pot-stand mode is common to other Early Classic period ceramic complexes.

Vessel 2 from Room 10, Building B, Group II, Holmul (Figure 6.13b2) is a composite silhouette bowl with black and red on orange polychrome. It has composite sides, a basal flange, direct rim, rounded lip, and ring bases. Rim diameter is 21 cm, wall thickness 0.7 cm, and height 9 cm.

Intraregional locations and contexts: These polychromes are rare in the Holmul region and can only be found in tombs at Building B, Group II at Holmul (see Appendix A).

Interregional locations and contexts: The pot-stand vessel has been commented on before and similar pieces have been found in Belize, namely Nohmul (Hammond 1984:11; Pring 2000:77–78). All date to the early Early Classic or even Terminal Preclassic periods. Vessel 2 from Room 10 may be a local polychrome or imported polychrome from unknown area. Again, it is not similar to Dos Arroyos or Actuncan Orange Polychromes.

Comments: These ceramics appear to be deposited during the K'ak 2-3 facets.

Illustrations: Figure 6.15b.

Unnamed Red Slipped (K'ak 2-3)

Established: Callaghan in this study.
Group: Unnamed
Ware: Petén Gloss
Complex: K'ak 2-3

Figure 6.15. Japon Resist: Japon Variety: (a1) BLDG.B.GRP.2.V1.R2.S10 and (a2) BLDG.B.GRP.2.V2. R2.S10. Unnamed Polychrome (K'ak): (b1) BLDG.B.GRP.S.V11.R1.S1, (b2) BLDG.B.GRP.2.V2.R10. Unnamed Red Slipped (K'ak 2-3): (c1) BLDG.B.GRP.2.V9.R1.S1, (c2) BLDG.B.GRP.2.V3.R1.S6, and (c3) BLDG.B.GRP.2.V5.R1.S6. Drawings by Fernando Alvarez (Holmul Archaeological Project).

Sphere: Tzakol 2-3

Sample: 3 vessels, 3 total, 100 percent of group, 0.1 percent of complex.

Principal identifying attributes: (1) Red slip, (2) polished glossy surface finish, and (3) cylinders with supports.

Paste, firing, and temper: Because these three vessels were museum pieces, I was not able to perform a paste analysis.

Surface finish and decoration: Vessel interior and exterior surfaces are well smoothed and polished. Slip is a deep red like that of the K'ak 1-2 facet Dos Hermanos Red (10R4/8).

Forms: These are all rare pieces. Forms are

1. a miniature jar with gadrooning; rim diameter is 5 cm, wall thickness 0.8 cm, and height 17 cm; and

2. bowls with outcurving or flaring sides, direct rims, rounded lips, flat bases and supports; rim diameters measure 18 to 20 cm, wall thicknesses 0.7 to 0.8 cm, and heights 10 to 12 cm. The two bowls are not identical. Vessel 3 from Room 1 in Building B, Group II at Holmul has three slab supports and a chamfer on the exterior. Vessel 9 from Room 1 also has a chamfer, but has four cylinder supports and is taller and less wide.

Intraregional locations and contexts: These rare vessels were found in tombs at Building B, Group II at Holmul.

Interregional locations and contexts: At first, I wanted to place these vessels in the Dos Hermanos Red type, but the form and potential time-period of production and deposition make me hesitate doing so. These vessels do not share open-form characteristics of Dos Hermanos Red types from Uaxactun (Smith and Gifford 1966:154), El Mirador (Forsyth 1989:66), or Barton Ramie (Gifford 1976:160–161). Furthermore, they do not resemble other red types such as Caribal Red (Adams 1971:21) in the Pasión River region or Minanha Red (Gifford 1976:157–159) at Barton Ramie. Therefore, they remain unclassified for now.

Comments: These ceramics appear to have been deposited during the K'ak 2-3 facet.

Illustrations: Figure 6.15c.

Balanza Black: Balanza Variety

Established: Smith and Gifford at Uaxactun (1966:154–155, 171).

Group: Balanza
Ware: Petén Gloss
Complex: K'ak 1-3
Sphere: Tzakol 1-3

Ceramic Group Frequency: 246 rims, 1,479 bodies, 9 vessels, 1,734 total, 66.9 percent of group, 11.8 percent of complex.

Principal identifying attributes: (1) Black slip and (2) highly polished vessel surfaces.

Paste, firing, and temper: Balanza Black in the Holmul region may have three paste variants. The first is a medium- to fine–textured paste with many crystalline calcite inclusions. Paste color is gray (10R5/1) to black. The second paste is also medium to fine in texture with many small crystalline calcite inclusions, but the color tends toward a pink-brown (5YR4/4). The third variant is fine–textured with volcanic ash inclusions and is gray to buff (10YR6/1) in color. Like Aguila Orange and Dos Hermanos, Balanza paste variants show some chronological sensitivity. While the calcite pastes crosscut K'ak 1-3 facets, the volcanic ash-tempered paste appears to be a K'ak 3 facet mode.

Surface finish and decoration: Highly polished vessel surfaces. Two types of slip treatment crosscut the paste groups. One treatment is a deep, even coat of black on vessel interiors and exteriors. The second type of surface finish involves the application of a thin slip that fires to black, but more often remains mottled black-brown or even gray. Occasionally "screwhead" or "coffee bean" appliqués occur on vessel exteriors. Screwheads are usually found near the base of cylinder vase tripods. These types of decorations appear on K'ak 2-3 Balanza Black sherds.

Forms:

1. Bowls with composite sides, basal flanges, direct rims, rounded lips, and ring bases; rim diameters measure 18 to 35 cm, wall thicknesses 0.6 to 0.9 cm, and heights 8 to 12 cm;

2. cylinders with vertical walls, direct rims, rounded or pinched lips, flat bases, and occasional slab tripod vessels; rim diameters measure 7 to 30 cm, wall thicknesses 0.5 to 0.8 cm, and heights 6 to 15 cm;,

3. bowls with round sides, direct rims, rounded lips, and flat or round bases; rim diameters measure 11 to 25 cm, wall thicknesses 0.6 to 0.8 cm, and heights 6 to 10 cm;

4. jars with short, vertical necks, direct rims, and rounded lips; rim diameters measure 8 to 10 cm and wall thicknesses 0.6 to 1.2 cm;

5. round bowls with spouts; rim diameters measure 11 to 25 cm, wall thicknesses 0.6 to 0.8 cm, and heights 6 to 10 cm; and

6. scutate lids (no measurements available).

Balanza Black forms are more difficult to isolate chronologically than Aguila Orange forms. While the cylinder vase may be a K'ak 3 facet marker, other forms seem to crosscut facets.

Intraregional locations and contexts: Balanza Black is found at every major site in the region, but is more common in its incised type of Lucha Incised.

Interregional locations and contexts: Balanza Black: Balanza Variety appears at Uaxactun (Smith and Gifford 1966:154–155, 171), Tikal (Culbert 1993:13, 2006), Altar de Sacrificios (Adams 1971: 24), Becan (Ball 1977:33), Colha (Valdez 1987:173), La Milpa (Sagebiel 2005:280–287), and Calakmul (Dominguez-Carrasco 1994:52). It appears as a local variety and Unspecified Variety at Barton Ramie (Gifford 1976:161–164), as an Unspecified Variety at Seibal (Sabloff 1975:107–108), as an Unspecified Variety at El Mirador (Forsyth 1989:71–73), as an Unspecified Variety at K'axob (Lopez Varela 2004), and as an Unspecified Variety at Yaxchilan (Lopez Varela 1989:144). It is defined at the group level and as an Unspecified Variety at Edzná (Forsyth 1983:76), as an Unspecified Variety at Chan (Kosakowsky 2012:62), at Piedras Negras (Muñoz 2004:15–18) as the established named variety and local varieties, and as an Unspecified Variety in the Petexbatun region (Foias and Bishop 2013:130–132).

Comment: Balanza Black crosscuts the K'ak 1-3 facets. Form, surface, and paste modes are much more difficult to isolate chronologically than ceramics of the Aguila group. It is interesting to note that one black jar rim may be an example of Mount Maloney Black of the Pine Ridge Carbonate Ceramic Group (Figure 6.16a24). Mount Maloney was established at Barton Ramie by Gifford (1976:243). This single sherd has the characteristic drag marks and possible thin black slip that Gifford mentions as a principal identifying attribute. Also note the fluted sherd illustrated as Figure 6.16a14. This could be Paradero Fluted, but because the sample only consisted of one sherd that does not meet all the criteria of Paradero Fluted (see Adams 1971:48), I choose not to define the type: variety here. But I felt it worth noting.

Illustration: Figures 6.16 and 6.17.Note that the color convention in Figure 6.16 of solid black is not followed for all drawings, but all pieces are slipped black.

Lucha Incised: Lucha Variety

Established: Smith and Gifford at Uaxactun (1966: 159, 171).
Group: Balanza
Ware: Petén Gloss
Complex: K'ak 1-3

Sphere: Tzakol 1-3
Ceramic Group Frequency: 101 rims, 105 bodies, 11 vessels, 217 total, 29.4 percent of group, 5.2 percent of complex.
Principal identifying attributes: (1) Black slip, (2) glossy surface finish, and (3) post-slip incision.
Paste, firing, and temper: Paste, temper, and firing can be found in the same three variants as described above for Balanza Black.
Surface finish and decoration: Surface finish is identical to Balanza Black with the addition of post-slip incision in the form of horizontal circumferential lines on basal flanges and rims, more complicated geometric or naturalistic patterns on walls and lids, and small vertical slashes on basal flanges. Incision can range from excellent to extremely poor in quality.
Forms:
   1. Bowls with composite sides, basal flanges, direct rims, rounded or squared lips, and ring bases; rim diameters measure 12 to 35 cm, wall thicknesses 0.6 to 0.9 cm, and heights 8 to 12 cm;
   2. cylinders with vertical sides, direct rims, and rounded lips; rim diameters measure 7 to 30 cm, wall thicknesses 0.5 to 0.8 cm, and height 6 to 15 cm;
   3. bowls with round sides, direct rims, and rounded or pinched lips; rim diameters measure 11 to 25 cm, wall thicknesses 0.6 to 0.8 cm, and heights 6 to 10 cm; and
   4. scutate lids with 12- to 3-cm diameter rims and 0.6- to 0.9-cm thick walls.

Intraregional locations and contexts: Lucha Incised has been found in greatest quantities at La Sufricaya, but has also been found at Holmul, Cival, and K'o.
Interregional locations and contexts: Lucha Incised: Lucha Variety can be found at Uaxactun (Smith and Gifford 1966:159), Tikal (Culbert 1993:14, 2006), Altar de Sacrificios (Adams 1971:43), Calakmul (Dominguez-Carrasco 1994:52), Becan (Ball 1977:85), and in the Petexbatun region (Foias and Bishop 2013:132–134). It appears as an Unspecified Variety and local variety at Barton Ramie (Gifford 1976:164–166 and as an Unspecified Variety at Seibal (Sabloff 1975:110–112), El Mirador (Forsyth 1989:73), Chan (Kosakowsky 2012:62), La Milpa (Sagebiel 2005:291–294), K'axob (Lopez Varela 2004), Colha (Valdez 1987:175), and Piedras Negras (Muñoz 2004:17).
Comments: Like Balanza Black, Lucha Incised crosscuts the K'ak 1-3 phases. Form, surface, and paste modes are much more difficult to isolate chronologically than ceramics of the Aguila group.

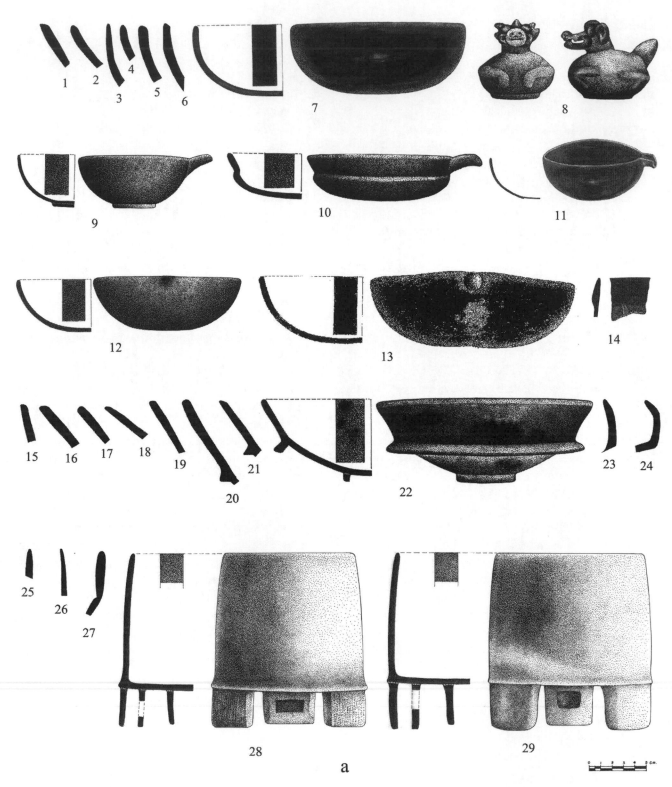

Figure 6.16. Balanza Black: Balanza Variety: (a1) ST.08.80, (a2–a3) ST.08.71, (a4) ST.08.80, (a5–a6) ST.08.08, (a7) BLDG.B.GRP.2.V4.R1.S1, (a8) BLDG.B.GRP.2.V12.R1.S1, (a9) BLDG.B.GRP.2.V6.R1.S6, (a10) BLDG.B.GRP.2.V14. R1.S1, (a11) KOL.L.T.01, (a12) BLDG.B.GRP.2.V5.R2.S5-12, (a13) BLDG.B.GRP.2.V18.R1.S1, (a14–a15) ST.08.80, (a16) ST.08.55, (a17–a19) ST.08.71, (a20–a21) ST.08.08, (a22) BLDG.B.GRP.2.V1.R2.S5-12, (a23–26) ST.08.80, (a27) ST.08.34, (a28) HOL.T.84.14.02.03, and (a29) HOL.T.84.14.02.01. Drawings by Michael G. Callaghan (a1–a6, a15–a21, a23–a27) and Fernando Alvarez (a7–a14, a22, a28–29). See Figure 6.17 for a photo of vessels a28 and a29.

Figure 6.17. Balanza Black: Balanza Variety (left and right vessels, HOL.T.84.14.02.03 and HOL.T.84.14.02.01) and Urita Gouged-Incised: Urita Variety vessel (center, HOL.T.84.14.02.02). Photo by Diana Méndez-Lee. The Balanza Black: Balanza Variety vessels are also illustrated in Figure 6.16 (a28 and a29); the Urita Gouge-Incised: Urita Variety vessel is also illustrated in Figure 6.22(a17).

Illustration: Figures 6.18a1–20, 6.19, and 6.20a1-7. Note that color conventions of solid black are not followed in all drawings, but all of the vessels are slipped black.

Lucha Incised: Variety Unspecified

Established: Type by Smith and Gifford at Uaxactun (1966:159, 171), Variety by Callaghan in this study.
Group: Balanza
Ware: Petén Gloss
Complex: K'ak 1-3
Sphere: Tzakol 1-3
Ceramic Group Frequency: 2 whole vessels, 0.5 percent of group, 0.1 percent of complex.
Principal identifying attributes: (1) Black slip, (2) glossy surface finish, (3) post-slip incision in abstract designs, and (4) rare vessel forms.
Paste, firing, and temper: Paste, temper, and firing are the first and third variants of Balanza Black. The first is a medium- to fine-textured paste with many crystalline calcite inclusions. Paste color is gray (10R5/1) to black. The third variant is fine-textured with volcanic ash inclusions and is gray to buff (10YR6/1) in color.
Surface finish and decoration: Surface finish is identical to Lucha Incised, but the composition of the incision is more complex than simple bands or slash marks.

For example, Figure 6.18a22 shows a conventionalized design, possibly a bleeding heart with obsidian knife and blood droplets.
Forms:
1. Large bucket with vertical sides, wide everted rim, and rounded lip; rim diameter is 28 cm, wall thickness 0.8 cm, and heights 16 to 25 cm; and
2. cotton-reel pot stand with solid supports; rim diameter 8 cm, wall thickness 0.8 cm, and height 14 cm.

Intraregional locations and contexts: This Unspecified Variety of Lucha Incised has been found Building B, Group II (Vessel 4, Room 7) at Holmul and in Structure 1 at La Sufricaya.
Interregional locations and contexts: This Unspecified Variety of Lucha Incised is not equivalent to Unspecified Varieties at other sites. I defined it as Unspecified because the sample is too small to adequately classify the material at this time.
Comments: This Variety of Lucha Incised crosscuts the K'ak 1-3 facets. It is set apart from Lucha Incised: Lucha Variety primarily due to its special forms and more complicated designs.
Illustration: Figures 6.18a21–22 and 6.21. Note that the color conventions of solid black are not followed in Figure 6.18, but both vessels are slipped black.

Figure 6.18. Lucha Incised: Lucha Variety: (a1–a2) ST.08.71, (a3) KOL.LT.01, (a4) ST.08.02, (a5) ST.18.26, (a6) SUF.01. STR.40, (a7–a8) ST.08.71, (a9) ST.08.02, (a10) ST.08.80, (a11) BLDG.B.GRP.2.V16.R1.S1, (a12) KLT.01.03.02.01, (a13) BLDG.B.GRP.2.POT.C.R2.S5-12, (a14) ST.08.71, (a15–a19) Unknown provenance, and (a20) BLDG.B.GRP.2.V6.R1.S1. Lucha Incised: Variety Unspecified: (a21) BLDG.B.GRP.2.V4.R7 and (a22) ST.08.08.02.01. Drawings by Michael G. Callaghan (a1–a2, a4, a7–a10) and Fernando Alvarez (a3, a5–a6, a11–a22) (Holmul Archaeological Project).

Figure 6.19. Lucha Incised: Lucha Variety: (a1) BLDG.B.GRP.2.V1-2.R2.S13-14, (a2) BLDG.B.GRP.2.V8-9.R2.S13-14, and (a3) BLDG.B.GRP.2.V10-11.R2.S13-14. Drawings by Fernando Alvarez (Holmul Archaeological Project).

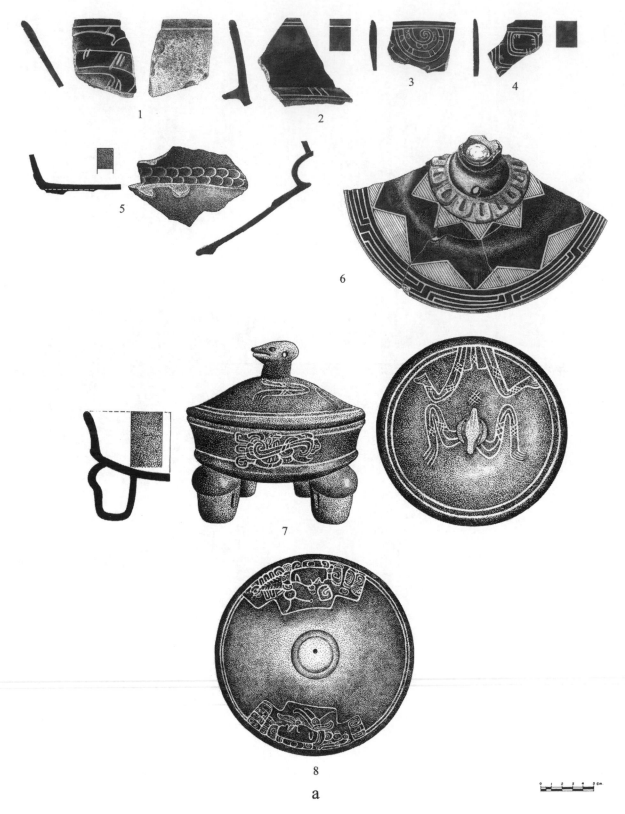

Figure 6.20. Lucha Incised: Lucha Variety: (a1) SUF.T.28.05, (a2) SUF.T.26.08, (a3–a4) ST.08.52, (a5) CIV.T.56.03, (a6) ST.08.55.02.01, and (a7) BLDG.B.GRP.2.V5-6.R7. Urita Gouged-incised: Urita Variety: (a8) BLDG.B.GRP.2.V12.R2.S13-14. Drawings by Fernando Alvarez (Holmul Archaeological Project).

Figure 6.21. Lucha Incised: Variety Unspecified (ST.08.08.02.01). Photo by Diana Méndez-Lee.

Urita Gouged-incised: Urita Variety

Established: Smith and Gifford (1966:164, 171).
Group: Balanza
Ware: Petén Gloss
Complex: K'ak 1–3
Sphere: Tzakol 1–3
Ceramic Group Frequency: 10 rims, 22 bodies, 2 whole vessels, 34 total, 3.1 percent of group, 0.6 percent of complex.
Principal identifying attributes: (1) Black slip; (2) preslip gouge-incision in the form of geometric, conventionalized, naturalistic, and glyphic elements; (4) cylinders with vertical sides; and (5) bowls with round sides.
Paste, firing, and temper: Paste is similar to the first two variants of Balanza Black. The first is medium to fine in texture with many crystalline calcite inclusions. This paste color is gray (10YR5/1) to black. The second paste is also medium to fine in texture with many small crystalline calcite inclusions, but this paste color is pinkish brown (5YR4/4).
Surface finish and decoration: Surface treatment is similar to the two variants within Balanza Black. One treatment is a deep even coat of black on vessel interiors and exteriors. The second type of surface finish involves the application of a thin black slip that remains mottled or gray. Gouge-incision was performed preslip and takes the form of geometric, naturalistic, conventionalized, or glyphic elements. Sometimes negative areas were filled with purple paint or pigment. Occasionally "screwhead"

or "coffee bean" appliqué occurs on vessel exteriors. Screwheads usually appear on vessel exteriors near the base of cylinder vases with tripod supports.
Forms:
1. Cylinder vases with vertical sides, direct rims, rounded lips, and flat bases sometimes with supports; rim diameters measure 7 to 30 cm, wall thicknesses 0.5 to 0.8 cm, and heights 6 to 15 cm; and
2. bowls with round sides, direct rims, and rounded lips; rim diameters measure 11 to 25 cm, wall thicknesses 0.6 to 0.8 cm, and heights 6 to 10 cm.

Intraregional locations and contexts: Urita Gouged-Incised has been found at La Sufricaya and in Building B, Group II at Holmul (see Appendix A).
Interregional locations and contexts: Urita Gouged-Incised appears at Uaxactun (Smith and Gifford 1966:164, 171), Tikal (Culbert 1993:15, 2006), and Piedras Negras (Muñoz 2004:17). It appears as an Unspecified Variety at Seibal (Sabloff 1975:11), Altar de Sacrificios (Adams 1971:52), Colha (Valdez 1987:178), and in the Petexbatun region (Foias and Bishop 2013:135).
Comment: Urita Gouged-Incised appears to be a relatively late type in the Early Classic period. It is found in association with K'ak 3 contexts at La Sufricaya.
Illustration: Figures 6.17 (middle vessel), 6.20a8, and 6.22a. Note that color conventions are not followed in Figures 6.20 and 6.22, but all examples are slipped black.

Positas Modeled: Positas Variety

Established: Smith and Gifford at Uaxactun (1966:161,171)
Group: Balanza
Ware: Petén Gloss
Complex: K'ak 2–3
Sphere: Tzakol 2–3
Ceramic Group Frequency: 0 rims, 10 bodies, 10 total, less than 0.01 percent of group, less than 0.01 percent of complex.
Principal identifying attributes: (1) Black slip, (2) small modeled effigy figures, and (3) cross-hatching incision.
Paste, firing, and temper: Paste is fine-textured with many small crystalline calcite inclusions. Paste color is gray (10YR5/1).
Surface finish and decoration: Exterior surfaces are covered in black slip. Preslip incised cross-hatching decoration appears on the exterior of the few pieces

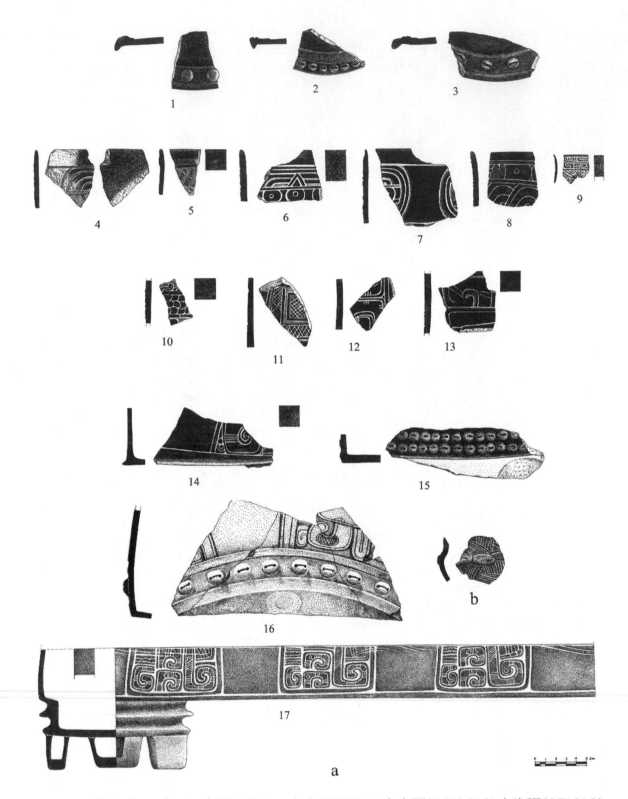

Figure 6.22. Urita Gouged-incised: Urita Variety: (a1) SUF.T.29.06, (a2) ST.08.71A.01.01, (a3) ST.08.71.01.02, (a4) ST.08.80, (a5) ST.08.34, (a6) ST.08.55, (a7) ST.08.80, (a8) SUF.T.29.06, (a9) CIV.T.32.02.01.01, (a10) (SUF. LT.01.STR.1, (a11) ST.08.71.01.06, (a12) ST.08.80.01.03, (a13) ST.08.80.01.04, (a14) ST.08.08.01.03), (a15) SUF.T.37.03, (a16) SUT.05.09, and (a17) HOL.T.84.14.02.02. Positas Modeled: Positas Variety: (b) ST.08.80.01. Drawings by Fernando Alvarez (Holmul Archaeological Project). Figure 6.17, center, is a photo of vessel a17.

of material that exist. Appliqué filets also appear on some sherds.

Forms: While this type is extremely rare, a number of small, modeled body fragments have been recovered; among them an arm, shoulder, and possibly part of a head. Other than this, no form data or measurements are available.

Intraregional locations and contexts: This type has only been found in the fill of Structure 1 at La Sufricaya.

Interregional locations and contexts: Positas Modeled: Positas Variety appears at Uaxactun (Smith and Gifford 1966:161, 171), Tikal (Culbert 1993:14, 2006), and as an Unspecified Variety at La Milpa (Sagebiel 2005:295–296).

Comment: Positas Modeled may be a K'ak 2-3 facet marker.

Illustration: Figure 6.22b. Note that color conventions are not followed in this figure, but all examples are slipped black.

CHAPTER SEVEN

Chak Complex

Michael G. Callaghan

The Chak Complex dates between AD 550 and 950. Unfortunately, the Chak Complex sample available at the time of this study is small. In addition, at present, no radiocarbon dates can be associated with the Chak Complex. Contextual classification of ceramics associated with hieroglyphic inscriptions and polychrome ceramic styles have, however, allowed me to separate the Chak Complex into three facets: an early (Chak 1), middle (Chak 2), and late (Chak 3). Although Chak 1 ceramics have been typologically related to the Tepeu 1 Sphere (see Callaghan 2005, 2008), they have only recently been found in association with hieroglyphic inscriptions that verify this assertion. Chak 1 ceramics were found in a tomb located in a substructure of Building A, Group II at Holmul (Estrada-Belli 2013). The tomb contained the body of a possible early Late Classic period Holmul ruler. The frieze on the exterior of the building containing the tomb recorded a potential relationship between the deceased Holmul ruler and the Late Classic ruler of Naranjo, *Aj Wasal*, who reigned from AD 546 to 615 (Martin and Grube 2008:70).

Chak 2 facet ceramics from the middle Late Classic period can be contextually dated through the presence of Tepeu 2 Sphere diagnostic ceramics and, more specifically, by the presence of Cabrito Cream Polychromes of the Zacatel Group. Merwin found examples of Cabrito Cream Polychrome in sealed tomb deposits in Building F, Group I and Ruin X in his original excavations in 1911 (Merwin and Vaillant 1932). Vessel 1 from Building F displays a primary standard sequence (PSS) around the rim below the lip on the exterior. This PSS states that Lord *B'at K'awil*, ruler of Naranjo between AD 780 and 785, commissioned the vessel (Tokovinine 2005:359–360). The

vessel was gifted to the individual in Tomb 1 of Group F and buried with this person's body (Callaghan 2014).

Archaeologists have discovered Cabrito Cream Polychrome with PSSs that mention Naranjo lords in other sites outside of the Holmul region. The most notable example comes from Buena Vista del Cayo, Belize, where a Cabrito Cream Polychrome vessel was found in association with the burial of a provincial lord (Ball and Taschek 1992). The PSS on that vessel names the original owner as *K'ak Tiliw Chan Chak,* who ruled the polity of Naranjo between AD 693 and 728. This type of cream polychrome is not found in association with contexts later than AD 800. Based on these dates I believe it is safe to place the production and distribution of Cabrito Cream Polychrome, and contextually related Chak 2 ceramics in the Holmul region to between AD 693 and 800. Finally, Chak 3 ceramics of the Tepeu 3 Sphere can be contextually dated between AD 800 and 900. Although there are no hieroglyphic inscriptions associated with ceramics of this facet, I am able to date the facet based upon presence or absence of strong Terminal Classic period diagnostics and distinguishable decorative modes.

Descriptions of Chak material included in this study come from 954 rim sherds, 2,981 diagnostic body sherds, and 44 vessels, for a total of 3,979 samples. Three definable wares, 9 groups, and 24 type: varieties define the Chak Complex (Table 7.1). The majority of type: varieties are slipped (68.9 percent). Typologically, Chak ceramics resemble material of the Tepeu 1–3 Spheres during the Late Classic period in the Maya lowlands. As noted previously, I have separated the Chak Complex into three facets: Chak 1 (i.e., Tepeu 1), Chak 2 (i.e., Tepeu 2), and Chak 3 (i.e., Tepeu 3). It is important to note that these

Table 7.1. Ceramic Wares, Groups, Types, and Varieties of the Late Classic Period (Chak Complex)

Ware	Group (% of complex)	Type: Variety	Numbers			Percentages	
			Rims	Bodies	Vessels	Group	Complex
Uaxactun Unslipped	Cambio (31.1%)	Cambio Unslipped: Cambio Variety	299	818	1	96.8	30.1
		Encanto Striated: Encanto Variety	6	255	0	1.9	0.6
		Miseria Appliquéd: Miseria Variety	4	3	0	1.3	0.4
Petén Gloss	Tinaja (42.3%)	Tinaja Red: Tinaja Variety	239	1542	0	56.6	23.9
		Chinja Impressed: Floresas Variety	71	9	0	16.8	7.1
		Chinja Impressed: Tuspán Variety	51	20	0	12.1	5.1
		Chaquiste Impressed: Chaquiste Variety	10	4	0	2.4	1.0
		Cameron Incised: Cameron Variety	44	33	1	10.7	4.5
		Cameron Incised: Variety Unspecified	6	0	0	1.4	0.6
	Saxche (4.9%)	Saxche Orange Polychrome: Saxche Variety	19	7	23	100.0	4.2
	Palmar (3.3%)	Palmar Orange Polychrome: Palmar Variety	20	13	0	100.0	2.0
	Zacatel (3.1%)	Zacatel Cream Polychrome: Zacatel Variety	17	10	5	71.0	2.2
		Cabrito Cream Polychrome: Cabrito Variety	5	23	4	29.0	0.9
	Achote (16.6%)	Achote Black: Achote Variety	16	150	0	100.0	1.6
	Maquina (0.5%)	Maquina Brown: Maquina Variety	5	0	0	100.0	0.5
	Asote (0.9%)	Asote Orange: Asote Variety	9	0	0	100.0	0.9
Fine Orange Paste Ware	Altar (0.1%)	Trapiche Incised: Trapiche Variety	0	1	1	100.0	0.1
Unspecified	Unnamed (14.2%)	Unnamed Polychrome (Chak 1)	0	0	3		0.3
		Unnamed Black-on-orange (Chak 1)	0	0	1		0.1
		Unnamed Polychrome (Chak 2-3)	117	49	5		12.2
		Unnamed Black-on-orange (Chak 2-3)	7	9	0		0.7
		Unnamed Red-on-cream (Chak 2-3)	4	2	0		0.4
		Unnamed Modeled and Painted (Chak 2-3)	0	0	1		0.1
		Unnamed Modeled (Molded)-carved (Chak 3)	5	33	1		0.6
		TOTALS	**954**	**2981**	**44**		

facets do not represent distinct and separate ceramic complexes at this time. As I explain here and in the type-descriptions that follow, these facets are distinguished from one another based on the appearance and disappearance of diagnostic types, as well as changes in modes of established Late Classic type: varieties. In earlier publications I (Callaghan 2005, 2008, 2013) presented the facets as three separate complexes. Upon further typological work, however, I have yet to find strong enough evidence of complete assemblage replacement, or quantifiable change, in serving, utilitarian, and trade types to warrant the identification of three separate complexes. This does not preclude the identification of separate complexes in the future, but for now I feel more comfortable with labeling these phases as facets.

Chak 1 ceramics belong to the Tepeu 1 Sphere, first defined by Smith (1955:40; see also Willey et al. 1967:299–301) for Uaxacatun; they date between AD 550 and 693. During Chak I, the ceramics from the Cambio, Tinaja, and Saxche groups make an appearance. Saxche Orange Polychrome is a Chak 1 diagnostic type. Some modal differences in serving vessels distinguish Chak 1 types from later Chak 2 and 3 types. Form and decorative modes are the most sensitive indicators of chronological change within long-spanning Chak types. Open plate forms have small lateral ridges during the Chak 1 facet. Cylinder vases with vertical sides are not frequent during the Chak 1 facet. Small round-sided or barrel-shaped bowls are more common during Chak 1 as opposed to flaring-sided bowls in the later Chak 2 facet. Red slip color tends toward red-orange during Chak 1 and may represent a local outgrowth from earlier Aguila Group types. Significant deposits of Chak 1 ceramics were found in Building A, Group II, and other contexts at the site of Holmul.

Chak 2 facet ceramics are contemporaneous with Tepeu 2 Sphere material as defined by Smith (1955:40; see also Willey et al. 1967:299–301) for Uaxactun; they date between AD 693 and 800. During the Chak 2 facet Saxche Orange Polychrome disappears. Palmar Orange Polychrome, Zacatel Cream Polychrome, and Cabrito Cream Polychrome appear. Forms of polychrome vessels change in frequency. Barrel-shaped bowl forms are absent and round-sided bowl forms diminish in frequency, while flaring and outcurving–side bowl forms increase. Open plate forms often lack lateral ridges or flanges, have flat bases, and have three hollow supports. A new type: variety appears within the Tinaja group, Chinja Impressed: Floresas Variety. Significant deposits of Chak 2 material have been found in Building F, Group I, and in Ruin X at Holmul.

Chak 3 material is affiliated with the Tepeu 3 Sphere as defined by Smith (1955:40; see also Willey et al. 1967:301–303) at Uaxactun; it dates between AD 800 and 900. The Chak 3 facet is characterized by the disappearance of Zacatel Group Polychromes. New type: varieties include Miseria Appliquéd within the Cambio Group. Type: varieties also diversify in the Tinaja Group including the addition of Chinja Impressed: Tuspán Variety (in accordance with the disappearance of Chinja Impressed: Floresas Variety), Cameron Incised, and Chaquiste Impressed. Strong Terminal Classic period Petén diagnostics like Asote Orange, Maquina Brown, and Achote Black all appear (although in small frequencies). Also present are small frequencies of Altar Group ceramics and potential local type: varieties of molded-carved or modeled-carved ceramics in the tradition of Pabellon Modeled-carved. New polychrome type: varieties appear, but samples are so small and eroded that they remain unspecified at this time. One example of a coarse-paste effigy vessel was found in a stela cache at Homul (Estrada-Belli 2001). The most significant Chak 3 deposits are found at Holmul in the palace structure of Group III. Here I present a brief description of major wares, followed by type-descriptions for the Chak Complex. I offer interpretations in the Chapter 8.

UAXCATUN UNSLIPPED WARE

Smith and Gifford (1966:169) established this ware at Uaxactun. It is characterized by roughly smoothed unslipped surfaces. Decoration includes striation and applique. Vessel surfaces are the color of pastes (7.5YR5/2, 4/2). Pastes are coarse to medium textured with primary inclusions of crystalline calcite. Type: varieties within Uaxactun Unslipped Ware that date to the Chak Complex include

Cambio Group
    Cambio Unslipped: Cambio Variety
    Encanto Striated: Encanto Variety
    Miseria Appliquéd: Miseria Variety

PETÉN GLOSS WARE

Smith and Gifford (1966:167–168) defined Petén Gloss Ware at Uaxactun. Surfaces are smoothed and polished to a shine. No polish or burnish marks are visible. Slip color in the Late Classic is predominantly red-orange (2.5YR4/8, 4/6) or black. Decoration includes incision, punctation, impression, polychrome painting (red-

and-black-on-orange, red-and-black-on-buff), black-on-orange painting, modeling, and applique. Pastes are light-colored and range from yellow (10YR6/4, 7/3) to gray (10YR5/1). Common inclusions are volcanic ash and crystalline calcite. Groups and type: varieties within Petén Gloss Ware of the Chak Complex include

Tinaja Group
    Tinaja Red: Tinaja Variety
    Chinja Impressed: Floresas Variety
    Chinja Impressed: Tuspán Variety
    Chaquiste Impressed: Chaquiste Variety
    Cameron Incised: Cameron Variety
    Cameron Incised: Variety Unspecified
Saxche Group
    Saxche Orange Polychrome: Saxche Variety
Palmar Group
    Palmar Orange Polychrome: Palmar Variety
Zacatel Group
    Zacatel Cream Polychrome: Zacatel Variety
    Cabrito Cream Polychrome: Cabrito Variety
Achote Group
    Achote Black: Achote Variety
Maquina Group
    Maquina Brown: Maquina Variety
Asote Group
    Asote Orange: Asote Variety

FINE ORANGE PASTE WARE

Smith and Gifford (1966:165–166) established Fine Orange Paste Ware at Uaxactun. Surfaces are well-smoothed and can be unslipped, slipped red, or black. Although presently in the Holmul region there is only one example of true Fine Orange Paste Ware (Trapiche Incised: Trapiche Variety) and it displays a black slip. Decoration includes incision, gouged-incision, modeling, molding, impression, and punctation. The example from the Holmul region displays deep incision. Its paste is fine-textured and orange in color (5YR6/8; 7.5YR6/8) with no visible inclusions. It does not react to HCL indicating that it is not a carbonate-based paste.

Altar Group
    Trapiche Incised: Trapiche Variety

UNSPECIFIED WARES

The Chak Complex also includes type: varieties that do not belong to the Uaxactun Unslipped, Petén Gloss, or Fine Orange Paste Wares. Because of the limited size and eroded nature of the sample, I cannot define specific wares for these type: varieties at this time. These type: varieties include

Unnamed
    Unnamed Polychrome (Chak 1)
    Unnamed Polychrome (Chak 2-3)
    Unnamed Black-on-orange (Chak 1)
    Unnamed Black-on-orange (Chak 2-3)
    Unnamed Red-on-cream (Chak 2-3)
    Unnamed Modeled and Painted (Chak 2-3)
    Unnamed Modeled (Molded)-Carved
      (Chak 3)

TYPE DESCRIPTIONS

Cambio Unslipped: Cambio Variety

Established: Smith and Gifford at Uaxactun (1966: 155, 173).
    Group: Cambio
    Ware: Uaxactun Unslipped
    Complex: Chak 1-3
    Sphere: Tepeu 1-3
    Ceramic Group Frequency: 299 rims, 818 bodies, 1 vessel, 1,118 total, 96.8 percent of group, 30.1 percent of complex.
    Principal identifying attributes: (1) Unslipped surfaces and (2) large jars with outcurving necks, direct rims, and squared lips.
    Paste, firing, and temper: Paste is coarse in texture with many large crystalline calcite inclusions. Paste color is gray (10YR5/1), yellow (10YR7/4), or pink (5YR6/4). Paste cores are not common.
    Surface finish and decoration: Exterior vessel surfaces are smoothed and remain unslipped. Surfaces are porous and gritty with paste inclusions often showing through. Fire-clouding can occur on body sherds. Surface color is similar to paste, gray (10YR5/1), yellow (10YR7/4), or pink (5YR6/4).
    Forms: Large, wide-mouthed jars with outcurving necks, direct rims, and squared lips. Rim diameters measure 16 to 20 cm, wall thicknesses 0.6 to 0.8 cm, neck heights 5 to 6 cm, and vessel heights 35 to 45 cm.
    Intraregional locations and contexts: Cambio Unslipped is found in Chak complex deposits at South Group 1 at Holmul, other locations at Holmul, and La Sufricaya.
    Interregional locations and contexts: Cambio Unslipped: Cambio Variety has been found at Uaxactun (Smith

and Gifford 1966:155), Altar de Sacrificios (Adams 1971:18), Tikal (Culbert 1993:13, 2006), Calakmul (Dominguez-Carrasco 1994:53), and El Mirador (Forsyth 1989:114). It appears as an Unspecified Variety at Yaxchilan (1989:101), Becan (Ball 1977:9), La Milpa (Sagebiel 2005:326–330, 388–398, 484–493), and Seibal (Sabloff 1975:153–155); and as an Unspecified Variety and local varieties in the Petexbatun region (Foias and Bishop 2013:148–156),. Aside from the site of La Milpa in Belize and Calakmul in Mexico, unslipped types generally diverge from established Petén types in the Late Classic period at many other Belizean and Mexican sites.

Comment: Although Cambio Unslipped jars span the entire Chak Complex, modal differences in form distinguish earlier from later types. The main difference between Cambio Unslipped of the earlier Chak 1 and 2 facets and the later Chak 3 facet is the presence of piecrust impression on the lips of jar rims on Chak 3 material. Piecrust impressions do not occur on Chak 1 or Chak 2 jars.

Illustration: Figure 7.1a.

Encanto Striated: Encanto Variety

Established: Smith and Gifford at Uaxactun (1966: 157, 173).

Group: Cambio
Ware: Uaxactun Unslipped
Complex: Chak 2-3
Sphere: Tepeu 1-3
Ceramic Group Frequency: 6 rims, 255 bodies, 261 total, 1.9 percent of group, 0.6 percent of complex.

Principal identifying modes: (1) Unslipped surfaces, (2) crisscrossing medium to heavy striations on exterior surfaces, and (3) large jars with outcurving necks, direct rims, and squared lips.

Paste, firing, and temper: Paste, temper, and firing are the same as Cambio Unslipped.

Surface finish and decoration: Surface treatment is the same as Cambio Unslipped with the addition of medium to deep striations on vessel exteriors. Paste color is gray (10YR5/1), yellow (10YR7/4), or pink (5YR6/4).

Forms: Large wide mouth jars with outcurving necks. Rim diameters measure 16 to 20 cm, wall thicknesses 0.6 to 0.8 cm, and neck heights 5 to 6 cm.

Intraregional locations and contexts: Encanto Striated has been found in South Group 1 at Holmul other locations at Holmuland at La Sufricaya.

Interregional locations and contexts: Encanto Striated: Encanto Variety has been found at Uaxactun (Smith and Gifford 1966:157), Altar de Sacrificios (Adams 1971:19),

Calakmul (Dominguez-Carrasco 1994:53), Tikal (Culbert 2006), and El Mirador (Forsyth 1989:114-117). It appears as an Unspecified Variety at Seibal (Sabloff 1975:155-158), Yaxchilan (Lopez Varela 1989:113), and La Milpa (Sagebiel 2005:331-333, 405, 499–504); as local varieties at Becan (Ball 1977:15) and Piedras Negras (Muñoz 2004:19, 22 also as Encanto Variety); and as an Impressed Variety in the Petexbatun region (Foias and Bishop 2013:161–162). It is similar to Tu-Tu Camp striated found at Barton Ramie (Gifford 1976:273–277), Chan (Kosakowsky 2012:62) and Colha (Valdez 1987:191–193), but is not the same type.

Comment: Currently Encanto Striated occurs in Chak 2 and 3 facet contexts.

Illustration: Figure 7.1b.

Miseria Appliquéd: Miseria Variety

Ceramic Group Frequency: 4 rims, 3 bodies, 7 total, 1.3 percent of group, 0.4 percent of complex.

Established: Smith and Gifford at Uaxactun (1966: 159, 173).

Group: Cambio
Ware: Uaxactun Unslipped
Complex: Chak 3
Sphere: Tepeu 3
Principal identifying attributes: (1) Unslipped vessel surfaces, (2) censerware, (3) coarse, gritty paste, and (4) small bowls or composite vessels with appliquéd spikes on the exterior.

Paste, firing, and temper: Paste, firing, and temper are the same as Cambio Unslipped. Paste color is gray (10YR5/1), yellow (10YR7/4), or pink (5YR6/4). Pastes are carbonate-based with medium to large crystalline calcite inclusions. Fire clouds occur, but could be due to use as censers and not part of the production process.

Surface finish and decoration: Vessel surfaces are smoothed but remain unslipped. Appliquéd spikes decorate vessel exteriors. Surface color is the color of the paste: gray (10YR5/1), yellow (10YR7/4), or pink (5YR6/4).

Forms:

1. Small bowls with flaring sides, direct rims, and rounded lips; rim diameters measure 10 to 14 cm and wall thicknesses 0.6 to 0.9 cm; and

2. hourglass-shaped vessels and other composite forms (no measurements available).

Intraregional locations and contexts: An excellent example of Miseria Appliquéd comes from South Group 1 at Holmul. Miseria can also be found at Holmul.

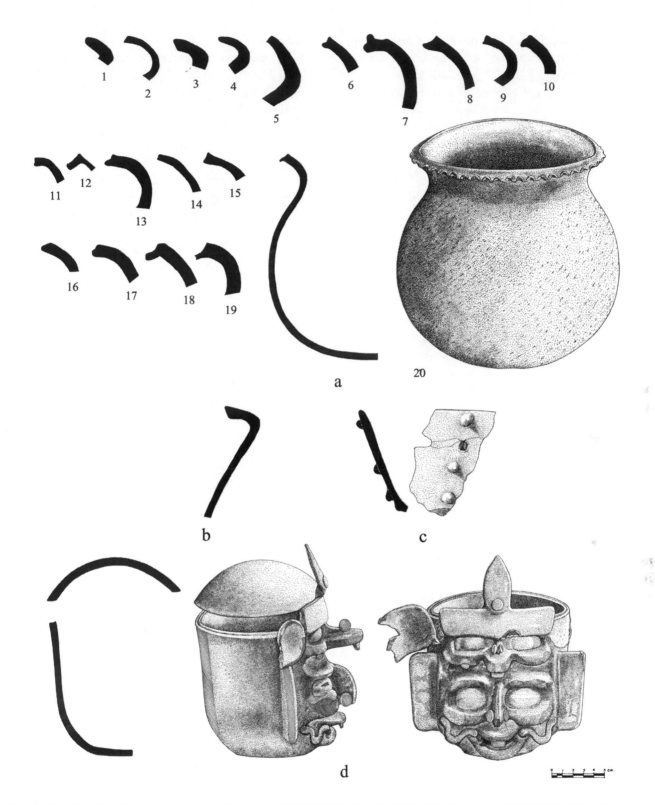

Figure 7.1. Cambio Unslipped: Cambio Variety: (a1) HOL.T.53.01, (a2) HOL.T.47.02, (a3 –a4) HOL.T.46.03, (a5) HOL.T.53.01, (a6) HOL.T.57.22, (a7) HOL.T.48.03, (a8) HOL.T.58.02, (a9–a10) HOL.T.48.03, (a11) HOL.T.58.03, (a12) HOL.T.53.01, (a13) HOL.T.50.04, (a14) HOL.T.58.01, (a15–a16) HOL.T.47.02, (a17) HOL.T.57.13, (a18) HOL.T.53.01, (a19) HOL.T.57.32, and (a20) SUF.T.11.05.02.01. Encanto Striated: Encanto Variety: (b1) HOL.T.57.08. Miseria Appliquéd: Miseria Variety: (c1) HOL.LT.13.01.01.02. Unnamed Modeled and Painted (Chak 2-3): (d1) HOL.TP.1.L7. Drawings by Michael G. Callaghan (a1–a19, b) and Fernando Alvarez (a20, c, d) (Holmul Archaeological Project).

Interregional locations and contexts: Miseria Appliquéd: Miseria Variety appears at Uaxactun (Smith and Gifford 1966:159, 173), and Calakmul (Dominguez-Carrasco 1994:53). It appears as an Unspecified Variety and local variety at Yaxchilan (Lopez Varela 1989:153), as local varieties at Piedras Negras (Muñoz 2004:22), as an Unspecified Variety at Seibal (Sabloff 1975:174) and La Milpa (Sagebiel 2005:494–498), and as an Unspecified Variety in the Petexbatun region where it is named Miseria "Applique" (Foias and Bishop 2013:166). Adams (1971:53–56) identifies local varieties of Miseria "Applique" at Altar de Sacrificios, but these are Late Preclassic and Early Classic types, part of his Salinas, Ayn, and early Veremos Complexes.

Comments: Presently, Miseria Appliquéd appears to be a Chak 3 facet marker in the Holmul region.

Illustration: Figure 7.1c.

Tinaja Red: Tinaja Variety

Established: Smith and Gifford at Uaxactun (1966: 163, 172).

> *Group:* Tinaja
> *Ware:* Petén Gloss
> *Complex:* Chak 1–3
> *Sphere:* Tepeu 1–3

Ceramic Group Frequency: 239 rims, 1,542 bodies, 1781 total, 56.6 percent of group, 23.9 percent of complex.

Principal identifying attributes: (1) Red slip, (2) jars with short vertical necks and everted rim, (3) bowls with round sides, and (4) open plates with tripod supports.

Paste, firing, and temper: There are two paste variants, the first is fine-textured with mixed calcite and volcanic ash inclusions (the calcite is not visible even under magnification, but the paste reacts heavily to HCL). This paste is yellow (10YR7/3) and reserved for serving vessels. The second variant is gritty and gray with visible crystalline calcite inclusions. This paste color is gray (10YR5/1) or brown-yellow (10YR6/4) and reserved for larger jars and basins as well as serving bowls. Firing cores are not common in either variant.

Surface finish and decoration: On smaller bowls, vessel interiors and exteriors are smoothed. Red-orange slip (2.5YR4/8, 4/6) is applied to vessel interiors, over the lip, and about half way down the exterior surface. Plates are slipped entirely with a relatively even red or red-orange slip. Jars are slipped an even red. Fire-clouding is extremely common on jar forms.

Forms:

> 1. Round-sided bowls with direct rims and rounded or squared lips; rim diameters measure 15 to 37 cm, wall thicknesses 0.6 to 0.8 cm, and heights 6 to 10 cm;
>
> 2. plates with open flaring sides, convex bases, and tripod supports; rim diameters measure 29 to 36 cm, wall thicknesses 0.6 to 0.8 cm, and heights 8 to 10 cm; and
>
> 3. jars with short vertical necks, everted rims, and rounded lips; rim diameters measure 10 to 15 cm and wall thicknesses 0.6 to 0.8 cm.

Intraregional locations and contexts: Tinaja Red vessels are mostly found at Holmul, especially in South Group 1, but do occur at K'o, and La Sufricaya.

Interregional locations and contexts: Tinaja Red was established as the predominant red type at Uaxactun (Smith and Gifford 1966:163, 172) where Smith and Gifford (1966:171–172) differentiated between Tepeu 3 Tinaja Red, Tepeu 2 Nanzal Red, and Tepeu 1 Tasital Red. Although Smith and Gifford may have been able to distinguish differences among red ceramics of different complexes within the Late Classic period, I have not been able to do this with the Holmul sample. Tinaja Red: Tinaja Variety is also present at Altar de Sacrificios where it also occurs in local varieties (Adams 1971:23), at Becan (Ball 1977:23), Tikal (Culbert 1993:15, 2006), and Calakmul (Dominguez-Carrasco 1994:52); as an Unspecified Variety at Chan (Kosakowsky 2012:62), Colha (Valdes 1987:194), Yaxchilan (Lopez Varela 1989:125), and Seibal (Sabloff 1975:158–160); as an Unspecified Varieties at La Milpa in the Late Classic II and III facets (Sagebiel 2005:412–417, 507–511); and as local varieties at Piedras Negras (Muñoz 2004:19),. At El Mirador Forsyth (1989:79–86) identifies a Tinaja Red: Tinaja Variety as well as a Tinaja Red: Nanzal Variety, and in the Petexbatun region it is identified as Variety Unspecified (Foias and Bishop 2013:166–172).

Comment: Tinaja Red is currently found more frequently in Chak 3 contexts, but does appear in small frequencies in Chak 1 and 2 contexts. Unlike Aguila Group ceramics of the Early Classic K'ak Complex, I have not been able to correlate time sensitive differences in paste, form, and surface modes within Tinaja Red, nor have I found any meaningful pattern related to paste differences between sites. Paste differences appear to be related to vessel form and function. Coarse pastes with crystalline calcite are associated with larger cooking, storage, and food processing jars and bowls. Finer pastes with volcanic inclusions are associated with smaller serving bowls and plates.

Illustration: Figure 7.2a. Note that Figure 7.2a19–20 are shaded as unslipped; they are not unslipped but are extremely eroded.

Chinja Impressed: Floresas Variety

Established: Type named by Smith and Gifford at Uaxactun (1966:156, 172), Variety named by Callaghan in this study.

Group: Tinaja
Ware: Petén Gloss
Complex: Chak 2
Sphere: Tepeu 2
Ceramic Group Frequency: 71 rims, 9 bodies, 80 total, 16.8 percent of group, 7.1 percent of complex.

Principal identifying attributes: (1) Large open bowl or "olla" forms; (2) ring of deep fingernail impressions encircling the vessel exterior; and (3) red-slipped interior—the slip runs up and over lip and extends down to the row of fingernail impressions on exterior.

Paste, firing, and temper: The paste is the second variant of Tinaja Group ceramics. Paste is medium in texture with many large crystalline calcite inclusions. Past color is gray (10YR5/1) or brown-yellow (10YR6/4). Firing cores are not common, but do occur.

Surface finish and decoration: Vessel interiors and exteriors are well-smoothed and polished. A row of deep, gouged fingernail impressions encircles the vessel exterior. The entire interior is slipped red or red-orange (2.5YR4/8; 10R4/8). The slip continues up and over the lip and extends down to the row of fingernail impressions on vessel exteriors. The remainder of the vessel exterior below the row of impressions is left unslipped.

Forms: Large open bowls or "ollas" with direct rims and rounded lips. Rim diameters measure 25 to 40 cm and wall thicknesses 0.7 to 0.9 cm.

Intraregional locations and contexts: Chinja Impressed: Floresas Variety can be found in highest frequency in the South Group 1 at Holmul.

Interregional locations and contexts: This type: variety is similar, but not identical to Chinja Impressed: Chinja Variety, which appears at Uaxactun (Smith and Gifford 1966:156, 172), Tikal (Culbert 1993:13, 2006), Seibal (Sabloff 1975:168–171), Calakmul where Dominguez-Carrasco (1994:52) places it in the Nanzal Group, as an

Unspecified Variety at La Milpa in Late Classic III (Sagebiel 2005:512–514), and at El Mirador (Forsyth 1989:86–89). Chinja Impressed: Floresas Variety is similar to Pascua Impressed (Gifford 1976:178), Gloria Impressed (Gifford 1976:200, 202), and Kaway Impressed (Gifford 1976:239–240) at Barton Ramie, but these are different types.

Comment: Chinja Impressed: Floresas Variety is a Chak 2 diagnostic.

Illustration: Figure 7.2b.

Chinja Impressed: Tuspán Variety

Established: Type named by Smith and Gifford at Uaxactun (1966:156, 172), Variety named by Callaghan in this study.

Group: Tinaja
Ware: Petén Gloss
Complex: Chak 3
Sphere: Tepeu 3
Ceramic Group Frequency: 51 rims, 20 bodies, 71 total, 12.1 percent of total, 5.1 percent of complex.

Principal identifying attributes: (1) Large open bowl or "olla" forms, (2) ring of shallow "slash" fingernail impressions encircling the vessel exterior, and (3) red-slipped interiors with slip running up and over lip and extending down to a row of fingernail impressions on the vessel exterior.

Paste, firing, and temper: Paste is the second variant of Tinaja Red. Pastes are medium textured with crystalline calcite inclusions. Paste color is gray (10YR5/1) or brown-yellow (10YR6/4). Firing cores are not common, but do occur.

Surface finish and decoration: Vessel interiors and exteriors are well-smoothed and polished. A row of shallow, slash-like fingernail-made impressions encircles the vessel exterior. The entire interior is slipped red (2.5YR4/8; 10R4/8). The slip continues up and over the lip and extends down to the row of slash impressions. The remainder of the vessel exterior below the row of impressions is usually left unslipped.

Forms: Large open bowls or ollas with incurving walls, direct rims, and squared lips. Rim diameters measure 36 to 45 cm and wall thicknesses 0.7 to 0.9 cm.

Intraregional locations and contexts: Chinja Impressed: Tuspan Variety can be found in largest quantities in contexts at Holmul.

Interregional locations and contexts: This type: variety is similar, but not identical to Chinja Impressed: Chinja

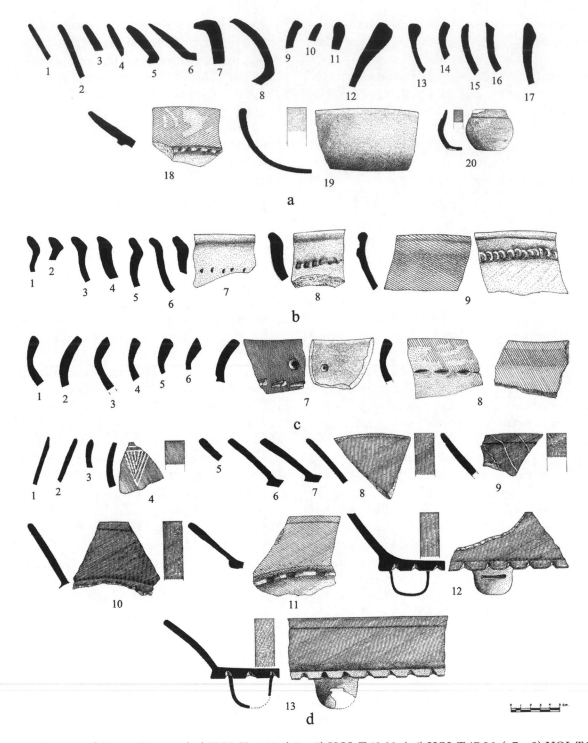

Figure 7.2. Tinaja Red: Tinaja Variety: (a1) HOL.T.47.02, (a2–a5) HOL.T.48.03, (a6) HOL.T.47.06, (a7–a9) HOL.T.50.02, (a10–a11) HOL.T.47.06, (a12) HOL.T.57.22, (a13–a14) HOL.T.53.01, (a15) HOL.T.57.02, (a16) HOL.T.47.19, (a17) HOL.T.47.02, (a18) HOL.T.48.03, (a19) HOL.T.35.04.02.01, and (a20) SUF.T.37.03.02.01. Chinja Impressed: Floresas Variety: (b1–b5) HOL.T.48.03, (b6) HOL.T.57.32, (b7–b8) HOL.T.48.03, and (b9) HOL.T.47.13. Chinja Impressed: Tuspán Variety: (c1) HOL.T.57.02, (c2) HOL.T.47.02, (c3) HOL.T.53.01, (c4) HOL.T.57.32, (c5) HOL.T.53.01, (c6) HOL.T.58.01, (c7) HOL.T.15.19.01, and (c8) HOL.T.57.32. Cameron Incised: Cameron Variety: (d1) HOL.T.28.40, (d2) HOL.T.55.03, (d3) HOL.T.58.02, (d4) HOLT.T.77.05, (d5) HOL.T.57.02, (d6) HOL.T.53.01, (d7) HOL.T.58.01, (d8–d12) HOL.T.23.10, (d13) SUF.T.11.10.02.01. Drawings by Michael G. Callaghan (a1–17, b1–b6, c1–c6, d1–d3, d5–d7) and Fernando Alvarez (a18–20, b7–9, c7–c8, d4, d8–d13) (Holmul Archaeological Project).

Variety, which occurs at Uaxactun (Smith and Gifford 1966:156, 172), Tikal (Culbert 1993:13, 2006), Seibal (Sabloff 1975:168–171), and Calakmul where Dominguez-Carrasco (1994:52) places it in the Nanzal Group, and at El Mirador (Forsyth 1989:86–89). and as an Unspecified Variety at La Milpa in Late Classic III (Sagebiel 2005:512–514). Chinja Impressed: Floresas Variety is similar to Pascua Impressed (Gifford 1976:178), Gloria Impressed (Gifford 1976:200, 202), and Kaway Impressed (Gifford 1976:239–240) at Barton Ramie, but these are different types.

Comments: Chinja Impressed: Tuspán Variety is a Chak 3 diagnostic marker. The two varieties of Chinja Impressed do not appear to overlap chronologically. The distinguishing characteristics of Floresas Variety and Tuspán Variety are associated with form, style of fingernail impressions, and chronological context. Tuspán Variety displays slash-like impressions whereas Floresas Variety displays true fingernail impressions.

Illustration: Figure 7.2c.

Cameron Incised: Cameron Variety

Established: Smith and Gifford at Uaxactun (1966: 155, 172).

Group: Tinaja
Ware: Petén Gloss
Complex: Chak 3
Sphere: Tepeu 3
Ceramic Group Frequency: 44 rims, 33 bodies, 1 vessel, 78 total, 10.7 percent of group, 4.5 percent of complex.

Principal identifying attributes: (1) Red-orange slip, (2) plates with tripod supports and basal ridges, and (3) thin bands of incision on exterior surface just below the lip, and tick marks on basal ridges.

Paste, firing, and temper: Cameron Incised plates are made with the first of the two paste variants described for Tinaja Red. Paste color is orange or yellow (10YR7/3) with volcanic ash inclusions and possibly finely crushed calcite inclusions. Calcite is not visible even with magnification, but pastes react strongly to HCL.

Surface finish and decoration: Interior and exterior surfaces are smoothed, polished, and slipped red or red-orange (2.5YR4/8, 4/6). A single or double horizontal circumferential band of incision is executed just below the lip on vessel exteriors. A circumferential band of dentate stamping is also common on plate exteriors near the basal break. Tick marks can appear on basal flanges.

Forms:
1. Plates with flaring sides, direct rims, rounded lips, flat bases, tripod supports, and basal flanges or ridges;

rim diameters measure 28 to 38 cm, wall thicknesses 0.5 to 0.8 cm, and heights 7 to 11 cm; and

2. vases with incurving sides, direct rims, and rounded lips; rim diameters measure 13 to 18 cm and wall thicknesses 0.5 to 0.7 cm.

Intraregional locations and contexts: Cameron Incised: Cameron Variety has only been found at Holmul.

Interregional locations and contexts: Cameron Incised: Cameron Variety also appears at Uaxactun (Smith and Gifford 1966:155, 172), Tikal (Culbert 1993:13, 2006) Altar de Sacrificios (Adams 1971:44), Calakmul (Dominguez-Carrasco 1994:52), Becan (Ball 1977:88), Seibal (Sabloff 1975:179-181), and as an Unspecified Variety at Yaxchilan (Lopez Varela 1989:104) and La Milpa in Late Classic II (Sagebiel 2005:419–421).

Comment: Cameron Incised: Cameron Variety plates from the Holmul region bear a striking resemblance to Belize Red plates from the Belize River Valley (Xunantunich in particular, personal observation 2005). Cameron Incised: Cameron Variety is a Chak 3 diagnostic marker.

Illustration: Figure 7.2d.

Cameron Incised: Variety Unspecified

Established: Type named by Smith and Gifford at Uaxactun (1966), Variety named by Callaghan this study.

Group: Tinaja
Ware: Petén Gloss
Complex: Chak 3
Sphere: Tepeu 3
Ceramic Group Frequency: 6 rims, 0 bodies, 0 vessels, 6 total, 1.4 percent of group, 0.6 percent of complex.

Principal identifying modes: (1) Red-orange slip, (2) plates with tripod supports and basal ridges, (3) bands of grooved-incision on exterior surface just below the lip, and (4) occasional smudging on exterior surfaces near the rim and grooved-incision.

Paste, firing, and temper: Cameron Incised: Variety Unspecified plates are made with the first of the two paste variants described for Tinaja Red. Paste color is orange or yellow (10YR7/3) with volcanic glass inclusions and possibly finely crushed calcite inclusions. Calcite is not visible even with magnification, but pastes react strongly to HCL.

Surface finish and decoration: Interior and exterior surfaces are smoothed, polished, and slipped red or red-orange (2.5YR4/8, 2.5YR4/6). A single or double horizontal circumferential band of grooved-incision is executed just below the lip on vessel exteriors. A circumferential band of dentate stamping is also common on plate exteriors near the basal break. Tick marks can appear on basal flanges. On these type: varieties, black smudges occur on the exterior of vessels near the rim and covering the fine-line incision. I think this smudging is intentional and is one trait that distinguishes this Unspecified Variety from the established Cameron Variety Forms of the Unspecified Variety are exclusively open plates, which also distinguishes this variety from the established variety.

Forms: Forms consist of plates with flaring sides, direct rims, rounded lips, flat bases, tripod supports, and basal flanges or ridges (no measurements available).

Intraregional locations and contexts: Cameron Incised: Variety Unspecified has been found only at Holmul.

Interregional locations and contexts: This variety does not appear in the literature on other lowland Maya sites.

Comment: Like Cameron Incised: Cameron Variety, Cameron Incised: Variety Unspecified is a Chak 3 diagnostic marker. Because of the small sample size I feel more comfortable identifying this variety as unspecified.

Illustration: Figure 7.3a.

Chaquiste Impressed: Chaquiste Variety

Established: Adams at Altar de Sacrificios (1971:47).
Group: Tinaja
Ware: Petén Gloss
Complex: Chak 2-3
Sphere: Tepeu 2-3
Ceramic Group Frequency: 10 rims, 4 bodies, 14 total, less than 2.4 percent of group, 1 percent of complex.

Principal identifying attributes: (1) Large incurving bowls or ollas, (2) finger impressed appliqué fillet encircling vessel exterior, and (3) red slip that extends from the interior lip down to top of fillet on exterior.

Paste, firing, and temper: Paste is the second variant of Tinaja Red. Pastes are medium textured with crystalline calcite inclusions. Paste color is gray (10YR5/1) or brown-yellow (10YR6/4). Firing cores are not common, but do occur.

Surface finish and decoration: Vessel exteriors are smoothed and polished. A finger-impressed appliquéd fillet encircles the vessel exterior. Red slip (2.5YR4/8; 10R4/8) extends down from the interior lip to the top of the fillet on vessel exteriors.

Forms: Large open bowls or ollas with incurving sides, folded rims, and rounded lips. Rim diameters measure 35 to 44 cm and wall thicknesses are 0.7 to 0.9 cm.

Intraregional locations and contexts: Chaquiste Impressed: Chaquiste Variety has been found in the South Group 1 at Holmul.

Interregional locations and contexts: Chaquiste Impressed: Chaquiste Variety is more prevalent in the Pasión River region and has been found at Altar de Sacrificios (Adams 1971:47); as an Unspecified Variety at Seibal (Sabloff 1975:168), and Calakmul (Dominguez-Carrasco 1994:52); as an Unspecified Variety and Appliqué Variety at Yaxchilan (Lopez Varela 1989:107, 109), and as Unspecified and Stamped varieties in the Petexbatun region (Foias and Bishop 2013:188–194).

Comments: Chaquiste Impressed is rare, but is a late Chak 2 and Chak 3 ceramic diagnostic.

Illustration: Figure 7.3b.

Achote Black: Achote Variety

Established: Smith and Gifford at Uaxactun (1966: 154, 172).
Group: Achote
Ware: Petén Gloss
Complex: Chak 3
Sphere: Tepeu 3
Ceramic Group Frequency: 16 rims, 150 bodies, 166 total, 100 percent of group, 1.6 percent of complex.

Principal identifying modes: (1) Black slip, (2) smooth polished vessel surfaces, and (3) small dishes or bowls.

Paste, firing, and temper: Paste color varies from yellow (10YR7/4), gray (10YR5/1) to black. All pastes have crystalline calcite inclusions. Firing cores are common and when they do appear compose one hundred percent of the cross section.

Surface finish and decoration: Surfaces are smoothed and polished. Slips can appear mottled with brown or orange showing through from underneath.

Forms: Late Classic monochrome blacks are rare in the Holmul region and only a few rims are present. Definite forms include

1. small dishes or bowls with flaring sides, direct rims, and rounded lips; rim diameters measure 13 to 21 cm and wall thicknesses 0.5 to 0.7 cm;

2. bowls with round sides, direct rims, and rounded lips; rim diameters measure 12 to 22 cm and wall thicknesses 0.5 to 0.7 cm;

3. a possible jar form with an outcurving neck, direct rim, and rounded lip (no measurements available); and

4. a possible vase with recurving sides, direct rim, and rounded lip (no measurements available).

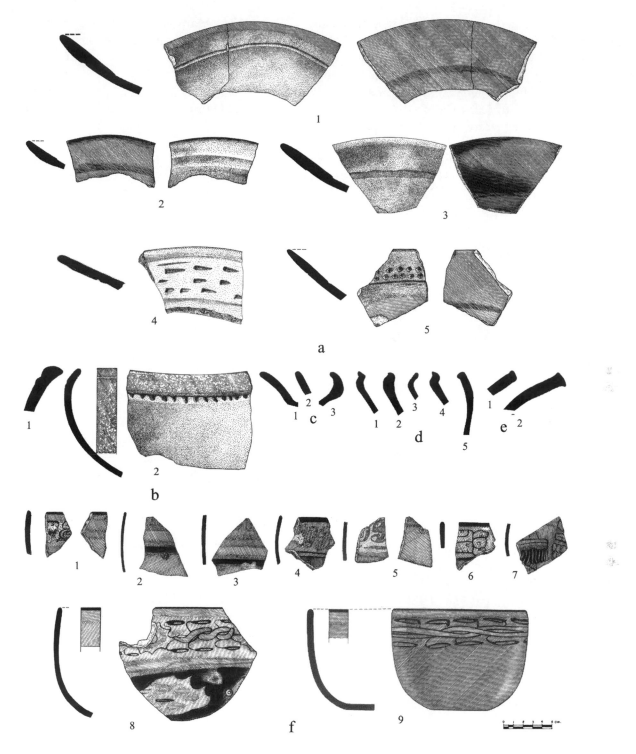

Figure 7.3. Cameron Incised: Variety Unspecified: (a1) HOL.T.83.01, (a2) HOL.L.20.16, (a3) HOL.L.21.01, (a4) HOL.T.57.32, and (a5) HOL.L.21.01. Chaquiste Impressed: Chaquiste Variety: (b1) HOL.T.58.03 and (b2) HM.LT.61.00.02.04. Achote Black: Achote Variety: (c1) HOL.T.57.02, (c2) HOL.T.49.02 and (c3) HOL.T.48.03. Asote Orange: Asote Variety: (d1) HOL.T.57.13, (d2–d3) HOL.T.57.02, (d4) HOL.T.57.13, and (d5) HOL.T.47.02. Maquina Brown: Maquina Variety: (e1) HOL.T.57.01 and (e2) HOL.T.57.15. Saxche Orange Polychrome: Saxche Variety: (f1) SUF.STR.138, (f2–f3) HOL.T.29.03, (f4–f6) N/A, (f7) SUF.STR.113, (f8) DAG.T.19.15.0106, and (f9) HOL.L.20.21.02.15. Drawings by Fernando Alvarez (a, b2, f) and Michael G. Callaghan (b1, c, d, e) (Holmul Archaeological Project).

Intraregional locations and contexts: Achote Black has been found only in Group III at Holmul.

Interregional locations and contexts: Achote Black: Achote Variety is often identified as the black-slipped type ceramic during the Tepeu 3 Sphere at sites in the Petén, but it is also found in earlier complexes at sites in Belize. It can be found at Uaxactun (Smith and Gifford 1966:154), Altar de Sacrificios (Adams 1971:25), Becan (Ball 1977:34), Tikal (Culbert 1993:13, 2006), and Calakmul (Dominguez-Carrasco 1994:52). It appears as an Unspecified Variety at Seibal (Sabloff 1975:181, 184), El Mirador (Forsyth 1989:119), Colha (Valdez 1987:197), Yaxchilan (Lopez Varela 1989:101), and at La Milpa during Late Classic II and III times (Sagebiel 2005:425–432, 515–518). It has been defined on the group level at Barton Ramie (Gifford 1976:248), and identified as the "Infierno Black: Achiote Variety" in the Petexbatun region (Foias and Bishop 2013:272–274).

Comment: Achote Black is a Chak 3 diagnostic marker, but is rare in Terminal Classic contexts at Holmul. This is not surprising, as black-slipped pottery of the Infierno Group was absent in samples of the preceding Chak 1 and 2 facets. This low frequency of black ceramics could, however, be a product of our small sample at the present time.

Illustration: Figure 7.3c.

Maquina Brown: Maquina Variety

Established: Smith and Gifford at Uaxactun (1966: 159, 172).

Group: Maquina
Ware: Petén Gloss
Complex: Chak 3
Sphere: Tepeu 3
Ceramic Group Frequency: 5 rims, 5 total, 100 percent of group, 0.5 percent of complex.

Principal identifying attributes: (1) Brown slip, (2) small flaring-walled incurving-lip bowls, and (3) large restricted bowls or ollas.

Paste, firing, and temper: Paste is medium to fine in texture with mixed volcanic ash and crystalline calcite inclusions. Paste color is yellow to orange (10YR7/3).

Surface finish and decoration: Vessel surfaces are well-smoothed and slipped a light brown (7.5YR5/4) on vessel interiors and exteriors. Patches of orange are also present. Vessels are polished to a dull shine.

Forms:
1. Small flaring-sided bowls with slightly incurving rims and rounded lips; rim diameters measure

20 to 24 cm and wall thicknesses 0.5 to 0.8 cm. This form variant is identical to Asote Orange as recorded at Uaxactun (see Smith and Gifford 1966:154, 159); and
2. large bowls or ollas with incurving rims and rounded lips (no measurements available).

Intraregional locations and contexts: Found in Chak 3 deposits in Group III, Holmul.

Interregional locations and contexts: Maquina Brown: Maquina Variety is very rare, but has been found at Uaxactun (Smith and Gifford 1966:159, 172), Tikal (Culbert 2006), Calakmul (Dominguez-Carrasco 1994:52), and in the Dolores Valley (Laporte et al. 1993:117).

Comment: Maquina Brown is a Chak 3 diagnostic marker. It is quite possible that Maquina Brown and Asote Orange are the same type, but because of mottling during the firing process they appear orange or brown depending on the sherd that is being classified. This is a product and flaw of the type: variety classification system. Regardless, both these types are rare in the Holmul region. Elsewhere in the Petén lowlands these two types are diagnostic of the Tepeu 3 Sphere.

Illustration: Figure 7.3e.

Asote Orange: Asote Variety

Established: Smith and Gifford at Uaxactun (1966: 154, 172).

Group: Asote
Ware: Petén Gloss
Complex: Chak 3
Sphere: Tepeu 3
Ceramic Group Frequency: 9 rims, 9 total, 100 percent of group, 0.9 percent of complex.

Principal identifying attributes: (1) Orange slip, (2) small flaring-walled incurving lip bowls, and (3) large restricted bowls or ollas.

Paste, firing, and temper: Paste is medium to fine in texture with mixed volcanic ash and calcite inclusions. The paste color is yellow to orange (10YR7/3, 7/4).

Surface finish and decoration: Vessel interiors and exteriors are well-smoothed and polished. An orange slip may have been applied to the entire surface. Slip color is orange (2.5YR5/8), but surfaces are extremely eroded and this reading may not be representative.

Forms: The forms are the same as Maquina Brown with the exception of large restricted ollas. The main form is a small, outflaring bowl with a slightly incurving rim and rounded lip; rim diameters measure 20 to 24 cm and wall thicknesses 0.5 to 0.8 cm.

Intraregional locations and contexts: Like Maquina Brown, Asote Orange has been found only at Holmul.

Interregional locations and contexts: Asote Orange: Asote Variety has been identified as a Tepeu 3 type at Uaxactun (Smith and Gifford 1966:154, 172). It has also been found in the Dolores Valley (Laporte et al. 1993:133) and Calakmul (Dominguez-Carrasco 1994:52).

Comments: Asote Orange is a Chak 3 Terminal Classic diagnostic marker. As noted previously, it is possible that Maquina Brown and Asote Orange are the same type, but because of mottling during the firing process they appear orange or brown depending on the sherd that is being classified. This is a product and flaw of the type: variety classification system. Regardless, both these types are rare in the Holmul region. Elsewhere in the Petén lowlands these two types are diagnostic of the Tepeu 3 Sphere.

Illustration: Figure 7.3d.

Saxche Orange Polychrome: Saxche Variety

Established: Smith and Gifford at Uaxactun (1966: 162–163).

Group: Saxche
Ware: Petén Gloss
Complex: Chak 1
Sphere: Tepeu 1
Ceramic Group Frequency: 19 rims, 7 bodies, 23 vessels, total 49, 100 percent of group, 4.2 percent of complex.

Principal identifying attributes: (1) Orange slip, (2) red and black painted designs, (3) glossy surface, (4) bowls with round or slightly incurving sides, (5) barrel-shaped bowls, and (6) open plates with lateral ridges and tripod supports.

Paste, firing, and temper: Paste is fine to medium in texture and can be either carbonate based with white and crystalline calcite inclusions, volcanic with crushed ash inclusions, or mixed. Paste color is yellow (10YR7/3) to orange (7.5YR7/6).

Surface finish and decoration: Vessel surfaces were well-smoothed and slipped with a thin, cream-colored underslip. An orange slip (7.5YR6/8, 6/6) applied over the cream underslip served as the background for painting. Glyphic designs and fine figural elements were painted in black and red (10R4/8) and the surface was then polished.

Forms:

1. Plates with open flaring sides, direct rims, rounded lips, basal ridges, flat or convex bases, and tripod supports; rim diameters measure 30 to 36 cm, wall thicknesses 0.5 to .7 cm, and heights 5 to 7 cm;

2. bowls with round or slightly incurving sides, direct rims, and rounded lips; rim diameters measure 14 to 21 cm, wall thicknesses 0.5 to 0.7 cm, and heights 8 to 12 cm; and

3. barrel-shaped bowls with flat bases; rim diameters measure 13 to 20 cm, wall thicknesses 0.5 to 0.7 cm, and heights 8 to 13 cm.

Intraregional locations and contexts: The site of Holmul contains the most Saxche Orange Polychrome; a few pieces have been found in contexts at La Sufricaya. The most significant context is the recently excavated tomb in the substructure of Building A, Group II, at Holmul.

Interregional locations and contexts: Saxche Orange Polychrome: Saxche Variety was used throughout the lowlands during the early part of the Late Classic Period. It occurs at Uaxactun (Smith and Gifford 1966:162–163), Tikal (Culbert 1993:14, 2006), Calakmul (Dominguez-Carrasco 1994:52), Becan (Ball 1977:68–72), and Altar de Sacrificios as both the established and local varieties (Adams 1971:37–38). It is grouped with Palmar at Seibal because of poor preservation (Sabloff 1975:123–132). It occurs at Chan where Kosakowsky (2012:62) also combines the Saxche and Palmar types. As an Unspecified Variety it occurs at La Milpa in Late Classic I contexts (Sagebiel 2005:351–357), at Colha (Valdez 1987:204), at Piedras Negras where Muñoz (2004:20) places it in the Palmar Group, and at Barton Ramie (Gifford 1976:205–209).

Comment: Saxche is an excellent marker of Chak 1 contexts.

Illustration: Figure 7.3f, 7.4, 7.5, 7.6, 7.7 (left and right bowls), and possibly 7.15c.

Palmar Orange Polychrome: Palmar Variety

Established: Smith and Gifford at Uaxactun (1966: 160, 172).

Group: Palmar
Ware: Petén Gloss
Complex: Chak 2 facet
Sphere: Tepeu 2
Ceramic Group Frequency: 20 rims, 13 bodies, 33 total, 100 percent of group, 2 percent of complex.

Principal identifying attributes: (1) Orange slip, (2) red and black painted designs, and (3) glossy surface.

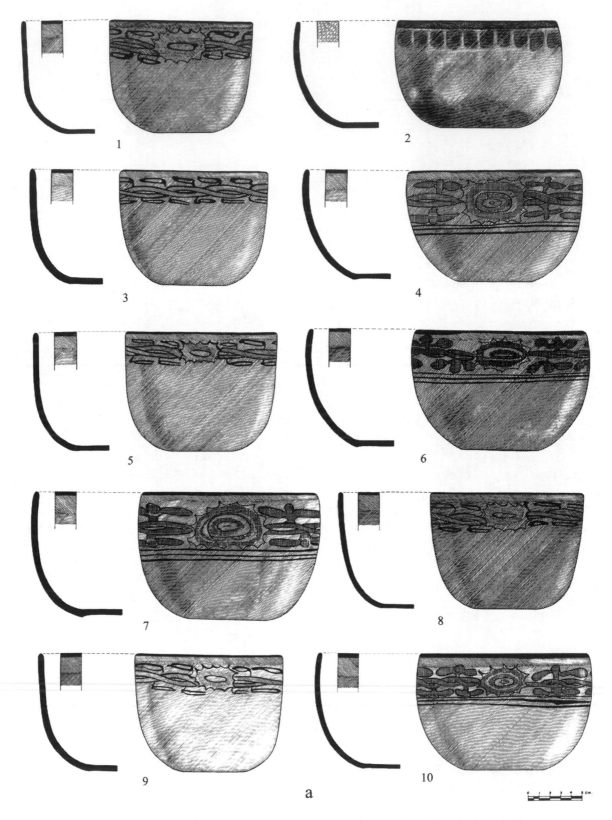

Figure 7.4. Saxche Orange Polychrome: Saxche Variety bowls: (a1) HOL.L.20.21.02.12, (a2) HOL.L.20.15.02.01, (a3) HOL.L.20.21.02.01, (a4) HOL.L.20.21.02.02, (a5) HOL.L.20.21.02.03, (a6) HOL.L.20.21.02.04, (a7) HOL.L.20.21.02.05, (a8) HOL.L.20.21.02.06, (a9) HOL.L. 20.21.02.07, and (a10) HOL.L.20.21.02.08. Drawings by Fernando Alvarez (Holmul Archaeological Project).

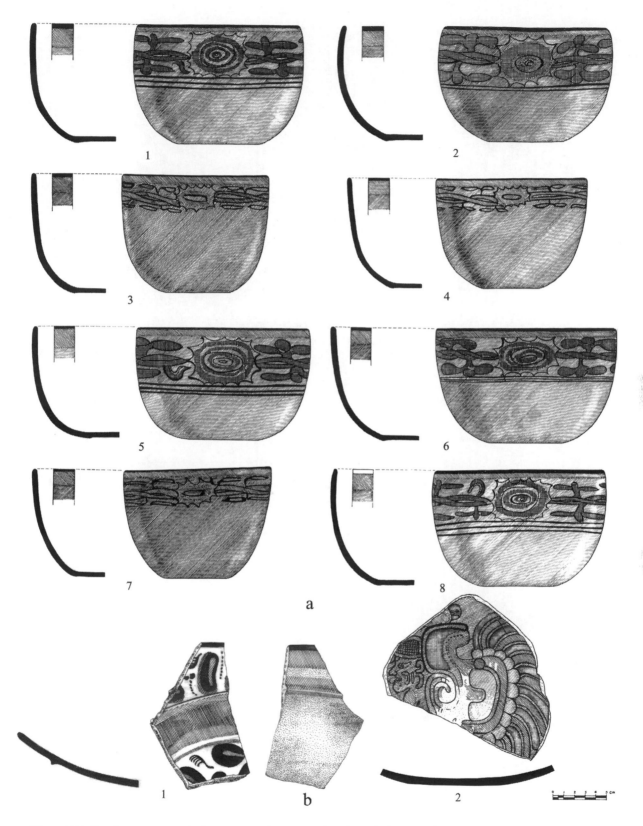

Figure 7.5. Saxche Orange Polychrome: Saxche Variety bowls and plates: (a1) HOL.L.20.21.02.10, (a2) HOL.L.20.21.02.11, (a3) HOL.L.20.21.02.13, (a4) HOL.L.20.21.02.14, (a5) HOL.L.20.21.02.16 (see Figure 7.8 for photo of this vessel), (a6) HOL.L.20.21.02.17, (a7) HOL.L.20.21.02.18, (a8) HOL.L.20.21.02.09, (b1) HOL.T.56.01, and (b2) DAG.T.29.25.03.05. Drawings by Fernando Alvarez (Holmul Archaeological Project).

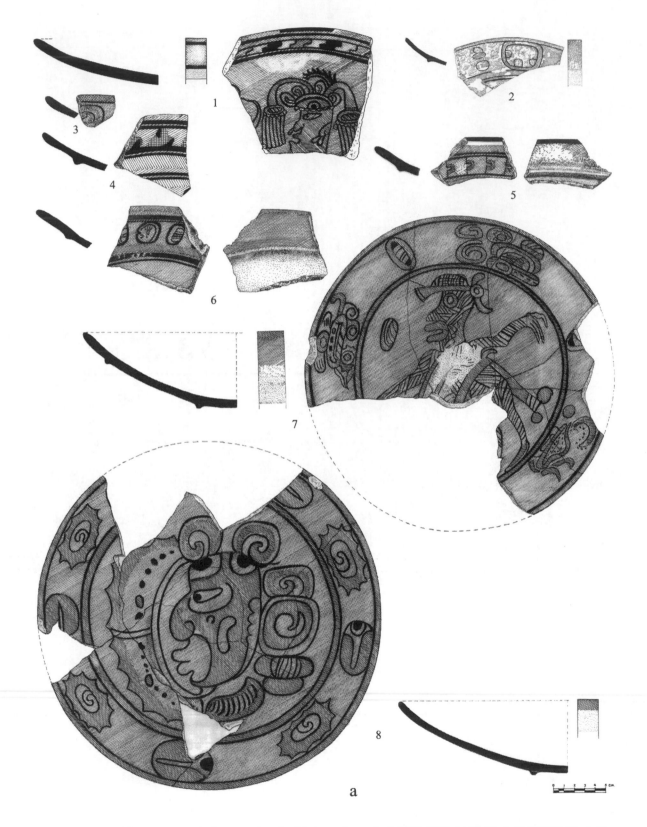

Figure 7.6. Saxche Orange Polychrome: Saxche Variety plates: (a1) HOL.T.78.44.03.01, (a2) SLT.01.01, (a3) Unknown provenance, (a4) ST.08.02, (a5) Unknown provenance, (a6) SUF.STR.113, (a7) DAG.T.19.15.02.02, (a8) and. DAG.T.19.15.02.01. Drawings by Fernando Alvarez (Holmul Archaeological Project).

0   CM   10

Figure 7.7. Saxche Orange Polychromes at left (HOL.T.57.02) and right (HOL.L.20.21.02.16), Unnamed Polychrome (Chak 1) in middle (HOL.L.20.21), and Nitan Composite: Nitan Variety Vessel center back (HOL.L.20.21.02.20). Photo by Diana Méndez-Lee. See Figures 7.4a5, 7.5a5, and 7.14 for additional illustrations of these vessels.

Paste, firing, and temper: Paste is fine to medium in texture and can be either carbonate-based with white and crystalline calcite inclusions, volcanic with crushed ash, or mixed. Paste color is yellow (10YR7/3) to orange (7.5YR7/6).

Surface finish and decoration: Vessel surfaces are well-smoothed and slipped with a thin cream underslip. Orange slip (7.5YR6/6, 6/8) applied over the cream underslip served as the background for black and red (10R/48) painted design of abstract or conventionalized elements. Vessels are well-polished.

Forms:

1. Plates with flaring walls, direct rims, rounded lips, basal ridges, flat or convex bases, and tripod supports; rim diameters measure 22 to 33 cm, wall thicknesses 0.6 to 0.9 cm, and heights 7 to 11 cm;

2. bowls with outflaring sides, direct rims, rounded lips, and flat bases; rim diameters measure 22 to 27 cm, wall thicknesses 0.6 to 0.9 cm, and heights 7 to 10 cm;

3. bowls with round sides, direct rims, and rounded lips; rim diameters are 15 to 26 cm, wall thicknesses 0.6 to 0.9 cm, and heights 7 to 10 cm; and

4. cylinder-vases with vertical walls, direct rims, and rounded lips; rim diameters measure 16 to 19 cm, wall thicknesses 0.6 to 0.9 cm, and heights 17 to 20 cm.

Intraregional locations and contexts: The residential contexts at South Group 1 at Holmul contain the most Palmar Orange Polychrome found to date. Some pieces have also been found at K'o.

Interregional locations and contexts: Palmar Orange Polychrome: Palmar Variety is common throughout the lowlands during the Late Classic Period. It appears at Uaxactun (Smith and Gifford 1966:10, 162), Tikal (Culbert 1993:14, 2006), and Calakmul (Dominguez-Carrasco 1994:52). It occurs as an Unspecified Variety at La Milpa during Late Classic II (Sagebiel 2005:452–459); as an Unspecified Variety combined with Saxche at Chan

(Kosakowsky 2012:62); as an Unspecified Variety and local variety at Piedras Negras (Muñoz 2004:20); and as an Unspecified Variety at Colha (Valdez 1987:200–204), El Mirador (Forsyth 1989:107-109), and Barton Ramie (Gifford 1976:249). It occurs as local varieties at Altar de Sacrificios (Adams 1971:37–39). Because of poor preservation, Palmar Orange Polychrome is grouped with Saxche at Seibal (Sabloff 1975:123–132) and with Zacatel in the Petexbatun region (Foias and Bishop 2013:221–232). It occurs as the established variety and a Resist Variety at Becan (Ball 1977:74).Comment: Palmar is a Chak 2 marker and is not present in earlier Chak 1contexts at sites in the Holmul region.

Illustration: Figure 7.8.

Zacatel Cream Polychrome: Zacatel Variety

Established: Smith and Gifford at Uaxactun (1966: 164, 172).

Group: Zacatel
Ware: Petén Gloss
Complex: Chak 2 facet
Sphere: Tepeu 2
Ceramic Group Frequency: 17 rims, 10 bodies, 5 vessels, 32 total, 71 percent of group, 2.2 percent of complex.

Principal identifying attributes: (1) Cream slip, (2) highly polished glossy surfaces, (3) red and black painted designs over cream, (4) cylinder vases, and (5) bowls with flaring or outcurving walls.

Paste, firing, and temper: Paste is fine–textured with volcanic ash inclusions. Paste color is yellow (10YR7/3) to buff (10YR8/2; 2.5Y8/2). Firing cores are uncommon.

Surface finish and decoration: Vessel interiors and exteriors are smoothed and polished. Cream slip (10YR8/1; 2.5Y8/1) is applied as a background for painting. Red (10R4/8) and black designs in the form of bands and simple geometric or abstract patterns decorate the exteriors of vessels. Orange slip (7.5YR6/6, 6/8) may occur on vessel interiors, accompanied by simple horizontal bands of black and red paint.

Forms:

1. Cylinder vases with vertical sides, direct rims, and rounded lips; rim diameters are 11 to 15 cm, wall thicknesses 0.6 to 0.9 cm, and heights 15 to 18 cm; and

2. bowls with flaring or outcurving sides, direct rims, and rounded lips; rim diameters measure 18 to 24 cm, wall thicknesses 0.6 to 0.9 cm, and heights 7 to 10cm.

Intraregional locations and contexts: Zacatel Cream polychromes have been found at La Sufricaya and in the residential contexts of South Group I at Holmul.

Interregional locations and contexts: Zacatel Cream Polychrome: Zacatel Variety is found at Uaxactun (Smith and Gifford 1966:10, 164, 172), Tikal (Culbert 1993:15, 2006), Yaxchilan (Lopez Varela 1989:132), and Altar de Sacrificios (Adams 1971:41). It occurs as an Unspecified Variety at Barton Ramie (Gifford 1976:251), Colha (Valdez 1987:204), El Mirador (Forsyth 1989:112), Becan (Ball 1977:78), and in Late Classic II contexts at La Milpa (Sagebiel 2005:460–472). It is grouped with Palmar in the Petexbatun region because of poor preservation (Foias and Bishop 2013:220–232).

Comment: Zacatel Cream Polychrome is a Chak 2 facet marker. It is important to note that Culbert (1993:12), Gifford (1976:249–251), and Foias and Bishop (2012:220) place Palmar Orange Polychrome and Zacatel Cream Polychrome in the same group. Forsyth (1989:9) places these two types in different groups. Based on attributes of Palmar and Zacatel sherds in the Holmul region sample, I prefer to place these two types in two different groups as well. In the Palmar Group, black and red designs are painted on an orange-slipped surface. In the Zacatel Group, black and sometimes only red designs are painted on a cream surface. Furthermore, design composition varies with Palmar compositions comprised of more naturalistic and conventionalized elements, while on Zacatel Group polychromes there is a preference for geometric patterns. Both Zacatel and Palmar Group polychromes can display glyphs or pseudoglyphs, but this is rare in the current sample.

Illustration: Figures 7.9 and 7.10a.

Cabrito Cream Polychrome: Cabrito Variety

Established: Named as a type Reents (1985) for sites in the northeast Petén region, originally named as a variety of Zacatel Cream Polychrome by Smith and Gifford (1966:172).

Group: Zacatel
Ware: Petén Gloss
Complex: Chak 2 facet
Sphere: Tepeu 2
Ceramic Group Frequency: 5 rims, 23 bodies, 4 vessels, 32 total, 29 percent of group, 0.9 percent of complex.

Principal identifying attributes: (1) Cream slip, (2) fine-line painting using only red and orange paint with occasional black, (3) design elements include

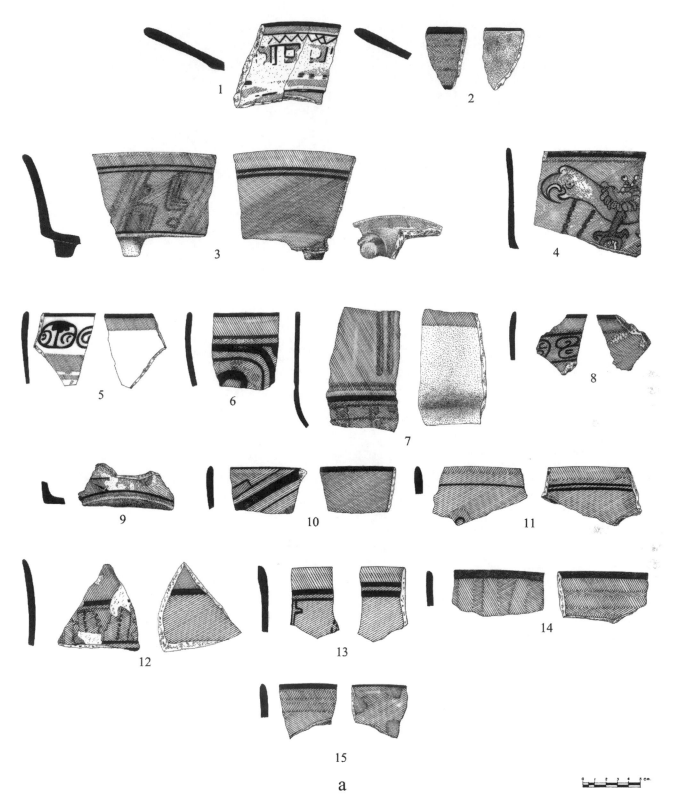

Figure 7.8. Palmar Orange Polychrome: Palmar Variety: (a1) Unknown provenance, (a2) HOL.T.57.15, (a3) STP.01.03.01, (a4) SUF.STR.113, (a5) SUF.STR.138, (a6) Unknown provenance, (a7) HAP.03.T.31. NORTE, (a8) SUF.STR.138, (a9) HOL.T.57.02, (a10)HAP.03.T.31.NORTE, (a11) HOL.T.26.01, and (a12 –a15) N/A. Drawings by Fernando Alvarez (Holmul Archaeological Project).

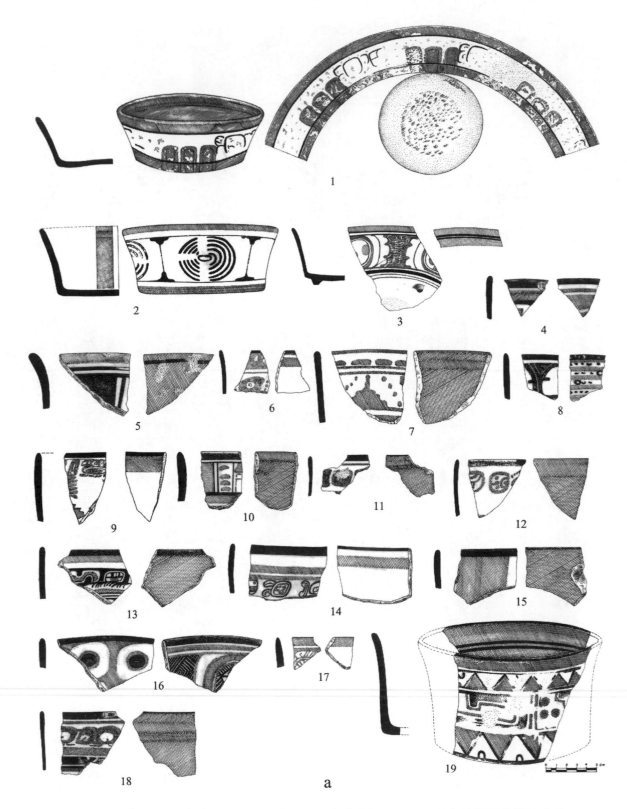

Figure 7.9. Zacatel Cream Polychrome: Zacatel Variety: (a1) SUF.L.17.7.57.06, (a2) BLDG.F.V4, (a3) HOL.T.34.03.01, (a4) SUF.STR.113, (a5) Unknown provenance, (a6) SUF.STR.113, (a7) Unknown provenance, (a8) SUF.STR.138, (a9) DAG.T.19.15.01.02, (a10) HAP.00GH.L.01.00, (a11) Unknown provenance, (a12) ST.07.03.05, (a13) SUF.STR.110, (a14) SUF.STR.113, (a15–a16) SUF.STR.138, (a17) HOL.T.20.E16, (a18) SUF.STR.138, (a19) SUF. STR.110. Drawings by Fernando Alvarez (Holmul Archaeological Project).

Figure 7.10. Zacatel Cream Polychrome: Zacatel Variety: (a1) Unknown provenance, (a2) SUF.STR.113, (a3–a4) SUF.STR.138, (a5) Unknown provenance, (a6) HOL.T.30.OESTE, and (a7) Unknown provenance. Cabrito Cream Polychrome: Cabrito Variety: (b1) T.30.HAP.03, (b2) SUF.01.STR.138, (b3) N/A, (b4) HAP.03.T30.03, (b5) SUF.01.STR.110, (b6) SUF.STR.138, (b7) GRIII.HAP.00.L.1.0, (b8)HAP.03.T30.03, (b9) HAP.03.T31. NORTE, (b10) GRIII.HAP.00.L.1.0, (b11) SUF.STR.110, (b12) HOL.BLDG.F.V5, and (b13) HOL.BLDG.F.V1. Drawings by Fernando Alvarez (Holmul Archaeological Project).

human figures and hieroglyphs, and (4) cylinder vases and plates.

Paste, firing, and temper: Paste color is light buff or light gray (10YR8/2). Pastes are fine with few fine inclusions. Pastes tend to be volcanic-based with crushed ash.

Surface finish and decoration: Vessel surfaces are smoothed and polished. A cream slip (10YR8/1; 2.5Y8/1) is applied as a background for painting. Human figures, animals, other life-like designs, and bands of hieroglyphs are often depicted, frequently repeating, around the vessel exteriors. Orange and red paint (10R4/8; 2.5YR5/8) predominate, but black occurs occasionally.

Forms:

1. Cylinder vases with vertical sides, direct rims, and rounded lips; rim diameters measure 11 to 13 cm, wall thicknesses 0.6 to 0.8 cm, and heights 22 to 27 cm;

2. plates with flaring walls, direct rims, rounded lips, flat bases, and tripod supports; rim diameters measure 22 to 33 cm, wall thicknesses 0.6 to 0.9 cm, and heights 7 to 11 cm; and

3. bowls with flaring or outcurving sides, direct rims, and rounded lips; rim diameters are 15 to 23 cm, wall thicknesses 0.6 to 0.9 cm, and heights 7 to 10cm.

Intraregional locations and contexts: Whole vessels have been found in burials at the site of Holmul in Ruin X and Building F, Group I (Merwin and Vaillant 1932; see also Appendix A). Sherds have also been found in South Group 1 at Holmul and in surface finds at La Sufricaya.

Interregional locations and contexts: This type is relatively rare in the lowlands and represents a local regional ceramic style (Reents 1985; Reents-Budet 1994). Cabrito Cream Polychrome: Cabrito Variety has been identified at Uaxactun (Smith and Gifford 1966:172), Naranjo, Guatemala, and Buena Vista del Cayo, Belize (Reents-Budet et al. 2000).

Comments: Cabrito Cream Polychrome is a Chak 2 facet marker. Despite Holmul being known for its Cabrito Cream Polychrome vessels from Merwin's original excavations, the finer quality examples of this type were probably not produced in the Holmul region and seem to have been gifted into Holmul and out of the Naranjo area (Callaghan 2014; Reents-Budet et al. 2000).

Illustration: Figures 7.10b and 7.11a.

Trapiche Incised: Trapiche Variety

Established: Smith and Gifford at Uaxactun (1966: 163, 173).

Group: Altar

Ware: Fine Orange Paste Ware
Complex: Chak 3 facet
Sphere: Tepeu 3
Ceramic Group Frequency: 1 whole vessel, 1 body, 2 total, 100 percent of group, 0.1 percent of complex.

Principal identifying attributes: (1) Fine orange paste, (2) incurving bowls with hollow tripod supports, (3) deep incised lines on interior base of bowl ("grater bowl" form), and (4) black or red slip.

Paste, firing, and temper: Paste color is orange (5YR6/8; 7.5YR6/8). Paste texture is fine with little to no visible inclusions. This paste does not react to HCL and therefore does not contain calcite.

Surface finish and decoration: The vessel surface is well-smoothed. The interior base of the bowl is incised with deep lines. A black slip is applied to the interior vessel surface. The exterior surface is eroded.

Forms: Bowl with incurving walls, direct rims, convex bases, and hollow tripod supports. Rim diameter is 19 cm, vessel walls are 0.5 cm thick, and height is 6 cm.

Intraregional locations and contexts: Found in Group III at Holmul.

Interregional locations and contexts: Trapiche Incised: Trapiche Variety is a definitive Terminal Classic marker at many lowland sites. It can be found at Uaxactun (Smith and Gifford 1966:163, 173), Calakmul (Dominguez-Carrasco 1994:53), and Becan (Ball 1977:88). It occurs as established and local varieties at Altar de Sacrificios (Adams 1971:45); and as the established and Interior-decorated Variety at Seibal (Sabloff 1975:192, 194), in the Petexbatun region (Foias and Bishop 2013:283–286), at Yaxchilan (Lopez Varela 1989:173, 176)

Comments: Trapiche Incised is a Chak 3 facet diagnostic. This single example was probably gifted into the region.

Illustration: Figure 7.12d. Note that the color convention indicates unslipped; this vessel is actually eroded.

Unnamed Polychrome (Chak 2-3)

Established: Callaghan this study.
Group: Unnamed
Ware: Unspecified
Complex: Chak 2-3
Sphere: Tepeu 2-3
Ceramic Group Frequency: 117 rims, 49 bodies, 5 vessels, 171 total, 12.2 percent of complex.

Principal identifying attributes: (1) Orange slip, (2) red and black painted designs, and (3) matte surface finish.

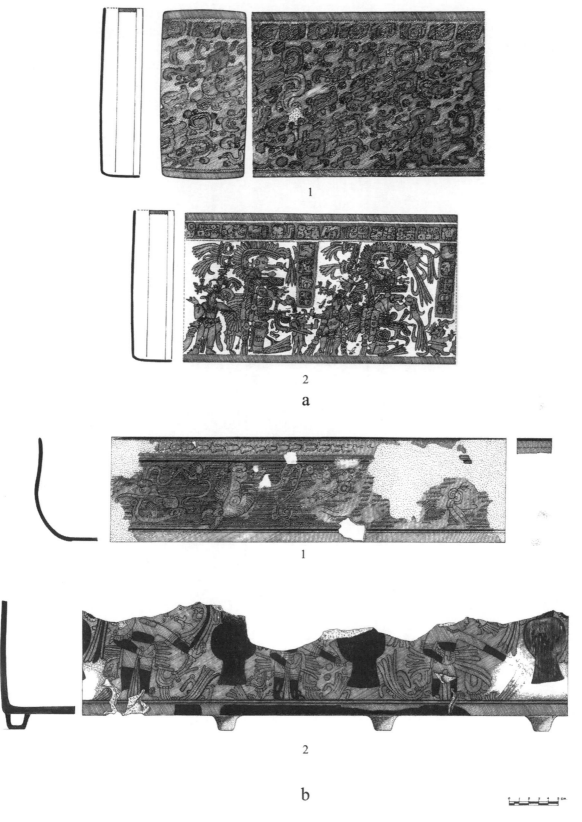

Figure 7.11. Cabrito Cream Polychrome: Cabrito Variety: (a1) HOL.RUIN.X.V3, (a2) HOL. BLDG.F.V3. Unnamed Polychrome (Chak 2-3): (b1) HOL.T.24.10.03.01, (b2) HOL.T.35.02.02.01. Drawings by Fernando Alvarez (Holmul Archaeological Project).

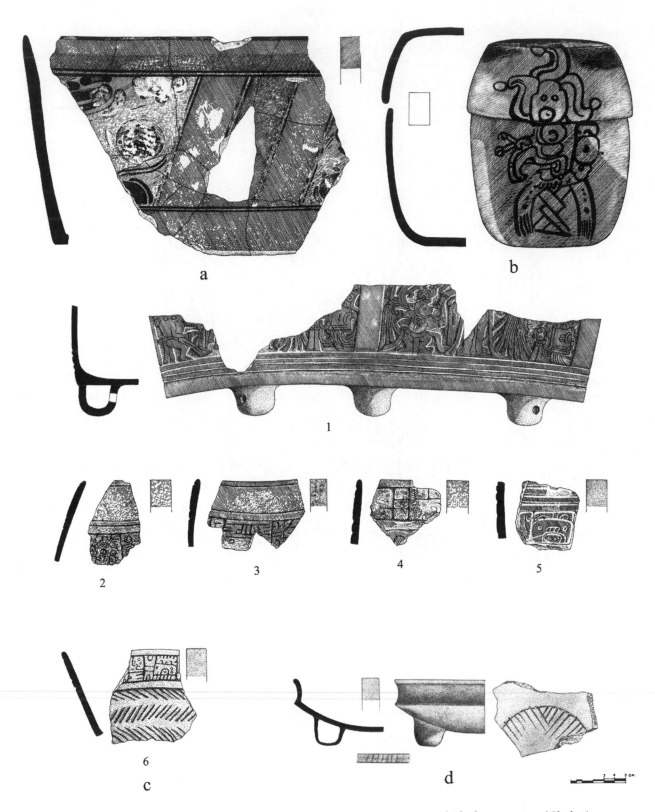

Figure 7.12. Unnamed Polychrome (Chak 2-3): (a1) HOL.T.71.01. Unnamed Black-on-orange (Chak 1) composite vessel: (b1) HOL.T.20.19. Unnamed Modeled (Molded)-carved (Chak 3): (c1) HOL.T.35.04.02.02, (c2–c3) HOL.T.69.02, (c4–c5) HOL.T.67.03, and (c6) HOL.T.69.05.01.01. Trapiche Incised: Trapiche Variety: (d) HOL.T.65.02.01.01. Drawings by Fernando Alvarez (Holmul Archaeological Project).

Paste, firing, and temper: Paste is similar to the first variant of Tinaja Red. Pastes are fine-textured with mixed volcanic glass and possibly crushed calcite inclusions. Although calcite inclusions are not visible, pastes react strongly to HCL. Paste color is yellow to orange (10YR7/3).

Surface finish and decoration: Orange (7.5YR6/8) underslip serves as a background for black and red painted bands and geometric patterns. This type of polychrome is not placed in the Petén Gloss Ware because surfaces remain slightly dull and not highly polished. Surfaces are usually highly eroded, but when paint is present designs are simple and geometric.

Forms:

1. Plates with flaring walls, direct rims, rounded lips, basal ridges, flat or convex bases, and tripod supports; rim diameters measure 22 to 33 cm, wall thicknesses 0.6 to 0.9 cm, and heights 7 to 11 cm;

2. bowls with outflaring sides, direct rims, rounded lips, and flat bases; rim diameters measure 22 to 27 cm, wall thicknesses 0.6 to 0.9 cm, and heights 7 to 10 cm;

3. bowls with round sides, direct rims, and rounded lips; rim diameter measure 15 to 26 cm, wall thicknesses 0.6 to 0.9 cm, and heights 7 to 10 cm; and

4. cylinders with vertical walls, direct rims, and rounded lips; rim diameters measure 16 to 19 cm, wall thicknesses 0.6 to 0.9 cm, and heights 17 to 20 cm.

Intraregional locations and contexts: This unnamed polychrome has been found in South Group 1 and other contexts at Holmul.

Interregional locations and contexts: This unnamed polychrome resembles ceramic material of the Vinaceous Tawny Ware from Belize, specifically Benque Viejo Polychrome (Smith and Gifford 1966:155; Gifford 1976:269–272).

Comments: This unnamed painted type is a Chak 2-3 facet marker. At this time I am uncomfortable with assigning this type an actual name, because the present sample is so highly eroded. There is the possibility that this one type is actually two or more. Regardless, this kind of matte-finish polychrome with simple geometric designs does not appear in earlier Chak 1 deposits. It most likely represents a locally produced serving vessel tradition that dates to the late Late Classic and Terminal Classic periods.

Illustration: Figures 7.11b and 7.12a.

Unnamed Black-on-orange (Chak 2-3)

Established: Callaghan this study
Group: Unnamed
Ware: Unspecified
Complex: Chak 2-3 facet
Sphere: Tepeu 2-3
Ceramic Group Frequency: 7 rims, 9 bodies, 16 total, 0.7 percent of complex.

Principal identifying attributes: (1) Orange slip, (2) black on orange painted designs, and (3) matte surface.

Paste, firing, and temper: The paste is similar to the Unnamed Polychrome (Chak 2-3) and the first variant of Tinaja Red. Pastes are fine-textured with mixed volcanic glass and possibly crushed calcite inclusions. Calcite inclusions are not visible, but the pastes react strongly to HCL. Paste color is yellow to orange (10YR7/3).

Surface finish and decoration: Orange (7.5YR6/8) underslip serves as a background for black bands and geometric patterns. Like the Unnamed Polychrome just described, this type of black-on-orange pottery is not placed in the Petén Gloss Ware because surfaces remain slightly dull and not highly polished.

Forms:

1. Plates with flaring walls, direct rims, rounded lips, basal ridges, flat or convex bases, and tripod supports; rim diameter are 22 to 33 cm, wall thicknesses 0.6 to 0.9 cm, and heights 7 to 11 cm;

2. bowls with outflaring sides, direct rims, rounded lips, and flat bases; rim diameters measure 22 to 27 cm, wall thicknesses 0.6 to 0.9 cm, and heights 7 to 10 cm;

3. bowls with round sides, direct rims, and rounded lips; rim diameters measure 15 to 26 cm, wall thicknesses 0.6 to 0.9 cm, and heights 7 to 10 cm; and

4. cylinders with vertical walls, direct rims, and rounded lips; rim diameters measure 16 to 19 cm, wall thicknesses 0.6 to 0.9 cm, and heights 17 to 20 cm.

Intraregional locations and contexts: This unnamed black-on-orange is relatively rare, but has been found in South Group 1 and other contexts at Holmul.

Interregional locations and contexts: This Unnamed Black-on-orange type resembles ceramic material of the Vinaceous Tawny Ware from Belize more than sites in the central Petén, specifically Xunantunich Black-on-orange (Gifford 1976:268–269).

Comments: Like the Unnamed Painted type previously described, this Unnamed Black-on-orange type is

Figure 7.13. Unnamed Red-on-cream (Chak 2-3). Photo by Michael G. Callaghan.

a Chak 2-3 facet diagnostic. At this time I am uncomfortable with assigning this type an actual name, because the sample is small and highly eroded.

Illustrations: no illustration

Unnamed Red-on-cream (Chak 2-3)

Established: n/a
Group: Unnamed
Ware: Unspecified
Complex: Chak 2-3
Sphere: Tepeu 2-3
Ceramic Group Frequency: 4 rims, 2 bodies, 6 total, 0.4 percent of complex.

Principal identifying attributes: (1) Red on cream painting, (2) carved design band on rim, and (3) cylinder vase form.

Paste, firing, and temper: Paste is fine-textured with crushed volcanic ash. Paste color is buff to yellow (10YR8/2, 8/3; 10YR7/4). Cores are not present in the sample.

Surface finish and decoration: Surfaces are well-smoothed. Interior is usually eroded, but may have been slipped. On vessel exteriors a red (10R4/8) band decorates the rim. The paint contains specular hematite. Beneath the rim is a band of carved and incised repeating glyphs or pseudo-glyphs. Beneath the band the vessel is fluted. The pseudo-glyphs and fluting are covered with cream slip (10YR8/1).

Form: This type is found in one form, a cylinder vase with a direct rim, rounded lip, and flat base. The rim diameter is 10 cm and wall thickness 0.6 cm.

Intraregional locations and contexts: This unnamed type has been found only in Chak 2-3 contexts at Holmul.

Interregional locations and contexts: I have not come upon this type of pottery in other lowland sites. These combinations of vessel form and surface modes are more common in the southern lowlands or northern highlands (see Smith 1952). Carving like this is, however, a common decorative mode in the Terminal Classic period throughout the lowlands (see Smith 1955:25).

Comments: Like the Unnamed Painted types previously described, this Unnamed Red-on-cream ceramic is only found in Chak 2-3 deposits.

Illustration: Figure 7.13.

Unnamed Modeled and Painted (Chak 2-3)

Established: Callaghan this study
Group: Unnamed
Ware: Unspecified
Complex: Chak 2-3
Sphere: Tepeu 2-3
Ceramic Group Frequency: 1 whole vessel, 1 total, 100 percent of group, 0.1 percent of complex.

Principal identifying attributes: (1) Bowl with barrel shaped sides, (2) modeled and appliqué design elements, and (3) red, blue, and white paint.

Paste, firing, and temper: Paste is medium-textured with crystalline calcite inclusions. Paste color is gray to yellow (10YR5/1, 6/4). There is no firing core.

Surface finish and decoration: The interior of the vessel is heavily eroded. The exterior is well-smoothed. A supernatural face is created by modeled and appliqué design. Traces of red (7.5Y3/8), blue, and white or cream (10YR8/1) paint are visible on the exterior.

Forms: Vase with barrel-shaped sides, direct rim, and squared lip. Rim diameter is 17cm, wall thickness 0.8 cm, and height 27 cm.

Intraregional locations and contexts: One example of this type is found in the main plaza at Holmul in a cache associated with Stela 7 (Estrada-Belli 2001).

Interregional locations and contexts: This type is most similar to Pedregal Modeled, which was established by Smith and Gifford (1966:161) at Uaxactun. Pedregal Modeled: Appliquéd Head Variety is common at Seibal (Sabloff 1975:114–116), the Petexbatun region (Foias and Bishop 2013:162–166), and in local varieties at Altar de Sacrificios (Adams 1971:57).

Comment: While the Holmul type is similar to Pedregal Modeled, it differs in surface decoration. The appliquéd head is not human in appearance, but supernatural. I prefer not to place this type in the Uaxactun Unslipped Ware because it is clearly painted and the vessel form and paste characteristics are not completely consistent with Uaxactun Unslipped Ware.

Illustration: Figure 7.1d.

Unnamed Modeled (Molded)-carved (Chak 3)

Established: Callaghan in this study,
Group: Unnamed
Ware: Unspecified
Complex: Chak 3
Sphere: Tepeu 3
Ceramic Group Frequency: 5 rims, 33 bodies, 1 vessel, 39 total, 0.6 percent of complex.
Complex: Chak 3
Principal identifying attributes: (1) Orange paste, (2) vases with insloping or vertical sides, (3) occasional annular bases or supports, (4) occasional incision, and (5) modeled (molded)-carved designs in the form of anthropomorphic figures, glyphs, and pseudoglyphs.

Paste, firing, and temper: Paste is similar to first variant of Tinaja Red. Pastes are fine-textured with mixed volcanic glass and crushed calcite inclusions. Paste color is yellow to orange (10YR7/3, 7/4). The paste is extremely compact and sherds are fired to a hard state. Firing cores are not present.

Surface finish and decoration: Surfaces are very highly polished and slipped an orange-red color (7.5YR6/8; 5YR6/8; 2.5YR5/8). Occasionally, thin bands of pre- or post-slip incision are present on vessel rims. The main design is a combination of modeled-carving (to create actual glyphs around the exterior rim) and molded-carving (to create scenes on the main exterior body of the vessel). A mold may have been applied to vessel exteriors when the clay was still malleable. The mold creates impressions of human figures dressed in regal or military regalia. Surfaces are usually highly eroded and no slip is visible. One partial vessel is slipped red-orange (2.5YR4/6) on the exterior. One sherd with hieroglyphs names a local Holmul region title, Chak Tok Wayaab, which was also found on an incised bone in Room 2 Building B, Group II, at Holmul. This title reaches back into the late Early Classic period in the region. Firing clouds may occur on vessel exteriors, but are not common.

Forms:
1. Vases with insloping or vertical walls, direct rims, rounded lips, and, on occasion, annular bases or supports (no measurements available) and
2. bowls with flaring sides, direct rims, and rounded lips (no measurements available).

Intraregional locations and contexts: This type of pottery has been found at Holmul in contexts within Group III and South Group 1.

Interregional locations and contexts: This type is similar, but not the same as, Pabellon Modeled-carved. Pabellon Modeled (Molded)-carved can be found at Uaxactun (Smith and Gifford 1966:160, 173), Altar de Sacrificios (Adams 1971:49), Seibal (Sabloff 1975:195), Tikal (Culbert 1993:14, 2006), Calakmul (Dominguez-Carrasco 1994:53), Piedras Negras (Muñoz 2004:25), Yaxchilan (Lopez Varela 1989:161), the Petexbatun region (Foias and Bishop 2013:287–289), and Becan (Ball 1977:98).

Comments: The type is a strong Chak 3 Terminal Classic period marker. It appears to be a local reproduction of fine paste pottery of the Altar Group found in many Terminal Classic contexts in the Pasión River region and Central Petén at this time (see Adams 1971; Sabloff 1975). This type is very similar to Pabellon Modeled (Molded)-Carved of the Pasión River region, but lacking the fine orange paste.

Illustration: Figure 7.12c.

Unnamed Polychrome (Chak 1)

Established: Callaghan this study.
Group: Unnamed
Ware: Unspecified
Complex: Chak 1
Sphere: Tepeu 1
Ceramic Group Frequency: 3 vessels, 3 total, 0.3 percent of complex.
Complex: Chak 1
Principal identifying attributes: (1) Orange slip, (2) red and black painted designs, (3) glossy surface, (3) open plates, (4) bowl with barrel shape.
Paste, firing, and temper: Paste is fine to medium in texture and has crushed volcanic ash inclusions. Paste color is yellow (10YR7/3) to orange (7.5YR7/6).
Surface finish and decoration: The vessel surface was first smoothed and slipped orange (7.5YR6/8, 6/6). On one plate (Figure 7.7, 7.14, and 7.15b), a black slip was then applied, except for the middle interior of the plate where an anthropomorphized snail was painted in black and red (10R4/8).
  Forms:
    1. Plate with open, slightly flaring sides, a direct rim, rounded lip, flat base, and a spout. Rim diameter is 29 cm, wall thickness 0.7 cm, and height 2 cm;
    2. plate with open, slightly flaring sides, a direct rim, rounded lip, convex base, and three supports (scars). Rim diameter is 30 cm, wall thickness 0.7 cm, and height is 6 cm without supports; and
    3. bowl with barrel-shaped sides, direct rim, rounded lip, and flat base. Rim diameter is 15 cm, wall thickness 0.7 cm, and height 12 cm.

Intraregional locations and contexts: All of these vessels are associated with tombs at Holmul. The black-slipped plate with snail design came from a recently excavated tomb in the substructure of Building A, Group II, at Holmul (HOL.L.20.21). The plate with supports scars and fish design came from Ruin X at Holmul (HOL.RUIN.X.V1). The bowl came from Building F, Group 1 at Holmul (HOL.BLDG.F.POT.A).
Interregional locations and contexts: The vessel form and design composition resembles Saxche Orange Polychrome, which can be found throughout the lowlands during the early part of the Late Classic Period. Because the plate is predominantly black, however, I hesitate to classify it as an orange polychrome. I prefer to leave the typed Unnamed at this time.

Figure 7.14. Unnamed Polychrome (Chak 1) plate (HOL.L.20.21). Photo by Michael G. Callaghan. See Figure 7.15 for additional illustration of this vessel. Also on front cover in background.

Illustration: Figures 7.7 (center), 7.14, and 7.15c (possible Saxche Orange Polychrome: Variety Unspecified.

Unnamed Black-on-orange (Chak 1)

Established: Callaghan in this study.
Group: Unnamed
Ware: Unspecified
Complex: Chak 1
Sphere: Tepeu 1
Ceramic Group Frequency: 1 vessel, 1 total, 0.1 percent of complex.
Principal identifying attributes: (1) Orange slip, (2) black painted designs, (3) dull surface, finish, and (4) bowls with slightly barrel-shaped sides.
Paste, firing, and temper: Paste is fine to medium in texture and contains crushed volcanic ash inclusions. Paste color is yellow (10YR7/3) to orange (7.5YR7/6).
Surface finish and decoration: Vessel surfaces are smoothed and slipped orange (7.5YR6/8, 6/6). A fine black design has been painted on both vessels. The design appears to be a "Jester God" (Fields 1991); it begins on the exterior of one vessel and continues on the next. Surface finish is dull.

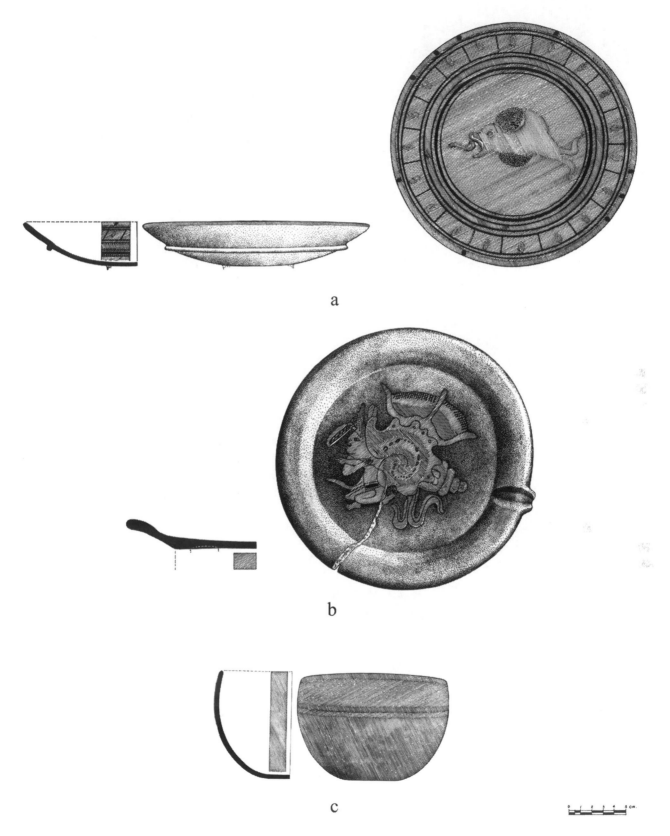

a

b

c

Figure 7.15. Unnamed Polychrome (Chak 1): (a) HOL.RUIN.X.V1, (b) HOL.L.20.21 (also on front cover in background), (c) HOL.BLDG.F.POT.A. Drawings by Fernando Alvarez (Holmul Archaeological Project).

Figure 7.16. Unnamed Black-on-orange (Chak 1) composite vessel (HOL.T.20.19). Photo by Diana Méndez-Lee. See also Figure 7.12b for additional illustration of this vessel.

Forms: The vessel is composed of two separate bowls, both with slightly barrel-shaped sides, direct rims, and rounded lips. Rim diameters are 14 and 15 cm, wall thicknesses 0.7 cm, and heights 8 and 12 cm. The smaller bowl inverts over the larger bowl to create the complete design.

Intraregional locations and contexts: This vessel comes from the recently excavated tomb in the substructure of Building A, Group II at Holmul (HOL.T.20.19).

Interregional locations and contexts: The vessel form and design composition resembles Saxche Orange Polychrome, but the decoration is in black-on-orange and not polychrome. The vessel forms are characteristic of Tepeu 1 modes, which make me comfortable placing the vessel as a Special Unnamed Black-on-orange within the Chak 1 facet.

Illustration: Figures 7.12b and 7.16.

CHAPTER EIGHT

Summary

Michael G. Callaghan

I stated in the introductory chapter that this classification was created in an effort to accomplish three primary goals. The first was to use ceramic artifacts to establish site-wide and regional chronological and spatial frameworks for the Holmul region. The second was to compare local and regional temporal-spatial frameworks to other sites in the southern Maya lowlands and to a lesser extent the northern Maya lowlands, southern Maya highlands, and Pacific coast. The third goal was to address specifically defined issues within particular ceramic complexes. I believe I have realized the first two goals and have come closer to understanding the specific issues listed within the third. In this chapter, I present a summary of type: variety-mode information in relation to the temporal-spatial frameworks for each ceramic complex. I also discuss how the classification and sequence created by type: variety-mode analysis can be used as low-level theory (Trigger 2006:30-31) to address specific issues related to cultural practice, particularly mid and high-level theory about the ancient Maya during individual complexes. As I stated in the introduction, I still emphasize that the primary product of this study is descriptive rather than interpretative. Excavations in the Holmul region are ongoing, so the Holmul region sequence and interpretations based on that sequence are subject to revision. The interpretations of cultural process in this chapter are informed by type: variety-mode classifications, but they remain speculative until supported by more archaeological research in the Holmul region and other areas.

THE K'AWIL COMPLEX

The Early Middle Preclassic in the Holmul region is represented by pre-Mamom sherds found in mixed deposits with Mamom material. Based on radiocarbon dates and typological comparisons, the pre-Mamom presence can be estimated to date between 1000 and 840 BC (see Chapter 2). Descriptions of pre-Mamom material included in this study come from 1,271 rim sherds and 560 diagnostic body sherds for a total of 1,831 samples. Four definable wares, 12 groups, and 30 type: varieties define the pre-Mamom presence. Contexts of pre-Mamom material come from subplatform excavations in Buildings B, N, and F in Group II at Holmul (see Estrada-Belli 2008; Neivens de Estrada 2014). Pre-Mamom sherds have been found occasionally in excavations in the epicenter of Cival. Pre-Mamom contexts are complicated, because they appear to be mixed-fill deposits containing small amounts of Yax Te (Mamom Sphere) and Itzamkanak (Chicanel Sphere) material. Because of the mixed nature of these deposits, lack of whole vessels, and the small sample size, I am not comfortable calling the pre-Mamom presence a legitimate complex at this time. But, Neivens de Estrada has more experience with the material than I do at this point and I defer to her judgment in this study. I am, however, hopeful that future excavations in the Holmul region will uncover an unmixed deposit. The Pre-Mamom sample includes varieties of types present in the Cunil Complex of the neighboring Belize River Valley (e.g., Mo Mottled and Kitam Incised) and the Eb Complex of Tikal (e.g., Calam Buff), but the presence of these types is not enough to include it within the Cunil or Eb spheres. The pre-Mamom sample is roughly contemporaneous with the Early Eb Complex at Tikal (Culbert 1993, 2003, 2006; Laporte and Fialko 1995; Laporte and Valdes 1993), the Cunil Complex at Cahal Pech (Awe 1992; Cheetham 1995, 1996, 2005; Cheetham et al. 2003; Clark and Cheetham 2002) and Xunantunich (Strelow and LeCount 2001), Kanocha at Blackman Eddy (Garber et al. 2002), the Early Ah Pam Complex in the Lake Yaxha-Sacnab region (Rice 1979), Xe at Altar de Sacrificios (Adams 1971), Real at Seibal (Sabloff 1975), the Swasey Complex at Cuello originally defined by Pring (1977b) and later split into Swasey and Bladen by Kosakowsky (1987), Early Chaakk'ax at K'axob (Lopez Varela 2004), and Bolay at Colha (Valdez 1987). The following summary is based upon Neivens de Estrada's study presented in Chapter 2.

Slipped Ceramics

The majority of pre-Mamom type: varieties are slipped or burnished (91.7%) vs. unslipped (8.3%). Table 8.1 illustrates type: varieties as a percentage of total sherds within the slipped and burnished, and unslipped wares of the pre-Mamom sample. For slipped and burnished ceramics, type: varieties Calam Buff: Calam Variety predominates at 16.6 percent followed K'atun Red: K'atun Variety (15.6%), K'atun Red: Lak Variety (11%), Sak White: Sak Variety (10.2%), and K'atun Red: Incised Variety (8.9%). Black ceramics of the Eknab Group within K'an Slipped Ware are present, but appear in smaller frequencies than red and white slipped ceramics. Eknab Black: Eknab Variety and Eknab Black: Eknab Incised Variety account for only 3.9 percent and 0.4 percent of slipped ceramics respectively. Although present in smaller quantities than ceramics of K'an Slipped Ware and Belize Valley Dull Ware, red slipped ceramics of the Río Holmul Slipped Ware also slightly outnumber black ceramics of K'an Slipped Ware with Jobal Red: Jobal Variety and Jobal Red: Incised Variety accounting for 4.8 percent and 1.5 percent of slipped ceramics respectively. These preliminary typological data suggest that the red, white, and black slipped macrotraditions began during the early Middle Preclassic period. Because of the problematical sample sizes and contexts, I am unwilling to offer any more interpretations based on these preliminary frequency data at this time.

Surface finishes within K'an Slipped Ware, Belize Valley Dull Ware, and Río Holmul Slipped Ware are similar in that they exhibit a smooth texture and dull shine. Preference of surface decoration is also consistent with post-slip incision predominating in the incised varieties of red, white, and black types within the three slipped wares. Designs embody what have come to be known as Middle Preclassic Pan-Mesoamerican motifs including the cleft head, shark's tooth, and music bracket patterns (Cheetham et al. 2003). Incision appears on the exterior of

vessels as well as the interior bases and rims of more open forms like plates and dishes. Another decorative technique is zone slipping, or at least, differential slipping of vessel exteriors and interiors. K'atun Red: Lak Variety and K'atun Red: Lak'ek Variety both display red slip on vessel interiors that runs up and over the rim to the exterior. The remainder of the vessel is either unslipped (i.e., Lak Variety) or smudged black (i.e., Lak'ek Variety). The same differential slipping also appears on Aac Red on Buff: Aac Variety. These three types are precursors to Chito Red-and-unslipped: Chito Variety within the Joventud Group of the later Yax Te Complex, as well as more open forms of Joventud Red: Ixtoc Variety. The Preclassic red-on-cream slipped macrotradition also begins during the early Middle Preclassic period as evidenced in Lak'in Red-on-white: Lak'in Variety of K'an Slipped Ware and Xaman Red-on-white: Xaman Variety. Muxanal Red-on-cream later replaces these types during the Yax Te Complex.

Forms of slipped ceramics of the pre-Mamom sample include bowls, dishes, plates, jars, and tecomates. Bowls are a frequently occurring form; they have either flat or slightly convex bases and flaring, outcurving, incurving, or rounded sides. Rim and lip treatments vary according to bowl forms.. Bolstered or folded rims appear on bowls with incurving sides. Direct rims and rounded lips are more common on medium and smaller sized bowls. So are pointed lips. Bowls with incurving sides eventually gave way to bowls with outcurving sides during the Yax Te Complex, but bolstered and pointed lips on bowl forms appear to be an early Middle Preclassic mode. Tecomate forms often display folded or bolstered rims with rounded lips.

For slipped plates, the most common form is a plate with outflaring sides, wide everted rim, and rounded lip. On incised type: varieties, the everted rim serves as the medium for decoration (as well as the interior base). Plate forms also commonly display folded and pointed rims and lips. Like bowls, plates also have flat or slightly convex bases. Slipped jar forms are also common. Jar rims are vertical or sometimes slightly outflaring with either a direct rim and rounded lip or very slightly everted rim with rounded lip.

Callaghan (2008:240–270) and Neivens de Estrada (see Chapter 2) have separated paste composition within early Middle Preclassic slipped ceramics into four variants. The most common variant is fine- to medium-textured and yellow in color (10YR7/4, 7/6; 7.5YR8/6). The primary inclusion in this paste variant is volcanic ash. Unlike other paste variants, there is no form of calcite present in this

Table 8.1. Percentages of K'awil Complex Slipped and Unslipped Type: Varieties

Ware	Group	Type: Variety	% Slipped
K'an Slipped	K'an	K'atun Red: K'atun Red Variety	15.6
		K'atun Red: Incised Variety	8.9
		K'atun Red: Lak Variety	11.0
		K'atun Red: Lak'ek Variety	4.5
	Ochkin	Ochkin Orange: Ochkin Variety	0.6
		Ochkin Orange: Incised Variety	0.6
	Baadz	Baadz Tan: Incised Variety	0.2
	Sak	Sak White: Sak Variety	10.2
		Sak White: Incised Variety	1.9
		Lak'in Red-on-white: Lak'in Variety	4.3
		Lak'in Red-on-white: Incised Variety	0.3
	Eknab	Eknab: Eknab Variety	3.9
		Eknab: Incised Variety	0.4
Belize Valley Dull	Uck	Mo' Mottled: Mo' Variety	3.8
		Mo' Mottled: Fluted Variety	1.0
		Kitam Incised: Kitam Variety	5.2
La Lila Burnished	Calam	Calam Buff: Calam Variety	16.6
		Ante Incised: Ante Variety	2.8
		Aac Red-on-buff: Aac Variety	0.4
Río Holmul Slipped	Jobal	Jobal Red: Jobal Variety	4.8
		Jobal Red: Incised Variety	1.5
	Ainil	Xpokol Incised: Xpokol Variety	0.3
	Chicin'a	Chicin'a Black: Chicin'a Variety	0.3
		Chicin'a Black: Incised Variety	0.3
	Unnamed	Xaman Red-on-white: Xaman Variety	0.4
			% Unslipped
Unspecified	Canhel	Canhel Unslipped: Canhel Variety	41.5
	Cabcoh	Cabcoh Striated: Cabcoh Variety	4.7
	Unnamed	Ramonal Unslipped: Variety Unspecified	26.4
		Unamed Unslipped	8.5
		Unnamed Unslipped Red Paste	18.9

paste. Microscopic examination and exposure to diluted HCL do not indicate the inclusion of calcite minerals in this paste. This paste-variant crosscuts slipped vessel forms and can be found in type: varieties within K'an Slipped Ware and Belize Valley Dull Ware. This variant, however, is reserved for vessels with a lighter slip color, namely red and cream slipped type: varieties of the K'an Slipped and Belize Valley Dull Wares. The second paste variant is medium-textured with rounded gray calcite and less rounded crystal calcite inclusions. This variant is less compact and more porous. Color is buff (10YR8/2, 8/3), and firing cores are almost non-existent. This paste occurs exclusively within types of the Calam Group. The third paste variant is medium-textured with angular pieces of crystalline calcite as the main inclusion. This paste is gray in color (7.5YR6/1; 10YR5/1). This paste-variant occurs in ceramics of the Eknab Group, which are slipped black. The practice of using crystalline calcite pastes for the production of black-slipped vessels continues from the early Middle Preclassic period all the way through to the Terminal Classic facet of the Chak Complex. The fourth paste variant can only be found within type: varieties of Río Holmul Slipped Ware. This variant is medium-textured and dark brown (10YR4/4, 4/6; 10YR5/3, 5/4, 5/6) to gray in color. Inclusions are a mixture of small angular pieces of crystalline calcite, volcanic ash, and occasional pieces of mica as well as round ferruginous particles. This paste is compact, dense, and easily distinguishable from the other two variants, which crosscut K'an Slipped Ware and Belize Valley Dull Ware. One of the more interesting aspects of paste composition within the slipped ceramics of the pre-Mamom sample is the frequent occurrence of volcanic ash as the primary inclusion. This pattern persists into the succeeding Yax Te Complex and I address this issue in the discussion of that complex.

Ceramics of the early Middle Preclassic period also include type: varieties within La Lila Burnished Ware. Most of the type: varieties within this ware have been established at other central Petén sites. Rice (1979) established the Calam Buff Group in the Lake Yaxha-Sacnab area during the Ah Pam Complex. Culbert identified Calam Buff at Tikal during the Eb Complex (1993, 2003, n.d.). Laporte and Valdes (1993:51-52) established Ante Incised and Aac Red-on-buff within the Calam Buff Group at Tikal during the Eb Complex. The Calam Buff Group is composed of Calam Buff: Calam Variety (83.5 percent), Ante Incised: Ante Variety (14.3 percent), and Aac Red-on-buff (2.2 percent). Ceramics of La Lila Burnished Ware are well-smoothed, left unslipped, but highly burnished. Although the unslipped surface does not "shine," it can often appear white or milky. Microscopic examination does not reveal any slip. Decoration on Ante Incised takes the form of post-burnish incision. Design includes combinations of horizontal and vertical lines on the exterior of round-sided bowls and outcurving dishes, as well as more complicated Pan-Mesoamerican motifs on the interiors of everted rim dishes.

Forms of La Lila Burnished Ware include bowls, dishes, jars, and one possible example of a special mushroom form. According to Neivens de Estrada, the most common bowl form within the Calam Buff is a bowl or plate with outflaring or outcurving sides, bolstered rim, and rounded lip. Ante Incised forms include an outflaring side bowl with wide everted rim and rounded lip. The everted rim and interior of the vessel provide the background for incised design. Neivens de Estrada reports that Ante Incised occurs on plates, as well as round-sided bowls with direct rim and rounded lip. Jar forms are rare.

My initial study (Callaghan 2008:250–253) and Neivens de Estrada's subsequent typological data suggest there are two paste variants within the Calam Buff Group. The first is fine to medium in texture and buff in color (10YR8/2). The primary and in many cases exclusive inclusion for this paste is spherical balls of gray calcite. This paste is correlated to Calam Buff: Calam Variety plates and bowls with outflaring sides and bolstered rims. The second variant occurs more frequently within Ante Incised: Ante Variety forms. This paste variant is fine in texture and buff (10YR8/2) or sometimes yellow (10YR 7/4) in color. The primary inclusion is volcanic ash. This paste is more similar to pastes of K'an Slipped Ware. The presence of the ash-tempered paste variant within the Ante Incised type is problematic. Because it is also found in K'an Slipped Ware, there remains the possibility that Ante Incised sherds are simply eroded incised sherds of the K'atun Red Group. Neivens de Estrada will continue to investigate this problem in future studies.

Unslipped Ceramics

Unslipped ceramics of the early Middle Preclassic period are type: varieties within the Canhel, Cabcoh, and Unnamed Groups. Canhel Unslipped: Canhel Variety occurs most frequently, comprising 41.5 percent of all early Middle Preclassic unslipped ceramics. Canhel Unslipped: Canhel Variety is followed by Ramonal Unslipped: Variety Unspecified (26.4%), Unnamed Unslipped Red Paste (18.9%), an Unnamed Unslipped type (8.5%), and Cabcoh Striated: Cabcoh Variety (4.7%). Unfortunately, I can say little about the unslipped ceramics of the early Middle Preclassic period because they have not been studied as well as the slipped ceramics. The presence or absence of type: varieties within the present sample can, however, tell us something about interregional affiliation, all indicating ties to the central Petén. Canhel Unslipped: Canhel Variety and Cabcoh Striated: Cabcoh Variety are both established unslipped types of the Eb Complex at Tikal (Culbert 1993:5). Neivens de Estrada defined Ramonal Unslipped: Variety Unspecified in the current study and believes this type: variety occurs at Tikal after viewing collections at that site (see Chapter 2). Neivens de Estrada defines the Unnamed Unslipped type as having forms similar to Achiotes Unslipped of the succeeding Yax Te (late Middle Preclassic) Complex. Unnamed Unslipped Red Paste appears to be a type: variety local to the Holmul region.

Aside from the Unnamed Unslipped type, forms for early Middle Preclassic Unslipped ceramics are mainly tecomates. Tecomates of the Canhel Group often display bolstered or folded rims—a common early Middle Preclassic mode on slipped ceramics. Decoration on unslipped ceramics is minimal and infrequent, but does occur on Canhel Unslipped and Cabcoh Striated. Rows of fingernail impressions can appear on the exterior surfaces of Canhel Unslipped incurving side bowls. Striation occurs on the exterior surfaces of Cabcoh Striated. According to Neivens de Estrada's descriptions, paste texture and composition can vary within and among the unslipped type: varieties. Pastes of the Canhel and Cacoh Groups are medium in texture, with few inclusions of white calcite and silica, and are light brown in color (7.5YR6/4). Pastes of Ramonal Unslipped are medium-textured with rounded gray calcite and less rounded crystal calcite inclusions, and are yellow (10YR7/4) to buff (10YR8/2) in color. Neivens de Estrada believes this paste is similar to Calam Buff: Calam Variety. Pastes of the Unnamed Unslipped type are medium to coarse in texture, with many fine-grained inclusions of silica, some volcanic ash, and unidentified red inclusions. This paste is gray (5YR5/1). Finally, Unnamed Unslipped Red Paste is characterized by a coarse paste with quartz inclusions and is red (2.5YR6/8) in color. The most I am able to conclude at this point is that the unslipped ceramics of the early Middle Preclassic period in the Holmul region represent local production of Petén region types (e.g., Canhel Unslipped, Cacoh Striated, and Ramonal Unslipped) along with local production of local Holmul region types (e.g., Unnamed Unslipped and Unnamed Unslipped Red Paste). Forms and decorative treatments are well within the range of early Middle Preclassic unslipped ceramics in other areas of the lowlands at this time. Having summarized the characteristics of slipped and unslipped ceramics of the early Middle Preclassic period, I now offer some brief initial interpretations its relationship to other established complexes.

Discussion

Upon the completion of Neivens de Estrada's classification, I had hoped to address two specific issues using her typological data of early Middle Preclassic period ceramics. The first issue regarded the adoption and use of pottery within the Holmul region in pre-Mamom times. More specifically, where did the technology used in making this pottery come from and what were the processes or reasons that led to its adoption? The second issue regarded assessing qualitative changes in production patterns between this early pottery and the succeeding Yax Te Complex. More specifically, how does this pre-Mamom sample compare to the Mamom Sphere sample? Did type: varieties and modes demonstrate continuity or disjunction? And what could these similarities and differences tell us about other social processes occurring in the Holmul region? Suffice it to say I have not unequivocally answered any of these questions. Neivens de Estrada's type: variety-mode data have, however, provided some insight into these issues.

Where did this pre-Mamom pottery come from, when was it adopted, and how did this process take place? Comparison of dates, types, and modes between the Holmul material and other pre-Mamom Complexes produces some insights, but no conclusive evidence. In terms of dating, the Holmul sample is not the earliest ceramic complex in the Maya lowlands. The earliest dated lowland ceramics appear in northern Belize at Cuello (i.e., Swasey Complex) and in the Belize River Valley (i.e., Cunil Complex) between 1200 and 900 BC (Andrews and Hammond 1990; Kosakowsky 1987; Sullivan and Awe 2013; Sullivan et al. 2009). As I mentioned previously, there are no radiocarbon samples associated with pure pre-Mamom deposits in the Holmul region. There is, however, carbon from a pure Yax Te (Mamom) deposit that dates between 895 and 840 BC. Therefore, one can speculate that the pre-Mamom material must have existed at least as early as 895 BC. Because the ceramics in the complex appear to have been locally made and are quite sophisticated in regard to production technology, one can conservatively estimate that at least two generations, but perhaps as many as three, must have been involved in their production. This brings one back approximately 100 years to the estimated start date of the early Middle Preclassic presence of ceramics at around 1000 BC. Modal and typological comparison to neighboring pre-Mamom complexes strengthens this assertion. Modally, and in two cases typologically (i.e., Kitam Incised: Kitam Variety and M'o Mottled: Mo' Variety), pre-Mamom Holmul ceramics are very similar to neighboring ceramics of the Belize River Valley Cunil Complex, which dates to approximately 1100 to 900 BC (Sullivan and Awe 2013). Calam Group ceramics at Holmul are typologically and modally similar to Calam Buff ceramics found in the Eb Complex at Tikal, which dates to approximately 800 to 600 BC (Culbert 1993). Based on this information, it can be suggested that the Holmul pre-Mamom pottery dates to sometime between the onset of pottery production in the neighboring Belize River Valley and the central Petén, Guatemala. A conservative speculation would be that ceramic technology was adopted toward the beginning of the early Middle Preclassic period through the interaction of peoples living in the Holmul region, the neighboring Belize River Valley, and the central Petén. At this point, it appears unlikely that ceramic-producing peoples settled the Holmul region. Wahl and colleagues (2013) demonstrate that anthropogenic changes to the local environment began around 1300 BC. To date, this predates any archaeological remains in the Holmul region and, more importantly, this predates the earliest ceramic production in the Belize River Valley, northern Belize, and Tikal. Equally as difficult to answer are questions related to why and how pre-Mamom pottery was adopted in the Holmul region. At this time, the typological data are too preliminary to support anything more than unfounded assertions. I believe on this last point that it is better to let the typological data serve future researchers than to create loose interpretations based on an incomplete dataset. What can be affirmed is that the pottery-making traditions revealed from classification of early Middle Preclassic ceramics serve as the foundation for pottery making in the succeeding late Middle Preclassic Yax Te Complex. As I discuss next, many Yax Te Complex ceramics are the definitive outgrowth of traditions that were established during pre-Mamom times.

THE YAX TE COMPLEX

Yax Te is the late Middle Preclassic period complex in the Holmul region. Based on radiocarbon dates and typological comparisons, I estimate that the complex dates between 840 and 400 BC (see Chapter 3). Descriptions of Yax Te material included in this study come from 2,616 rim sherds, 5,666 diagnostic body sherds, and 20 whole vessels for a total of 8,300 samples. Four wares (1 Unspecified), 7 groups, and 21 type: varieties define the Yax Te Complex. The majority of Yax Te material was recovered from excavations at the site of Cival, although sherds have occasionally been found mixed into fill at the sites of Holmul, K'o, and La Sufricaya. Yax Te ceramics share 72 percent of type: varieties with the Mamom ceramic sphere. This places the percentage of Mamom sphere types well over the 60 percent threshold suggested by Ball (1976:323) for full inclusion in a ceramic sphere. Typologically and modally, Yax Te ceramics are contemporaneous with Mamom material at Uaxactun (Smith 1955), Tzec at Tikal (Culbert 1993, 2003, 2006), Monos at El Mirador (Forsyth 1989), Escoba at Seibal (Sabloff 1975), San Felix at Altar de Sacrificios (Adams 1971), Jenny Creek at Barton Ramie (Gifford 1976), Chaakk'ax at K'axob (Lopez Varela 2004), Chiwa at Colha (Valdez 1987), Hol at Piedras Negras (Muñoz 2002), Boden at Chan (Kosakowsky 2012), Zihnal at Calakmul (Dominguez-Carrasco 1994), Excarvado in the Petexbatun region (Foias and Bishop 2013), Yancotil in the Lake Yaxha-Sacnab region (Rice 1979), Acachen at Becan (Ball 1977), and Lopez at Cuello (Kosakowsky 1987). As I demonstrate here, however, modes of Yax Te ceramics represent a unique regional assemblage within the larger Mamom Sphere.

Slipped Ceramics

The majority of Yax Te type: varieties are slipped (93.1%) vs. unslipped (6.9%). Table 8.2 illustrates type: varieties as a percentage of rims and whole vessels within the slipped and unslipped wares of the Yax Te Complex. For slipped ceramics, type: varieties within Flores Waxy Ware are predominant, with Joventud Red: Ixtoc Variety appearing most frequently at 31.6 percent followed by Guitara Incised: Noctún Variety (20%), Joventud Red: Joventud Variety (9%), Savana Orange: Savana Variety (8%), and Chunhinta Black: Chunhinta Variety (7.8%) rounding out the top five type: varieties. Within the Joventud Group, local varieties outnumber established varieties. These varieties include the Joventud Red: Ixtoc Variety and Guitara Incised: Noctún Variety, as well as Chito Red-and-unslipped: Chito Variety and Desvario Chamfered: Horqueta Variety. It is interesting to note that there is, as of yet, no documented local varieties of

Table 8.2. Percentages of Yax Te Complex Slipped and Unslipped Type: Varieties

Ware	Group	Type: Variety	% Unslipped
Uaxactun Unslipped	Achiotes	Achiotes Unslipped: Achiotes Variety	98.4
	Jocote	Jocote Orange-brown: Jocote Variety	1.1
		Chacchinic Red-on-orange-brown: Chacchinic Variety	0.5

Ware	Group	Type: Variety	% Slipped
Mars	Savana	Savana Orange: Savana Variety	8.0
		Reforma Incised: Reforma Variety	4.9
Unspecified	Joventud	Joventud Red: Ixtoc Variety	31.6
		Guitara Incised: Noctún Variety	20.0
		Chito Red-and-unslipped: Chito Variety	3.9
		Chito Red-and-unslipped: Variety Unspecified	1.1
		Desvario Chamfered: Horqueta Variety	2.2
Flores Waxy	Joventud	Joventud Red: Joventud Variety	9.0
		Guitara Incised: Guitara Variety	0.5
		Desvario Chamfered: Desvario Variety	1.1
	Tierra Mojada	Tierra Mojada Resist: Tierra Mojada Variety	0.3
	Pital	Pital Cream: Pital Variety	4.4
		Paso Danto Incised: Paso Danto Variety	0.4
		Muxanal Red-on-cream: Muxanal Variety	0.6
		Unnamed Red-on-cream Incised	0.1
	Chunhinta	Chunhinta Black: Chunhinta Variety	7.8
		Deprecio Incised: Deprecio Variety	2.6
		Centenario Fluted: Centenario Variety	1.6

Chunhinta Black or Pital Cream types. Of further note, red-on-cream ceramics are present, but in small numbers, with Muxanal Red-on-cream types comprising less than 1 percent of slipped ceramics. Also occurring, but in low numbers, is Tierra Mojada Resist (less than 1%). These data indicate that although Yax Te ceramics are typologically similar to ceramics of the Mamom Sphere, the high frequency of local varieties and lack of more common affiliated varieties implies slight regionalism during the late Middle Preclassic.

Slipped ceramics are classified into two wares. Established type: varieties exhibit the characteristic waxy or greasy texture of Flores Waxy Ware. Local varieties, however, differ from conventional established varieties in a number of qualitative ways, leading me to place them in an Unspecified Ware. For example, Joventud Group local varieties like Joventud Red: Ixtoc Variety, Guitara Incised: Noctún Variety, Desvario Chamfered: Horqueta Variety, and Chito Red-and-unslipped: Chito Variety display a thin, flaky, red slip reminiscent of pre-Mamom red ceramics. Local varieties of Joventud Group ceramics are also polished to a dull shine. In contrast, established varieties like Joventud Red: Joventud Variety, Guitara Incised: Guitara Variety, and Desvario Chamfered: Desvario Variety all exhibit the more conventional thick red-orange slips and greasy feel of Flores Waxy Ware ceramics found in other lowland sites. These differences between surface treatment in local and established varieties correlate to differences in surface decoration, paste, and form modes as well. It is interesting to note that established varieties of types within the Chunhinta, Pital, Tierra Mojada, and Muxanal groups all exhibit surface-finish modes more consistent with conventional Mamom Sphere ceramics (i.e., waxy surface finish, thick coats of slip, and high shine).

I think these typological and modal data suggest two different systems of Yax Te Complex red-slipped ceramics. One system, which contains the local varieties of Mamom Sphere types, has roots in pre-Mamom red ceramics and is characterized by thin red-orange slips, slightly waxy surface finish, and a dull shine. The other system is the more conventional lowland Maya Mamom Sphere tradition of red ceramics, which is characterized by established varieties that display thick red-orange slips, waxy surface finish, and a highly polished surface. As I mentioned in Chapter 3, this system of red pottery is part of a larger tradition related to earlier material of the Pre-Mamom period. The dull glossy red slip, yellow-orange ash-based paste, and forms of Joventud Red: Ixtoc Variety represent a clear continuity in pottery-making tradition from pre-Mamom times. I prefer not to use the ware defined by Neivens de Estrada for Pre-Mamom material, however, because her study is ongoing and not yet complete. Therefore, the ware for these local varieties of Joventud Group ceramics remains Unspecified. The presence of these local varieties in the Yax Te Complex supports my earlier argument (see Chapter 1) that ware cannot be integrated into type: variety-mode classification in a hierarchical manner. In this case, ware crosscuts varieties of Joventud Red and cannot be integrated above the level type: varieties, much less ceramic groups. Finally, analysts may question why I chose to create a new variety within an unspecified ware, and not an entirely new group of red-slipped ceramics. At this time, I do not think that the differences between the local and established varieties of Joventud Red warrant the creation of a new group. This material is clearly a local manifestation of an established tradition of pottery and I think if I were to create a new group and ware

designation, I would highlight the differences between the two more than the similarities, leading readers to believe the Holmul region was somehow more isolated from the rest of the lowlands during the late Middle Preclassic period than it actually was. I do not think this is the case. If anything the presence of these local varieties of established types indicates contact (at the least) and appropriation (at the most) of a ceramic system outside of the immediate geographical area.

Surface decoration of slipped ceramics includes preslip incision, post-slip incision, preslip grooved-incision, differential slipping and/or smudging, chamfering, and resist decoration. Preslip grooved-incision is the most common form of decoration and characterizes the local Joventud Group type: varieties of Guitara Incised: Noctún Variety and Chito Red–and-unslipped: Unspecified Variety. Grooved-incision can occur as single, double, or triple lines on the interior everted rim of open forms, and on the exterior rim of more closed forms including round-sided bowls and incurving rim bowls and dishes. Preslip incision is the second most common form of decoration and occurs on the established varieties of Joventud, Chunhinta, and Pital Group types. The post-slip incision so common in pre-Mamom ceramics declines dramatically in frequency during Yax Te times. This type of incision is very rare and occasionally only seen in simple lines or geometric patterns on Deprecio Incised: Deprecio Variety, Centenario Fluted: Centenario Variety, and Paso Danto Incised: Paso Danto Variety sherds.

Differential slipping, sometimes including black smudging, is the third most common decorative treatment. Slipped and unslipped ceramics include the local Chito Red-and-unslipped: Chito Variety and Chito Red-and-unslipped: Variety Unspecified. On these ceramics the interior of the vessel is slipped red. The red slip continues up over the rim and extends down about a quarter of the vessel exterior. The remainder of the exterior is left unslipped or smudged black. In this way potters create a dichrome effect. Differential slipping, in this case a true dichrome effect, is also present on Muxanal types. With Muxanal, however, the colors are red on cream.

Chamfering is the next most common surface decoration and occurs on established type: varieties like Desvario Chamfered: Desvario Variety and Centenario Fluted: Centenario Variety. It also appears on the local Desvario Chamfered: Horqueta Variety. The Horqueta and Desvario varieties of Desvario Chamfered differ in form and in the placement and number of chamfers on their exteriors. Desvario Chamfered: Desvario Variety forms are outflaring side bowls with direct rim and rounded lip. Chamfers run horizontally down the exterior of vessels. Desvario Chamfered: Horqueta Variety forms are incurving sided bowls with a slightly outcurving rim and rounded lip. One or two horizontal chamfers appear on vessel exteriors just below the rim. Paste modes of these local and established varieties of Joventud Group ceramics also correlate with the form, surface finish, and surface decoration modes have already discussed.

Finally, resist decoration also occurs on the established variety of Tierra Mojada Resist. This type is rare in the current sample. Taken together, surface decoration modes on slipped vessels reflect both a movement away from pre-Mamom norms as well as desire to continue working within established traditions. Surface-decoration modes also reflect both interactions with other lowland sites, as well as a continued preference for regional traditions during Yax Te times.

Forms of slipped ceramics of the Yax Te complex include bowls, dishes, and jars. Tecomates diminished in frequency from pre-Mamom to Yax Te times. Bowls are the most frequently occurring form. They range in size, shape of sides, rim, and lip treatment. However, they all have either flat or slightly convex bases. I have not found any evidence of supports. Medium-sized and smaller bowls include forms with flaring sides, outcurving sides, incurving sides, and rounded sides. Rim and lip treatments vary slightly according to bowl forms, but are rather consistent in that they are usually rounded. Bolstered or folded rims no longer appear on bowls with incurving sides. Direct rims and rounded lips are more common on medium- and smaller-sized bowls. Pointed lips are quite rare. Tecomate forms do not display the folded or bolstered rims of pre-Mamom forms. Bowls with incurving sides from the early Middle Preclassic have given way to wider, shallower dishes and bowls with incurving sides during the Yax Te Complex. These incurving side dishes and bowls are most commonly associated with local varieties of Joventud Group types. Within slipped dishes, the most common form is a bowl with outcurving sides, everted rim, and rounded lip. The sharp break between everted rims and vessel bodies which seemed to be a hallmark mode of pre-Mamom bowls and dishes gave way to a more gradually everted rim during Yax Te times. These gradually everted rim bowls and dishes are associated with local varieties of Joventud Group types.

Slipped jar forms are also common. Jars are approximately 30 to 40 cm tall with small apertures (about 10 cm); they were most likely used for storing and serving liquid. Jars are globular or teardrop-shaped with round or narrow, flat bases. Jar rims are vertical or sometimes slightly outflaring with either a direct rim and rounded lip or very slightly everted rim with rounded lip. Small round jar handles begin to appear on Yax Te jars. Taken together, I think these changes in form represent a gradual shift away, yet outgrowth from, pre-Mamom modes.

I separated paste composition within slipped ceramics into three variants. The variants correlate to specific type: varieties. The most common variant is fine to medium in texture and yellow in color (10YR7/4, 7/6; 7.5YR8/6). The primary inclusion in this paste variant is volcanic ash. Unlike other paste variants, there is no form of calcite present in this paste. Microscopic examination and exposure to diluted HCL do not indicate the inclusion of calcite minerals in this paste. This paste-variant can be found in local varieties within the Joventud Group including Joventud Red: Ixtoc Variety, Guitara Incised: Noctún Variety, Desvario Chamfered: Horqueta Variety, Chito Red-and-unslipped: Chito Variety, and Chito Red-and-unslipped: Unspecified Variety.

The second paste variant is medium in textured and yellow (10YR7/4), buff (10YR8/3), or even pink (5YR7/4) in color. It contains angular pieces of crystalline calcite, sherd temper, and occasionally burnt organics. This paste: variant occurs in type: varieties within the Pital Group, Tierra Mojada Group, and established varieties of the Joventud Group (i.e., Joventud Red: Joventud Variety, Guitara Incised: Guitara Variety, and Desvario Chamfered: Desvario Variety). The third paste variant is medium in texture and gray or black (10YR4/1) in color, with angular pieces of crystalline calcite as the main inclusions. This variant is found within type: varieties of the Chunhinta Group.

Paste modes correlate with established and local varieties of Yax Te ceramics. Paste mode data also suggest the presence of at least two paste-making traditions that correlate with slip traditions. The first paste-making tradition has its roots in pre-Mamom ceramics and is characterized by a fine, yellow, volcanic ash-based paste. This variant is found on local varieties of Joventud types. The second paste-making tradition is new to the region during Yax Te times and is characterized by medium-textured buff, yellow, pink pastes with crystalline calcite and other inclusions (e.g., sherd, burnt organics, white calcite, etc.). While pre-Mamom pastes did include a variant with crystalline calcite, grog and organics were never included. This paste variant is found within established Mamom Sphere type: varieties. As I discuss in the proceeding discussion of Itzamkanak Complex ceramics, paste modes of established varieties within the Yax Te Complex become the most common modes within Itzamkanak Complex ceramics. Therefore, paste modes (and surface modes of established types) of the Late Preclassic period in the Holmul region have their roots in production patterns of the late Middle Preclassic period.

Slipped ceramics of the Yax Te Complex also contained a substantial number of Mars Orange Ware types. In fact, Mars Orange Paste Ware ceramics comprise 12.9 percent of Yax Te Complex slipped ceramics. Mars Orange Ware is composed of one group and two type: varieties. All ceramics within the current sample belong to the Savana Group. Savana Orange: Savana Variety comprises the majority of the ware (62.3%) and Reforma Incised: Reforma Variety makes up the rest of the group and ware (37.7%). Their fine, bright orange paste distinguishes Mars Orange Ware ceramics from other wares. Pastes are not uniform, however, and can vary between a very fine untempered variant to a fine, volcanic ash-tempered variant. Forms of Savana Orange and Reforma Incised include bowls, dishes, and small serving jars (some with spouts). Bowls or dishes with outcurving sides, direct or gradually everted rims with rounded lips are common. Incurving side forms are not uncommon. Some weathered sherds exhibit signs of red slip, which would classify them as Savana Orange: Rejolla Variety. These sherds were very rare, however, and when found are extremely eroded, so I chose to classify them at the group level. Like Jocote Orange-brown, Savana Orange types have previously been found in greater frequency at neighboring Belize River Valley sites (Gifford 1976:63–70). The presence of Savana Group material in such quantities implies some kind of interaction with sites to the east.

A Note on Volcanic Ash Temper

At this point I find it appropriate to address a specific paste mode that I have observed in both pre-Mamom and Yax Te Complex ceramics, but which all but disappears in the succeeding Itzamkanak Complex. I am specifically referring to the presence of volcanic ash in many pre-Mamom and Yax Te slipped serving vessels. The presence of volcanic ash has been well-documented in lowland Maya Late Classic period ceramics and some Middle Preclassic period ceramics, but its origins are currently unknown (Coffey et al. 2014; Ford and Glicken 1987; Ford and Rose 1995; Shepard 1939, 1942, 1955). Since there are no volcanoes in the lowlands, volcanic ash must have been transported to the lowlands by environmental or anthropogenic means. Environmental means of transport include the movement of ash in the form of pumice balls or dissolved dust downstream from rivers in the highlands. Another probable means of environmental transport would be ash falling on lowland sites in the form of windblown dust from large volcanic eruptions in the highlands. Human transport would include the movement of ash from highland areas in the form of dust, pumice, or tuff stones for use in trade. There is currently no support for any of these types of movement. Typological and modal data of pre-Mamom and Yax Te Complex ceramics may be able to inform research into the transport of volcanic ash.

Based on typological and modal data, I am currently leaning in the direction of the ash fall hypothesis. Serving vessels with pastes containing ash are so frequent in the pre-Mamom and Yax Te Complex I believe any hypothesis for ash transport must account for a great quantity of ceramics created through local production. Although this does not rule out the river and trade hypotheses completely, it does present some problems for them. Because the Holmul region is not connected to any great waterways originating in the highlands, the likelihood of pumice balls or dissolved dust reaching the region from the highlands is quite low. Similarly, while trade with highland areas was certainly important during the Middle Preclassic period in the Holmul region (as evidenced in the presence of jade and obsidian), it does not appear that interregional contact was robust enough to support such a seemingly vigorous trade in volcanic dust, pumice, or tuff. This brings me to the ash fall hypothesis.

In previous publications, Ford and colleagues (Coffey et al. 2014; Ford and Glicken 1987; Ford and Rose 1995) have hypothesized that ash present in Late Classic period ceramics found at the site of El Pilar, Belize, originated from wind-blown ash of large volcanic eruptions in the Salvadoran and Guatemalan highlands. Although Ford and her colleagues have yet to find support for this hypothesis, recent research from the reservoirs of Tikal are lending credence to their ideas. Tankersely and colleagues (Tankersley et al. 2011; Tankersley et al. 2015) have reported on deposits of volcanic ash used as possible filtering mechanisms in the walls of some of Tikal's reservoirs. They hypothesize, and their data is beginning to show, that degraded volcanic ash is present in local smectite clay sediments associated with still water sources in the Tikal area (i.e., lakes, bajos, and reservoirs). A likely source for the presence of ash in these water sources is airborne ash fall. More contemporary reports of volcanic eruptions both in the Maya lowlands (Ford and Rose 1995:154; Rose et al. 1984:163) and South America (e.g., the Calbuco eruption in Chile, April 2015) emphasize the large amounts of airborne ash transported through the atmosphere to areas hundreds of miles from the source of eruption. While volcanic ash degrades quickly if left exposed in tropical climates (see Ford and Rose 1995; Tankersley et al. 2011) it is possible that ash was deposited and preserved in still-water sources (lakes, bajos, ponds spread by springs) or was collected by residents living far from the original volcanic blasts. It is possible that white or gray volcanic dust falling from the sky would have been thought of as an important symbolic substance – something physical and tangible that was connected to the powerful supernatural forces associated with the sky that we know were worshiped by occupants of the Holmul region during the Middle Preclassic period (Estrada-Belli 2006b, 2010). Ash could have been an important ideological component to paste recipes of serving vessels used in commensal events of the Middle Preclassic period. Ash temper would have embodied the supernatural forces associated with the heavens and could have been directly incorporated into the ceramic vessels used in celebrating those same forces. At this point, this discussion is extremely speculative, but the ash fall hypothesis is intriguing and I look forward to further research on the topic.

Unslipped Ceramics

Unslipped ceramics of the Yax Te complex are type: varieties within the Achiotes and Jocote Groups. Achiotes Unslipped: Achiotes Variety comprises 98.4 percent of unslipped ceramics whereas Jocote Orange-brown and Chacchinic Red-on-orange-brown make up only 1.6 percent of unslipped ceramics combined. Achiotes Unslipped: Achiotes Variety is part of Uaxactun Unslipped Ware characterized by unslipped, roughly smoothed exterior surfaces, and a coarse gray (10YR4/1) calcite paste. Jocote Group ceramics are unslipped, but paste is different from Achiotes Group ceramics. Pastes are relatively fine to medium in texture. Paste colors are more yellow (10YR7/5, 6/8), appearing "orange-brown." Primary inclusions consist of small crystalline calcite grains and undefined white inclusions.

Forms for Achiotes Unslipped are mainly jars with globular sides, round bases, short necks, outcurving rims, and rounded lips. The rounded bases and coarse pastes suggest a cooking function for many of these jars.

The Jocote Group consists of Jocote Orange-brown: Jocote Variety and Chacchinic Red-on-orange-brown: Chacchinic Variety. Jocote Group types differ from Achiotes Group types in terms of paste, form, and surface decoration. Jocote pastes are coarse, yellow-brown, and loaded with angular pieces of crystalline calcite grains and unidentified white inclusions. The two forms of Jocote Orange-brown in the Holmul region are jars with short necks and large bowls or ollas. Jocote Group ceramics are distinguished by a twisting applique and impressed fillet on the exterior of bowl and jar forms. On Chacchinic Red-on-orange-brown, red wash decorates the rim and extends down the exterior to the level of the fillet. Jocote Group ceramics are more prevalent in the neighboring Belize River Valley (Gifford 1976) while Achiotes Unslipped is an established Petén type (Smith and Gifford 1966). The presence of these two groups reflects some kind of interaction between Holmul region potters and neighbors to the east, but emphasizing a preference for Petén modes.

Discussion

What can the typological and modal data reveal about cultural processes during Yax Te or late Middle Preclassic times? Quantitatively, the greater frequencies and greater distribution of Yax Te types at sites in the Holmul region points to population growth, especially at the site of Cival. This growth is also reflected in architectural development both inside and outside Cival's epicenter (Estrada-Belli 2008, 2010). Qualitatively in terms of modes, Yax Te Complex ceramics represent both continuity and change when compared to pre-Mamom Complex ceramics. The presence of a new red tradition resembling established Joventud Group ceramics signals interaction with peoples and ideas at other central Petén and Belize River Valley lowland sites. The production of local varieties of Joventud Group ceramics within the older red tradition that has its origins in pre-Mamom complex times embodies a continued preference for regional production technologies, and perhaps practices to go along with them. The low number of other established Mamom Sphere types (e.g., Muxanal Red-on-cream, Tierra Mojada Resist, Palma Daub) supports the notion that although Holmul region potters were willing to accept some aspects of Pan-Maya lowland ceramic traditions, they did not accept them all—or perhaps were not exposed to them. Despite the preference for regional tradition during the Yax Te Complex, potters appear to have abandoned any semblance of older pre-Mamom complex traditions in the succeeding Itzmakanak Complex. As discussed in the next section, many modes embodied by the newer red-slipped tradition that characterized established varieties of the Joventud Group during Yax Te times came to eclipse any vestiges of an early Middle Preclassic past by Itzamkanak times.

THE ITZAMKANAK COMPLEX

Itzamkanak is the Late Preclassic period ceramic complex in the Holmul region. Based on radiocarbon dates and typological comparison, the complex is estimated to date between 400 BC and AD 230 (see Chapter 4). Descriptions of Itzamkanak material included in this study come from 4,376 rim sherds, 16,108 diagnostic body sherds and 11 whole vessels for a total of 20,492 samples. Two wares, 7 groups, and 20 type: varieties define the Itzamkanak Complex. Itzamkanak material is found at Cival, Holmul, La Sufricaya, K'o, Hamontun, T'ot, and Dos Aguadas, with the largest quantities of material found in the construction fill of monumental buildings at Cival. Itzamkanak ceramics share 100 percent of type: varieties with the Chicanel Sphere. Typologically, Itzamkanak ceramics resemble material of the Chicanel Sphere during the Late Preclassic period in the Maya lowlands and are contemporaneous with Chicanel Complex ceramics at Uaxacatun (Smith 1955); Chuen, Cauac, and Cimi Complex ceramics at Tikal (Culbert 1993, 2003, 2006); the Cascabel Complex at El Mirador (Forsyth 1989); the Plancha through early Salinas Complexes at Altar de Sacrificios (Adams 1971); the Cantutse Complex at Seibal (Sabloff 1975); the Barton Creek and Mount Hope Complexes at Barton Ramie (Gifford 1976); the Xakal Complex at Cahal Pech (Awe 1992); the Cadle and Potts Complexes at Chan (Kosakowsky 2012); the Abal Complex at Piedras Negras (Muñoz 2004); the Kaynikte Complex at Calakmul (Dominguex-Carrasco 1994); the K'atbche'k'ax Complex at K'axob (Lopez Varela 2004);Yaxek at Yaxchilan (Lopez Varela 1989); Baluartes at Edzná (Forsyth 1983); the Onecimo Complex at Colha (Valdez 1987); the Ixtabaie, C'oh, and Tulix Complexes at Cerros (Robertson-Freidel 1980);the Faisan Complex in the Petexbatun region (Foias and Bishop 2013); the Late Preclassic Complex at La Milpa (Sagebiel 2005);and the Cocos Complex at Cuello (Kosakowsky 1987).

Slipped Ceramics

The majority of type: varieties are slipped (86%) vs. unslipped (14%). Table 8.3 illustrates type: varieties as a percentage of rims and whole vessels within slipped and unslipped ceramics of the Itzamkanak Complex. These numbers indicate a slight increase in the frequency of unslipped ceramics from Yax Te Complex times. There is a no dramatic change in wares, groups, types, and varieties compared to the Yax Te Complex, although Itzamkanak contains only two wares, Paso Caballo Waxy Ware and Uaxactun Unslipped Ware. Paso Caballo Waxy Ware contains all slipped ceramics. Type: varieties within the Sierra Group dominate the assemblage with Sierra Red: Sierra Variety appearing most frequently at 65.8 percent followed by Polvero Black: Polvero Variety (15.2%), Society Hall: Society Hall Variety (5.4%), Flor Cream: Flor Variety (3.7%), and Laguna Verde Incised: Laguna Verde Variety (3.5%) rounding out the top five type: varieties.

Surface finishing techniques of slipped ceramics exhibit the characteristic waxy or greasy texture of Paso Caballo Waxy Ware. Surface decoration within slipped ceramics of Paso Caballo Waxy Ware includes streaky slips, preslip incision, fluting, preslip grooved-incision, post-fire scratching, and punctation. While incision remains popular as the primary form of surface decoration on red-slipped ceramics (as seen on Laguna Verde type: varieties), preference for streaky red slip appears to be quite popular during the Itzamkanak Complex as well. This is particularly noticeable in Society Hall: Society Hall Variety. Pre- and post-slip incision are both present on cream- and black-slipped ceramics, namely Accordian Incised: Accordian Variety and Lechugal Incised: Lechugal Variety respectively. Incision usually takes the form of single or double lines encircling rims or on flanges of open forms. Post-slip scratching begins to resemble conventionalized aspects of Maya iconography (such as the Maize God on one sherd, see Figure 4.4a13). Fluting is more rare than incision, but does occur on Altamira Fluted: Altamira Variety vessels. Punctation or impression is also rare, but is present on Lagartos Punctated: Lagartos Variety within the Sierra group, as well as on Polvero Black jars at the shoulder break. Repasto Black-on-red (within the Sierra group) also makes a very infrequent appearance (see Figure 4.6). Along with these changes in surface decoration comes an increase in the number of vessel form modes, rim, and lip treatments.

Forms of slipped ceramics of the Itzamkanak Complex include bowls, dishes, and jars. Bowls and dishes are the most frequently occurring forms. They range greatly in size, shape of sides, rim, and lip treatment. Preference is given to flat bases. Supports begin to make an appearance. Large tecomate forms are very rare. Medium-sized

Table 8.3. Percentages of Itzamkanak Complex Slipped and Unslipped Type: Varieties

Ware	Group	Type: Variety	% Unslipped
Uaxactun Unslipped	Achiotes	Achiotes Unslipped: Achiotes Variety	95.8
		Achiotes Unslipped: Variety Unspecified	0.8
		Sapote Striated: Sapote Variety	3.4

Ware	Group	Type: Variety	% Slipped
Paso Caballo Waxy	Sierra	Sierra Red: Sierra Variety	65.8
		Laguna Verde Incised: Laguna Verde Variety	3.5
		Laguna Verde Incised: Grooved-incised Variety	1.1
		Altamira Fluted	0.9
		Repasto Black-on-red	0.1
		Society Hall	5.4
		Unnamed Punctated	0.0
		Unnamed Modeled	0.1
		Unnamed Dichrome	0.3
		Unnamed Red-and-unslipped	0.1
	Caramba	Unnamed Red-on-orange	0.0
	Zapatista	Unnamed Trickle-on-gray	0.0
	Flor	Flor Cream: Flor Variety	3.7
		Accordian Incised: Accordian Variety	0.3
	Polvero	Polvero Black: Polvero Variety	15.2
		Lechugal Incised: Lechugal Variety	0.8
	Boxcay	Boxcay Brown: Boxcay Variety	2.8

and smaller bowls include forms with flaring sides, outcurving sides, incurving sides, round sides, and composite sides (recurving, z-angle, and slightly rounded z-angle). Lip flanges and medial flanges make an appearance and are common on bowls and dishes of Itzamkanak slipped ceramics. On incised forms, these flanges usually serve as the background for decoration with simple tic marks, zig-zags, or squiggly lines. Rim treatments vary greatly and include direct, everted, incurving, exterior thickened, and interior thickened modes. Lip treatments also vary and include round, pointed, beveled, and beaded modes among others. Slipped jar forms are also common, some with spouts. Jars vary greatly in size and therefore function. Jars can be large with wide openings, short necks, and outcurving rims. They can also be medium in size, approximately 30 to 40 cm tall with small apertures (about 10 cm). Most were likely used for storing and serving liquid. Jar forms frequently occur in Polvero Black: Polvero Variety and Sierra Red: Sierra Variety. Miniature vessels also appear during the Itzamkanak Complex in both slipped (Sierra Group) and unslipped (Achiotes Group) type: varieties. As others (Fields and Reents-Budet 2005; Reents-Budet 2006) and I (Callaghan 2017) argue elsewhere, it is possible that style and potential value of Itzamkanak slipped vessels resided in their form more than their surface decoration.

This fascination with vessel form continued into the Terminal Preclassic Wayab Subcomplex and reached its height later in the Early Classic K'ak Complex.

Paste variants of slipped ceramics are almost all carbonate-based. All pastes contain some form of calcite. There are few pastes with volcanic ash inclusions. Paste texture and color corresponds to vessel form, size, and slip color. Smaller bowls, dishes, and jars of the Sierra Group are made with medium-textured pastes varying in color from buff to yellow to gray. Inclusions within these pastes could be angular crystalline calcite, round grey calcite, sherd temper (grog), burnt organic material, and, rarely, volcanic ash. Dishes, bowls, and medium-sized jars within the Flor Group are lighter in color, but contain similar inclusions. Polvero Group ceramics have pastes that are darker and more frequently contain only crystalline calcite inclusions (this preference for crystalline calcite inclusion goes back to black ceramics from pre-Mamom times). It is important to remember that this crystalline calcite based paste variant, often containing grog, was found within established Mamom type: varieties. It has now become the most common mode within Itzamkanak Complex slipped ceramics.

Unslipped Ceramics

Unslipped ceramics of the Itzamkanak Complex are type: varieties within Uaxactun Unslipped Ware. Uaxactun Unslipped Ware consists of one group and three type: varieties. Achiotes Unslipped: Achiotes Variety continues to be the most common type: variety of unslipped ceramic (95.8% of ware). A decorated type: variety, Sapote Striated: Sapote Variety, appears during Itzamkanak and comprises 3.4 percent of unslipped ceramics. Finally, I have identified another decorated variety of Achiotes Unslipped (Achiotes Unslipped: Unspecified Scratched Variety) that makes up less than 0.8 percent of ware. It is characterized by post fire scratching in simple lines—usually beginning at the shoulder break and continuing vertically down the exterior of jar walls. Achiotes Unslipped ceramics are made from a variety of coarse-grained pastes containing large angular pieces of crystalline calcite, but varying in color from yellow (10YR6/4) to gray (10YR5/1). Forms for Achiotes Group ceramics are mainly jars with globular sides, round bases, short necks, outcurving rims, and rounded lips. The rounded bases and coarse pastes suggest cooking or storage functions for many of these jars. Strap handles became common on jar forms at this time as opposed to the round handles of the Middle Preclassic Yax Te Complex. As a note, it is difficult to differentiate Achiotes Unslipped: Achiotes Variety jars between Yax Te and Itzamkanak deposits. Typologically and modally, these jars are quite similar. As I noted within the type-descriptions in Chapters 3 and 4, Achiotes Unslipped of the Yax Te Complex more frequently exhibit handles and are, on average, slightly smaller in diameter and potentially height than Itzamkanak Achiotes Unslipped types. Because of these similarities, both Yax Te and Itzamkanak Achiotes Unslipped frequencies were tabulated using contextually reliable deposits.

Discussion

Taken together, the typological and modal data of Itzamkanak ceramics paint a portrait of population growth and internationalism during the Late Preclassic period. Quantitatively, the greater frequencies and distribution of Itzamkanak types at all sampled sites in the Holmul region points to large-scale population growth. This growth is reflected in architectural development at almost every center with significant monumental architecture being erected at Cival and Holmul (Estrada Belli 2006b, 2010, 2012). Qualitatively in terms of modes, Itzamkanak Complex ceramics represent continuity with specific traditions of Yax Te ceramics. These are the red tradition that included *established varieties* of the Joventud Group, the black tradition characterized by Chunhinta Group ceramics, the cream tradition embodied in ceramics of the Pital Group, and the unslipped tradition characterized by the Achiotes Group. These red, black, cream, and unslipped Yax Te traditions continued in Sierra, Polvero, Flor, and Achiotes Group ceramics respectively during Itzamkanak times. These traditions are not solely defined by slip color and texture, but also by paste composition. Continuity in paste composition within red, black, cream, and unslipped ceramics can be seen in potters' preferences for crystalline calcite and sherd inclusions in many slipped serving vessels, as opposed to the volcanic ash found in local varieties of Joventud Group ceramics during Yax Te. Despite all this continuity in surface and paste modes, however, there are changes in form modes.

During Itzamkanak times there was an expansion in the diversity of form modes, especially in terms of wall, rim, and lip treatments of bowls and dishes. Unfortunately, this is an area of inquiry less suited for type: variety classification. Because type: variety focuses on surface treatment and decoration, only through separate modal analyses could I discern the great variety in form modes during Itzamkanak. At present, I cannot offer any one explanation as to why form modes diversified. The numerous forms could be due to the scale of production, with more potters creating more vessel forms. Or it could be due to changes in food preparation and serving, with more diverse liquid and solid foods being prepared and served during Late Preclassic times. Despite not being able to isolate specific reasons for the proliferation in vessel forms, I believe form may have been the vehicle for value in Late Preclassic ceramics (Callaghan 2008, 2013, 2017).

A greater range of forms and smaller range of decorative modes would have increased gradations of value in vessel forms, while decreasing gradations of value in surface decoration. As Lesure (1999) notes, more gradations of value within a characteristic of an artifact class (in this case vessel form) allow that characteristic to become a determining variable in the transformation of objects in that artifact class into social valuables. This relationship between gradations of value in form and creation of ceramic social valuables is supported by data from sites within and outside the Holmul region. Elaborate forms like jars with spouts, urns or tall vases, and dishes with supports appear to be found in greater quantities in ritual or high status contexts during the Late Preclassic period (see Culbert 1993; McAnany et al. 1999; Powis et al. 2002; Robin 1989). The combination of conservatism in surface decoration and elaboration in form would enable vessels to signify both inclusive and exclusive relationships. The elaboration in form within established modes of surface treatment may have enabled emerging groups and authority figures to both maintain community identity through surface modes, while simultaneously creating an exclusive identity for themselves through form modes. These dual identities would have been materialized and reinforced during commensal gatherings where the sharing of sacred foods would have further enhanced the authority of the food-givers (see Callaghan 2017 for more on Late Preclassic ceramic social valuables).

As speculative as this hypothesis may seem, it gains support when we look to the Wayab subcomplex of the Terminal Preclassic period. As I show in the next section, the Wayab subcomplex is composed of specific serving vessels that are characterized by further elaboration in form, as well as the first attempts at painted decoration of the Classic periods. As many Maya ceramicists have suggested, Terminal Preclassic subcomplex serving vessels may serve as the evolutionary link between predominantly monochrome Late Preclassic period ceramics and Early Classic polychromes. What I try to demonstrate,

however, is that form modes are just as important as surface decorative modes in supporting this evolutionary argument (see also Callaghan 2008, 2013; Callaghan et al. 2013). Elaboration in both form and surface modes were predicated upon the specific social contexts in which these vessels were used: namely, increasingly intimate commensal gatherings between authoritative groups and individuals.

THE WAYAB SUBCOMPLEX

The Wayab Subcomplex dates between AD 120 and 230 BC. The subcomplex dates were determined through a combination of radiocarbon samples and typological comparison to other sites (see Chapter 5). The Wayab Subcomplex is not a complete ceramic assemblage and does not represent a full ceramic complex. It is best described as a collection of serving vessels of types and modes that crosscut the Late Preclassic and Early Classic periods (see also Brady et al. 1998). Descriptions of Wayab material included in this study come from 14 whole vessels, 11 rim sherds and 4 diagnostic body sherds for a total of 29 representative samples. Two wares, 5 groups, and 8 type: varieties define the Wayab Subcomplex. Whole vessels of this subcomplex are restricted to ritual contexts at Holmul. Significant contexts include Room 8, the Room 8 Vault, and Room 9 in Building B, Group II as well as Burial 10 (Appendix A; Callaghan 2013; Merwin and Vaillant 1932; Neivens 2005). Wayab Subcomplex material represents diagnostic ceramics from the second phase of Brady and colleagues' (1998) proposed Terminal Preclassic ceramic period, which dates from AD 150 to 400. Wayab is contemporaneous with the proposed Matzanel Complex at Uaxactun (Smith 1955:22), Cimi Complex ceramics at Tikal (Culbert 1993, 2003, 2006), the Paixbancito Subcomplex at El Mirador (Forsyth 1989:51–60), the early Salinas Complex at Altar de Sacrificios (Adams 1971:93–94), the Poderes Complex (Sepos Subcomplex) at Edzná (Forsyth 1983:62–65), Blossom Bank at Colha (Valdez 1987), and the Floral Park Complex at Barton Ramie (Gifford 1976:127–153).

Slipped Ceramics

All type: varieties are slipped. Table 8.4 illustrates type: varieties as a percentage of rims and whole vessels within the Wayab Subcomplex. Wayab ceramics resemble a combination of types and modes from both the Itzamkanak Late Preclassic Complex and the first facet of the K'ak Early Classic Complex. Wares include the Late Preclassic

Table 8.4. Percentages of Wayab Subcomplex Slipped and Unslipped Type: Varieties

Ware	Group	Type: Variety	% Slipped
Petén Gloss	Aguila	Aguila Orange: Variety Unspecified	20.7
	Ixcanrio	Ixcanrio Orange Polychrome: Ixcanrio Variety	27.6
		Ixcanrio Orange Polychrome: Turnbull Variety	6.9
		Ixcanrio Orange Polychrome: Variety Unspecified	13.8
	Actuncan	Actuncan Orange Polychrome: Variety Unspecified	3.4
Paso Caballo Waxy	Sierra	Sierra Red: Variety Unspecified	6.9
	Flor	Flor Cream: Variety Unspecified	3.4
		Accordian Incised: Variety Unspecified	3.4

Paso Caballo Waxy Ware with its Sierra and Flor Groups and the Classic Period Petén Gloss Ware with its Aguila, Ixcanrio, and Actuncan groups. Within Paso Caballo Waxy Ware Sierra Red: Unspecified Variety comprises 50 percent of the ware (6.9% of the Subcomplex), while Flor Cream: Unspecified Variety and Accordian Incised: Unspecified Variety each account for 25 percent of the ware (3.4% of the Subcomplex). Within Petén Gloss Ware, Ixcanrio Orange Polychrome: Ixcanrio Variety is most frequent (32 percent of ware and 27.6% of the Subcomplex) followed by Aguila Orange: Unspecified Variety (29% of ware and 20.7% of the Subcomplex), Ixcanrio Orange Polychrome: Unspecified Variety (19% of ware and 13.8% of the Subcomplex), Ixcanrio Orange Polychrome: Turnbull Variety (10% of ware and 6.9% of the Subcomplex), and Actuncan Orange Polychrome: Unspecified Variety (5% of the ware and 3.4% of the Subcomplex).

Surface treatment within the Paso Caballo Waxy Ware type: varieties is more or less consistent with other examples of these ceramics from the Itzamkanak Complex. Surface texture on the Sierra Red pot-stand, Flor Cream jar with spout, and Accordian Incised jar with spout are waxy or greasy and vessels are relatively shiny. In contrast, the Sierra Red vase with mammiform tetrapod supports is slightly dull. Surface decoration on the Flor jars is more complex than anything I have seen in the regular Itzamkanak assemblage. The Accordian Incised jar displays post-slip incision in the form of circular patterns on the exterior of the vessel. The Flor Cream jar was slipped, polished, possibly fired, then covered in stucco and painted with bluish green, red, and black colors. The design is geometric with simple step patterns and single lines.

The Sierra Red vase with tetrapod supports is slipped red on the interior and exterior. The exterior of the Sierra Red pot stand is slipped red, but is almost completely covered in a fire cloud. Similar to surface decoration, the four vessels represent as yet unseen forms of serving vessels in the Late Preclassic Itzamkanak Complex. Jars with spouts have been found for type: varieties within Paso Caballo Waxy Ware (specifically Sierra Red types), but they lack the bridge-spouts of the two Flor Group examples within the Wayab Subcomplex. The Sierra vessel forms (vase with tetrapod supports and pot stand) have not yet been encountered in contemporary Holmul region collections.

The pastes of these vessels was hard to study because they are currently museum pieces and no cross section is available. The Accordian Incised jar appeared to display the buff-colored crystalline calcite paste consistent with Flor Group ceramics, but the pastes of the other three vessels are undetermined. Individually, and together as a group, these vessels represent singularities within Paso Caballo Waxy Ware in the Holmul region. They appear to embody a combination of Late Preclassic, Early Classic, and idiosyncratic surface, form, and paste modes. Late Preclassic modes include waxy surface texture, pitcher forms, post-slip incision, and heavy fire-clouding on the Sierra pot-stand. Early Classic modes include the stucco-painted surface of the Flor spouted jar and the pot stand form of the single Sierra vessel. Idiosyncratic modes include the dull slip and tetrapod mammiform supports on the Sierra Red vase, and the bridge-spouts on Flor Group jars. It is highly probable that these Wayab Subcomplex vessels were made during a period of overlap in ceramic production systems at the end of the Late Preclassic and beginning of the Early Classic periods. The Petén Gloss Ware ceramics exhibit similar combinations of Late Preclassic, Early Classic, and idiosyncratic modes.

The Ixcanrio Group contains the largest number of Petén Gloss Ware ceramics. Surface finish and decoration vary on Ixcanrio vessels and cannot be correlated to type: varieties. Like the Paso Caballo Waxy Ware vessels discussed previously, these Petén Gloss Ware vessels exhibit a combination of Late Preclassic and Early Classic finishing techniques with some appearing and feeling more waxy than glossy. It is, however, their decorative modes that place them more firmly within Early Classic decorative traditions. The plain monochrome type: varieties are slipped orange, one of the defining characteristics of Aguila Orange. The painted vessels present a range of designs including simple geometric patterns (e.g., the vertical squiggly lines of Ixcanrio: Turnbull Variety), abstract designs (e.g., the more complicated combination of shapes and lines on Ixcanrio: Ixcanrio Variety, as well as Actuncan: Unspecified Variety), and conventionalized objects (e.g., the macaw, swirling smoke, and mat pattern on Ixcanrio: Unspecified Variety). Despite differences in composition, all vessels display the characteristic red and black on orange or cream background painting style of Early Classic period polychromes. Petén Gloss Ware vessel forms represent a mixture of Early Classic and idiosyncratic attributes. While some attributes are reminiscent of Early Classic form modes (i.e., composite silhouette bowl and bowl with annular base), others are rarely seen in the current collection of Early Classic material (i.e., hollow tetrapod supports some with mammiform shapes). Like the Paso Caballo Waxy Ware vessels, pastes of Petén Gloss Ware vessels were difficult to study because they were museum pieces. Sherds of these gloss wares that were found in excavation units, however, show that paste composition varied and contained crystalline calcite, gray calcite, sherd, volcanic ash, or a combination of inclusions. Taken together, these Petén Gloss Ware ceramics of the Wayab Subcomplex represent singularities much like the Paso Caballo Waxy Ware vessels. What then can type: variety-mode data tell us in regard to the dating, frequency, function, and meaning of these Wayab Subcomplex serving vessels?

Discussion

In terms of quantity, Wayab Subcomplex type: varieties are extremely rare. While Holmul may be known for its Terminal Preclassic period ceramic material, the present sample does not indicate that potters in the Holmul region were producing these vessels in any great quantity. Qualitatively, type: variety-mode data reveal that the specific collection of vessels and sherds from Holmul represent a combination of surface, form, firing, and paste modes from both the Late Preclassic and Early Classic periods. These vessels were most likely produced during a time of overlap during the end of the Late Preclassic Itzamkanak Complex and beginning of the Early Classic K'ak Complex. In order to understand the function and meaning of these vessels, and why they appeared at Holmul during this time, it is necessary to understand the broader cultural and historical context of the Terminal Preclassic period. I have presented more detailed discussions of Terminal Preclassic subcomplex pottery in previous publications (see Callaghan 2008, 2013; Callaghan et al. 2013), but I offer a brief explanation here.

The Terminal Preclassic period bridges the end of the Late Preclassic period and beginning of the Early Classic period in the Maya lowlands, and in its greatest estimation falls between 75 BC and AD 400 (Brady et al. 1998). This time period has been previously referred to as the Protoclassic period in Maya archaeology and its nature and significance have long been the subject of intense debate (Brady et al. 1998; Hammond 1974, 1977, 1984; Pring 1977a, 1977b, 2000; Sharer and Gifford 1970; Sheets 1979a, 1979b; Willey and Gifford 1961; Willey et al. 1967). At the center of much Terminal Preclassic period research is the study of the Petén Gloss Ware ceramics discussed previously. As the type: variety-mode data show, these orange gloss ceramics exhibit a combination of Preclassic and Classic period ceramic traits along with their own unique characteristics (see also Smith 1955:22). These orange gloss ceramics are actually part of a second wave of ceramic innovation taking place during the Terminal Preclassic period, and it is important to understand these two waves of innovation in order to understand the function and meaning of the orange gloss ceramics (I return to the Paso Caballo Waxy Ware ceramics at the end of this discussion).

Brady and colleagues (1998) suggest that the Terminal Preclassic period can be divided into two ceramics facets; an early (75 BC–AD 150) and a late (AD 150–400), both based upon significant changes in ceramic modes. In brief, the first facet witnessed the introduction of matte- or waxy-finish orange-brown ceramic types (for example, Iberia Orange and Ixobel Orange) as well as production and exchange of pottery displaying the Usulutan mode of drip-like decoration (through application of true-resist technology or positive painting). The second facet saw the introduction of glossy-finished orange types (ceramics of the Aguila Group) including those with polychrome painted decoration (for example, Ixcanrio Orange Polychrome) as well as continued production and exchange of matte-finished types (ceramics of the Aguacate Group).

Sites containing tombs with early phase Terminal Preclassic ceramic material are rare, but include Tikal Burials 167, 166, and 85, and PD 87 (Coe 1965; Culbert 1993; Estrada-Belli 2010); Jabalí Group Tomb 1 at San Bartolo, Guatemala (Pellecer 2006); and possibly Tombs 1, 2, and 3 at Wakna, Guatemala (Hansen 1998). It is important to note that no early phase Terminal Preclassic material has yet to be identified in the Holmul region. In contrast to phase one material, phase two material appears to be more widespread yet still rare in the lowlands. Sites that contain notable examples of late facet Terminal Preclassic ceramics include *chultunes* at Tzimin Kax, Belize (Thompson 1931:284–288); *chultunes* and caches at Topoxte, Guatemala (Hermes 1999); a tomb at Cahal Cunil, Belize (Thompson 1931:291); a burial mound at Nohmul, Belize (Anderson and Cook 1944:84; Gann and Gann 1939); a potential "port mound" at Nohmul, Belize (Pring and Hammond 1985); Burials 19, 30, and 31 at Barton Ramie, Belize (Pring 2000:106; Willey and Gifford 1961); a *chultun* at El Mirador, Guatemala (Forsyth 1989:10; Hansen 1990:88–94; Pring 2000:117); "ritual contexts" (Lopez Varela 1996:302) and burials at K'axob, Belize (Berry et al. 2004); contexts of an "elite element of society" (Pring 2000:122) at Kichpanha, Belize (Meskill 1992); a tomb and cave at La Lagunita, Guatemala (deposit C-48) (Ichon and Arnauld 1985); a cave at Naj Tunich, Guatemala (Brady 1989); Tomb 2 at Chan Chich, Belize (Houk et al. 2010); construction fill of a large mound in the epicenter of El Pozito, Belize (Case 1982); a large midden deposit at Salinas de los Nueve Cerros, Guatemala (Dillon 1977); construction fill of Building B, Group II at Holmul, Guatemala (Callaghan 2008); construction fill of Structure 1 at La Sufricaya, Guatemala (Callaghan 2008); and Tikal burials PNT-21 and PNT-10, both in Structure 5D-86 of the east platform of the E-Group structure at Mundo Perdido (Laporte 1995; Laporte and Fialko 1995).

Maya archaeologists have tested many models to understand the function and meaning of the second-facet Terminal Preclassic orange gloss ceramics. Because of their combination of Preclassic and Classic period traits, they were once thought to be representative of a transitional cultural phase between the Preclassic and Classic periods (Willey et al. 1967). After years of excavations at other Maya sites yielded relatively few examples of Terminal Preclassic orange gloss ceramics (see discussions in Brady et al. 1998; Callaghan 2008; and Pring 2000); however, it became clear that the vessels could not be indicative of a pan-lowland phase of cultural development. The presence of these vessels in the Maya Lowlands was also thought to be the result of major migrations of populations from southeastern Mesoamerica in the wake of volcanic eruptions (Sharer 1978; Sharer and Gifford 1970; Sheets 1979a, 1979b). Refined modal analysis and revised dating of the volcanic event proved to falsify these hypotheses (Dull et al. 2001; Hammond 1974, 1977, 1984; Pring 1977a).

The introduction of Petén Gloss Ware is best understood in relation to larger culture-historical processes that took shape in the Terminal Preclassic period. Reese-Taylor and Walker (2002) cite a number of significant culture-historical changes that occurred during this time, including

1. increased signs of warfare and site abandonment along pre-existing trade routes;
2. a massive reorganization of trade patterns after the collapse of El Mirador;
3. signs of the first royal burials in tombs and plazas of major centers such as Tikal, Caracol, and Holmul;
4. usurpation of the supernatural realm by elites through the construction of ceremonial architecture in the form of mythical places at major site centers and the possibility that elite shamans began taking on roles of deities and sacred ancestors at important ceremonial events, and, most important as concerns this research; and
5. the introduction of a subcomplex of orange-slipped polychrome pottery displaying "tags" of ideology representing re-birth (such as mammiform supports, which Reese-Taylor and Walker [2002] relate to representations of breasts from the goddess Ix'chel, as well as peccary imagery) and symbols that eventually become associated with Classic period

elites (such as the weave, mat, or *pop* pattern, as well as early representations of the *ahau* or Lord glyph).

In light of these emerging culture-historical patterns, scholars are currently applying models derivative of more traditional political economy approaches to understand the introduction of orange gloss ceramics during the late facet of the Terminal Preclassic period. In these models, Petén Gloss Ware constituted part of a new political economy and served as a form of social currency that materialized political or trade relations (Brady et al. 1998:33; Fields and Reents-Budet 2005:214–217; Pring 2000:42; Reese-Taylor and Walker 2002:104-105; Walker et. al 2006:665). In this type of model Petén Gloss Ware would have been considered a type of prestige good with its production and distribution controlled by groups of elites seeking to gain or maintain social status and political authority.

I agree with these models, but would also like to qualify or expand upon them further. I have argued that Terminal Preclassic polychrome vessels were social valuables that simultaneously integrated communities while reinforcing political and social hierarchies within them (Callaghan 2008; Callaghan et al. 2013). This process began in the Late Preclassic period when highly elaborate forms of monochrome-slipped vessels were being used as food serving vessels during commensal gatherings. My typological and modal analyses of paste, form, finishing, and firing modes of these Terminal Preclassic serving vessels and contemporaneous Sierra Red types at Holmul have shown that this early painted pottery was produced by numerous production units often with similar technologies as seemingly unrestricted Sierra Red serving vessels (Callaghan 2008; Callaghan et al. 2013). These data do not suggest restricted access to resources or technology at every single stage of the production process. When combined with data about the segmented nature of the ceramic production process from ethnographic (D. Arnold 1985, 2008; P. Arnold 1991; Druc 2000; Reina and Hill 1978) and archaeological (Beaudry 1984; Coggins 1975; Reents-Budet 1994; Rice 2009) data it is quite reasonable to assume that the first orange-slipped polychromes were produced not by few elite craftspeople, but by many people possibly of different socioeconomic statuses. This would have integrated regional producers into one economic and possibly even social and political unit centered on a Terminal Preclassic polity.

Although production may have been segmented and multiple producers were responsible for the creation of these vessels, I argue that some of these producers may not have had access to their final products, specifically some of those responsible for the production of vessels in Building B, Group II at Holmul. As I suggest elsewhere, the vessels found in the rooms of Building B, Group II at Holmul may have been used only by the Terminal Preclassic and early facet Early Classic period elite in what Dietler (1996:92–99, 2001:75–88) calls "diacritical feasts" (Callaghan 2008; Callaghan et al. 2013). Diacritical feasts are exclusive gatherings of elites where rich and rare food is served. The function of these feasts was to legitimate social inequalities between exclusive elite participants and those non-elites (and also other elites) that were not in attendance. Unlike "empowering" or "patron-role" feasts (Dietler 1996:92–99, 2001:75–88), it is not the quantity of food that was important in these feasts, but its quality and the performance or ritual surrounding its serving. Preparation, ceremonious serving, and appreciation of rare foods of exceptional quality serves as a marker of cultural "distinction" and simultaneously demonstrates and boosts one's level of cultural capital (sensu Bourdieu 1984).

LeCount (2001) and others (Foias 2007; Reents-Budet 1994, 2000, 2006) have used ceramic remains and ethnohistoric documents to suggest that Classic period Maya elites practiced exclusive, potentially diacritical, feasting rituals. Painted scenes on Late Classic period polychrome vases support the idea that diacritical feasts may have been practiced by Maya elites. Pictorial scenes on these vessels often portray a king sitting on a throne eating or speaking as he receives visitors (sometimes carrying tribute), and attended by servants or ritual persons such as dwarves or hunchbacks (Reents-Budet 1994, 2000, 2006). These scenes sometimes depict actual historical occasions. It is possible to extend these interpretations back in time to the Terminal Preclassic period when polychrome painting began to appear more frequently in the lowlands.

Because some producers may have been alienated from their final products, and more than likely not granted access to the diacritical feasts in which these vessels were used, the vessels and the feasts they were used in simultaneously contributed to community integration while reinforcing newly forming social and political hierarchies. I argue Terminal Preclassic period orange polychrome serving vessels were representations of changes in feasting strategies and material tools of social integration and separation (Callaghan 2008; Callaghan et al. 2013). The polities who took part in the production and consumption of these types of ceramics, and the elites who used and gifted them at diacritical feasts, were able to survive the political turmoil of the Terminal Preclassic period. The vessels in Building B, Group II at Holmul may have been a testament to that community's ability to integrate itself and survive the political and economic events that caused the collapse of other major lowland polities like Cerros, El Mirador, and even Cival in the Holmul region itself.

While much of the discussion surrounding Terminal Preclassic pottery focuses on Petén Gloss Ware serving vessels, less emphasis is placed on the interpretation of Terminal Preclassic Paso Caballo Waxy Ware vessels. This is unfortunate, because without understanding changes in Paso Caballo Waxy Ware we can create only a partial reconstruction of ceramic production and distribution patterns during the Terminal Preclassic period and perhaps write-out entire groups of important political actors. The typological and modal data at Holmul show that even though Paso Caballo Waxy Ware disappears during the onset of the Early Classic period, potters were integrating Early Classic form modes (such as the pot stand and basal flanges) and decorative modes (such as painted stucco) into their repertoire. While we are gaining a better understanding of the function and meaning of early Petén Gloss Ware ceramics, much work needs to be completed on changes in Paso Caballo Waxy Ware during the Terminal Preclassic period in an effort to better understand the socio-political events taking place during this time. I return to this theme in my concluding remarks.

THE K'AK COMPLEX

K'ak is the Early Classic period complex in the Holmul region. Based on radiocarbon dates and typological comparisons, the complex dates between AD 230 and 550 (see Chapter 5). Descriptions of K'ak material included in this study come from 2098 rim sherds, 10,984 diagnostic body sherds, and 64 whole vessels for a total of 13,145 samples. Three definable wares (1 Unspecified), 8 groups, and 25 type: varieties define the K'ak Complex. K'ak material is found at Cival, Holmul, La Sufricaya, K'o, Hamontun, and Dos Aguadas, with significant deposits occurring in Structure 1 at La Sufricaya and Rooms 1 and 2 in Building B, Group II at Holmul. K'ak ceramics share almost 100 percent of type: varieties with the Tzakol ceramic sphere. Typologically and modally, K'ak ceramics are contemporaneous with Tzakol material at Uaxactun (Smith 1955),

Manik at Tikal (Culbert 1993, 2003, 2006), Acropolis at El Mirador (Forsyth 1989), Junco at Seibal (Sabloff 1975), Jordan Tzakol in the Petexbatun region (Foias and Bishop 2013), Kaynikte at Calakmul (Dominguez-Carrasco 1994), Burrell at Chan (Kosakowsky 2012), the Early Classic complex at La Milpa (Sagebiel 2005), Poderes (Full) at Edzná (Forsyth 1983), Yaxcab at Yaxchilan (Lopez Varela 1989), Nohalk'ax at K'axob (Lopez Varela 2004), Cobweb at Colha (Valdez 1987), and Hermitage at Barton Ramie (Gifford 1976).

The K'ak Complex is separated into three facets: K'ak 1 (early), K'ak 2 (middle), and K'ak 3 (late). It is important to note that these facets do not represent distinct and separate ceramic complexes. As I explained in Chapter 6, these facets are distinguished from one another based on the appearance and disappearance of diagnostic types, as well as changes in modes of established Early Classic type: varieties. K'ak 1 facet ceramics belong to the Tzakol 1 facet of the Tzakol Sphere, first defined by Smith (1955:23–24; see also Willey et al. 1967:298–299) and Smith and Gifford (1966:171). The K'ak 1 facet dates between AD 230 and 300. K'ak 1 is distinguished by the introduction of Aguila, Balanza, Actuncan, and Quintal Group ceramics. Diagnostic types of the K'ak 1 facet include Actuncan Orange Polychrome and Boleto Black-on-orange. K'ak 2 facet ceramics are contemporaneous with Tzakol 2 facet ceramics of the Tzakol Sphere (Smith 1955:23–24; Smith and Gifford (1966:171; see also Willey et al. 1967:298–299) and date between AD 300 and 450. They are also contemporaneous with Manik 2 Complex ceramics at Tikal (Culbert 1993, 2003, 2006). During the K'ak 2 facet in the Holmul region, Actuncan Orange Polychrome and Boleto Black-on-orange disappeared and Dos Arroyos Orange Polychrome and Caldero Buff Polychrome appeared. K'ak 3 facet material is part of the Tzakol 3 facet of the Tzakol Sphere (Smith 1955:23–24; Smith and Gifford 1966:171; Willey et al. 1967:298–299) and dates between AD 450 and 550. It is also contemporaneous with Manik 3 ceramics at Tikal (Culbert 1993, 2003, 2006; Laporte et al. 1992). The K'ak 3 facet is characterized by the addition of Paxbán Unslipped within an Unspecified Ware, and two new type: varieties (Bocul Orange-on-cream: Bocul Variety and Bocul Orange-on-cream: Variety Unspecified).

Slipped Ceramics

The majority of type: varieties within the current sample are slipped (79%) vs. unslipped (21%). Table 8.5 lists type: varieties as a percentage of rims and whole vessels

Table 8.5. Percentages of K'ak Complex Slipped and Unslipped Type: Varieties

Ware	Group	Type: Variety	% Unslipped
Uaxactun Unslipped	Quintal	Quintal Unslipped: Quintal Variety	76.4
		Triunfo Striated: Triunfo Variety	8.6
		Quintal Unslipped: Variety Unspecified	0.4
		Triunfo Striated: Variety Unspecified	0.2
	Unnamed	Unnamed Unslipped and Modeled (K'ak)	0.2
Unspecified	Paxbán	Paxbán Unslipped: Paxbán Variety	14.1

Ware	Group	Type: Variety	% Slipped
Petén Gloss	Aguila	Aguila Orange: Aguila Variety	54.3
		Pita Incised: Pita Variety	4.5
		Nitan Composite: Nitan Variety	7.2
		Bocul Orange-on-cream: Bocul Variety	2.9
		Bocul Orange-on-cream: Variety Unspecified	0.4
		Unnamed Modeled	0.0
	Dos Hermanos	Dos Hermanos Red: Dos Hermanos Variety	0.4
	Balanza	Balanza Black: Balanza Variety	14.9
		Lucha Incised: Lucha Variety	6.6
		Lucha Incised: Variety Unspecified	0.1
		Urita Gouged-incised: Urita Variety	0.7
		Positas Modeled: Positas Variety	0.0
	Actuncan	Actuncan Orange Polychrome: Actuncan Variety	1.3
		Boleto Black-on-orange: Boleto Variety	1.3
	Dos Arroyos	Dos Arroyos Orange Polychrome: Dos Arroyos Variety	3.7
		Caldero Buff Polychrome: Caldero Variety	1.2
	Japon	Japon Resist: Japon Variety	0.1
	Unnamed	Unnamed Polychrome (K'ak)	0.1
		Unnamed Red Slipped	0.2

within the slipped and unslipped wares of the K'ak Complex. These numbers indicate an increase in frequency of unslipped ceramics from Itzamkanak times. There is also a notable increase in wares, groups, types, and varieties compared to the Itzamkanak Complex. Within slipped ceramics Aguila Orange: Aguila Variety comprises the majority (54.3% of ware) followed by Balanza Black: Balanza Variety (14.9% of ware), Nitan Composite: Nitan Variety (7.2% of ware), Lucha Incised: Lucha Variety (6.6% of ware), and Pita Incised: Pita Variety (4.5% of ware) rounding out the top five type: varieties.

Surface finishing techniques of slipped ceramics changed from the preceding Itzamkanak Complex. Surface textures are less waxy or greasy. Monochrome slips are thinner and glossy. Surface decoration within slipped ceramics of Petén Gloss Ware are primarily orange slips, not red. Decoration includes some previously used techniques such as post-slip incision, as well as new techniques such as black-on-orange or polychrome painting, gouge-incision, applique, and resist. Incision usually takes the form of single or double lines encircling rims or on flanges of open forms in the Aguila and Balanza Groups. Some examples of post-slip incision and gouge-incision on Lucha Incised or Urita Gouged-Incised types are glyphs, pseudoglyphs, complicated geometric designs, anthropomorphic faces, and animals. Incision appears on the exterior surfaces of bowl and vase forms. Incision also appears on lids for bowls, not to mention the appearance of lids themselves. Balanza Group rims and vessels displaying incision and gauge-incision outnumber polychrome sherds of the Actuncan, Dos Arroyos, and Caldero groups combined. In addition, incision and gouge-incision designs and techniques are more sophisticated than polychrome decoration. Incision on Balanza Group vessels is often found in combination with appliquéd beads, especially in K'ak 2 and 3 facet examples.

Painting, which began on Wayab Subcomplex serving vessels, proliferated during the K'ak Complex; it was done on the exterior and interior of bowl forms, as well as basal flanges. Polychrome designs on red-and-black-on-orange (i.e., Actuncan Orange Polychrome and Dos Arroyos Orange Polychrome) or red-and-black-on-buff (i.e., Caldero Buff Polychrome) ceramics range from complicated geometric patterns to conventionalized forms of animals and humans. Designs on black-on-orange vessels (i.e., Boleto Black-on-orange) are exclusively geometric. At this point, I cannot say that painted decoration became more complicated, or even moved from geometric to conventional compositions from K'ak 1 through K'ak 3. Some of the earliest painted designs on Wayab Subcomplex Ixcanrio Polychromes are also some of the more complex examples. This pattern changed in the Chak Complex with the introduction of sophisticated calligraphic painting of glyphs and conventional designs on vessel exteriors and interiors. Painting on stucco-covered vessels is another decorative mode of the K'ak Complex, although it is very rare. Even more rare is resist decoration on the exterior of vessel surfaces. The only resist types of the K'ak Complex are two Japon Resist vases found in Room 2 of Building B, Group II at Holmul. Taken together, the increase in number and sophistication of decorative modes suggests an emphasis on the importance of surface modes during the K'ak Complex.

Forms of slipped ceramics of the K'ak Complex include bowls, vases, and jars. Form modes are particularly sensitive to changes in chronology during the larger K'ak Complex, especially within certain groups. Forms of K'ak 1 Aguila Orange include flaring sided bowls with direct rims, rounded lips, and flat bases; composite silhouette bowls with rounded z-angles, direct rims, rounded lips, and flat bases; and composite silhouette bowls with z-angles, direct rims, rounded lips, and flat bases. Basal flanges appear on Aguila and Actuncan Group ceramics, but are small in size. Composite silhouette bowl forms within the Aguila and Actuncan Groups are shorter during K'ak 1. Ring bases became frequent in K'ak 1 and continued through K'ak 2 and 3. K'ak 1 supports are rare, but when they do occur they are large, hollow tetrapods. During K'ak 2 composite bowl forms with basal flanges in the Aguila, Balanza, Dos Arroyos, and Caldero Groups are wider and taller, and flanges became much larger. Lids appeared during K'ak 2 in the Balanza and Dos Arroyos Groups. Rounded z-angle and z-angle forms diminished in frequency and almost disappeared. Finally, bowls with round sides and small spouts are also a K'ak 2 form mode; they are mostly found within the Balanza Group. Forms indicative of K'ak 3 facet ceramics include large bucket shapes with everted rims (both in the Aguila and Balanza Groups). They also include vases with small solid cylindrical-shaped or slab-shaped tripod supports. Plates began to appear in the Dos Arroyos Group. Flanges on composite silhouette bowls and these new more open plate forms are smaller and resemble lateral ridges more than they do true basal flanges.

Throughout all three facets, bowls are the most common form. Tecomates are not present. Large bowls and ollas are extremely rare. Bowls are medium to small in size. The most common form is a composite silhouette bowl with z-angle, rounded z-angle, or basal flange. As noted previously, differences in the frequencies of vessel profiles are chronologically sensitive. Bowls with flaring walls are also common, as are bowls with round sides. Both flaring and round-sided bowls are found within the Aguila and Balanza Groups. Flaring and round-sided polychrome bowls are not present in the current sample. The variety of rim and lip treatments greatly diminishes during the K'ak Complex, with a preference for direct rims and rounded lips, although flat or squared lips are not uncommon in K'ak 3 forms. Bases on bowls are flat, but ring-bases are extremely common on composite silhouette forms with basal flanges. Supports are rare overall, but are stylistically sensitive to temporal phases (e.g., tetrapod hollow supports in K'ak 1-2, tripod solid supports in K'ak 3). Jar forms are present in the Aguila and Balanza Groups. They are similar to one another in that they are medium in size with vertical necks, direct rims, and rounded lips. There are currently no examples of polychrome jars in the collection. Taken together, modal data on form suggest that the sophistication and fascination with vessel forms continued from the Late Preclassic period into the first two facets of the Early Classic period. At the same time, there is less diversity and more consistency in many modes (e.g., vessel size, vessel profile, rim treatment, and lip treatment). This pattern continues into the Late Classic period when form modes take a back seat to decorative surface modes.

Paste variants of K'ak Complex slipped ceramics are also chronologically sensitive, especially within particular groups. K'ak 1-2 Aguila Group pastes are made almost exclusively of clays that fire to a buff color and are loaded with small spheres of gray calcite (i.e., peloid calcite). By K'ak 3, Aguila Group pastes are mostly composed of light firing clays that include volcanic ash. Balanza Group pastes are not temporally sensitive. Balanza pastes during the K'ak Complex are made from dark firing clays with angular pieces of crystalline calcite. Polychrome ceramics of the Actuncan, Dos Arroyos, and Caldero Groups vary greatly. While they are all light firing clays, primary inclusions can include angular pieces of crystalline calcite, round balls of gray calcite, or volcanic ash. Pastes of polychrome vessels do not appear to be chronologically sensitive either. Taken together, paste data obtained from modal analyses of K'ak Complex slipped ceramics suggests a relatively dramatic change in production patterns. While all variants appear to be local and somewhat present in type: varieties of the Preclassic complexes, the frequency in which they occur changed since Itzamkanak times. It is important to remember that aside from a few examples of Actuncan Orange Polychrome in the K'ak 1 facet, no pastes included sherd temper during the Early Classic period. This is in contrast with Itzamkanak Complex times, when sherd temper was a popular mode for slipped ceramics. The addition of a paste variant containing gray spheres of calcite is also an innovation of K'ak Complex ceramics. This type of inclusion appeared before (e.g., Calam Buff Group during the early Middle Preclassic), but it became the exclusive variant for Aguila Group ceramics in the K'ak 1 and 2 Early Classic facets. Interestingly, great change in paste recipes took place not only between Itzamkanak and K'ak times, but also within the K'ak Complex itself. Local potters abandoned recipes containing gray calcite in K'ak 1 and 2 in preference for light-firing clays with volcanic ash by K'ak 3. These preferences for pastes are not correlated to specific sites, but to specific type: varieties. Based on these data, it is reasonable to say that the Early Classic period was a time of great change and innovation of surface, form, and paste modes. This is a pattern reflected in the surface and form modes of unslipped pottery as well.

Unslipped Ceramics

Unslipped ceramics of the K'ak Complex are type: varieties within Uaxactun Unslipped Ware and a new Unspecified Ware. Uaxactun Unslipped Ware consists of one group and two established type: varieties. Quintal Unslipped: Quintal Variety is the most common type: variety within Uaxactun Unslipped Ware (76.4% of unslipped ceramics) with Triunfo Striated: Triunfo Variety second (8.6% of unslipped ceramics). Paxbán Unslipped: Paxbán Variety within an Unspecified Ware are found in less frequency than Quinta Unslipped, but in higher frequencies than Triunfo Striated composing 14.1 percent of unslipped ceramics. Although the Triunfo and Quintal types are not diagnostic of any one phase within the K'ak Complex, Paxbán Unslipped is a clear K'ak 3 facet marker. As it was for slipped ceramics, the K'ak Complex was also a time of innovation in surface and form modes of unslipped ceramics. Not only is there an increase in the percent of unslipped ceramics during the K'ak Complex (79% slipped and 21% unslipped, compared to 86% slipped and 14% unslipped for Itzamanak times), there is also an increase in the diversity of surface and form modes.

Type: varieties in the Quintal Unslipped group within Uaxactun Unslipped Ware begin to exhibit decorative modes during the K'ak Complex. Triunfo Striated is characterized by deep striations on vessel exteriors that extend down from the rim or shoulder break to the rest of the vessel. Some Quintal Unslipped and Triunfo Striated vessels exhibit applique and impressed filets encircling the shoulder-break. One spouted jar form from Building B at Holmul is decorated with a modeled peccary face while another spouted jar form shows black slip extending down from the lip to the shoulder break on the vessel exterior (see Figure 6.1b). Jars are the most common forms of Quintal Unslipped and Triunfo Striated. But excavators have encountered sherds of large flat forms that I have yet to positively identify as lids, comales, or large flaring-side bowls. Quintal Unslipped jar forms are large and often characterized by their high necks and exterior bolstered rims. Shorter outcurving and outflaring jar necks also occur. Triunfo jar forms are similar in overall form, but differ in terms of rim treatment. Triunfo Striated rims are not bolstered, but often exhibit a small notch on the interior of the lip. Outcurving forms are rare, but do occur. Pastes of Quintal Unslipped and Triunfo Striated are dark gray and contain many pieces of angular crystalline calcite. There does not seem to be any differences in paste between the two types.

As I discussed above, Paxbán Unslipped was introduced during the K'ak 3 facet and does not resemble type: varieties of the Quintal group within Uaxactun Unslipped Ware. Paxbán Unslipped is part of a new Unspecified Ware that contains only the Paxbán type. Paxbán Unslipped is a censer type. Paxbán Unslipped sherds can be decorated with applique, impression, or modeling. One applique form from La Sufricaya resembles a corncob. Other forms are more abstract and often too fragmented to decipher any identifiable form or image. Paxbán Unslipped ceramics are found in two form classes, small bowls with flaring sides, direct rims, squared lips, and flat bases; and composite censer forms. The small bowls often display burn marks on the interior and exterior base. Paxbán Unslipped ceramics are also easily distinguished from unslipped ceramics within Uaxactun Unslipped Ware by their paste. Paxbán Unslipped was created using light-firing clays with volcanic ash as the main inclusion. The introduction of Paxbán Unslipped during K'ak 3 signals not merely increased diversity in unslipped ceramics, but the introduction of new ritual practices. Paxbán Unslipped is a ware of portable censers, something not seen before the end of the Early Classic period. This ritual tradition appears to be a characteristic of Classic period culture and it is an institution that continues to grow throughout the proceeding Late Classic period.

Discussion

What do the typological and modal data say about cultural processes during the Early Classic period in the Holmul region? Quantitative and distributional data of type: varieties indicate contraction at certain sites and expansion at others during specific facets of the K'ak Complex. K'ak 1 and 2 facet data suggest that occupation at Cival greatly diminishes. Architectural data correlate with these ceramic data and reveal that monumental construction ceased between AD 150 and 200 and never again reached heights of the Late Preclassic period

(Estrada-Belli 2006b, 2008, 2010). This, however, is not the case at Holmul, Hamontun, or K'o. K'ak 1 and 2 facet data indicate that Holmul continued to grow during the first two thirds of the Early Classic period, exemplified in the continued growth of Building B, Group II, and the entombment of local elites in Rooms 1 and 2. Hamontun also experienced growth at this time with much of its monumental epicenter being constructed during the early facet of the Early Classic period. Finally, K'o experienced significant growth with at least one temple mound being constructed during K'ak 2 times. This pattern changes during the latter third of the Early Classic period. The only significant K'ak 3 deposits come from the site of La Sufricaya. The site may have been established as early as the Late Preclassic period, but it did not experience significant growth until the end of the Early Classic period (Estrada-Belli et al. 2009). Some researchers suggest that La Sufricaya may have been home to a rival political faction in the Holmul region during K'ak 3 times (Estrada-Belli et al. 2009; Tokovinine and Estrada-Belli 2015). This faction may have usurped the power of Holmul elites and established a new political seat at La Sufricaya. This is evidenced in the art, architecture, and ceramics found in and around Structure 1, the palace type structure at that site. This shift in political fortune was short-lived. The palace was abandoned and filled by the beginning of the Late Classic period. Monumental architecture and stelae erection also ceased at the end of the Early Classic period. While areas of La Sufricaya were occupied during the Late Classic period, it never again experienced the growth and political importance of its late facet Early Classic apogee.

Qualitatively, typological and modal data reveal a stark contrast between the K'ak Complex and ceramics of the preceding Late Preclassic period Itzamkanak Complex. Surface, form, paste, and firing modes change dramatically during K'ak times. This change began at the end of the Late Preclassic period and is evidenced in the Terminal Preclassic Wayab Subcomplex serving vessels found in Rooms 8 and 9 of Building B, Group II at Holmul. A true Early Classic ceramic complex, however, does not exist until K'ak 1 times. Major Early Classic modes for slipped ceramics include orange slip, polychrome painting, complex incised designs, elaborate vessel forms, lack of sherd inclusions in paste fabrics, and the increase in gray calcite based pastes. By the end of the K'ak 3, modes changed again with the introduction of vase forms and the increased use of volcanic ash-based pastes. Within unslipped ceramics, decorative treatments became more frequent, and overall percentages increased from Itzamkanak times. These qualitative changes in K'ak Complex modes suggest an intentional break from previous production patterns of the Late Preclassic Itzamkanak Complex. As I noted in reference to the quantitative and distributional data, qualitative changes in ceramic modes are also correlated with construction and occupation data at specific sites in the Holmul region. Unfortunately, at this moment I cannot state how or why changes in ceramic production correlate with local population movements and political fortunes. What the typological and modal data do suggest, however, is that Holmul region ceramic producers were interacting heavily with people from other sites of the central Petén to the west, north, and south, and to a lesser extent the Belize River Valley to the east. Local authority figures at Holmul may have played an important role in interregional politics during K'ak 1 and 2 times, as evidenced by the ceramic inventory in Rooms 1 and 2 in Building B, Group II at Holmul. Political fortunes changed by the last third of the Early Classic period, however, and the seat of power in the region may have shifted to La Sufricaya. It is this particular cultural-historical event that I address next.

The smaller Early Classic center of La Sufricaya is located on the west side of the Río Holmul approximately 1.2 km west of Holmul. According to Estrada-Belli (2001:12; Tokovinine and Estrada-Belli 2015), the site was discovered and its monuments first documented by Ian Graham in 1984. The majority of architecture at the site sits atop a narrow ridge measuring approximately 150 m long. The site is best known for its seven fragmentary stelae and palace structure with painted murals (Estrada-Belli et al. 2009; Tokovinine and Estrada-Belli 2015). The murals and stelae date to the Early Classic period (AD 350–500) and document historical events occurring around the time of the potential arrival of Pre-Columbian Mexican elites around AD 378 in the southern Maya lowlands. Combining archaeological and epigraphic data Tokovine and Estrada-Belli (2015; Estrada-Belli et al. 2009) suggest that La Sufricaya was home to a rival (yet local) political faction in the Holmul region that came to power sometime between AD 350 and 450. This faction may have been supported by elites from Tikal who were at that time utilizing imagery and ideology from the central Mexican site of Teotihuacan to legitimate their political power. What do modal and typological data of K'ak 3 facet ceramics add to this story?

Typological and modal data of K'ak 3 facet ceramics found in and around Structure 1 (in some cases directly associated with the murals) appear to support Tokovinine and Estrada-Belli's (2015; Estrada-Belli et al. 2009) interpretation. To begin, none of the ceramic types are foreign to the Holmul region. All ceramics are common type: varieties within established K'ak Complex groups and wares. Aspects of decorative modes and forms are distinct within some examples of pottery collected from Structure 1 deposits. The most striking example is a Lucha Incised: Variety Unspecified bucket-shaped bowl with everted rim and tripod supports (see Figure 6.18a22). The main design on the vessel exterior has been identified as the Teotihuacan inspired motif of a bleeding heart pierced by an obsidian blade. Despite the motif and slightly unique form, the paste and surface treatment of the vessel are consistent with local modes of Petén Gloss Ware pottery. The paste is medium to fine in texture and light gray in color. The primary inclusion is volcanic ash. The interior and exterior surfaces are covered in a highly polished, yet slightly mottled black slip. Taken together, modal data indicate the vessel was produced regionally, but inspired by interregional style. The same can be said for other ceramics found in deposits within the Structure 1 compound at La Sufricaya. Other examples include ceramics within the Aguila and Balanza Groups that exhibit short cylinder vase forms, sometimes with accompanying slab tripod supports. Like the Lucha Incised vessel, all pastes and surface decorative techniques on these sherds are local variations.

In an important publication discussing ceramic interaction between Teotihuacan and lowland Maya sites, Ball (1983) made the distinction between what he called "identities" or direct imports from Teotihuacan and "homologies" or local imitations of Teotihuacan pottery. At La Sufricaya, it is difficult to say that either of these kinds of ceramics is present. There are currently no examples of imports (identities) in the collection. On the other hand, the Teotihuacan-inspired pottery does not seem to be replicating any one type, or combination of modes, of actual Teotihuacan pottery (c.f. Rattray 2001). Instead, local Holmul region potters apparently borrowed certain form and decorative modes from Teotihuacan pottery (i.e., cylinder vases, everted rim bowls, solid tripod supports, stylistic motifs) and recombined them in their own way. In this way, the K'ak 3 facet ceramics associated with Teotihuacan-related murals in Structure 1 at La Sufricaya offer yet another important and unknown perspective on interregional interaction during the close of the Early Classic period. This perspective comes from local elites who may not have been in contact with people from Teotihuacan directly, but may have been in contact with elites from Tikal who experienced more direct influence from Teotihuacan (although this is currently being debated). Regardless, this interaction was short-lived and the seat of political power soon returned to Holmul in the beginning of the Late Classic period. I discuss these culture-historical processes in relation to typological and modal data from the Chak Late Classic complex next.

THE CHAK COMPLEX

Chak is the Late Classic period ceramic complex in the Holmul region. Based on epigraphic data and typological comparison, the complex dates between AD 550 and 950 (see Chapter 7). Descriptions of Chak material included in this study come from 954 rim sherds, 2,981 diagnostic body sherds, and 44 whole vessels for a total of 3,979 pieces. Three definable wares, 9 groups, and 24 type: varieties define the Chak Complex. Chak material is found at Holmul, La Sufricaya, K'o, and Hamontun. Chak ceramics share 76 percent of type: varieties with the Tepeu 1–3 Spheres. Typologically and modally, Chak ceramics are contemporaneous with Tepeu 1–3 material at Uaxactun (Smith 1955); Ik, Ixim, and Eznab at Tikal (Culbert 1993, 2003, 2006); Lac Na at El Mirador (Forsyth 1989); Yaxkin and Yaxmuc at Yaxchilan (Lopez Varela 1989); Late Classic I-III at La Milpa (Sagebiel 2005); Balche, Yaxche, and Chalcalhaaz at Piedras Negras (Muñoz 2004); Ku and Halibe at Calakmul (Dominguez-Carrasco 1994); Nacimiento Tepeu and Sepens Boca in the Petexbatun region (Foias and Bishop 2013); Chixoy, Pasión, and Boca at Altar de Sacrificios (Adams 1971); and Tepejilote and Bayal at Seibal (Sabloff 1975).

The Chak Complex is separated into three facets: Chak 1 (early), Chak 2 (middle), and Chak 3 (late). It is important to note that these facets do not represent distinct and separate ceramic complexes. As I explained in Chapter 7, these facets are distinguished from one another based on the appearance and disappearance of diagnostic types, as well as changes in modes of established Late Classic type: varieties.

Chak 1 ceramics belong to the larger Tepeu 1 Sphere, first defined by Smith (1955:40; see also Willey et al. 1967:299–301) for Uaxacatun and date between AD 550 and 693. During Chak 1 the ceramics from the Cambio, Tinaja, and Saxche Groups appear. Saxche Orange Polychrome is a Chak 1 diagnostic type.

Chak 2 facet ceramics are contemporaneous with Tepeu 2 Sphere material as defined by Smith (1955:40; see also Willey et al. 1967:299–301) for Uaxactun and date between AD 693 and 800.During the Chak 2 facet Saxche Orange Polychrome disappears. Palmar Orange Polychrome, Zacatel Cream Polychrome, Cabrito Cream Polychrome, and Chinja Impressed: Floresas Variety appear at this time.

Chak 3 facet material is part of the Tepeu 3 Sphere as defined by Smith (1955:40; see also Willey et al. 1967:301–303) at Uaxactun and dates between AD 800 and 950. The Chak 3 facet is characterized by the disappearance of Zacatel Group polychromes. New type: varieties include Miseria Appliquéd within the Cambio Group. Type: varieties also diversify in the Tinaja Group including the addition of Chinja Impressed: Tuspán Variety (in accordance with the disappearance of Chinja Impressed: Floresas Variety), Cameron Incised, and Chaquiste Impressed. Strong Terminal Classic period diagnostics like Asote Orange, Maquina Brown, and Achote Black all appear (although in small frequencies). Also present are small frequencies of Altar Group ceramics and potential local type: varieties of molded-carved and modeled-carved ceramics in the tradition of Pabellon Modeled-carved. New polychrome type: varieties appear, but samples are so eroded they remain Unnamed at this time.

Slipped Ceramics

The majority of type: varieties within the current sample are slipped (69%). Table 8.6 illustrates type: varieties as a percentage of rims and whole vessels within slipped and unslipped type: varieties of the Chak Complex. These numbers indicate an increase in the number of unslipped type: varieties and decrease in frequency of slipped type: varieties from K'ak Complex times. There is also an increase in wares, groups, types, and varieties compared to the K'ak Complex. Within slipped ceramics Tinaja Red: Tinaja Variety comprises the majority (34.7% of slipped ceramics) followed by Unnamed Polychromes of Chak 2-3 (17.7%), Chinja Impressed: Floresas Variety (10.3%), Chinja impressed: Tuspán Variety (7.4%), and Cameron Incised: Cameron Variety (6.5%) rounding out the top five type: varieties.

Surface-finishing techniques of slipped ceramics are similar to the preceding K'ak Complex. Monochrome slips are thin and glossy. Surface decoration within slipped ceramics of Petén Gloss Ware changed during Chak, however, and emphasized red over orange slips. Red remains the preferred slip color of monochrome vessels throughout all facets of the Chak Complex, but other modes of surface decoration are somewhat temporally

Table 8.6. Percentages of Chak Complex Slipped and Unslipped Type: Varieties

Ware	Group	Type: Variety	% Unslipped
Uaxactun Unslipped	Cambio	Cambio Unslipped: Cambio Variety	96.8
		Encanto Striated: Encanto Variety	1.9
		Miseria Appliquéd: Miseria Variety	1.3

			% Slipped
Petén Gloss	Tinaja	Tinaja Red: Tinaja Variety	34.7
		Chinja Impressed: Floresas Variety	10.3
		Chinja Impressed: Tuspán Variety	7.4
		Chaquiste Impressed: Chaquiste Variety	1.5
		Cameron Incised: Cameron Variety	6.5
		Cameron Incised: Variety Unspecified	0.9
	Saxche	Saxche Orange Polychrome: Saxche Variety	6.1
	Palmar	Palmar Orange Polychrome: Palmar Variety	2.9
	Zacatel	Zacatel Cream Polychrome: Zacatel Variety	3.2
		Cabrito Cream Polychrome: Cabrito Variety	1.3
	Achote	Achote Black: Achote Variety	2.3
	Maquina	Maquina Brown: Maquina Variety	0.7
	Asote	Asote Orange: Asote Variety	1.3
Fine Orange	Altar	Trapiche Incised: Trapiche Variety	0.1
Unspecified	Unnamed	Unnamed Polychrome (Chak 1)	0.1
		Unnamed Black-on-orange (Chak 1)	0.1
		Unnamed Polychrome (Chak 2-3)	17.7
		Unnamed Black-on-orange (Chak 2-3)	1.0
		Unnamed Red-on-cream (Chak 2-3)	0.6
		Unnamed Modeled and Painted (Chak 2-3)	0.1
		Unnamed Modeled (Molded)-carved (Chak 3)	0.9

sensitive. Polychrome decoration is most frequent in the Chak 1–2 facets. Surface penetrating techniques like preslip incision and fingernail impression become more popular during Chak 2. Preslip incision is a more popular decorative mode by Chak 3. Modeled-carving and molded-carving both occur frequently in Chak 3, but are not present in the preceding Chak 1 and 2 facets. Some Early Classic K'ak Complex decorative modes disappear completely by Chak 1 times, namely, gouge-incision, painting on stucco, and resist decoration. It is important to note that although incision carries over from the K'ak Complex, Chak ceramics display more preslip than post-slip incision and designs are not nearly as complicated as K'ak Complex motifs. Preslip incision during Chak takes the form of simple single or double lines below interior or exterior rims on open forms. Polychrome design motifs and sophistication also change from the preceding K'ak Complex. Chak 1 and 2 red-and-black-orange and red-on-cream polychrome ceramics display complicated geometric, abstract, and conventionalized motifs that did not appear on K'ak Complex ceramics. Sophistication and preference for polychrome painting declines by Chak 3 times, with modeled and molded-carved types possibly replacing polychromes as the most prized ceramic valuables. Taken together, Chak decorative surface modes represent growth out of and away from K'ak Complex modes. This finding is reflected in form and paste modes.

Forms of slipped ceramics of the Chak Complex include bowls, vases, plates, and jars. Form modes are particularly sensitive to chronological change. Chak 1 forms include bowls with barrel-shaped sides, direct rims, rounded lips, and flat bases (especially within Saxche Orange Polychrome); and plates with rounded sides, direct rims, rounded lips, lateral ridges, and ring bases. Chak 2 forms include bowls with outcurving or flaring sides, direct rims, rounded lips, and flat bases sometimes with three solid nubbin supports; plates with flaring sides, direct rims, rounded lips, and flat bases with three hollow cylindrical-shaped supports; large bowls (ollas) with incurving sides, exterior bolstered rims, rounded lips, and flat bases; and cylinder vases with vertical sides, direct rim, rounded lips, and flat bases. Chak 3 forms include vases with incurving or insloping sides, direct rim, pointed or rounded lip, and annular bases; cylinder vases with vertical sides, direct rims, squared lips, and flat bases, sometimes with three hollow rounded supports; plates with composite sides, direct rims, rounded lips, and convex bases with three hollow rounded supports; plates with flaring sides, direct rims, rounded lips, lateral ridges, and flat bases with three hollow rounded supports; and large bowls (ollas) with incurving sides, incurving rims, squared lips, and flat bases. In the current sample jar forms are only present in the Tinaja Group. They are larger than slipped jars of the preceding K'ak Complex. Taken together, Chak modal data suggest a kind of conservatism in regard to form. The complicated and elaborate bowl and vase forms of the K'ak Complex gave way to simple bowl, dish, plate, and vase forms during the Chak Complex. This correlates with elaboration in surface decoration, especially polychrome painting. These data show that within Chak ceramics, decorative treatments emphasize surface attributes and not form.

Paste variants of Chak Complex slipped ceramics are not particularly chronologically sensitive. Aside from the addition of fine untempered ceramics during the Chak 3 facet, paste variants appear to correlate more with vessel size and function rather than ceramic facet. Polychrome serving vessels of the Saxche, Palmar, Zacatel, and Unspecified Groups are produced from medium to fine light-firing clays with either volcanic ash or crystalline calcite as the primary inclusions. Smaller and medium-sized Tinaja Group serving plates and bowls are made from light firing clays with volcanic ash and no visible traces of calcite. However, clays react strongly to dilute HCL indicating the presence of crushed or naturally occurring microscopic particles of calcite in the clay fabrics. Larger Tinaja Group bowls (ollas) are produced using darker-firing clays whose primary inclusion is crystalline calcite. Only in the Chak 3 facet are there fine paste serving vessels that do not appear to contain temper material. These fine paste ceramics belong to Fine Orange Paste Ware and an Unnamed Group containing local type: varieties of fine orange ceramics. Taken together, Chak paste data from slipped ceramics indicates that potters were working within established ranges of paste composition for the Holmul region. While fine paste ceramics appear during the Chak 3 facet, only a very small percent (0.1%) resemble actual imported ceramics of Fine Orange Paste Ware. The local molded-carved type: variety is made from a local variant with volcanic ash inclusions.

Unslipped Ceramics

Unslipped ceramics of the Chak Complex are type: varieties within Uaxactun Unslipped Ware. Uaxactun Unslipped Ware consists of one group and three established type: varieties. Cambio Unslipped: Cambio Variety is the most common type: variety within Uaxactun Unslipped Ware (96.8%) with Encanto Striated: Encanto Variety at a far second (1.9%), and Miseria Appliquéd: Miseria Variety third (1.3%). Although Cambio and Encanto appear in all three facets, Miseria does not appear until Chak 2. They belong to the same ware category, but Uaxactun Unslipped Ware of the Chak Complex is distinguishable from Uaxactun Unslipped Ware of the K'ak Complex.

Cambio Unslipped and Encanto Striated are almost exclusively found in large jar forms. Cambio and Encanto rim forms are easily distinguished from earlier Quintal and Triunfo forms. The Late Classic types almost exclusively have outcurving rims with flat lips. By the Chak 3 facet, piecrust decoration is found on almost every Cambio Unslipped rim sherd. Cambio and Encanto never exhibit the high vertical necks with bolstered or notched lips of Quintal and Triunfo. Striations on the exterior of Encanto vessels are markedly different than striations on Triunfo vessels. Encanto Striated is characterized by light shallow striation marks beginning on the shoulder break and continuing down vertically on the vessel exterior, while Triunfo Striated exhibits deep pronounced striation beginning on the rim in horizontal directions and continuing down the vessel exterior in multiple directions. Miseria Appliquéd of the Chak 2–3 facets is also easily distinguishable from Paxbán Unslipped of the K'ak Complex. Miseria is made from the same crystalline calcite-based paste of other Cambio group ceramics (not volcanic ash as in Paxbán Unslipped). Miseria Appliquéd forms are more consistent and conservative. Miseria forms include small ladle censers composed of a cylindrical handle attached to a bowl with flaring sides, direct rims, squared lips, and flat bases that sometimes have small holes. Another popular Miseria mode is a composite form composed of two small bowls that fit base-to-base to form an hourglass shape. Each bowl has flaring sides, a direct rim, rounded lip, and spike appliques on the exterior. None of these forms existed during the K'ak Complex. It appears there may have been a gap in censerware production between K'ak 3 and Chak 2, as I have not yet identified censerware ceramics in the Chak 1 (Tepeu 1) collections. These data pertaining to unslipped ceramics corroborate changes in slipped ceramics and indicate great change in the production and use of ceramic vessels from K'ak to Chak Complex times. But what can some of these specific changes in type: varieties tell us about culture-historical processes during the Late Classic period?

Discussion

Distribution of Chak ceramics indicates that Holmul, K'o, and Hamontun experienced population growth during the Late Classic period. Archaeological data from these sites also indicates significant architectural growth during Chak Complex times (Estrada-Belli 2010; Paling et al. 2011; Tomasic 2009). Quantitatively, Chak Complex ceramics indicate an increase in the number and diversity of wares, groups, and type: varieties. Although Chak 1 and 2 diagnostic types reflect interaction and

internationalism during Tepeu 1 and 2 times, the proliferation in currently unspecified local type: varieties during Chak 3 indicate increasing regionalism in the Terminal Classic period (Tepeu 3 times)—as is common among many other lowland sites. Typological and modal data are better understood when they are integrated with information about interregional political interaction between Holmul and other sites in the lowlands during the Late Classic period. Specific types of ceramics were important indicators of interaction and were often instruments of political alliance building.

Cabrito Cream Polychromes can provide insight into sociopolitical processes during the Chak 2 facet in the Holmul region. Cabrito Cream Polychromes display a design style that Reents-Budet (1994:179–187) has classified as the "Holmul" regional style. It is defined by the application of fine-line red-and-orange designs to a cream background on wide dishes, dishes, vases, and bowls. Painted subjects often include pairings of a dancer with a dwarf. Subjects also include repeating water bird motifs. Vessels displaying the Holmul style of painting date to the Late Classic period in the Maya Lowlands and are found at sites in the northeastern Petén and western Belize. Paste chemical composition of Holmul-style vessels also indicates that they were produced from clay mined in the northeast Petén and western Belize. Some of these vessels display painted inscriptions that name the person who commissioned the piece and the contents of the vessel. These inscriptions appear on the interior or exterior rim of vessels (depending on the form). This specific type of inscription has come to be termed the primary standard sequence, or PSS. In the early 1970s, Michael Coe (1973:18) discovered and formulated the PSS. He recognized a pattern of painted hieroglyphs with a familiar syntax wrapping around the rim of many Late Classic-period vases and dishes. Later studies (Houston and Taube 1987; MacLeod and Reents-Budet 1994:109–134; Stuart 1989) revealed that this band of glyphs had regional variations but could be broken into segments related to (1) the presentation or divine creation of the vessel, (2) the inscribing of the vessel by the painter, (3) the form of the vessel, (4) the contents of the vessel, and (5) the owner–patron who commissioned the vessel. At least two whole vessels of Cabrito Cream Polychrome with PSS's have been found at the site of Holmul. Both were discovered by Merwin in Building F, Group I (Merwin and Vaillant 1932).

The PSS on Vessel 1 names the original owner of the wide dish as *B'at K'awil*, ruler of the polity of Naranjo,

Guatemala, for a short period of time around C.E. 780 to 785 (Figure 7.10b13; Tokovinine 2005:359–360). That the vessel was not found within the polity of Naranjo, but in an elite tomb at Holmul, indicates the vessel must have been gifted to the person in the tomb at some time during his or her life or even upon death. Vessel 3 also contains a PSS and painted scene in the same Holmul style. Vessel 3 is a cylinder vase with vertical sides, direct rim, rounded lip, and flat base (Figure 7.11a2). The cream-slipped exterior boasts painted red-and-orange designs. A red-and-orange band encircles the base. As on Vessel 1, the main design shows a "Holmul Dancer" theme. The rim contains a horizontal band of hieroglyphs, with one vertical column of glyphs extending down into the main design frame. In contrast to Vessel 1, Tokovinine (2005:360–361) believes the glyphs are written in an idiosyncratic style compared to earlier and contemporary cream-slipped polychromes of Holmul style. Unlike the wide bowl commissioned by a king of Naranjo and possibly made in a production unit in that area, an unknown patron at a currently unknown site commissioned Vessel 3. Tokovinine (2005:360–361) does not identify the name of the original owner but does state that the PSS mentions an unknown toponym or place-name, *yuk'ite*. He concludes that the vessel represents independent innovation or development in an artistic style of the Holmul polychrome tradition.

Cabrito Cream Polychrome vessels with PSSs were part of a tradition of elite gifting during Chak 2 times in the northeastern lowlands. The tradition was probably focused on the site of Naranjo in Guatemala. Support for this argument comes from the presence of a Naranjo vessel in Building F, Group I at Holmul as well as another vase found in the tomb of a provincial ruler at Buena Vista del Cayo, Belize. Tomb 1 at Buena Vista del Cayo contained a Cabrito Cream Polychrome cylinder vase (Ball and Taschek 1992). This cylinder displays the Homul dancer theme and a PSS naming the original owner of the vessel as a lord of Naranjo, *K'ak Tiliw Chan Chaak*, who reigned from approximately AD 693 to 728 (Houston et al. 1992). As I have argued elsewhere (Callaghan 2014), Cabrito Cream Polychromes may have functioned as inalienable possessions that were gifted by Naranjo lords to lords at provincial capitals like Holmul and Buenavista in an effort to secure political alliances. Once in the possession of these provincial lords, these pots would enhance and legitimate the authority of local leaders by way of connecting them to the powerful king of the Naranjo polity.

Cabrito Cream Polychromes with PSSs were not produced at Holmul, but excavation and modal analyses from this study reveal that Holmul region potters may have produced lesser quality examples. In 2003 and 2005, outside the epicenter of Holmul in South Group 1 and La Sufricaya, architectural fill contexts containing a large amount of Holmul-style polychrome sherds were discovered (Estrada-Belli 2003) (see Figure 7.10b1-11). Modal analyses of painting style reveal that these sherds do not display any examples of legible hieroglyphs. Also, though these sherds display red-and orange on cream fine-line painting, the quality of line and thematic content does not equal that of Vessels 1 and 3 in Building F. It is interesting to note that archaeologists also uncovered a large sherd deposit of lesser-quality Holmul-style ceramics at Buenavista del Cayo (Ball 1993; Ball and Taschek 1992; Reents-Budet et al. 2000). Similar to sherds from the South Group at Holmul, they lack the PSS on the vessel rims; however, some do display pseudoglyphs (i.e., unreadable representations of real hieroglyphics) wrapping around vessel rims. The fine-line painting on the Buenavista sherds also lacks the detail and skill of execution of the Holmul-style polychromes painted by artisans attached to royal courts. This suggests to Reents-Budet and colleagues (1994:184) that the artisans painting these ceramics did not have the ability to read or paint glyphs, or they were specifically creating these vessels for a less-discerning group of consumers. I argue that the production of these lesser quality Cabrito Cream Polychromes may have helped increase the value of inalienable Cabrito Cream Polychromes with PSSs (Callaghan 2014). Because these less well-executed copies produced in provincial sites like Holmul and Buena Vista del Cayo circulated among lesser elites, they enabled nonroyal individuals to possess something that resembled a greatly valued ceramic singularity and simultaneously added value to the original masterpieces through emulation. The presence of at least two of these finer quality Cabrito Cream Polychromes at Holmul in conjunction with locally produced Cabrito Cream Polychromes of lower quality reveals to us that while they were not the most powerful people in the northeastern lowlands, Holmul region elites played an important role in Late Classic period politics during the Chak 2 facet.

Finally, I had hoped that typological and modal data could contribute to a better understanding of the events surrounding the abandonment of sites in the Holmul region during the Terminal Classic period (AD 800–950). Unfortunately, I have much less to contribute about

Terminal Classic abandonment than originally anticipated. The majority of Chak 3 facet (Tepeu 3) material was concentrated at the site of Holmul in Group III. This group contains palace-type buildings with midden deposits in certain rooms (Mongelluzzo 2011). These middens produced a number of well-preserved whole and partial vessels of Chak 3 diagnostic types. One significant find was a partially complete vessel of Trapiche Incised: Trapiche Variety. Also found in these middens was a small sample of Pabellon Modeled (Molded)-carved ceramics and locally produced molded-carved varieties. One example of the local molded-carved variety displays a glyph signifying the local Holmul-region *Chak-Tok-Wayab* title (Figure 7.12c; Estrada-Belli et al. 2009:Figures 10 and 11). The presence of the Trapiche Incised partial vessel and the Pabellon Modeled (Molded)-carved sherds indicates relations with contemporaneous polities in the Pasión River region, like Seibal or Altar de Sacrificios, around AD 830. The *Chak-Tok-Wayab* glyph indicates elite presence of at Holmul during the Terminal Preclassic period and that Group III may have been the seat of power for Holmul region elites during the Chak 3 facet. Another significant context at the site of Holmul was a cache associated with Stela 7 in the main plaza on the west side of Ruin X. The cache contained a modeled effigy bowl in the shape of a Chak god that had remnants of red, blue, and cream paint (Figure 7.1d). The presence of the cache in front of the plain stela 7 indicates that Holmul region elites were still erecting monuments during Chak 2–3 times. Taken together, these archaeological and ceramic data indicate Holmul region elites were present during the Terminal Classic period. They also indicate that elites possessed enough power and influence to secure social valuables from foreign sites, erect monuments, and construct a palace at the site of Holmul. The middens and deposits containing ash layers within certain rooms of the palace structure in Group III at Holmul, however, indicate termination of the building sometime prior to the close of the Terminal Classic period. I currently do not know how or why these buildings were abandoned. Recently, Wahl and colleagues have discovered that the Holmul region may have experienced significantly drier conditions than normal between approximately AD 730 and 950 (Wahl et al. 2013). Their data also reveal the Holmul region was densely occupied until about AD 1050 when maize (*Zea* sp.) pollen completely disappears from the environmental record, disturbance taxa drop, and forest taxa dramatically increase. At this point, environmental, archaeological, and ceramic data do not appear to indicate drought-like conditions were the immediate cause of abandonment. Future archaeological, environmental, and ceramic research in the Holmul region will seek to address this final issue in Holmul region culture-history.

DIRECTIONS FOR FUTURE STUDY

Through type: variety-mode classification I have demonstrated how Holmul region ceramics can be used as low-level theory that create site and regional chronologies, compare Holmul ceramic datasets to other lowland Maya sites, and eventually to address particular questions of mid- and high-level theory concerning economic, social, religious, and ecological regional and interregional processes. In reference to creating temporal-spatial parameters for the region and comparing them to other lowland sites, typological and modal data were used to distinguish the presence of an Early Middle Preclassic population, and four complexes that span the Late Middle Preclassic period through the Terminal Classic period. Early Middle Preclassic ceramics share type: variety-mode affiliations with the Belize River valley Cunil Sphere and the Eb Sphere of Tikal. The late Middle Preclassic Yax Te Complex contains type: varieties common within central Petén ceramics of the Mamom Sphere, but local varieties outnumber established ones. The presence of two red-slipped traditions within the Joventud Group—one with paste and slip modes similar to earlier local pre-Mamom ceramics and the other more similar to established lowland Joventud modes—suggests that although Yax Te potters were interacting more with the central Petén and Belize, they still preferred older, regionally inspired production traditions. Late Preclassic period Itzamkanak material contains types and modes firmly within the Chicanel Sphere in all aspects of production—paste preparation, form, firing, and surface. The Terminal Preclassic Wayab Subcomplex is composed of type: varieties of serving vessels that represent a new form of political economy at the end of the Late Preclassic period and beginning of the Early Classic period. Wayab vessels exhibit modes affiliated with pottery from the same time period that have been found in ritual contexts at sites in Belize and central Petén. K'ak Complex ceramics of the Early Classic period contain type: varieties firmly within the Early Classic Tzakol Sphere in the Maya lowlands. The complex can be separated into three facets and each one of the phases contains established type: varieties of its respective Tzakol 1–3 facet equivalent. The Chak

Late Classic complex can also be separated into three facets. Each facet contains type: varieties and modes firmly established within the Tepeu 1–3 Spheres. While Chak 1–2 contain type: varieties and modes common to neighboring lowland sites and indicates continued internationalism from the K'ak Complex, the Chak 3 facet witnesses an increase in local type: varieties and suggests a pattern of regionalism before abandonment during the Terminal Classic period.

As I noted in the introduction, the current ceramic sequence for the Holmul region is the result of many scholars working over the course of a century. Although the sequence has been established, analysis of specific aspects of Holmul region ceramics will continue. Future work includes further typological study of pre-Mamom material, as well as modal studies of pastes and forms in conjunction with production studies emphasizing paste composition through petrography and INAA. I anticipate a similar approach will be taken to ceramics of the two red macrotraditions within the Yax Te Complex. Analysis of Late Preclassic material will continue, specifically within Sierra Red types, in an effort to potentially split this larger complex into smaller units of time based on form modes. Analysis of the Terminal Preclassic subcomplex will continue, but study will emphasize previously understudied Paso Caballo Waxy Ware vessels. Within K'ak Complex ceramics, utilitarian and monochrome vessels will become the focus of study in an attempt to better define these three ceramic phases based on form and paste modes. Also of interest within the Early Classic period is the study of black incised and polychrome painted serving types in order to correlate style within these types to potential production areas and possibly political relationships between sites in the Holmul region and other Early Classic Maya sites. In the Chak Complex, study will emphasize Cambio and Tinaja Group ceramics in an effort to distinguish form and paste modes that may lead to a better understanding about chronology during the larger Late Classic period. Cabrito Cream Polychromes will continue to form part of the focus of Late Classic period ceramic studies, specifically identifying modal differences in painting style and form as well as mineral and chemical composition through petrography and INAA. Finally, Terminal Classic material will be studied with an eye toward social and political relations with both foreign and local polities through the further refinement of our classifications of local polychrome types, as well as the study of authentic and local varieties of Fine Orange Paste Ware.

I would like to conclude this study with a brief discussion about the future of ceramic classification in the Maya area. I argued in the introduction that ceramic classification is one of the most important steps in discerning temporal-spatial relationships within and between sites. It is the low-level theory necessary to begin answering questions of mid- and high-level theory about ancient practices and processes. Regardless of one's preference for method (type: variety, mode, contextual), some kind of ceramic classification is standard operating procedure in any archaeological research design. Despite its importance and the frequency at which it is practiced, however, publications on ceramic classifications are surprisingly few. Publications on new sequences have become increasingly rare. There are a number of reasons behind this trend and I would like to address some of them in the hope of turning things around.

One critique of ceramic classification is articulated by Dunnell (1971:117–118) who states, "If classifications of any kind are to be devices useful in constructing explanations . . . they must be hypotheses about the ordering of data for a specific problem . . . only with specifically defined problems is it possible to evaluate the utility, parsimony, elegance, and sufficiency of a given classification." I fully agree. But since the beginning of processual archaeology in the 1960s, what Mesoamerican ceramic classification has *not* been implemented in an effort to answer a "specifically defined problem?" See Adams (1971), Ball (1977), Bryant et al. (2005), Forsyth (1983, 1989), Gifford (1976), Kosakowsky (1987), Love (2002), Rattray (2001), Sabloff (1975), and Smith (1971) for examples. Even authors of the seminal modal classifications predating processual archaeology were concerned with establishing temporal-spatial relationships within and between the sites in their regions (e.g., Kidder et al. 1946; Longyear 1952; Smith 1955) – and these are certainly significant, specifically defined problems. Dunnell's comment is certainly valid, but I am not sure it necessarily applies to ceramic classifications in Mesoamerica.

John Clark raises more immediate and relevant comments regarding the publication of ceramic classifications (in Bryant et al. 2005:654–655). Clark notes that

> any ceramic monograph that manages to get published is an improbable success; all others are predictable failures. I am familiar with many classic failures, the forever-promised NWAF monograph on Chiapa de Corzo ceramics being the most obvious one. Over the years I have easily expended 30 times more effort

on ceramics than I have on obsidian or other artifacts, but a review of my CV would indicate the reverse. Therein lies the problem. Ceramic studies demand menial labor of the lowest order, take forever to finish, don't count for much in tenure review, may lead to premature brain-death, and erode any writing skills. That they are expensive to publish, with most outlets having dried-up, is a final indignity.

Clark writes as only he can and emphasizes issues of time, money, and perceived value to the academic community. Clark also adds that the classification and publication process are usually performed by the same person or persons, making it an "all or nothing" endeavor. He critiques not only the process, but also the product of classification. He creates a list addressing the major flaws in even the most meticulously compiled and amply illustrated publications (see Clark in Bryant et al. 2005:655). In addition to the time, money, and careers needed to complete just one ceramic report, Clark notes the best ceramic reports still (1) contain only black and white drawings photos that are not the best representations of ceramic artifacts, or both; (2) illustrate types that are abstracted from their contexts; (3) contain descriptions that are not useful when looking at actual artifacts; (4) contain only a sample of illustrations of the whole collection; and (5) are, overall, poor substitutes for traveling to a collection and handling actual artifacts. Clark argues that classification and publication cannot continue in this fashion and sadly announces that his present co-authored monograph on the Upper Grijalva ceramic sequence (Bryant et al. 2005) will be the last classification that the New World Archaeological Foundation publishes. He concludes by offering a few suggestions for future analyses and publications. I agree with some of Clark's comments and address his suggestions here.

Clark's first suggestion is that the classification process be split up among multiple researchers. This helps to avoid the "all or nothing" scenario that leads to the consumption of single careers. He and his colleagues successfully implemented this group-work policy. I tried this approach in the current study and although it was helpful, I feel I could have used more researchers, at least one for each complex. Clark points out that splitting up the work inevitably leads to issues regarding intellectual property. If all ceramic data is entered into a centralized database, then who has the right to first publication of synthesized data collected by multiple authors? Some kind of agreement would have to be reached before the classification process begins to avoid publication problems in the future.

Clark offers digital publication of classifications as an alternative to traditional print publications. In the short term electronic publication offers many benefits. It is certainly less expensive to produce a digital PDF than a traditional print copy. Electronic documents allow for the inclusion of countless high quality color photos of sherds and whole vessels. Finally, if the manuscript is published online in html format, it could potentially be revised as classification continues making more of working document rather than a fixed publication. However, digital publication is not without its problems. If the document is to be stored on a server, some individual or institution must be willing to pay for that server and its maintenance in perpetuity. The publication still needs to undergo peer-review, content editing, copy-editing, and illustration formatting. These are all stages of traditional print production and they do not disappear with a transfer to digital format. Another problem with digital publications is the issue of user-access. Although digital publications are excellent when you have access to the Internet or electricity for portable devices, they are worthless in more remote areas of field research. Portable print copies are still important for these reasons. Finally, digital publications do not address Clark's final critique of ceramic classifications in general—they do not make classifications any more valuable to the academic community. While ceramic classifications currently count little toward tenure-review at many universities, digital versions (especially if self-published) would count for nothing. If anything this would deter any ceramicist from ever embarking on larger classification projects in the future, much less trying to publish them. This would be an enormous setback to Mesoamerican archaeology. Now more than ever we need ceramic classifications from newly excavated areas in an effort to expand our knowledge about ancient Mesoamerican culture, practice, and process.

In closing, I think that the future of ceramic classification, and therefore publication of ceramic classifications, lay in this final concern of Clark's. If classifications are to survive, we must show how they are valuable and relevant to archaeological and anthropological endeavor. That is, we must show how classification can be used to address important questions of practice and process in the past (sensu Dunnell 1971). I have tried to accomplish this in the current study by showing how type: variety-mode data can address specific questions of culture process particular to each ceramic complex—how classification represents low-level theory necessary for later mid- and high-level theoretical endeavors.

We must continue to impart how important basic artifact description and illustration are to archaeological studies. Although it is true that the illustrations in the current study are divorced from their contexts and represent only a small sample of each type: variety, they are also the only examples of ceramic material from the Holmul region that many archaeologists will ever see or have access to. The drawings and descriptions contained in this study are invaluable as they are the only ones of their kind.

Finally, despite rising publication costs and the lack of interest to many publishers, I believe that print publication by academic presses is still the best manner of publishing classifications. Cost-sharing between projects and publishing houses, as well as building publishing costs into research grants may help lessen the cost to any one party. Softcover print formats published by academic presses as part of a series, or as stand-alone manuscripts, make classifications affordable and accessible. Most importantly, they confer much needed (and deserved) value upon classifications that many digital publications have yet to achieve. To conclude, although I am fully aware of the shortcomings in the current study, I hope this contribution helps others to better understand specific issues of lowland Maya cultural practice and process in the past, and reinvigorates the study of Maya ceramic material culture in the future. I look forward with cautious optimism to reading forthcoming classifications from analysts working in new and understudied regions of the ancient Maya world.

List of Whole Vessels from Holmul, Excavated by Merwin

Building B, Group II: Rooms 1 and 2, Skeleton 1

Pot	Description	C #	Type: Variety	Figure
1	Orange polychrome, basal flange, panel designs	5665	Caldero Buff Polychrome: Caldero Variety	6.14a9
2	Orange and cream, polished, basal flange	5426	Bocul Orange-on-cream: Bocul Variety	6.8a10
3	Orange, round bowl, ring base	5427	Aguila Orange: Aguila Variety	6.4a8
4	Black, round bowl	5428	Balanza Black: Balanza Variety	6.16a7
5	Orange and buff, unpolished, round bowl, ring base	5429	Nitan Composite: Nitan Variety	6.6b2
6	Black, incised, pot-stand	5430	Lucha Incised: Lucha Variety	6.18a20
7	Orange and buff, unpolished, round bowl, ring base	5431	Nitan Composite: Nitan Variety	6.6b1
8	Orange, incised, round bowl, annular base	5432	Pita Incised: Pita Variety	6.5e6
9	Red, cylinder, four short hollow cylinder supports	5533	Unnamed Red Slipped (K'ak 2-3)	6.15c1
10	Orange, basal flange, fire clouded	5434	Aguila Orange: Aguila Variety	6.4a40
11	White bowl on orange pot-stand	5435	Unnamed Polychrome (K'ak 2-3)	6.15b1
12	Black animal effigy and bowl, goes with Pot 19	5436-5439	Balanza Black: Balanza Variety	6.16a8
13	Black animal effigy, goes with Pot 14	5436-5439	Balanza Black: Balanza Variety	—
14	Black animal and bowl, goes with Pot 13	5436-5439	Balanza Black: Balanza Variety	6.16a10
15	Olla with spout, black slip, and applique decoration	5440	Quintal Unslipped: Variety Unspecified	6.1c
16	Black, incised, basal flange	5441	Lucha Incised: Lucha Variety	6.18a11
17	Red, basal flange	5442	Dos Hermanos Red: Dos Hermanos Variety	6.8c1
18	Black, round bowl, pinched sides, applique button	5443	Balanza Black: Balanza Variety	6.16a13
19	Black animal effigy and bowl, goes with Pot 12	5436-5439	Balanza Black: Balanza Variety	—

Building B, Group II: Rooms 1 and 2, Skeleton 5/12

Pot	Description	C #	Type: Variety	Figure
1	Black, basal flange	5476	Balanza Black: Balanza Variety	6.16a22
2	No record	—	—	—
3	Orange polychrome, cover for Pot 4, bird head handle	5477	Dos Arroyos Orange Polychrome: Dos Arroyos Variety	6.13a1
4	Orange polychrome, basal flange, goes with Pot 3	5478	Dos Arroyos Orange Polychrome: Dos Arroyos Variety	6.13a1
5	Black, round bowl, pinched sides	5479	Balanza Black: Balanza Variety	6.16a12

Building B, Group II: Room 2 West, Skeleton 5/12

Pot	Description	C #	Type: Variety	Figure
A	Orange polychrome, basal flange, flying man	5591	Dos Arroyos Orange Polychrome: Dos Arroyos Variety	6.13a3
A (lid)	Orange polychrome, Lid for Pot A, parrot handle	5592	Dos Arroyos Orange Polychrome: Dos Arroyos Variety	6.13a3
B	Orange, z-angle, four large hollow supports	5593	Aguila Orange: Aguila Variety	6.5b1
C	Black lacquer bowl, composite silhouette with bevel, incised on lip and bevel.	AMNH 30.0-6527	Lucha Incised: Lucha Variety	6.18a13

Building B, Group II: Rooms 1 and 2, Skeleton 6

Pot	Description	C #	Type: Variety	Figure
1	Orange and buff, unpolished, flaring bowl	5520	Nitan Composite: Nitan Variety	6.6b5
2	Orange and buff, unpolished, flaring bowl	5521	Nitan Composite: Nitan Variety	6.6b4
3	Red cylinder, three short slab feet	5522	Unnamed Red Slipped (K'ak 2-3)	6.15c2
4	No record	—	—	—
5	Red/orange, miniature gadrooned jar	5523	Unnamed Red Slipped (K'ak 2-3)	6.15c3
6	Black, round bowl, spout, ring base	5525	Balanza Black: Balanza Variety	6.16a9
7	Cream polychrome, basal flange, "bee man" design	5524	Caldero Buff Polychrome: Caldero Variety	6.14a10

Building B, Group II: Room 2, Skeleton 10

Pot	Description	C #	Type: Variety	Figure
1	Red and resist (smudge), cylinder with lid, monkey design in resist	5559	Japon Resist: Japon Variety	6.15a1
2	Red and resist (smudge), cylinder with lid, stylized design	5560	Japon Resist: Japon Variety	6.15a2

Building B, Group II: Room 2, Skeletons 13 and 14

Pot	Description	C #	Type: Variety	Figure
1	Black, incised, cover for Pot 2, jaguar head	5572	Lucha Incised: Lucha Variety	6.19a1
2	Black, incised, basal flange, with Pot 1	5572	Lucha Incised: Lucha Variety	6.19a1
3	Red, fire clouded, basal flange	5573	Dos Hermanos Red: Dos Hermanos Variety	6.8c2
4	Unslipped jar with spout, striated and impressed	5574	Triunfo Striated: Variety Unspecified	6.2a8
5	Unslipped jar with spout in shape of peccary	5575	Quintal Unslipped: Variety Unspecified	6.1b
6	Orange polychrome with stucco, cover for Pot 7	5576.1	Dos Arroyos Orange Polychrome: Dos Arroyos Variety	6.13a2
7	Orange polychrome with stucco, basal flange	5576	Dos Arroyos Orange Polychrome: Dos Arroyos Variety	6.13a2
8	Black, incised, cover for Pot 9, jaguar head	5577	Lucha Incised: Lucha Variety	6.19a2
9	Black, incised, basal flange, with Pot 8	5577	Lucha Incised: Lucha Variety	6.19a2
10	Black, incised, cover for Pot 11, monkeyhead handle	5578	Lucha Incised: Lucha Variety	6.19a3
11	Black, incised, basal flange, with Pot 10	5578	Lucha Incised: Lucha Variety	6.19 a3
12	Black, gauge-incised, lid, possible cover for Pot 16, Skeleton 1, Room 1	5579	Urita Gouged-incised: Urita Variety	6.20a8

Building B, Group II: Room 3

Pot	Description	C #	Type: Variety	Figure
1	Orange, flaring bowl	5622	Aguila Orange: Aguila Variety	6.4a26
2	Orange, flaring bowl	5623	Aguila Orange: Aguila Variety	6.4a27

Building B, Group II Room 7, Skeleton 16

Pot	Description	C #	Type: Variety	Figure
1	Polished black olla	5629	Not found	—
2	No record	—	—	—
3	Orange, rounded-z, bowl	5683	Aguila Orange: Aguila Variety	6.5a6
4	Black, incised, pot-stand with four solid supports	5630	Lucha Incised: Variety Unspecified	6.18a21
5	Black, incised, cover for Pot 6, animal head handle	5631	Lucha Incised: Lucha Variety	6.20a7
6	Black, incised, bowl with four supports, with Pot 5	5631	Lucha Incised: Lucha Variety	6.20a7

Building B, Group II: Room 8 Skeletons 17, 18, and 19

Pot	Description	C #	Type: Variety	Figure
1	Red flaring bowl	5641	Sierra Red: Sierra Variety	4.1a42
2	Red, cylinder with four supports	AMNH 30.0-6525	Sierra Red: Variety Unspecified	5.1a1
3	Red, rounded bowl	5643	Sierra Red: Sierra Variety	4.2a1
4	Orange Polychrome, basal flange bowl	5644	Actuncan Orange Polychrome: Variety Unspecified	5.2d
5	Red, fire clouded, pot-stand	5645	Sierra Red: Variety Unspecified	5.1a2
6	Red, flaring bowl	5651	Sierra Red: Sierra Variety	4.1a43
7	Red, flaring bowl	5651	Sierra Red: Sierra Variety	4.1a44

Building B, Group II: Room 8 Vault

Pot	Description	C #	Type: Variety	Figure
8	Orange, round bowl with annular base	5648	Aguila Orange: Aguila Variety	6.4a9
9	Cream, pitcher, stucco covered	5649	Flor Cream: Variety Unspecified	5.1b
10	Orange polychrome, tetrapod bowl, macaw design	5650	Ixcanrio Orange Polychrome: Variety Unspecified	5.2c1

Building B, Group II: Room 9, Skeleton 21

Pot	Description	C #	Type: Variety	Figure
1	Orange bowl, black wavy lines, annular base	5656	Ixcanrio Orange Polychrome: Turnbull Variety	5.2b1
2	Orange polychrome, tetrapod mammiform	5657	Ixcanrio Orange Polychrome: Variety Unspecified	5.2c2
3	Orange, tetrapod	5658	Aguila Orange: Variety Unspecified	5.1d1
4	Orange polychrome, tetrapod mammiform, triangles, bowl	5659	Ixcanrio Orange Polychrome: Ixcanrio Variety	5.2a2
5	Cream, incised, pitcher	5660	Accordian Incised: Variety Unspecified	5.1c
6	Orange polychrome, tetrapod, vase	5646	Ixcanrio Orange Polychrome: Ixcanrio Variety	5.2a1
7	Orange, plate with tetrapod cylinder supports	5647	Aguila Orange: Variety Unspecified	5.1d2

Building B, Group II: Room 10, Skeleton 22

Pot	Description	C #	Type: Variety	Figure
1	Orange polychrome, basal flange	5661	Dos Arroyos Orange Polychrome: Dos Arroyos Variety	6.12b13
2	Polychrome	AMNH 30.0-6528	Unnamed Polychrome (K'ak)	6.15b2
3	Black on orange, basal flange	5663	Boleto Black-on-orange: Boleto Variety	6.12a3
4	Black on Orange, z-angle	5664	Boleto Black-on-orange: Boleto Variety	6.12a4

Building F, Group I: Room 1, Skeleton 1

Pot	Description	C #	Type: Variety	Figure
1	Cream polychrome, plate with three supports, real glyphs	5666	Cabrito Cream Polychrome: Cabrito Variety	7.10b13
2	Tall cylinder, possible cream polychrome, extremely eroded		Indeterminate	—
3	Cream polychrome, cylinder vase, real glyphs (dancer)	5668	Cabrito Cream Polychrome: Cabrito Variety	7.11a2
4	Cream polychrome, bowl flaring sides	5669	Zacatel Cream Polychrome: Zacatel Variety	7.9a2
5	Cream polychrome, plate with three supports	5670	Zacatel Cream Polychrome: Zacatel Variety	7.10b12

Building F, Group I: Room 1, SW Wall Fill

Pot	Description	C #	Type: Variety	Figure
A	Red and buff, round bowl/barrel	5671	Unnamed Polychrome (Chak 1)	7.15c
B	Red/Orange and unpolished (ext.), polished (int.)	5673	Nitan Composite: Nitan Variety	6.6b3
C	Bowl with flat bottom, three support scars, cream polychrome,	5672	Indeterminate	—

Ruin X: Room 1, Skeleton 1

Pot	Description	C #	Type: Variety	Figure
1	Orange polychrome plate, three supports (scars), fish design	5709	Unnamed Polychrome (Chak 1)	7.15a
2	Large plain bowl	5711	Not found	—
3	Cream polychrome, cylinder vase, pelicans and fish	5710	Cabrito Cream Polychrome: Cabrito Variety	7.11a1

Ruin X: Room 2, Floor

Pot	Description	C #	Type: Variety	Figure
1	Incensario	5690	Not found	—

List of Contexts from Sites in the Holmul Region

Operation	Context
CIVAL	
CIV.STELA 1	Stela 1, Cival
CIV.L.05	Structure 7
CIV.L.06	Group 1 Platform
CIV.T.01	Structure 1
CIV.T.08	Structure 7
CIV.T.08	Structure 7
CIV.T.10	South defensive wall
CIV.T.11	Structure 7
CIV.T.12	Structure 9
CIV.T.13	Structure 7
CIV.T.14	Structure 7
CIV.T.15	Structure 9
CIV.T.16	Structure 1
CIV.T.17	E Group Plaza
CIV.T.18	Plaza between Structure 7 and Group 1
CIV.T.20	Structure 9
CIV.T.21	Structure 6 and 7
CIV.T.22	Midden, north sector
CIV.T.23	Potential center Structure of Triadic
CIV.T.24	Plaza west of Structure 7 (E-Group)
CIV.T.25	Plaza west of Structure 7 (E-Group)
CIV.T.26	Plaza west of Structure 7 (E-Group)
CIV.T.27	Plaza west of Structure 7 (E-Group)
CIV.T.28	Plaza in front of N. Pyramid
CIV.T.29	Structure 20
CIV.T.30	Defensive wall

Operation	Context
CIV.T.31	Structure 1 (Center), Triadic
CIV.T.32	Structure17, Group 7
CIV.T.33	Structure 1 (Center), Triadic
CIV.T.34	Defensive wall
CIV.T.64	Hill Group 1
CL.02	Structure 7
CL.04	Structure 31
CT.01	Structure 1
CT.02	Structure 7
CT.03	Beneath Stela 6
CT.05	Plaza west of Structure 7
CT.06	Structure 31
CT.07	Structure 7
CT.08	Beneath Stela 2, west of Structure 7
DOS AGUADAS	
DAG.L.07	Structure 15
HAMONTUN	
HM.LT.01.00	East Pyramid, Plaza 3
HM.LT.61	N/A
HOLMUL	
HOL.STR.44	Structure 44, Court A, Group III
HOL.STR.2	Structure 2, Court A, Group III
HOL.STR.2A	Plaza of Structure 2, Court A, Group III
HOL.L.14	Structure 7
HOL.L.20	Building A, Group II

Operation	Context
HOL.L.21	Building A, Group II
HOL.L.63	Building B, Group II
HOL.LT.11	Structure 2, Court A, Group III
HOL.LT.13	Structure 53, Court A, Group III
HOL.LT.17	Structure 65, Court B, Group III
HOL.T.08	Structure 43, Court B, Group III
HOL.T.15	Structure 43, Court B, Group III
HOL.T.21	Structure 43, Court B, Group III
HOL.T.22	Structure 43, Court B, Group III
HOL.T.23	Building B, Group II
HOL.T.23	Structure 60, Court B, Group III
HOL.T.24	Group 13
HOL.T.25	Group 13
HOL.T.28	Structure 1, South Group
HOL.T.29	Structure 1, South Group
HOL.T.30	Structures 1 and 6, South Group
HOL.T.31	Mound in Plaza, South Group
HOL.T.32	Plaza, Court A, Group III
HOL.T.32A	Plaza, Court A, Group III
HOL.T.33	South Group
HOL.T.34	South Group
HOL.T.35	Structure 43, Court B, Group III
HOL.T.36	Structure 63, Court B, Group III
HOL.T.37	Structure 63, Court B, Group III
HOL.T.38	Structure 43, Court B, Group III
HOL.T.39	Structure 43, Court B, Group III
HOL.T.40	Structure 60, Court B, Group III
HOL.T.40A	Structure 60, Court B, Group III
HOL.T.40B	Structure 60, Court B, Group III
HOL.T.40C	Structure 71, Court B, Group III
HOL.T.41	Building B, Group II (B. 10)
HOL.T.42	Structure's 57 and 58, Court B, Group III
HOL.T.43	Structure 43, Court B, Group III
HOL.T.44	Structure 2, Court A, Group III
HOL.T.46	Stela 1, South Group
HOL.T.47	Structure 103, South Group
HOL.T.48	Structure's 102 &103, South Group
HOL.T.49	Building B, Group II
HOL.T.50	Structure 59, Court B, Group III
HOL.T.51	South Group
HOL.T.52	South Group

Operation	Context
HOL.T.53	Structure 64, Court B, Group III
HOL.T.54	Structure 60, Court B, Group III
HOL.T.54A	Structure 60, Court B, Group III
HOL.T.54B	Structure 60, Court B, Group III
HOL.T.54C	Structure 60, Court B, Group III
HOL.T.54D	Structure 60, Court B, Group III
HOL.T.54E	Structure 60, Court B, Group III
HOL.T.55	Structure 64, Court B, Group III
HOL.T.56	Building B, Group II
HOL.T.57	Structure 64, Court B, Group III
HOL.T.58	Structure 64, Court B, Group III
HOL.T.59	Structure 61, Court B, Group III
HOL.T.60	Court's A and B, Group III
HOL.T.61	Structure 62, Court B, Group III
HOL.T.62	Structure 7
HOL.T.64	Defensive wall
HOL.T.65	Structure 43, Court B, Group III
HOL.T.66	Structure 43, Court B, Group III
HOL.T.67	Structure 43, Court B, Group III
HOL.T.68	Structure 43, Court B, Group III
HOL.T.69	Structure 43, Court B, Group III
HOL.T.71	Building B, Group II
HOL.T.74	Building B, Group II
HOL.T.75	Building B, Group II
HOL.T.76	Building B, Group II
HOL.T.77	Building B, Group II
HOL.TP.1.L7	Stela 7, Ruin X
K'O	
KLT.01	Structure 1
KOL.LT.01	Structure 1
KOL.L.2	Structure 3
KOL.L.3	Structure 94
KOL.T.01	Plaza west of Structure 20
KOL.T.02	Structure 67, 68 (ballcourt)
KOL.T.03	Structure 94
KOL.T.04	Defensive wall
KOL.T.05	Defensive wall
KOL.T.06	Structure 56
KOL.T.07	Structure 8
KOL.T.08	Plaza S. of Structure 8

Operation	Context
KOL.T.09	Plaza N of Structure 8
KOL.T.10	Plaza west of Structure 1
KOL.T.11	Defensive wall
KOL.T.12	Plaza E. of Structure 1
KOL.T.13	Structure 73
KOL.T.14	Structure 73
KOL.T.34	Chultun 19

LA SUFRICAYA

SL.07	Structure 146
SLT.05	Structure 1
SLT.06	Structure 1
ST.07	Structure 1
ST.08	Structure 1
ST.08E	Structure 1
ST.09	Structure 1
ST.11	Structure 110
ST.16	Structure 1
ST.17	Structure1
ST.18	Structure 146
ST.19	Platform 1, Group 1
ST.20	Structure1
ST.21	Structure 147
SUF.STELA 4	Beneath Stela 4, Sufricaya
SUF.STELA 8	Beneath Stela 8, Sufricaya
SUF.STELA 9	Beneath Stela 9, Sufricaya
SUF.STELA 6	Beneath Stela 6, Sufricaya

Operation	Context
SUF.L.08	Structure 3 (Pyramid)
SUF.L.13	Structure 44, Group 16
SUF.L.14	Structure 43, Group 16
SUF.L.15	Structure 43, Group 16
SUF.L.17	Structure 48 or 49
SUF.T.11	Structure 1
SUF.T.22	Structure 1, sub 3
SUF.T.23	Structure 146
SUF.T.24	Structure's 148, 149
SUF.T.25	Structure's 148, 149
SUF.T.26	Structure 48 (ballcourt)
SUF.T.27	Structure 3 (Pyramid)
SUF.T.28	Plaza, Group 16
SUF.T.29	Plaza, Group 16
SUF.T.30	Structure 49 (ballcourt)
SUF.T.31	Structure 48 or 49
SUF.T.32	Structure 48 or 49
SUF.T.35	Structure 54 south of ballcourt
SUF.T.37	Structure 1
SUF.T.38	Structure 54. south of ballcourt
SUF.T.41	Structure 48 or 49
SUF.T.42	Structure 54 south of ballcourt
SUT.05	Structure 1

T'OT

CAR.STR.3	Structure 1

References Cited

Adams, Richard E.
1971   The Ceramics of Altar de Sacrificios. *Papers of the Peabody Museum of Archaeology and Ethnology* 63:1. Harvard University, Cambridge.

Aimers, James John
2013   Problems and Prospects in Maya Ceramic Classification, Analysis, and Interpretation. In *Ancient Maya Pottery: Classification, Analysis, and Interpretation*, edited by James John Aimers, pp. 229–238. University Press of Florida, Gainesville.

Anderson, A. Hamilton, and Herbert J. Cook
1944   *Archaeological Finds near Douglas, British Honduras.* Notes on Middle American Archaeology and Ethnology No. 40. Carnegie Institution, Washington, D.C.

Andrews, Wyllys E. and George Bey III
2011   Early Ceramics in the Northern Maya Lowlands: New Interpretations from Komchen and Kiuic, Yucatan. Paper presented at the 8th Tulane Maya Symposium, New Orleans.

Andrews V., E. Wyllys, and Norman Hammond
1990   Redefinition of the Swasey Phase at Cuello, Belize. *American Antiquity* 55(3):570–584.

Arnold, Dean E.
1985   *Ceramic Theory and Cultural Process.* Cambridge University Press, New York.
2008   *Social Change and the Evolution of Ceramic Production and Distribution in a Maya Community.* University Press of Colorado, Boulder.

Arnold, Phillip
1991   *Domestic Ceramic Production and Spatial Organization: A Mexican Case Study in Ethnoarchaeology.* Cambridge University Press, New York.

Awe, Jaime
1992   *Dawn in the Land between the Rivers: Formative Occupation at Cahal Pech, Belize and Its Implications for Preclassic Development in the Maya Lowlands.* Ph.D. dissertation, University of London, London. University Microfilms, Ann Arbor.

Ball, Joseph
1976   Ceramic Sphere Affiliations of the Barton Ramie Ceramic Complexes. In *Prehistoric Pottery Analysis and the Ceramics of Barton Ramie, in the Belize Valley*, edited by James C. Gifford, compiled by Carol A. Gifford, pp. 323–330. Memoirs of the Peabody Museum of Archaeology and Ethnology Harvard University Vol. 18. Harvard, Cambridge.
1977   *The Archaeological Ceramics of Becan, Campeche, Mexico.* Middle American Research Institute Publication Vol. 43. Tulane University, New Orleans.
1983   Teotihuacan, the Maya, and Ceramic Interchange: A Contextual Perspective. In *Highland-Lowland Interaction in Mesoamerica: Interdisciplinary Approaches*, edited by Arthur G. Miller, pp. 125–145. Dumbarton Oaks, Washington DC.
1993   Pottery, Potters, Palaces, and Polities: Some Socioeconomic and Political Implications of Late Classic Maya Ceramic Industries. In *Lowland Maya Civilization in the eighth century AD: A Symposium at Dumbarton Oaks, 7th and 8th October 1989*, edited by Jeremy A. Sabloff and John S. Henderson, pp. 243–272. Dumbarton Oaks, Washington, D.C.

Ball, Joseph, and Jennifer Taschek
  1992   Lord Smoke Squirrel's Cacao Cup: The Archae-
         ological Context and Socio-Historical Signifi-
         cance of the Buenavista "Jauncy Vase." In *The
         Maya Vase Book*, Vol. 3, edited by Justin Kerr,
         pp. 490–497. Kerr and Associates,
         New York.
  2003   Reconsidering the Belize Valley Preclassic: A
         Case for Multiethnic Interactions in the Devel-
         opment of a Regional Culture Tradition. *Ancient
         Mesoamerica* 14(2):179–217.
Beaudry, Marilyn
  1984   Ceramic Production and Distribution in the
         Southeast Maya Periphery: Late Classic Painted
         Serving Vessels. *BAR International Series* 203.
         British Archaeological Reports, Oxford.
Berry, Kimberly A., Sandra L. Lopez Varela,
Mary Lee Bartlett, Tamarra Martz, and
Patricia A. McAnany
  2004   Pottery Vessels of K'axob. In *K'axob: Ritual,
         Work, and Family in an Ancient Maya Village*,
         edited by Patricia A. McAnany, pp. 193–262.
         Monumenta Archaeological 22. Cotsen Institute
         of Archaeology Press, Los Angeles.
Bill, Cassandra
  2013   Types and Traditions, Spheres and Systems: A
         Consideration of Analytic Constructs and Con-
         cepts in the Classification and Interpretation of
         Maya Ceramics. In *Ancient Maya Pottery: Clas-
         sification, Analysis, and Interpretation*, edited by
         James John Aimers, pp. 29–45. University Press
         of Florida, Gainesville.
Bourdieu, Pierre
  1984   *Distinction: A Social Critique of the Judgment of
         Taste*. Harvard University Press, Cambridge.
Brady, James
  1989   *An Investigation of Maya Ritual Cave Use
         with Special Reference to Naj Tunich, Petén,
         Guatemala*. Ph.D. dissertation. Department
         of Anthropology, University of California Los
         Angeles, Los Angeles. University Microfilms,
         Ann Arbor.
  1992   Function and Meaning of Lowland Maya Shoe-
         Pots. *Cerámica de cultura Maya* 16:1–9. Temple
         University, Philadelphia.
Brady, James, Joseph Ball, Ronald Bishop, Duncan Pring,
Norman Hammond, and Rupert Housley
  1998   The Lowland Maya Protoclassic: A Reconsid-
         eration of its Nature and Significance. *Ancient
         Mesoamerica* 9:17–38.

Braswell, Geoffrey (editor)
  2004   *The Maya and Teotihuacan: Reinterpreting
         Early Classic Interaction*. University of Texas
         Press, Austin.
Bryant, Douglas Donne, John E. Clark, and
David Cheetham
  2005   *Ceramic Sequence of the Upper Grijalva Region,
         Chiapas, Mexico*. Paper No. 67. New World
         Archaeological Foundation, Brigham Young
         University, Provo.
Callaghan, Michael G.
  2005   The Archaeological Ceramics of the Holmul
         Region, Guatemala. In *Archaeological Inves-
         tigations in the Holmul Region, Petén: Results
         of the sixth Season, 2005*, edited by Francisco
         Estrada-Belli, pp. 200–303. Vanderbilt Uni-
         versity, Nashville.
  2008   *Technologies of Power: Ritual Economy and
         Ceramic Production in the Terminal Preclassic
         Period Holmul Region, Guatemala*. Ph.D. disser-
         tation, Department of Anthropology, Vanderbilt
         University, Nashville.
  2013   Politics through Pottery: A View of the
         Preclassic-Classic Period Transition from Build-
         ing B, Group II, Holmul, Guatemala. *Ancient
         Mesoamerica* 24(2):307–341.
  2014   Maya Polychrome Vessels as Inalienable Posses-
         sions. In *The Inalienable in the Archaeology of
         Mesoamerica*, edited by Brigitte Kovacevich and
         Michael G. Callaghan, pp. 112–127. Archaeolog-
         ical Publications of the American Anthropologi-
         cal Association 23(1). Arlington, Virginia.
  2017   Ceramic Social Valuables of the Preclassic Maya
         Lowlands. In *Making Value, Making Meaning:
         Techné in the Pre-Columbian World*, edited by
         Cathy L. Costin, pp. 281-318. Dumbarton Oaks,
         Washington, D.C. In press.
Callaghan, Michael G., Francisco Estrada-Belli, and
Nina Neivens de Estrada
  2013   Technological Style and Terminal Preclassic
         Orange Ceramics in the Holmul Region, Gua-
         temala. In *Ancient Maya Pottery: Classification,
         Analysis, and Interpretation*, edited by James
         John Aimers, pp. 121–141. University Press of
         Florida, Gainesville.
Case, Robert P.
  1982   *Type: Variety Analysis and the Ceramics of El
         Pozito, Belize: A Critical View*. Unpublished
         Master's Thesis, Department of Anthropology,
         San Diego State University, San Diego.

Caso, Alfonso, Ignacio Bernal, and Jorge R. Acosta.
1967 *La cerámica de Monte Albán*. Instituto Nacional de Antropología e Historia, Mexico City.

Chase, Arlen F.
1994 A Contextual Approach to the Ceramics of Caracol, Belize. In *Studies in the Archaeology of Caracol, Belize*, edited by Diane Chase and Arlen Chase, pp. 157–182. Monograph No. 7. Pre-Columbian Art Research Institute, San Francisco.

Chase, Arlen F., and Diane Z. Chase
1994 Maya Veneration of the Dead at Caracol, Belize. In *Seventh Palenque Round Table, 1989*, edited by Merle Robertson and Virginia Fields, pp. 55–62. Monograph No. 7. Pre-Columbian Art Research Institute, San Francisco.
2013 Interpreting Form and Context: Ceramic Sub-complexes at Caracol, Nohmul, and Santa Rita Corozal, Belize. In *Ancient Maya Pottery: Classification, Analysis, and Interpretation*, edited by James John Aimers, pp. 46–73. University Press of Florida, Gainesville.

Cheetham, David
1995 Excavations of Structure B-4, Cahal Pech, Belize: 1994 Operations. In *Belize Valley Preclassic Maya Project: Report on the 1994 Season*, edited by Paul Healy and Jaime Awe, pp. 18–44. Occasional Papers in Anthropology Vol. 10. Trent University, Peterborough, Ontario.
1996 Reconstruction of the Formative Period Site Core of Cahal Pech, Belize. In *Belize Valley Preclassic Maya Project: Report on the 1995 Season*, edited by Paul Healy and Jaime Awe, pp. 1–33. Occasional Papers in Anthropology Vol. 12. Trent University, Peterborough, Ontario.
2005 Cunil: A Pre-Mamom Horizon in the Southern Maya Lowlands. In *New Perspectives on Formative Mesoamerican Cultures*, edited by Terry G. Powis, pp. 27–38. BAR International Series 1377. British Archaeological Reports, Oxford.

Cheetham, David, Donald Forsyth, and John E. Clark
2003 La cerámica Pre-Mamom de la cuenca del Río Belice y del centro Petén: Las correspondencias y sus implicaciones. In *XVI simposio de investigaciones arqueologicas en Guatemala, 2002*, edited by Juan Pedro Laporte, Barbara Arroyo, Hector Escobedo, and Hector Mejia, pp. 609–628. Ministerio de Cultura y Deportes, Instituto de Antropología e Historia, Asociación Tikal, Guatemala City, Guatemala.

Clark, John E., and David Cheetham
2002 Mesoamerica's Tribal Foundations. In *The Archaeology of Tribal Societies*, edited by William A. Parkinson, pp. 278–339. International Monographs in Prehistory, Archaeological Series 15. Oxbow Books, Oxford.

Coe, Michael
1973 *The Maya Scribe and His World*. Grolier Club, New York.

Coe, William R.
1965 Tikal, Guatemala, and Emergent Maya Civilization. *Science, New Series* 147(3664):1401–1419

Coffey, Kevin T., Axel K. Schmitt, Anabel Ford, Frank J. Spera, Constance Christensen, and Jennifer Garrison
2014 Volcanic Ash Provenance from Zircon Dust with an Application to Maya Pottery. *Geology* 42(7):595–598.

Coggins, Clemency C.
1975 *Painting and Drawing Styles at Tikal: An Historical and Iconographic Reconstruction*. Harvard University Press, Cambridge.

Colton, Harold S. and Lyndon L. Hargrave
1937 *Handbook of Northern Arizona Pottery Wares*. Bulletin, No. 11. Museum of Northern Arizona, Flagstaff.

Culbert, T. Patrick
1993 *The Ceramics of Tikal: Vessels from the Burials, Caches, and Problematical Deposits*. Tikal Report No. 25A. University Museum Monograph No. 81. University of Pennsylvania, Philadelphia.
2003 The Ceramics of Tikal. In *Tikal: Dynasties, Foreigners, and Affairs of State*, edited by Jeremy Sabloff, pp. 47–82. School of American Research Press, Santa Fe.
2006 Tikal Report No. 25B. Unpublished manuscript in the possession of the author (publication pending).

Culbert, T. Patrick, and Robert Rands
2007 Multiple Classifications: An Alternative Approach to the Investigation of Maya Ceramics. *Latin American Antiquity* 18:181–190.

Demarest, Arthur A.
1986 *The Archaeology of Santa Leticia and the Rise of Maya Civilization*. MARI Publication No. 52. Tulane University, New Orleans.

Dietler, Michael
1996 Feasts and Commensal Politics in the Political Economy: Food, Power and Status in Prehistoric Europe. In *Food and the Status Quest: An Interdisciplinary Perspective*, edited by Pauline

Dietler, Michael (*continued*)
  Wiessner and Wulf Schiefenhövel, pp. 87–125. Berghahn Books, New York.
  2001 Theorizing the Feast: Rituals of Consumption, Commensal Politics, and Power in African Contexts. In *Feasts: Archaeological and Ethnographic Perspectives on Food, Politics and Power*, edited by Michael Dietler and Brian Hayden, pp. 65–114. Smithsonian Institution Press, Washington, D.C.

Dillon, Brian
  1977 *Salinas de los Nueve Cerros Guatemala*. Studies in Mesoamerican Art, Archaeology, and Ethnohistory No. 2. Ballena Press, Socorro, New Mexico.

Dominguez-Carrasco, Maria del Rosario
  1994 Tipología cerámica de Calakmul, Campeche, México. *Mexicon* 16(3):51–53.

Driver, W. David
  2008 The Construction of Intrapolity Sociopolitical Identity Through Architecture at the Ancient Maya Site of Blue Creek, Belize. Unpublished Ph.D. dissertation, Department of Anthropology, Southern Illinois University, Carbondale.

Druc, Isabelle
  2000 Ceramic Production in San Marcos, Acteopan, Puebla, Mexico. *Ancient Mesoamerica* 11: 77–89.

Dull, Robert A., John R. Southon, and Payson Sheets
  2001 Volcanism, Ecology and Culture: A Reassessment of the Volcano Ilopango Tbj Eruption in the Southern Maya Realm. *Latin American Antiquity* 12(1):25–44.

Dunnell, Robert
  1971 *Systematics in Prehistory*. Free Press, New York.

Estrada-Belli, Francisco
  2006a Las épocas tempranas en el área de Holmul, Petén. *Las investigadores de la cultura Maya* No. 14, Vol. 2, pp. 307–316. Universidad Autonoma de Campeche, Campeche.
  2006b Lightning Sky, Rain, and the Maize God: the Ideology of Preclassic Maya Rulers at Cival, Petén, Guatemala. *Ancient Mesoamerica* 17(1): 57–78.
  2010 *The First Maya Civilization: Ritual and Power before the Classic Period*. Routledge, London.

Estrada-Belli, Francisco (editor)
  2000 *Archaeological Investigations at Holmul, Guatemala: Report of the First Field Season*. Vanderbilt University, Nashville.
  2001 *Archaeological Investigations at Holmul, Guatemala: Preliminary Report of the 2001 Season*. Vanderbilt University, Nashville.
  2002 *Archaeological Investigations at Holmul, Peten Guatemala: Preliminary Results of the Third Season, 2002*. Vanderbilt University, Nashville.
  2003 *Archaeological Investigations in the Holmul Region, Peten: Results of the Fourth Season, 2003*. Vanderbilt University, Nashville.
  2004 *Investigaciones arqueologicas en la region de Holmul, Peten, Guatemala: Informe preliminar de la temporada 2004*. Vanderbilt University, Nashville.
  2005 *Investigaciones arqueologicas en la region de Holmul, Peten, Guatemala: Informe preliminar de la temporada 2005*. Vanderbilt University, Nashville.
  2007 *Investigaciones arqueologicas en la region de Holmul, Peten, Guatemala: Holmul, Cival, La Sufricaya, y K'o. Informe preliminar de la temporada 2007*. Vanderbilt University, Nashville.
  2008 *Investigaciones arqueologicas en la region de Holmul, Peten, Guatemala: Cival y K'o. Informe Preliminar de la Temporada 2008*. Boston University, Boston.
  2009 *Investigaciones arqueologicas en la region de Holmul, Peten, Guatemala: Holmul y Hamontun. Informe preliminar de la temporada 2009*. Boston University, Boston.
  2012 *Investigaciones arqueologicas en la region de Holmul, Peten: Holmul y Dos Aguadas. Informe preliminar de la temporada 2012*. Tulane University, New Orleans.
  2013 *Investigaciones arqueologicas en la region de Holmul, Peten: Holmul y Cival. Informe preliminar de la temporada 2013*. Tulane University, New Orleans.

Estrada-Belli, Francisco, and Magaly Koch
  2007 Remote Sensing and GIS Analysis of a Maya City and Its Landscape: Holmul, Guatemala. In *Remote Sensing in Archaeology*, edited by Wiseman, James R., and Farouk El-Baz, pp. 263–281. Springer, New York.

Estrada-Belli, Francisco, Nikolai Grube, Marc Wolf, Kristen Gardella, and Claudio Guerra-Librero
  2003 Preclassic Maya Monuments and Temples at Cival, Peten, Guatemala. *Antiquity* 77:296.

Estrada-Belli, Francisco, and Alexandre Tokovinine
  2016 A King's Apotheosis: Iconography, Text, and Politics, from a Classic Maya Temple at Holmul. *Latin American Antiquity* 27(2): 149–168.

Estrada-Belli, Francisco, Alexandre Tokovinine,
Jennifer M. Foley, Heather Hurst, Gene A. Ware,
David Stuart, and Nikolai Grube
    2009   A Maya Palace at Holmul, Peten Guatemala
            and the Teotihuacan "Entrada": Evidence from
            Murals 7 and 9. *Latin American Antiquity*
            20(1):228–259.
Fields, Virginia M.
    1991   The Iconographic Heritage of the Maya Jester
            God. In *Sixth Palenque Round Table* (1986),
            edited by Merle Greene Robertson and Vir-
            ginia M. Fields, pp. 167–174. University of
            Oklahoma Press, Norman.
Fields, Virginia M., and Dorie Reents-Budet
    2005   *Lords of Creation: The Origins of Sacred Maya
            Kingship*. Scala Publishers Limited, London.
Flannery, Kent V., and Joyce Marcus, with technical ceramic
analysis by William O. Payne
    1994   *Early Formative Pottery of the Valley of Oaxaca*.
            University of Michigan Museum, Ann Arbor.
Foias, Antonia E.
    1996   *Changing Ceramic Production and Exchange
            Systems and the Classic Maya Collapse in the
            Petexbatun Region*. Doctoral dissertation,
            Vanderbilt University. University Microfilm,
            Ann Arbor.
    2004   The Past and Future in Maya Ceramic Studies.
            In *Continuities and Changes in Maya Archae-
            ology: Perspectives at the Millennium*, edited by
            Charles W. Golden and Gregory Borgstede,
            pp. 143–175. Routledge, New York.
    2007   Ritual, Politics, and Pottery Economies in the
            Classic Maya Southern Lowlands. In *Mesoameri-
            can Ritual Economy: Archaeological and Ethno-
            logical Perspectives*, edited by E. Christian Wells
            and Karla Davis-Salazar, pp. 167–196. University
            Press of Colorado, Boulder.
Foias, Antonia E., and Ronald L. Bishop
    2013   *Ceramics, Production, and Exchange in the
            Petexbatun Region: The Economic Parameters of
            the Classic Maya Collapse*. Vanderbilt University
            Press, Nashville.
Ford, Anabel
    1986   *Population Growth and Social Complexity: An
            Examination of Settlement and Environment in
            the Central Maya Lowlands*. Anthropological
            Research Papers No. 35. Arizona State Univer-
            sity, Tempe.
Ford, Anabel, and Harry Glicken
    1987   The Significance of Volcanic Ash Tempering in
            the Ceramics of the Central Maya Lowlands.

            In *Maya Ceramics: Papers from the 1985 Maya
            Ceramics Conference*, edited by Prudence M.
            Rice and Robert J. Sharer, pp. 479–502. BAR
            International Series No. 345. British Archaeo-
            logical Reports, Oxford.
Ford, Anabel, and William I. Rose
    1995   Volcanic Ash in Ancient Maya Ceramics of
            the Limestone Lowlands: Implications for
            Prehistoric Volcanic Activity in the Guatemala
            Highlands. *Journal of Volcanology and Geother-
            mal Research* 66:149–162.
Forsyth, Donald W.
    1983   Investigations at Edzna, Campeche, Mexico:
            Ceramics. *Papers of the New World Archaeolog-
            ical Foundation* 46(2). Brigham Young Univer-
            sity, Provo.
    1989   The Ceramics of El Mirador, Peten, Guatemala.
            El Mirador Series, Part 4. *Papers of the New
            World Archaeological Foundation* 63. Brigham
            Young University, Provo.
    1993   The Ceramic Sequence at Nakbe, Guatemala.
            Ancient Mesoamerica 4(1):31–53.
Gann, Thomas, and Mary Gann
    1939   Archaeological Investigations in the Corozal
            District of British Honduras. Bureau of Amer-
            ican Ethnology Bulletin 123. Smithsonian
            Institution, Washington, DC.
Garber, James F., M. Kathryn Brown, and
Christopher J. Hartman
    2002   The Early/Middle Formative Kanocha Phase
            (1200-850 B.C.) at Blackman Eddy, Belize.
            Reports submitted to FAMSI. http://www.famsi
            .org/reports/00090/index.html
Gifford, James C.
    1960   The Type-Variety Method of Ceramic Classifi-
            cation as an Indicator of Cultural Phenomena.
            American Antiquity 25(3):341–347.
    1963b   A Statement Concerning the Ceramic Group.
            Cerámica de Cultura Maya 1(2–3):23–24. Tem-
            ple University, Philadelphia.
    1963a   A Conceptual Approach to the Analysis of
            Prehistoric Pottery. PhD dissertation, Harvard
            University, Cambridge.
    1976   Prehistoric Pottery Analysis and the Ceramics
            of Barton Ramie in the Belize Valley. *Memoirs
            of the Peabody Museum of Archaeology and
            Ethnology* 18. Harvard University, Cambridge.
Gladwin, Winifred, and Harold S. Gladwin
    1930   *Some Southwestern Pottery Types, Series I*.
            Medallion Papers No. 8. Gila Pueblo, Globe,
            Arizona.

Hammond, Norman

1972   A Minor Criticism of the Type-Variety System of Ceramic Analysis. *American Antiquity* 37(3):450–452.

1974   Preclassic to Postclassic in Northern Belize. *Antiquity* 48:177–179.

1977   Ex Oriente Lux: A View from Belize. In *The Origins of Maya Civilization*, edited by R.E.W. Adams, pp. 45–76. University of New Mexico Press, Albuquerque.

1984   Holmul and Nohmul: A Comparison and Assessment of Two Maya Lowland Protoclassic Sites. *Cerámica de Cultura Maya* 13:1–17. Temple University, Philadelphia.

Hansen, Richard

1998   Continuity and Disjunction: The Pre-Classic Antecedents of Classic Maya Architecture. In *Function and Meaning in Classic Maya Architecture*, edited by Stephen D. Houston, pp. 49–122. Dumbarton Oaks, Washington, D.C.

Hermes, Bernard

1993   Adiciones tipológicas a los complejos Eb, Tzec, y Manik de Tikal, Guatemala. *Revista Espaniola de antropología Americana* 23.

1999   La Cerámica y otro tipo de evidencia anterior al Periodo Clásico en Topoxte, Petén. In *XII simposio de investigaciones arqueológicas en Guatemala, 1998*, edited by Juan Pedro Laporte and Hector L. Escobedo, pp.1–49. Ministerio de Cultura y Deportes, Asociación Tikal, Guatemala City, Guatemala.

Houk, Brett A., Hubert R. Robichaux, and Fred Valdez, Jr.

2010   An Early Maya Royal Tomb from Chan Chich, Belize. *Ancient Mesoamerica* 21(2):229–248.

Houston, Stephen, D., David Stuart, and Karl Taube

1992   Image and Text on the "Jauncy Vase." In *The Maya Vase Book,* Vol. 3, edited by Justin Kerr, pp. 498–512. Kerr and Associates, New York.

Houston, Stephen D., and Karl Taube

1987   "Name-tagging" in Classic Mayan Script. *Mexicon* 9(2):38–41.

Ichon, Alain, and Marie Charlotte Arnauld

1985   *Le protoclassique a La Lagunita, El Quiche, Guatemala.* Centre National de la Recherche Scientifique, Paris.

Inomata, Takeshi, Jessica MacLellan, Daniela Triadan, Jessica Munson, Melissa Burham, Kazuo Aoyama, Hiroo Nasu, Flory Pinzón, and Hitoshi Yonenobu

2015   Development of Sedentary Communities in the Maya Lowlands: Coexisting Mobile Groups and Public Ceremonies at Ceibal, Guatemala. *Proceedings of the National Academy of the Sciences* 112(14):4268–4273.

Inomata, Takeshi, Daniela Triadan, Kazuo Aoyama, Victor Castillo, and Hitoshi Yonenobu

2013   Early Ceremonial Constructions at Ceibal, Guatemala, and the Origins of Lowland Maya Civilization. *Science* 340(6131):467–470.

Kidder, Alfred Vincent, Jesse David Jennings, and Edwin M. Shook.

1946   *Excavations at Kaminaljuyu, Guatemala.* Vol. 561. Pennsylvania State University Press, State College, Pennsylvania.

Kosakowsky, Laura J.

1987   Preclassic Maya Pottery at Cuello, Belize. *Anthropological Papers* No. 47. University of Arizona Press, Tucson.

2001   The Ceramic Sequence from Holmul, Guatemala. Preliminary Results from the Year 2000 Season. *Mexicon* 23(4):85–91.

2012   Ceramics and Chronology of the Chan Site. In *Chan: An Ancient Maya Farming Community in Belize*, edited by Cynthia Robin, pp. 42–70. University Press of Florida, Gainesville.

Kosakowsky, Laura J., and Duncan C. Pring

1998   The Ceramics of Cuello, Belize: A New Evaluation. *Ancient Mesoamerica* 9 (1):55–66.

Laporte, Juan Pedro

1995   Preclasico a Clasico en Tikal: Proceso de transformacion en Mundo Perdido. In *The Emergence of Lowland Maya Civilization: The Transition from the Preclassic to the Early Classic*, edited by Nikolai Grube, pp. 17–33. Acta Mesoamericana Vol. 8. Verlag Anton Saurwein, Mockmuhl, Germany.

Laporte, Juan Pedro and Vilma Fialko

1995   Un Reencuentro con Mundo Perdido, Tikal, Guatemala. *Ancient Mesoamerica* 6(1):41–94.

Laporte, Juan Pedro and Juan Antonio Valdes

1993   *Tikal y Uaxactun en el Preclasico.* Universidad Nacional Autonoma de Mexico, Campeche.

Laporte, Juan Pedro, Lilian A. Corzo, Hector L. Escobedo, Rosa Maria Flores, K. Isabel Izaguirre, Nancy Monterroso, Paulino I. Morales, Carmen Ramos, Irma Rodas, Julia A. Roldan, Franklin Solares, and Bernard Hermes

1993   La sequencia ceramica del Valle de Dolores, Petén: La unidades ceramicas. *Atlas arqueologico de Guatemala* 1. Instituto de Antropologia e Historia, Guatemala City, Guatemala.

Laporte, Juan Pedro, Bernard Hermes, Lilian de Zea, and Maria Josefa Iglesias
1992 Nuevos Entierros y Escondites de Tikal: Subfases Manik 3a y 3b. *Ceramica de Cultura Maya* 16:30–101.

LeCount, Lisa J.
2001 Like Water for Chocolate: Feasting and Political Ritual among the Late Classic Maya at Xunantunich, Belize. *American Anthropologist* 103(4):935–953.

Leonard, Daniel
2003 Cival Looters' Trench CL04. In *Archaeological Investigations in the Holmul Region, Peten: Results of the Fourth Season, 2003*, edited by Francisco Estrada-Belli, pp. 139–144. Vanderbilt University, Nashville.

Lesure, Richard
1999 On the Genesis of Value in Early Hierarchical Societies. In *Material Symbols: Culture and Economy in Prehistory*, edited by John Robb, pp. 23–55. Center for Archaeological Investigations Occasional Paper No. 26. Southern Illinois University, Carbondale.

Lincoln, Charles
1985 Ceramics and Ceramic Chronology. In *A Consideration of the Early Classic Period in the Maya Lowlands*, edited by Gordon R. Willey and Peter Mathews, pp. 55–94. Institute for Mesoamerican Studies Publication No. 10. State University of New York, Albany.

Longyear, John Munro
1952 *Copan Ceramics: A Study of Southeastern Maya Pottery*. Publication No. 597. Carnegie Institution, Washington, D.C.

Lopez Varela, Sandra Lorena
1989 *Análisis y clasificación de la cerámica de un sitio Maya del clásico: Yaxchilán, México*. BAR International Series No. 535. British Archaeological Reports, Oxford.
1996 *The K'axob Formative Ceramics: The Search for Regional Interaction Through a Reappraisal of Ceramic Analysis and Classification in Northern Belize*. Ph.D. dissertation. London University, London.
2004 Ceramic History of K'axob, the Early Years. In *K'axob: Ritual, Work, and Family in an Ancient Maya Village*, edited by Patricia A. McAnany, pp. 169–191. Cotsen Institute of Archaeology, University of California, Los Angeles.

Love, Michael
2002 *Early Complex Society in Pacific Guatemala: Settlements and Chronology of the Río Naranjo, Guatemala*. Papers of the New World Archaeological Foundation Publication No. 66. Brigham Young University, Provo.

McAnany, Patricia A., Rebecca Storey, and Angela K. Lockard
1999 Mortuary Ritual and Family Politics at Formative and Early Classic K'axob, Belize. *Ancient Mesoamerica* 10:129–146.

MacLeod, Barbara, and Dorie Reents-Budet
1994 The Art of Calligraphy: Image and Meaning. In *Painting the Maya Universe: Royal Ceramics of the Classic Period*, edited by Dorie Reents-Budet, pp. 106–163. Duke University Press, Durham.

Martin, Simon, and Nikolai Grube
2008 *Chronicle of the Maya Kings and Queens: Deciphering the Dynasties of the Ancient Maya*. Thames & Hudson, London.

Mathews, Peter, and Peter Biro
2006 *The Maya Hieroglyphic Dictionary*. FAMSI. Available at http://research.famsi.org/mdp/mdp_index.php.

Meskill, Frances K.
1992 *Ceramics and Context: A Protoclassic Perspective from the Sites of Kichpanha and Colha*. Unpublished Master's Thesis, University of Texas, Austin.

Merwin, Raymond E., and George C. Vaillant
1932 *The Ruins of Holmul, Guatemala*. Memoirs of the Peabody Museum of Archaeology and Ethnology 3(2). Harvard University, Cambridge.

Moholy-Nagy, Hattula, and William R. Coe
2008 Appendix 12. In *Tikal Report 27, Part A: The Artifacts of Tikal: Ornamental and Ceremonial Artifacts and Unworked Material*. Tikal Report No. 27, University Museum Monograph No. 127. University Museum, University of Pennsylvania, Philadelphia.

Mongelluzzo, Ryan William
2011 Experiencing Maya Palaces: Royal Power, Space, and Architecture at Holmul, Guatemala. Ph.D. dissertation, Department of Anthropology, University of California, Riverside.

Morgan, Molly, and Jeremy Bauer
2003 Investigations of Structure 7 and Stela 2 at Cival, Petén, Guatemala. In *Proyecto Arqueologico Holmul: Informe Preliminar Temporada 2003*, edited by Francisco Estrada-Belli, pp. 100–136.

Morgan, Molly, and Jeremy Bauer (*continued*)
Proyecto Arqueologico Holmul, Vanderbilt
University, Nashville.

Muñoz, Rene
2004   The Ceramic Sequence of Piedras Negras, Guatemala: Type and Varieties. Report submitted
to FAMSI. Available at http://www.famsi.org/
reports/02055/02055Munoz01.pdf

Munsell Color
2000   *Munsell Soil Color Book: Year 2000 Revised
Washable Edition.* Munsell Color x-rite Gretag-
Macbeth, Grand Rapids, Michigan.

Neivens, Nina
2005   Group II, Building B, Excavation HT41. In
*Archaeological Investigations in the Holmul
Region, Peten: Results of the Fourth Season, 2003*,
edited by Francisco Estrada-Belli, pp. 88–90.
Vanderbilt University, Nashville.

Neivens de Estrada, Nina
2014   A Tangled Web. In *The Maya and Their Central
American Neighbours: Settlement Patterns, Architecture, Hieroglyphic Texts and Ceramics*, edited
by Geoffrey Braswell, pp. 177–200. Routledge,
New York.

Paling, Jason, Renee Morgan, Martin Rangel,
Varinia Matute Rodríguez, and Sean O'Brien
2011   *Entre dos rivales: Vida en un centro interme-
dio, Hamontun*, edited by B. Arroyo, L. Paiz,
A. Linares and A. Arroyave, pp. 296–319.
Museo Nacional de Arqueología y Etnología,
Guatemala.

Pellecer, Monica
2006   El Grupo Jabalí: Un complejo arquitectónico de
Patrón Tríadico en San Bartolo, Peten. In *XIX
simposio de investigaciones arqueológicas en Guatemala*, edited by Juan Pedro Laporte, Barbara
Arroyo, and Hector Mejia, pp. 937–948. Ministerio de Cultura y Deportes, Asociación Tikal,
Fundación Reinhart, Guatemala City, Guatemala.

Phillips, Philip
1958   Application of the Wheat-Gifford-Wasley Taxonomy to Eastern Ceramics. *American Antiquity*
24(2):117–125.

Phillips, Philip, and James C. Gifford
1959   A Review of the Taxonomic Nomenclature
Essential to Ceramic Analysis in Archaeology.
Manuscript on file, Department of Anthropology, Harvard University.

Poponoe de Hatch, Marion
1997   *Kaminaljuyu/San Jorge: Evidencia arqueologia de
la actividad economica en el Valle de Guatemala
300 a.C. A 300 d.C.* Universidad del Valle,
Guatemala.

Powis, Terry G., Fred Valdez Jr., Thomas R. Hester,
W. Jeffrey Hurst, and Stanley M. Tarka Jr.
2002   Spouted Vessels and Cacao Use among the Preclassic Maya. *Latin American Antiquity*
13(1):85–106.

Pring, Duncan C.
1977a   Influence or Intrusion? The "Protoclassic" in
the Maya Lowlands. In *Social Process in Maya
Prehistory*, edited by Norman Hammond,
pp. 135–165. Academic Press, London.

1977b   *The Preclassic Ceramics of Northern Belize.*
Doctoral dissertation, University of London.
University Microfilms, Ann Arbor.

2000   *The Protoclassic in the Maya Lowlands.* BAR
International Series No. 908. British Archaeological Reports, Oxford.

Pring, Duncan C., and Norman Hammond
1985   Investigation of a Possible River Port at Nohmul.
In *Nohmul: A Prehistoric Maya Community
in Belize*, edited by Norman Hammond, pp.
527–566. BAR International Series No. 205(ii).
British Archaeological Reports, Oxford.

Rattray, Evelyn Childs
2001   *Teotihuacan: Ceramics, Chronology, and Cultural
Trends.* Serie Arqueologia de Mexico. Instituto
Nacional de Antropologia e Historia and University of Pittsburgh, Pittsburgh.

Reents, Dorie
1985   The Late Classic Maya Holmul Style Polychrome
Pottery. PhD dissertation, Department of
Anthropology, University of Texas, Austin.

Reents-Budet Dorie
1994   *Painting the Maya Universe: Royal Ceramics
of the Classic Period.* Duke University Press,
Raleigh-Durham.

2000   Feasting among the Classic Maya: Evidence
from the Pictorial Ceramics. In *The Maya Vase
Book, 6*, edited by Barbara Kerr and Justin Kerr,
pp. 1032–1037. Kerr Associates, New York.

2006   The Social Context of Kakaw Drinking Among
the Ancient Maya. In *Chocolate in Mesoamerica:
A Cultural History of Cacao*, edited by Cameron
McNeil, pp. 202–223. University Press of Florida, Gainesville.

Reents-Budet, Dorie, Ronald Bishop, Jennifer Taschek,
and Joseph Ball
2000   Out of the Palace Dumps: Ceramic Production
and Use at Buena Vista del Cayo. *Ancient Mesoamerica* 11:99–121.

Reese-Taylor, Kathryn, and Debra Walker
2002   The Passage of the Late Preclassic in the
        Early Classic. In *Ancient Maya Political
        Economies*, edited by Marilyn A. Masson
        and David Freidel, pp. 87–122. Altamira
        Press, Oxford.

Reina, Ruben E., and Robert M. Hill II
1978   *The Traditional Pottery of Guatemala*. Univ-
        ersity of Texas Press, Austin.

Rice, Prudence
1976   Rethinking the Ware Concept. *American Antiq-
        uity* 41(4):538–543.
1979   Introduction and the Middle Preclassic Ceram-
        ics of Lake Yaxha-Sacnab, Guatemala. *Cerámica
        de la Cultura Maya* 10:1–36. Temple University,
        Philadelphia.
1987   *Pottery Analysis: A Sourcebook*. University of
        Chicago Press, Chicago.
1999   Rethinking Classic Lowland Maya Pottery
        Censers. *Ancient Mesoamerica* 10(1):25–50.
2009   Late Classic Maya Pottery Production: Review
        and Synthesis. *Journal of Archaeological Method
        and Theory* 16:117–156.
2013   Type Variety: What Works and What Doesn't.
        In *Maya Pottery: Classification, Analysis, and
        Interpretation*, edited by James John Aim-
        ers, pp. 11–28. University Press of Florida,
        Gainesville.

Robertson-Freidel, Robin A.
1980   *The Ceramics from Cerros: A Late Preclassic
        Site in northern Belize*. Doctoral dissertation,
        Department of Anthropology, Harvard Uni-
        versity, Cambridge. University Microfilms,
        Ann Arbor.

Robin, Cynthia
1989   *Preclassic Maya Burials at Cuello, Belize*. BAR
        International Series No. 480. British Archaeo-
        logical Reports, Oxford.

Rose, William I., Theodore J. Bornhorst, Sid P. Halsor,
William A. Capaul, Patrick S. Plumley,
Servando Dela Cruz-Reyna, Manuel Mena, and
Reynaldo Mota
1984   Volcán El Chichón, Mexico: pre-1982 S-rich
        Eruptive Activity. *Journal of Volcanology and
        Geothermal Research* 23(1):147–167.

Rouse, Irving
1939   *Prehistory in Haiti: A Study in Method*. Publica-
        tions in Anthropology No. 21. Yale University,
        New Haven.
1960   The Classification of Artifacts in Archaeology.
        American Antiquity 25(3):313–323.

Sabloff, Jeremy A.
1975   Ceramics. In *Excavations at Seibal, Department
        of Peten, Guatemala*. Memoirs of the Peabody
        Museum of Archaeology and Ethnology,
        Vol. 13(2). Harvard University, Cambridge.

Sabloff, Jeremy A., and Robert E. Smith.
1972   Ceramic Wares in the Maya Area: a Clarification
        of an Aspect of the Type Variety System and
        Presentation of a Formal Model for Compara-
        tive Use. In *Estudios de cultura Maya*, Vol. 8, pp.
        97–115. Universidad Nacional Autonoma de
        Mexico, Mexico City.

Sagebiel, Kerry
2005   *Shifting Allegiances at La Milpa, Belize: A
        Typological, Chronological, and Formal Anal-
        ysis of the Ceramics*. PhD Dissertation, Depart-
        ment of Anthropology, University of Arizona,
        Tucson.

Sharer, Robert J.
1978   Pottery and Conclusions, vol. 3, *The Prehistory
        of Chalchuapa, El Salvador*, University of Penn-
        sylvania Press, Philadelphia.

Sharer, Robert, and James C. Gifford
1970   Preclassic Ceramics from Chalchuapa, El Salva-
        dor, and Their Relationships with the Lowland
        Maya. *American Antiquity* 35:441–462.

Sheets, Payson D.
1979a   Environmental and Cultural Effects of the Ilo-
        pango Eruption in Central America. In *Volcanic
        Activity and Human Ecology*, edited by Payson
        D. Sheets and Donald K. Grayson, pp. 525–564.
        Academic Press, New York.
1979b   Maya Recovery from Volcanic Disasters Ilo-
        pango and Ceren. *Archaeology* 32:32–44.

Shepard, Anna O.
1939   Technological Notes on the Pottery of San Jose.
        In *Excavations at San Jose, British Honduras*,
        edited by J.E.S Thompson, pp. 251–277. Publica-
        tion 506. Carnegie Institution, Washington, D.C.
1942   Classification of Painted Wares. In *Late Ceramic
        Horizons at Benque Viejo, British Honduras*,
        edited by J.E.S Thompson, pp. 11–25. Publica-
        tion 528. Carnegie Institution, Washington, D.C.
1955   Technological Analysis: The Paste of Mars
        Orange Ware from Uaxactun. In *Ceramic
        Sequence at Uaxactun, Guatemala*, edited by
        Robert E. Smith, p. 32. MARI Publication
        No. 20. Tulane University, New Orleans.

Shetler, Anya
2013   Excavación HOL.T.84, Grupo I, Pirámide Norte
        (Edificio D), Holmul. In *Investigaciones*

Shetler, Anya (*continued*)
>
> *arqueologicas en la region de Holmul, Peten: Holmul y Cival. Informe preliminar de la temporada 2013*, edited by Francisco Estrada-Belli, pp. 76–88. Tulane University, New Orleans.

Smith, Robert E.

1952 *Pottery from Chipoc, Alta Verapaz, Guatemala.* Contributions to American Anthropology and History No. 56. Carnegie Institution, Washington, DC.

1955 *Ceramic Sequence at Uaxactun, Guatemala.* Middle American Research Institute Publication No. 20(I & II). Tulane University, New Orleans.

1971 *The Pottery of Mayapan: Including Studies of Ceramic Material from Uxmal, Kabah, and Chichen Itza.* Papers of the Peabody Museum of Archaeology and Ethnology, Vol. 66(I & II). Harvard University, Cambridge.

Smith, Robert E., and James C. Gifford

1963 The Type-Variety Content of Ceramic Groups in Pottery from Uaxactun (A Tentative Listing). *Ceramica de Cultura Maya* 2–3:26–33. Temple University, Philadelphia.

1966 Maya Ceramic Varieties, Types, and Wares at Uaxactun: Supplement to *Ceramic Sequence at Uaxactun, Guatemala.* pp. 125–174. Middle American Research Institute Publication No. 28. Tulane University, New Orleans.

Smith, Robert E., Gordon R. Willey, and James C. Gifford

1960 The Type-Variety Concept as a Basis for the Analysis of Maya Pottery. *American Antiquity* 25(3):330–340.

Strelow, Duane, and Lisa LeCount

2001 Regional Interaction in the Formative Southern Maya Lowlands: Evidence of Olmecoid Stylistic Motifs in a Cunil Assemblage from Xunantunich, Belize. Paper presented at the 75th annual meeting of the Society of American Archaeology Meetings, New Orleans.

Stuart, David

1989 Hieroglyphs on Maya Vessels. In *The Maya Vase Book*, Vol. 1, edited by Justin Kerr, pp. 149–160. Kerr and Associates, New York.

Sullivan, Lauren A., and Jaime J. Awe

2013 Establishing the Cunil Ceramic Complex at Cahal Pech, Belize. In *Ancient Maya Pottery: Classification, Analysis, and Interpretation*, edited by James John Aimers, pp. 107–120. University Press of Florida, Gainesville.

Sullivan, Lauren A., M. Kathryn Brown, and Jaime J. Awe

2009 Refining the Cunil Ceramic Complex at Cahal Pech, Belize. In *Research Reports in Belizean Archaeology: Papers of the 2008 Belize Archaeology Symposium*, edited by John Morris, Sherilyne Jones, Jaime Awe, George Thompson, and Christophe Helmke, pp. 161–168. Institute of Archaeology and National Institute of Culture and History, Belmopan, Belize.

Tankersley, Kenneth B., Nicholas P. Dunning, Vernon L. Scarborough, John G. Jones, Christopher Carr, and David L. Lentz

2015 Fire and Water: The Archaeological Significance of Tikal's Quaternary Sediments. In *Tikal: Paleoecology of an Ancient Maya City*, edited by David L. Lentz, Vernon L. Scarborough, and Nicholas P. Dunning, pp. 186–211. Cambridge University Press, New York.

Tankersley, Kenneth B., Vernon L. Scarborough, Nicholas Dunning, Warren Huff, Barry Maynard, and Tammie L. Gerke

2011 Evidence for Volcanic Ash Fall in the Maya Lowlands from a Reservoir at Tikal, Guatemala. *Journal of Archaeological Science* 38:2925–2938.

Taube, Karl

1985 The Classic Maya maize god: a reappraisal. In *Fifth Palenque Round Table 7* edited by Virginia Fields, pp. 171–181. Pre-Columbian Art Research Institute, San Francisco.

Thompson, J. Eric S

1931 *Archaeological Investigations in the Southern Cayo District, British Honduras.* Anthropological Series XVII, No. 3. Field Museum of Natural History, Chicago.

Thompson, Raymond H.

1958 *Modern Yucatecan Maya Pottery Making.* Memoirs No. 15. Society for American Archaeology, Salt Lake City.

Tokovinine, Alexandre

2005 Reporte epigrafico de la temporada 2005. In *Investigaciones arqueologicas en la region de Holmul, Petén, Guatemala: Informe preliminar de la temporada 2005*, edited by Francisco Estrada-Belli, pp. 322–364. Vanderbilt University, Nashville.

Tokovinine, Alexandre, and Francisco Estrada-Belli

2015 La Sufricaya: A Place in Classic Maya Politics. In *Classic Maya Polities of the Southern Lowlands: Integration, Interaction, Dissolution*, edited by Damien B. Marken and James L.

Fitzsimmons, pp.195–224. University Press of Colorado, Boulder.

Tomasic, John
2009   Investigating Terminal Preclassic and Classic Period Power and Wealth at K'o, Guatemala. PhD Dissertation, Department of Anthropology, Vanderbilt University, Nashville.

Tomasic, John, and Stephen Bozarth
2011   New Data from a Preclassic Tomb at K'o Guatemala. Paper presented at the 77th annual meeting of the Society of American Archaeology, Sacramento.

Trigger, Bruce G.
2006   *A History of Archaeological Thought,* 2nd edition. Cambridge University Press, Cambridge.

Urban, Patricia A., Edward M. Schortman, and Marne T. Ausec
2013   Looking for Times: How Type-Variety Analysis Helps Us "See" the Early Postclassic in Northwestern Honduras. In *Ancient Maya Pottery: Classification, Analysis, and Interpretation,* edited by James John Aimers, pp. 163–184. University Press of Florida, Gainesville.

Valdez, Fred, Jr.
1987   *The Prehistoric Ceramics of Colha, Northern Belize.* Doctoral dissertation, Department of Anthropology, Harvard University. Cambridge. University Microfilms, Ann Arbor.

Vaillant, George
1927   *The Chronological Significance of Maya Ceramics.* Doctoral dissertation, Department of Anthropology, Harvard University, Cambridge.

Wahl, David, Francisco Estrada-Belli, and Lysanna Anderson
2013   A 3400 year Paleolimnological Record of Prehispanic Human-Environment Interactions in the Holmul Region of the Southern Maya Lowlands. *Palaeogeography, Palaeoclimatology, Palaeoecology* 379:17–31.

Walker, Debra S., Kathryn Reese-Taylor, and Peter Mathews
2006   Después de la caída: Una redefinición del Clásico Temprano Maya. In *XIX simposio de investigaciones arqueológicas en Guatemala, 2005,* edited by Juan Pedro Laporte, Barbara Arroyo, and Héctor E. Mejía, pp. 659–671. Ministerio de Cultura y Deportes, IDAEH, Asociación Tikal, Fundación Arqueológica del Nuevo Mundo, Guatemala City, Guatemala.

Wentworth, C. K.
1922   A Scale of Grade and Class Terms for Clastic Sediments. *Journal of Geology* 30:377–392.

Wheat, Joe Ben, James C. Gifford, and William Wasley
1958   Ceramic Variety, Type Cluster, and Ceramic System in Southwestern Pottery Analysis. *American Antiquity* 24(1):34–47.

Willey, Gordon R.
1977   The Rise of Maya Civilization: A Summary View. In *The Origins of Maya Civilization,* edited by R.E.W. Adams, pp. 383–424. University of New Mexico Press, Albuquerque.

Willey, Gordon R., William R. Bullard Jr., John B. Glass, and James C. Gifford
1965   *Prehistoric Maya Settlements in the Belize Valley.* Papers of the Peabody Museum of Archaeology and Ethnology No. 54. Harvard University, Cambridge.

Willey, Gordon R., T. Pat Culbert, and R.E.W. Adams
1967   Maya Lowland Ceramics: A Report from the 1965 Guatemala City Conference. *American Antiquity* 32(3):289–315.

Willey, Gordon R., and James C. Gifford
1961   Pottery of the Holmul I Style from Barton Ramie, British Honduras. In *Essays in Pre-Columbian Art and Archaeology,* edited by Samuel K. Lothrop, pp. 152–170. Oxford University Press, London.

Index of Type: Varieties

Index of Type: Varieties by Surface Finish and Decorative Mode

Index of Type: Varieties by Complex, Ware, and Group

General Index

ABSTRACT

Ceramic classification is essential for the archaeological investigation of prehistoric complex societies. It allows archaeologists to quickly establish two important parameters of investigation: temporal range and spatial relations. Once determined, archaeologists are able to test hypotheses about past human behavior using other classes of artifacts along broad spectrums of theoretical inquiry. In the lowland Maya area ceramicists have used modal, type: variety-mode, and contextual ceramic classifications to create temporal-spatial frameworks that enable archaeologists to understand local and regional culture-historical events and to reconstruct the lifeway of a broad range of ancient Maya peoples. Although several subregions of the Maya lowlands contain at least one site where a sequence has been established, there are many areas where the Pre-Columbian ceramic record remains undefined.

One of these important and understudied areas is the Holmul region, located in the northeastern department of Petén, Guatemala. The region is composed of eight recorded sites varying in size and dates of occupation beginning in the early Middle Preclassic period (1300 BC) and ending in the Terminal Classic period (AD 900). Due to its strategic location between the Petén lowlands and Belize River Valley and the number of large sites spanning the Middle Preclassic through Terminal Classic periods, ceramic research in the Holmul region has the potential to refine and reshape our ideas about many aspects of ancient Maya cultural practice and process. This book presents a type: variety-mode classification of ceramic material from the Holmul region. The study incorporates ceramic material recovered from over a century of excavations. It includes material collected by Raymond Merwin in his 1911 investigations at Holmul, as well as multiple years of the Holmul Regional Archaeological Project directed by Francisco Estrada-Belli from 2000 to 2013.

This classification was created in an effort to accomplish three primary goals. The first was to use ceramic artifacts to establish site-wide and regional chronological and spatial frameworks for the Holmul region. The second was to compare site and regional temporal-spatial frameworks to other sites in the southern Maya lowlands and to a lesser extent the northern Maya lowlands,

RESUMEN

La clasificación cerámica es esencial para la investigación arqueológica de sociedades prehistóricas complejas. Permite a los arqueólogos establecer rápidamente dos parámetros importantes de investigación: rango temporal y relaciones espaciales. Una vez determinados, los arqueólogos son capaces de probar hipótesis sobre el comportamiento humano pasado al utilizar otras clases de artefactos, junto a amplios espectros de preguntas teóricas. En las tierras bajas mayas los ceramistas utilizan las clasificaciones modales, de tipo: variedad-modo y contextuales, para crear marcos temporales-espaciales que permitan a los arqueólogos entender los eventos culturales-históricos locales y regionales y la reconstrucción de los modos de vida de un amplio rango de antiguas personas mayas. Mientras que varias subregiones de las tierras bajas mayas contienen, por lo menos, un sitio dónde se ha establecido una secuencia hay otras áreas donde el registro cerámico Pre-Columbiano permanece impreciso.

Una de estas áreas importantes y poco estudiadas es la región Holmul localizada en el noreste del departamento de Petén, Guatemala. La región está compuesta de ocho sitios registrados que varían en tamaño y fechas de ocupación que inician en el período Preclásico Medio temprano (1300 a.C.) y terminan en el período Clásico Terminal (900 d.C.). Debido a su ubicación estratégica entre las tierras bajas de Petén y el valle del río Belice y el gran número de sitios grandes que van desde el período Preclásico Medio hasta el Clásico Terminal, la investigación cerámica en la región de Holmul tiene el potencial de refinar y remodelar nuestras ideas sobre muchos aspectos de la antigua práctica y procesos culturales mayas. Este libro presenta una clasificación tipo: variedad-modo para la cerámica de la región de Holmul. El estudio incorpora el material cerámico recuperado de más de un centenar de excavaciones. Incluye todo el material recolectado por Raymond Merwin en sus investigaciones de Holmul en 1911; así como de los múltiples años del Proyecto Arqueológico Regional Holmul dirigido por Francisco Estrada-Belli del 2000 al 2013.

Esta clasificación fue creada en un esfuerzo por alcanzar tres objetivos principales. El primero, utilizar artefactos cerámicos para establecer una secuencia y determinar,

southern Maya highlands, and Pacific coast. The third goal was to address specific issues within particular ceramic complexes including (1) understanding the adoption and use of pottery in the early Middle Preclassic period, (2) assessing the social and ecological reasons for qualitative changes in production patterns between Preclassic period ceramic complexes, (3) determining the function and meaning of the first polychrome painted ceramics of the Terminal Preclassic period, (4) assessing the strength and nature of ceramic influence from the central Mexican city of Teotihuacan in the Early Classic period, (5) understanding the role of Holmul in interregional politics as seen through cream polychrome ceramics during the Late Classic period, and (6) understanding the timing and possible reasons for permanent abandonment of sites in the Holmul region during the Terminal Classic period.

The result of this study is a ceramic typology created through type: variety-mode classification that addresses some of the most relevant issues in Maya studies both past and present. This classification defines a new subregion of ceramic production and distribution, and bridges the analytical gap between the Petén lowlands and Belize River Valley. It adds nuanced understanding to the interpretation of older ceramic datasets, contributes to ongoing ceramic studies, and poses new questions and predictions for future investigations into lowland Maya ceramic research, history, and practice.

a lo largo del sitio y la región, marcos cronológicos y espaciales para el área de Holmul. El segundo, comparar marcos temporales-espaciales del sitio y la región con otros sitios de las tierras bajas mayas del sur y en menor extensión con las tierras bajas mayas del norte, altiplano maya del sur y costa del Pacífico. El tercer objetivo, dirigirse a cuestiones específicas dentro de complejos cerámicos particulares incluyen lo siguiente (1) entender la adopción y uso de cerámica en el período Preclásico Medio temprano; (2) evaluar las razones sociales y ecológicas para los cambios cualitativos en los patrones de producción entre los complejos cerámicos del período Preclásico; (3) determinar la función y significado de la primera cerámica policromada pintada del período Preclásico Tardío; (4) valorar la fuerza y naturaleza de la influencia cerámica de la ciudad central de México, Teotihuacan en el período Clásico Temprano; (5) entender el papel de Holmul en la política inter-regional como se observa a través de la cerámica crema polícroma durante el período Clásico Tardío; y (6) utilizar la cerámica para entender el momento y posibles razones del abandono permanente de los sitios en la región de Holmul durante el período Clásico Terminal.

El resultado de este estudio es una tipología cerámica creada a través de la clasificación tipo: variedad-modo que aborda algunos de los temas relevantes de los estudios mayas, tanto pasados como presentes. La clasificación define una nueva subregión de producción y distribución cerámica y abarca la brecha analítica entre las tierras bajas de Petén y el valle del río Belice. Se añade una comprensión matizada a la interpretación de grupos de datos cerámicos anteriores, contribuye a los estudios cerámicos en marcha y brinda nuevas preguntas y predicciones para futuras investigaciones para el estudio de la cerámica, su historia y su práctica dentro de las tierras bajas mayas.

—Translated by Karla J. Cardona

ANTHROPOLOGICAL PAPERS OF THE UNIVERSITY OF ARIZONA